The University of Reading: *the first fifty years*

The University of Reading
the first fifty years

J. C. Holt

Professor of History in the University

Reading, 1977

Reading University Press

Published by
University of Reading Press Ltd
Whiteknights
Reading

© J. C. Holt, 1977

ISBN 0 7049 0500 0

Printed by
Bradley & Son Ltd
50–56 Portman Road
Reading

Contents

List of plates

The plates fall between pages 116 and 117

Preface

The story of a single British university in the twentieth century cannot make proper history. Part of it turns on the policies of the Ministry of Education and its successor, the Department of Education and Science, and on assessments reached and procedures devised in the University Grants Committee. Part again should properly be concerned with more general social problems: approaches towards higher education, the determination of professions to seek a graduate entry, the attitude of school-leavers towards employment on the one hand and three or four years' further study on the other; and in all these matters some elements of the tale must be concerned with changes related to the Second World War. Part finally should involve comparisons with other universities and with other institutions of higher education. Much of this lies outside the range of the history of one university, and I have been conscious throughout that I have been driven into making judgements and assessments which could not be tested as thoroughly as a practical historian, fully in charge of his material and the scope of his enquiry, would like. This, then, is not intended as a definitive history but as a contribution which some future historian of British universities may find useful.

I have sought to explain why there is a university at Reading at all, in what ways it has been affected by its environment, and why and how it has grown as it has. I have also tried to show what it was like to be at Reading. Necessarily for recent years the account has tended to become more anonymous. There are obvious difficulties attendant upon the writing of a history of a university in which the author is a working professor. Moreover, the more recent the period the more I have felt deprived of that essential historical tool: hindsight. Some of the topics I have discussed may no longer seem important when the University comes to celebrate its hundredth anniversary. It is to be hoped that this will be so, for the history of the University in the last fifteen years or so cannot but contain an intolerable deal of new buildings, new faculties and departments, new courses, and all the administrative impedimenta essential to their establishment and operation. In fifty years' time a centenary historian will be able to write more fully of other aspects of the life of the University in the 1960s and 1970s: the quality of its research, its teaching, and perhaps most important of all of the manner in which students make their own context for learning. He may also be fortunate enough to live in an age which does not confuse vigour and expansion.

This work was begun by Lady Stenton. At her death in 1971 she left only a few short fragments, the most complete of which, concerning the Library, is included below as Appendix 4. In carrying out the work I have had unstinted and generous aid from the Registrar, Mr J. F. Johnson, who has not only guided me to sources of information but also read the whole book in typescript. His comments have been invaluable. Mr J. A. Edwards and Mr G. M. C. Bott of the University Record Centre have also read most of the typescript, saved me from many errors of detail and helped in searching their files and providing information. Mrs Angela Tomlinson helped in correcting the proofs and has compiled the index. She has enabled me to eradicate many of the inconsistencies which tend to accrue during composition. I have benefited from the work of Miss Helen Crichton who, in the early stages, collected much of the oral evidence which I have used. The book has been edited and seen through the press by Professor M. L. Twyman. Mr I. Maclean and the staff of the University Photographic Department have produced many of the plates. The printers, Bradley and Son of Reading, have endured the delays which have affected the work with patience. Both Mr John and Mr Robert Bradley have taken a kind and personal interest in it.

In the course of the work I have been privileged to enjoy the interest and support of many colleagues. The Vice-Chancellor, Dr H. R. Pitt, in a few characteristically modest and sensible remarks, gave me my head; I can only hope that the book justifies the roving commission which he not only allowed, but required. I was helped at various stages by Miss June Brazier, Miss Nelia Rich and Miss Barbara Meade, all of whom answered queries or provided written information. Mr D. F. Batty met my requests for University records, all of which in retrospect seem to have been urgent, with unfailing efficiency and cheerfulness. Mr H. E. Bell and Mr W. D. Watts helped with illustrations, and Mr T. Bottomley on a number of matters concerned with University committees. I have used statistics of admission compiled by Mr R. M. G. Clark. Mr J. T. Mulholland assisted me on financial matters and Mr H. Bortoft on all questions concerned with buildings. There are two who contributed to this work whom it is now impossible to thank: Ernest Smith, Registrar from 1932 to 1955 and E. H. Carpenter, Bursar from 1946 to 1973. They need no book as their memorial for the University itself is a tribute to their memory.

The staff of the University Library, especially of the Education Library, went out of their way to meet my requests and provide me with material on long loan. I am also grateful to Professor P. Allen, Mrs Rosemary Chapman and Mrs Clare Snow for drawing my attention to evidence which I might otherwise have overlooked. For the account of student affairs since 1968 I owe a particular debt to Professor P. W. Campbell who supplied me with his own assiduously compiled collection of material.

The work would have been rendered much more difficult had not so many members of the University, past and present, students, academic and administrative staff, officers and members of Council, been ready to provide me with written and oral information. The extent of the debt to them, too numerous to name here, will be apparent in the footnotes. I have done my best to render their contributions *verbatim*. It is only here and there that their evidence, like that drawn from other sources, has been amended to conform to editorial conventions. I have allowed the witnesses to speak.

The book is therefore a result of shared interest and endeavour. It was a privilege to have been invited by the Council of the University to undertake the work. It has been an even greater privilege to minister to what many others, besides myself, have said or wanted to say. I am deeply grateful to all those who have helped.

I must record some special debts: to Mrs Audrey Munro, who produced most of the typescript; and to Mrs Janet Cory, Secretary of the Department of History, who not only helped with the typescript but also dealt with all the secretarial business and personal communications to which the author's part of the work gave rise. Finally, I owe much in completing the work, to my wife, Dr Elizabeth Holt. The book is the briefer and the clearer for her criticism.

I regret that Hubert Childs's interesting account of his father in *W. M. Childs: an account of his life and work* (Oxford, Alden Press, 1976) appeared too late for me to use.

J.C.H.
Whiteknights
November 1977

Acknowledgements

The author is indebted to the Bodley Head for permission to quote from J. F. Wolfenden, *Turning Points*; to Chatto and Windus and William Marrow & Co. for permission to quote from Elspeth Huxley, *Love among the Daughters*; to J. M. Dent and Sons, for permission to quote from W. M. Childs, *Making a University*; to the Oxford University Press for permission to quote from Bede's *Ecclesiastical History of the English People*, ed. Bertram Colgrave and R. A. B. Mynors; to the Royal Society for permission to quote from a bibliographical memoir of Professor H. L. Hawkins by Professor P. Allen; and to the *Times Higher Education Supplement* for permission to quote from an article by Sue Reid of 19 March 1976.

Plate 27 is produced by permission of Aerofilm Ltd, Boreham Wood; plates 31, 40 and 45 by permission of Bradley and Son, Reading; plate 46 by permission of P. Norman Bulton, Guildford; plate 43 by permission of the *Evening Post*, Reading; plate 34 by permission of Fairey Surveys Ltd, Maidenhead; plate 23 by permission of Frank Ormrod, and plate 19 by permission of Dr S. Smith. Plate 14 is the work of Norman Gruber of the National Institute for Research in Dairying. Members of the University Photographic Department have contributed plates 13, 17, 30-3, 36-45 and 47. Plate 6 is the work of the author.

It has not been possible to trace the originals of all the plates used in this work. Any resulting infringement of copyright is unintentional.

Chapter 1

Introduction

When H. C. Barnard was interviewed for appointment to the Chair of Education in the University of Reading in 1937, he was asked by Franklin Sibly, then Vice-Chancellor, whether he had ever considered the geographical position of Reading. 'I know what you mean', came the reply, 'it's halfway between London and Oxford'.[1] That effectively explains why a town of only moderate size, numbering a total population of roughly 100,000,[2] came in 1926 to be the site of the only university established in Great Britain between the two world wars. Reading was a market town; it had a biscuit factory, a brewery and a horticultural seed industry which were known nationally; it was also an important railway junction. All these features of its economy played an important part in the establishment and development of the University. But there was little in Reading to compare with the concentrated wealth and population which led to the establishment of colleges and universities as manifestations of civic pride and enterprise in the great industrial cities of the north and the midlands. By that standard Reading was small, too small to bear the load of a large and costly institution unless some inspiration were to conjure up a quite exceptional readiness to envisage and then realize such a possibility. It is no detraction from the effort and wisdom of the men who created the University to say that their ambition would never have been other than wildly impractical had it not been centred on a town which lay conveniently between the University of Oxford and the capital city.

This simple geographic consideration was emphasized by the Great Western Railway. However, it was effective long before the advent of modern transport. In 1209 a tawdry affair at Oxford led to the dispersal of the University. A woman was murdered; a scholar was thought to be the culprit; the townsfolk raided his hostel and executed summary justice by hanging two or three of the inmates, thereby infringing the privileges of both the University and the clerical order. The University was dispersed. Some of the scholars went to Paris; some to Cambridge, fated never to return; and some came to Reading. There they probably remained as a small community until the University was re-established at Oxford in 1214.[3]

---

[1] *Bulletin*, 55 (1974), p. 6. [2] The census return for 1931 was for 100,400.
[3] The main facts are covered in H. Rashdall, *The Universities of Europe in the Middle Ages*, ed. F. M. Powicke and A. B. Emden (Oxford, 1936), iii, pp. 33–5.

Reading was useful only when Oxford was inhospitable. It was a convenient funkhole rather than a serious alternative. It lay aside from the main routes of medieval England, whereas Oxford was sited where the ways up the Thames valley and over the Chilterns crossed the main artery which ran from the Solent north through Winchester and, beyond Oxford, to Brackley, Northampton and thence to Stamford and Lincoln. It was on this road that other possible alternatives for Oxford were available at Northampton and Stamford.[1] Reading was simply one of the less attractive of these alternative sites.

Nevertheless this earlier medieval settlement is of more than coincidental interest, for of all the modern universities Reading was the most medieval in the manner of its founding. As in 1209, the cause was a migration of scholars impelled this time not by fear of the townsfolk of Oxford, but by the missionary zeal of the University Extension movement. As the first *Calendar* of the University Extension College put it in 1892:

> The object of the College is to bring education of a university type
> within reach of those who cannot go to the university. Its function
> is to stimulate the desire for intellectual life, to diffuse both 'liberal'
> and technical education, to train good citizens, and to erect a ladder
> by which the chosen intellects of all classes may climb to the uni-
> versities themselves.

If that were to be achieved from Oxford, then Reading would be the obvious centre. There it lay, halfway to London, conveniently *en route* to and from the capital. The only other possible centre near Oxford was Swindon, smaller than Reading but more heavily industrial. All those who have ever had to change trains at Didcot will understand why Reading became the chosen base.

The first University Extension lectures in Reading were given in 1885. They were grafted on to the work of the local Schools of Science and Art which had been established in Valpy Street in 1882.[2] In 1891 the centre was vigorous enough to justify the founding of a college. Christ Church offered the services of H. J. Mackinder and on 29 September 1892 the University Extension College, in conjunction with the Schools of Science and Art, Reading, was opened by the Dean of Christ Church. The story of the early steps has been told in W. M. Childs's *Making a University*.[3] In that remarkable book the development of the first establishment in Valpy Street, the move to London Road, the gift by George William Palmer of the first endowment, the benefaction of Lady Wantage which led to the construction of the first hall of residence, and the first submission and ulti-

---

[1] *Ibid.*, iii, pp. 86–90. Salisbury also received a migration from Oxford in 1238 which survived for forty years (*ibid.*).

[2] The art classes were established in West Street in 1860 and the science classes ten years later in Vastern Lane, now Blagrave Street. They were brought together under the same roof in Valpy Street in 1882.

[3] London, 1933. Issues of the *Calendar* of the University College also contain brief but useful summaries of its history.

mate success in obtaining the University Charter are related as part of a personal Odyssey in which Childs appears to create a university almost with his own hands, through his energy, his extraordinary powers of persuasion, in great bounds of imaginative insight.[1] Childs's passionate advocacy played its part. But so also did Reading's capacity to attract and hold a group of scholars and teachers who were quite outstanding in what was then so small and insignificant an institution. Of this Reading's geographical location was the prime cause.

Among these scholars in the early years there were men who could easily have moved to chairs in other universities. Some moved, but some remained. Those who stayed acted in their turn as a magnet, attracting others to their company. Foremost among these was F. M. Stenton, Research Fellow of the College from 1908 to 1912, Professor of Modern History from 1912 to his appointment as Vice-Chancellor in 1946. Between the two world wars Stenton came to be acknowledged as one of the outstanding historians of medieval England. In the time of his pomp offers and invitations were showered on him. Yet he was never drawn away from Reading. For him the matter was complicated by the fact that his wife, Doris, was a lecturer in his department. On one occasion at least another institution sought to overcome this difficulty by offering to provide a lecturership for Doris along with a chair for Stenton. He was never a great letter-writer, but on this occasion he was moved to draft an immediate reply:

My dear Pollard,

Very many thanks for your letter which came this morning. I am sorry for the delay. Even now I cannot write conclusively, for my wife is at the Record Office until the evening and does not yet know the details contained in your letter. But I can indicate some of the points which have occurred to me.

The first is that I am extremely interested in the new university here. I have been associated with it in one way or another for more than twenty-five years, and I have always assumed that I should end my teaching days here. I should never, of my own motion, seek a professorship elsewhere. Of course the University is extremely small, and work is limited by the small scale of the place. Nevertheless, it is a quiet little community, including a number of close personal friends, and one's own work can be carried on without too much interruption from academic or administrative duties. Also experience has shown that now and then – on an average about once in five years – a first class research student comes along. And when that

[1] Childs's story turns on a pivotal scene of 4 July 1906, in which, after a private dinner party he unveiled to a few selected members of the University College his ultimate objective of establishing Reading as a university (*Making a University*, pp. 109–21). Stenton's comment on the book was simple and revealing – 'I wish he hadn't'. But it was natural enough for Childs to relate the history of the College in personal terms. All witnesses tend to do that. In Childs's case this was reinforced by the fact that he was indeed the central creative force behind the establishment of the University.

happens, he or she can be set to work in the British Museum or Record Office, 75 minutes away.

The simplicity of our departmental arrangements here is an attraction. I have a very senior lecturer, who does most of the strictly modern history. The Librarian is also a lecturer in history (mainly 16th and 17th century administrative and economic). For the rest, my wife and I divide out the work at our pleasure, both as regards lecturing and tutorial duties. It is of course a somewhat casual business, very different from the organization of a great department in the largest of London colleges.

I should like to thank you particularly for the suggestion that a lectureship might be found for my wife, and for your kind offer to undertake the onus or the odium. As the matter stands, unless my wife did receive such an appointment I should be seriously out of pocket by coming to London. In fact, after our interview, I realized that if or when any further proposal might be made I should have to decline it on this ground if on no other. But if the College is prepared to consider the anomalous if not unique situation created by the appointment of a professor whose wife follows him as lecturer, the least I can do is to consider the proposal anew! Naturally, I can take no step in this direction myself, and I must leave the whole matter to you and the College. I should never have proposed it, but I must say that quite apart from the financial question, it materially simplifies the academic situation, so far as I am concerned.

If I came to London, I should try to continue, with greater resources, the work I have begun here on Anglo-Saxon and Anglo-Norman history. This work has mainly dealt with the social and administrative sides of history. I do not know what danger there would be of a clash with others working on similar lines. Does Chambers, for example, deal with specifically historical problems? My wife deals with mainly legal and administrative matters. You may well already have someone who is handling Magna Carta in the light of plea rolls. These questions, of course, it is for you to consider, as also the wider question whether you particularly want a medievalist. Certainly, a professorship of Medieval English History would cover, very accurately, the work which I should hope to do. I quite understand the difficulty caused by the pre-existence of a professorship of medieval history.

These are disjointed observations raised by a consideration of your letter. They may be modified by talk with others – my wife in the first place, but also one or two discreet persons here. But I can do no less, in view of your full and kind letter, than give you my impressions at once. In a day or two (I gather that your crucial meeting takes place next week) I will write definitely.[1]

[1] URC, Stenton family papers, MS 1148 8/10. Undated, but ? 1927.

That letter reveals much of the quality of life at Reading in the formative years. Its theme was one to which Stenton returned on several occasions in his advice on the development of the College and University. He saw it always as a modest centre of learning, where small departments could educate well selected students, above all a place which gave easy access to the great libraries and repositories of London and Oxford. Until the Second World War he held a season ticket to London and counted it a bad day if he could not set out for the Public Record Office or the British Museum by lunchtime.

Others shared this view. Scientists found that Reading placed them within an inner circuit which included Oxford, Cambridge and London, with all its professional societies and institutions. They also tended to remain: F. J. Cole in Zoology, H. L. Hawkins in Geology, T. M. Harris in Botany and, later, E. A. Guggenheim in Chemistry and R. W. Ditchburn in Physics. The members of the Faculty of Agriculture not only found steadily increasing resources and an advancing reputation but also easy access to the Ministry of Agriculture and the various national boards and institutes. Reading seemed and was an attractive place. It was not simply that it was a convenient centre for research. From the beginning the College was indebted to Oxford, especially to Christ Church, for its teachers, some of whom came to be detached almost permanently, but many of whom simply called in either regularly or occasionally to help on this or that project.[1] This continuing interest formed the standards of the growing institution. Frederick York Powell, Regius Professor of Modern History in the University of Oxford, was the inspiration of the Reading Studies in Local History.[2] Hugh Allen, Director of the School of Music from 1908 to 1918, continued to act as guide and friend, with the formal title of Visitor to the School of Music until his death in 1946. Before the First World War Adrian Boult played the timpani in the orchestra under Allen's direction in a performance of Beethoven's second symphony, and he returned to conduct the University's orchestra and choir in 1919-20 and yet again in 1954 to conduct the orchestra's Fiftieth Anniversary Concert.[3] Gustav Holst succeeded Boult as conductor in 1920 and continued to come to Reading up to 1923. In the School of Art J. A. Betts found to his delight that he could tap the resources of the London schools of art and institutes of art history.[4] The traffic was not all one way. There was a continuing interchange between the departments of the Faculty of Agriculture and the national advisory councils or executive boards. Reading scholars were easily drawn into the

[1] None of the first staff of twenty teachers gave the whole of their time to the College. Of these, nine came over from Oxford. H. J. Mackinder, the first Principal, visited the College perhaps twice a week (Childs (1933), pp. 11, 17).
[2] *Ibid.*, pp. 27-8.
[3] Information supplied by Sir Adrian Boult.
[4] Information from Professor J. A. Betts. In Art this ability to draw on men from London was particularly important. The visiting teachers in art history have included Francis Wormald, C. R. Dodwell and George Zarnecki.

work of the national societies. Doris Stenton refounded the Pipe Roll Society as editor and secretary in 1923. When she retired from the office in 1961 she had seen through the press thirty-four volumes of the Society's new series. Most of these she edited herself.[1]

Such a community at Reading was bound to develop peculiar features of its own. It was remarkable among the early local colleges for its halls of residence, which in many respects were modelled on the colleges of Oxford. Halls or hostels were essential at Reading, for the town could not possibly provide accommodation for an academic institution of any size. However, the first move towards residential development, which led to the foundation of Wantage Hall in 1908, sprang not from any difficulty in finding rooms for students but from the decision, inspired by a disciplinary case, to turn the College into a residential community.[2] Thereafter the provision of residential places became and has remained an absolute prerequisite in the development of the College and University. The resulting flavour of the place was not unique. Durham, for example, was even more strongly collegiate. But through its emphasis on residence and in its small scale Reading stood apart from the great civic universities.

The influence of Oxford and the residential structure reinforced each other. They came together in the establishment in 1906 of a tutorial system which was a deliberate transfer to Reading of the 'Oxford idea of pastoral care'.[3] Just as the proximity to London and Oxford tended to produce a stable community, and financial limitations a small community, so the establishment of the Halls and the development of the tutorial system tended to produce a community which was peculiarly devoted to the proper management of its own affairs. All this was apparent enough to those outside. Hence its special attraction to those who wanted such an environment. Sibly came to it as Vice-Chancellor in 1929 after founding University College, Swansea, and acting as Principal of the University of London:

> It is certainly a charming place, in many ways; and a regular haven
> of refuge for such as 'oi'. There should be plenty to do, however, and
> the usual shortage of money for doing it.[4]

In 1950 the same spell was at work on J. F. Wolfenden:

> I was attracted by coming back to university life, where after all I
> had begun, and the picture I got of Reading, to be honest, was that
> it was very much like a good boarding school. It was small, compact,
> domestic, cosy. It had been pretty well unchanged for some time
> after the first great burst, and I felt that I should not be swamped

---

[1] J. C. Holt, 'Doris Mary Stenton', *American Historical Review*, lxxix (1974), pp. 265–7. See also Kathleen Major in *Proceedings of the British Academy*, lviii (1972), pp. 525–35 and C. F. Slade in the Pipe Roll Society, new series, xli (1976), pp. 1–32.
[2] Childs (1933), pp. 73–5.
[3] *Ibid.*, p. 104.
[4] Sibly to A. E. Morgan, Principal of University College, Hull, 19 May 1929 (URC, Registrar. box 256).

in a university as one might have been at Leeds or Liverpool or Manchester. Not least important, there was the emphasis at Reading on residence and halls of residence and the kind of life that grows up around them and in them. If there was a place outside Oxbridge and Durham that was like an Oxford college, this was it.[1]

The influence of Oxford penetrated deep into the structure of Reading. There it interacted with another development which became characteristic of the new University: agriculture. This went back to the transfer of the British Dairy Institute from Aylesbury to Reading in 1893–6 and to the establishment of the Department of Agriculture with the blessing of the Board of Agriculture in 1893–4.[2] This was the new college's response to the apparent need to find an individual flavour:

> It was felt that a distinctive study was essential if the College was to make a name. In a great city of the midlands or the north, a branch of technology relating to some leading local industry would have been chosen. In Reading the only great industries were biscuits and seeds. The biscuit factory, though an immense concern, was not dependent upon an annual supply of young men trained in applied science. For the raw material of manufacture it looked to the farmer. The seed firm had won world-wide fame by its application of specialized skill to the requirements of the grower. Outside Reading was a great agricultural area, which for many reasons it was important to serve. All these considerations pointed to agriculture.[3]

This, like the rest of the College's activities, benefited from the proximity of London. Here too, naturally, it looked to Oxford for help.[4] But agriculture at Reading, unlike the rest of its work, was not derived from Oxford or dependent on the zeal engendered by the University Extension movement. From its inception, therefore, the Reading College was an experiment in amalgamating an undiluted Oxford settlement, in which arts subjects were predominant, with a highly practical and applied subject which brought with it, sooner or later, all the major biological sciences, most of the physical sciences, and, in economics, one of the major social studies.

This, more than anything else, defined the public reputation of the place. As it changed from College to University it was known to a few for the distinguished work of some of its professors. To a wider circle it enjoyed esteem as one of the few residential institutions outside Oxford and Cambridge: school teachers, sending their pupils on to a university, knew that 'Reading looks after its students'.[5] But at large it was agriculture which made its name. This was also important in its internal development. From the start

[1] Conversation with Lord Wolfenden, 22 March 1975.
[2] Childs (1933), pp. 14, 17–19.
[3] *Ibid.*, p. 17.
[4] *Ibid.*, p. 18.
[5] Miss Winifred Pretty, senior history mistress, Nottingham High School for Girls, in conversation with the author *c.* 1950.

there was some concern about the balance between agriculture and the rest.[1] There was recurrent discussion of the comparative quality of the students in agriculture and the other faculties. There was mounting pressure that sciences which were first established as hand-maidens to agriculture should be developed as 'proper subjects' in their own right. There was a coherent argument on the other side that effective development would come the quicker the more it was oriented around agricultural studies; some maintained that the whole thrust of the University's work should be aimed at providing an agricultural complexion not only for its sciences but also for its humane studies. These overt arguments, fruitful though they were at times, were probably not as important in the development of the College and University as the practical conditions which the proper establishment of agriculture imposed. It required the amalgamation of a number of distinct disciplines, including bacteriology, botany, chemistry, animal physiology, geology and economics, in a single coherent course of study. In one area of its work, therefore, Reading was involved very thoroughly and at a very early date in interdisciplinary and interdepartmental co-operation. This too tended to emphasize and reinforce the small family characteristics of the enterprise.

These three interlocking influences: the geographical situation, the influence of Oxford, the importance of agriculture, moulded Reading's characteristic features. There were others, which, though negative, were equally important. At its foundation the University was desperately poor. Only two years earlier, in 1924, it had run out of the necessary money and credit to meet the bill for salaries, a default which was covered by the benevolent intervention of the President, J. H. Benyon, and Leonard Sutton.[2] It had accustomed itself to work on a shoe-string, as Sibly found to his surprise on his arrival:

> I displayed much curiosity about Psychology, in conversation with
> Childs and de Burgh. It seems that the lecturer in charge is very
> keen and very good on the experimental side. But the weakness lies
> in the fact that he is all alone; and if he falls ill, as happened on a
> recent occasion, things come pretty well to a standstill. It strikes me
> as a pretty unstable basis on which to offer an Honours course; but
> I don't think there is much likelihood of an improvement, this side
> of an increased Treasury Grant.[3]

But if it tried to do too much on meagre resources, or if time and energy were lost through money-pinching, at least it enjoyed the freedom which goes with the lack of financial ties. There was little hope that it would be rescued by the town. The corporation had helped by providing the first accommodation in Valpy Street, but after the move to London Road the

---

[1] Childs (1933), p. 19.
[2] Conversation with Ernest Smith.
[3] Sibly to A. E. Morgan, 19 May 1929 (URC, Registrar, box 256). The lecturer in question was A. W. P. Wolters, subsequently Professor of Psychology and Deputy Vice-Chancellor.

venture had gone well beyond what the interests of the town might require or could support. In the year ending 31 July 1926, the income of the University fell just short of £95,000. Of this the borough contributed £2,700 and the county of Berkshire nearly £5,000 of which nearly £4,000 was provided by the Agricultural Instruction Committee. The total contribution from all interested local authorities was less than half the contribution from the Ministry of Agriculture and Fisheries. Among the endowments the Reading Citizens' Fund stood at just over £9,000 in a total of over £305,000.[1] Despite the contribution of local authorities and the generosity of Reading's citizens the University was clearly more than a municipal enterprise. It could not expect to turn to the town for financial succour. But it was spared the self-important buildings, with their acres of cast iron and brown tiles, which municipal patronage provided for the civic universities.[2] Equally there was no danger that the town would seek to run it as though it were the municipal gas works.[3]

Hence the College had to find its own supports. That it advanced at all and ultimately achieved its Charter as a University is to be explained by the interest and benevolence of a small number of private patrons, the chief among whom were Alfred Palmer, George William Palmer and Lady Wantage. With them Childs established an extraordinary *rapport*. To them the college owed the site in London Road, the George Palmer Endowment Fund, the foundation of Wantage Hall, the University Endowment Fund, the Library, and much other encouragement both material and moral.[4] This left a stamp on the development of the institution. It gained interest and support not so much from institutions, whether of local government or concentrations of heavy industry, but from private individuals with a genuine personal interest in the adventure: after Alfred Palmer, from his grandson, Gerald Palmer, and from Gordon Palmer; from landowners in the shire, outstanding among whom in the early years of the University was Sir George Mowbray; and from senior civil servants, who on retirement moved into neighbouring villages of Berkshire. The Council of the College and University therefore took on a distinctive tone. It comprised men who were disposed to act on considered judgement with some speed and decision, and who were experienced in working together in a very informal way. But they were men too who found zest and enjoyment in their association in the University's work.

This also added to Reading's freedom of action. As it advanced from a

---

[1] *Proceedings and Reports*, 1925–6.
[2] The old Town Hall perhaps provides some indication of the form which a municipal building for the College might have taken.
[3] The phrase is A. C. Wood's. See his *History of University College, Nottingham, 1881–1948*, Oxford (1953), pp. 33–4 'Though the College and, for example, the gas works and the public wash-houses might all appear as parts of the mechanism of municipal enterprise, and by some myopic or ill-informed councillors were apt to be regarded on the same level, there were underlying differences which called for the exercise of much caution and tact'.
[4] Childs (1933), especially pp. 42–96, 131–6.

College to a University it was peculiarly unburdened except by its material circumstances. It bore no incubus of principles, political or religious, to restrict its development. It stood for nothing except the convictions and character which the conditions of its foundation and growth built into it. For the first thirty years of its existence it scarcely altered at all. It remained a small academic community slowly adding to its reputation for scholarship and as a residential institution which was also a major centre of agricultural studies. It relied on its own ways, themselves inherited from its earlier days as a college. With increasing security it became more self-contained, to the outside eye, perhaps even a little self-satisfied. At all events it had time enough to establish strong 'Reading' characteristics. To this the last twenty years of its history were in sharp contrast. The University had 793 undergraduate students under tutorial supervision in 1946 against 3,945 in 1975. In 1946 there were 74 postgraduates against 1,197 in 1975. In 1946 the academic staff numbered 143; in 1975, 600. In 1946 the University acquired a new site in Whiteknights. This made rapid expansion possible. The increasing use of this new base in turn emphasized the changes taking place. The University of 1946 was still recognizable as an immediate descendant of the College of 1925, even of 1919 or 1912. The University of 1975 was very different from that of 1946. That is the essence of Reading's history. It is a story of how a compact, self-made institution responded to demands and opportunities created by the expansion of university education after the Second World War. Reading was already a University. Its characteristics were more firmly established than those of the colleges which gained university status in the years immediately following the war. It was small. It could not take expansion so easily as the large civic universities of the midlands and the north. At Reading, therefore, the problems and consequences of change were highlighted and emphasized. In that lies the general importance of its history.

Chapter 2

The College and the University 1926

The second and final petition for the grant of a royal Charter to found the University of Reading was submitted to the King in Council in January 1925. The success of the application was announced by Childs on 30 May at the annual ceremony for the conferment of the Associateship of the University College.[1] He was chaired from the assembly by the students. The Charter which marked the foundation of the University was dated 17 March 1926. The act dissolving the College and transferring its property and liabilities to the University received the royal assent on 4 August 1926.

Among the many changes which marked the new status was a new edition of the *Calendar*. The last *Calendar* of the College was a slender volume of 107 pages issued in September 1925. The first *Calendar* of the new University, issued a year later, was more than twice the size for it included the Charter, Statutes and Ordinances, along with regulations for degrees. The old *Calendar* contained a list of the qualifications and honours which students of the College had obtained in the external examinations of the University of London over the previous ten years. It also made the residential character of Reading plain by entering the halls of residence on the front cover. The new *Calendar*, in contrast, offered the simple, plain, dignified title – *University of Reading, Calendar 1926–27*. No other advertisement was now necessary. This was not the only obvious change. The old *Calendar* contained a closely written note of some length, recording the history of the College. In 1925 this was prefaced by a bold announcement that the Charter had at last been granted. In the new *Calendar* the history was rewritten. The early developments were condensed and the story now quickly moved on to the quest for the Charter. There was one further change to note. The old *Calendar*, with touching practicality, included on the cover – price sixpence. On the new, the quieter dignity of the cover demanded the removal of the price to the spine. There, ominously, it appeared – two shillings.

The *Calendar* presented the formalities. It brought together all the carefully drafted provisions over which Childs and Francis Wright, the Registrar, had pored in the previous months. But it is only in these formal terms that

---

[1] The Associateship of the College was granted to those who passed the diploma examinations of the College or, in certain cases, pursued an approved course of study for two years and subsequently obtained academic qualifications elsewhere.

there was a transformation. In the memory of the few survivors of the staff of the old College the dramatic scene of Childs's announcement still survives as a great occasion. But none is conscious of the Charter marking some kind of millennium. Their work in teaching and research went on as before. Some recall that they were aware of an added dignity in their institution and increased responsibility in themselves, that their job had in some mysterious way become bigger. Some remember a feeling of mild surprise that Childs had managed to pull it off. But for all of them the Charter was simply a seal of approval on the work of the College. It did not mark the birth of a new institution.[1]

This is undoubtedly the right view. The grant of the Charter was itself the culmination of a long campaign. In 1906 Childs had already determined on achieving university status.[2] Even as early as that he had the powerful and independent support of Lord Haldane.[3] The College committed itself to the policy in 1911 when the University Endowment Fund of £200,000 was established by George William Palmer, Alfred Palmer and Lady Wantage.[4] It was delayed by the First World War, but that university status would ultimately be achieved was not in real doubt. When the first application of 1920 was rejected it was on the grounds that the College's financial resources were still inadequate and that the number of students reading for degrees was insufficient.[5] Despite that, the reply from the Privy Council was encouraging:

> While their Lordships feel that it would be premature to accede at
> the present stage to the application for a charter, they have been
> favourably impressed by certain features of the College organization,
> by the good work the Institution is doing, and the progress it has
> made particularly in the province of agriculture, and if the applica-
> tion is renewed when the College has increased its numbers, and
> raised its income to a figure approximating to £80,000, they will be
> willing to reconsider the matter.[6]

It was now simply a question of meeting these conditions. By 1924 it had been done: the College's revenue had risen from £52,000 in 1920 to £81,321; the endowment had been increased from £265,000 to £318,000; in the same period the number of students reading for degrees had gone up from 238 to 321. Some other important changes were obvious. New laboratories for chemistry and agricultural chemistry were brought into use in 1921. The Library was opened in 1923. The Shinfield estate was acquired in 1920 and the National Institute for Research in Dairying was

[1] This is based chiefly on conversations with Dr Nellie B. Eales. See also Stenton's comment, below p. 46.
[2] Childs (1933), pp. 109–21.
[3] *Ibid.*, p. 122.
[4] *Ibid.*, pp. 153–66.
[5] *Ibid.*, pp. 243–4.
[6] *Ibid.*

established there in 1924.[1] However, in the end success was due as much to Reading's special qualities as to the incremental process which met or approached the formal requirements stated by the Privy Council in 1921. In the earlier letter of rejection the work in agriculture had been specially commended. In the acceptance which Childs received on 22 May 1925 it was Reading's residential structure which was singled out:

> It is mainly owing to the well developed residential system estab-
> lished by the College, and its determination to concentrate its limited
> resources upon the Faculties of Arts, Pure Science and Agriculture,
> that their Lordships have felt able to accept in this case a consider-
> ably lower standard both of income and number of students than
> they would ordinarily have considered it necessary to require.[2]

Childs commented with a note of deep self-satisfaction:

> That was an interesting point about our residential system. The
> human side of our work, then, had carried the day. Our long struggle
> to make our College into a true university society did not depend
> for its rightness upon this or any external verdict. But its rightness
> would be reinforced by this historic proof of its wisdom.[3]

In some ways Childs's comment was misleading. It was certainly retro-spective and perhaps, looking back over his achievement, he placed too much emphasis on Reading's residential structure. Reading got its Charter for its qualities in scholarship, experiment and teaching. That it provided a nice billet for students which guarded their manners and morals was secondary. In 1925 Childs published a number of articles in the local press in which he gave some account of the development and underlying principles of the new University.[4] Much the most penetrating of these was entitled 'Universities and research'. In this Childs urged the argument forward with a confidence which was astonishing, coming as it did, from a new-born university:

> The primary business of all universities is to teach. . . . But it is an
> axiom that the best teaching can only be given when the teacher is
> himself a student and investigator. Since our theme is university
> teaching, this is the point to stress. If our theme were the teaching
> of young children . . . it would be right . . . to emphasize the value
> of a proper teaching method. When, however, those under instruc-
> tion are of the age of university students method matters less. The
> test question then is the amount of the teacher's knowledge. Does
> the teacher know his subject from outside and just enough of it to
> pass muster, or does he know it from the inside with the sure mastery

---

[1] *Ibid.*, pp. 251–2, 257–8.
[2] *Ibid.*, p. 260. In 1921 the Privy Council was advised by the UGC that £100,000 was the minimum requisite income for a small multi-faculty university (*ibid.*, p. 243).
[3] *Ibid.*
[4] He collected these under the title *The new University of Reading: some ideas for which it stands* (Reading, 1926).

that belongs to the master craftsman alone? In the one case, no method will save him; in the other case, no method will matter.

So long as a university is a vigorous centre for research, a 'factory of new knowledge', as Huxley expressed it, it matters little what particular line of research happens to be in the ascendant. . . . A university is the last place in the world to allow intellectual interests to be pared down at the dictates of a mean economy to the merely useful. A university is the highest form of intellectual association: it is for the benefit not of cliques and sections, but of man, whom Shakespeare proclaimed to be noble in reason and infinite in faculty. And who is to say what is useful and what is not? How many of the great discoverers and thinkers . . . have been regarded by their contemporaries as wastrels! How many of the prophets have been stoned! When Galileo brooded over the system of the universe, was he supposed to be 'usefully' engaged? Which of his contemporaries foresaw whither Darwin's first quiet and unadvertised researches would lead? How far were the brothers Wright held to be 'usefully' employed when they risked their lives in experiments with crazy flying machines?

Research for its own sake is a condition of university health and vigour.[1]

That is a statement of principle no longer regarded as orthodox by zealous educationists or cost-conscious governments. But Childs was no innocent. He had one professor whose control of students was so weak that his lectures were anarchic. He lived daily with the painful duty of allocating pitifully scarce resources to men and departments each one of whom was making just demands for support. Yet through these difficulties he saw the fundamental principles and ideals of university work clear. And he had done more than simply enunciate sound doctrine. He proudly pointed to the fact that in 1924 the College had established a Research Board with the duty of 'promoting and stimulating' research and that the Council of the College had already assigned £500 to it for the year 1925–6.[2] Already therefore, Reading had placed resources in the hands of a small committee of its senior men with instructions to direct them to the general development of research throughout the University.[3]

Childs also substantiated his argument along another line. As an appendix to his collection he included a list of publications which had been submitted along with the petition for the Charter in 1925.[4] It covered

---

[1] Childs (1926), pp. 34–7.
[2] Childs (1926), pp. 39–40.
[3] Stenton was the first Chairman of the Board. The other members were Childs as Principal, Cole, Crowther, H. A. D. Neville, Percival, Stiles and Alfred Palmer as Chairman of Council; Wolters was the first Secretary. The responsibilities of the Board did not extend to the National Institute for Research in Dairying.
[4] Childs (1926), pp. 53–64.

the six years since 1919. It included W. G. de Burgh's *Legacy of the Ancient World* (1924), P. N. Ure's *Greek Renaissance* (1921) and the *Origins of Tyranny* (1922), Stenton's *Documents illustrative of the social and economic history of the Danelaw* (1920) and *Transcripts of Gilbertine Charters* (1921), two monographs of E. H. Neville and a major book on *Prologomena to analytical geometry in anisotropic Euclidean space of three dimensions* (1922), J. Percival's great monograph on *The Wheat Plant* (1921),[1] W. Stiles on *Permeability* (1924), along with a long list of papers both literary and scientific. For so small a College this was good going. When Reading made its second application in 1925 it was clearly a centre of academic distinction. In the year of the Charter F. J. Cole was elected a Fellow of the Royal Society and Stenton a Fellow of the British Academy.

Despite, or perhaps because of, the firm priorities which Childs enunciated, the record in teaching was equally impressive. In 1926, the last year of the full operation of the London external degree for Reading students, thirty-eight candidates took the examination for Honours. Of eleven historians two took Firsts, and of eight candidates for French one took a First. Of the 159 students who obtained an Honours B.A. in the London examination between 1919 and 1926 fourteen took Firsts. Of the forty who read for Special Honours in the B.Sc. six took Firsts.[2] This is all the more remarkable in that those who read for Honours were only a small proportion of the students. Indeed those reading for degrees were very much a minority. Teaching the brilliant had to be fitted in to much more extensive commitments for a wide range of achievement, ability and ambition. Hence there was a link between research and the teaching of the Honours students. Without the real flair for research which was present in some outstanding members of the staff and which set a standard for the College as a whole, there would have been a greater danger of slipping into a comfortable round of teaching for the Intermediate Examination and the General Degree. This did not happen. Indeed one or two went to the other extreme. Looking back in 1943, E. H. Neville could roundly assert that he had only ever had three pupils at Reading who were worth teaching.[3] His memory was slightly at fault. Since 1926 the University had awarded just four Firsts in Mathematics.

The achievement both in teaching and research was noteworthy. It is well to dwell on it, not as a basis of comparison with the other university colleges of the day which were pursuing similar lines of their own with similar dedication, but as an indication of the high standard which was

[1] Reprinted 1975.
[2] This information is tabulated in the *Calendar 1925–6*, pp. 75–88, and for 1926 in the *Proceedings 1925–6*, pp. 64–5.
[3] 'I have said nothing of the value of first-class students to the staff. In the course of twenty years there have been in my Department three men worth teaching: this state of affairs is a lamentable waste of the abilities which Mr Broadbent, Mr Goodstein and I have brought to the service of our profession' (URC, Registrar, box 219).

then required of an institution which was seeking the privilege of granting its own degrees.

The achievement was all the more remarkable in that it was the work of an academic staff which in the first year of the University totalled 148. When spread across all the departments this was meagre indeed.[1] Some subjects, such as German and Spanish, were in the hands of sessional lecturers or teachers appointed from year to year. Others, like Psychology and Economics, were managed by just one lecturer. It was not uncommon in all faculties for a major subject to be in the hands of a professor with one lecturer to assist him and perhaps some ancillary help. De Burgh managed Philosophy along with one lecturer. In Geography there were two lecturers along with a sessional assistant lecturer. In Zoology, in addition to Cole, there was one lecturer, Dr Nellie Eales, and a museum assistant. In Agricultural Botany, in addition to Percival, there was one lecturer, Dr Adela Erith, and a demonstrator. In Agriculture, in addition to the professor, S. Pennington, there was a lecturer and an instructress. Some departments were fortunate enough to have two lecturers in addition to the professor. That was the case in English, where there were two Chairs, of Language and Literature, and also in History, French, Physics, Chemistry, Botany, Geology and Agricultural Chemistry. In some of these departments there was also ancillary assistance.[2] Only a handful of departments had larger establishments. In Classics Ure had three lecturers, along with his wife, Annie D. Ure, as an honorary research fellow. In Mathematics E. H. Neville had three lecturers. In Education there were five lecturers and three sessional teachers in addition to the senior lecturer in charge. That was the largest single teaching department in the University apart from the Schools of Art and Music.[3]

The University was no better off in other essential staffing. Excluding the National Institute for Research in Dairying, there were just nine laboratory assistants in the whole of the rest of the University in 1926–7. Physics and Agricultural Botany each had one steward. Agricultural Chemistry and Botany each had one attendant. Zoology had both a steward and an attendant and Chemistry the comparative luxury of a steward and two attendants. The picture was the same in other sectors of the University's work. In the Library, the Librarian, S. A. Peyton, was reinforced by two part-time assistants and a porter.[4] Among the Deans of Faculties, H. A. D. Neville in Agriculture and Horticulture was the

[1] The following analysis is based on the *Calendar 1926–7*.
[2] In History, S. A. Peyton, the Librarian, figured as an assistant lecturer. Childs was also an honorary professor of history. In French there was a French-speaking sessional assistant. In Chemistry there was a sessional lecturer and a technical teacher. In Agricultural Chemistry there was an adviser and two analysts.
[3] The School of Art listed nine teachers and the School of Music seventeen, but their staffing was on a different basis, many of the teachers being in effect part-time.
[4] The establishment was changed in 1928 to two graduate assistants, a part-time clerk and one porter.

only one to have a permanent secretary. The others had to call when necessary on the resources of the Registrar's staff. Professors and departments had no secretarial staff. Nor were they supplied with GPO telephones unless the nature of their work made it absolutely necessary. So straitened were the circumstances to which they were accustomed that it became difficult to distinguish between laudable economy and enervating parsimony. To the newcomer it could be forbidding. When J. A. Betts was appointed as Lecturer in Charge of the School of Art in 1933, he entered upon his empire to find a splendid studio for his personal use furnished with one single item, a kitchen chair.

There is no surviving witness to these early years who does not return again and again to the new University's lack of resources. It affected all its activities from the Library to the management of laboratories. From the foundation of 1926 up to the war the Library could rarely count on an annual income of much more than £2,000.[1] The purchase of essential periodicals was managed centrally by the Librarian. The remainder of his budget, when apportioned, provided roughly £60 a year for each of the major book-purchasing departments. Essentially the Library was dependent on the extraordinary skill with which the funds were managed, on gifts of books or money and on occasional non-recurrent grants from the University Grants Committee. Somehow few major opportunities to buy essential works of scholarship were missed. The budget for the day-to-day running of departments was equally parsimonious. In 1926–7 the total of the departmental and laboratory maintenance votes for the Faculty of Science was £875.[2] Only a proportion of this was available for the day-to-day running of the laboratories. In the Department of Zoology, where the total budget was £145, the laboratory was managed on £60 a year. This increased slowly over the years but was still little more than £100 at the outbreak of the Second World War. The Department had only five microscopes carefully acquired over the years. Cole bought his own slides: in his report for the *Proceedings 1926* he stated the facts bluntly:

> The laboratories are uncomfortably crowded. There is urgent need
> for more microscopes; the inadequate supply causes much incon-
> venience . . . [The Department] needs lecture-rooms, laboratories,
> equipment and especially a museum.

In the memory of the laboratory steward, F. C. Padley, the pattern of the working year was determined by the need to husband resources and hence,

---

[1] The vote of Council was £1,300, increased to £1,750 in 1930. The Library Endowment provided a further £225.

[2] The total was broken down as follows:

Mathematics (a moiety)	15	0	0	Zoology	145	0	0
Physics	160	0	0	Geography (a moiety)	15	0	0
Chemistry	285	0	0	Geology	65	0	0
Botany	190	0	0			

For further discussion and comparisons with other sections of the University's work see below pp. 22–3.

in this subject, partly by the seasons. In the second week in March his main duty was to visit ponds in Tilehurst where he collected frogs for use in the Department during the coming year. A wet night would bring him out on to the lawns adding to the departmental stock of worms.[1] Economical management, personal devotion and the readiness to make do and find time was a pattern repeated in department after department. Even the students were involved. In the Dairy the foreman, the formidable Jim Robinson, had the students scrubbing the floor. They still returned after many years to visit him.[2]

The inadequacy of the new University's accommodation was probably the most serious problem of all. In January 1926 Childs decided to conclude his first statement to the University Court on this theme. With the Charter not yet sealed and delivered, he turned to examine the real weakness of the new University's position:

> The perusal of this statement, even if not supplemented by a first-hand acquaintance with the circumstances of the University, will suggest two questions in practical policy which are now becoming urgent. The first is the question of accommodation for teaching and research. It is unnecessary to recapitulate the observations of deans and professors upon this subject. The situation is plain. With few exceptions, the accommodation afforded by the existing buildings is exhausted. Inconvenience already occurs; the marked over-crowding of the manual instruction room in the School of Art, and the wretched provision for Geology are only two of many instances that might be quoted; and if the University is to continue to grow, its quarters must be enlarged. Every faculty, and nearly every department, needs more space. The problem is, therefore, formidable; but it is useless to try to conceal its existence. The University of Reading may not be ambitious to attain great size. Such a prospect is far removed, and there are indeed convincing reasons in favour of a university of modest dimensions. But the University as it is today is almost dangerously small: it promises to grow and it ought to grow. To check growth before a reasonable university stature has been attained would be disastrous. When universities generally are expanding, Reading cannot afford to restrict its proportions to those of a college. Unwelcome though the present situation may be, there is in it nothing surprising. The attainment of university status has brought with it a new impetus and a new responsibility. Neither can be neglected without peril. It is to be borne in mind that our building schemes are in arrears. A small hall has long been badly wanted. A building was planned years ago

[1] Conversation with F. C. Padley, 26 September 1975.
[2] Conversation with F. C. Padley. See also his 'The Technical Staff before 1930' in *Staff Journal*, University of Reading, no. 7 (1969), pp. 13–16 and his 'Recollections', MS in the University Library.

to meet certain requirements of the Faculty of Letters. It proved impossible to erect it. Relief was secured by the generous action which placed at the disposal of the College the private houses in Portland Place. But valuable as the rooms there have proved, they do not suffice for all the requirements of today; and many of them are now useless for teaching, owing to the noise of motor traffic. The buildings of the Faculty of Science are practically what they were when they were erected twenty years ago. Their design has completely justified itself, but they should now be enlarged. The obvious method of enlargement is to carry out the idea contemplated and provided for when they were built, and raise them by one storey. The Faculty of Agriculture and Horticulture has never been adequately housed. Years ago a large building was planned, but only parts of it have materialized. Additions, some of them important (e.g. laboratories for Agricultural Chemistry and Agricultural Botany, and the Machinery Hall), have been made from time to time: but something more is now needed. The School of Art is overcrowded: the School of Music should be rebuilt. The University site still possesses unoccupied space which could be used without destroying the impression of its homely buildings set amongst lawns and gardens. I have already drawn the attention of the Council to this question of accommodation. I now lay it before the University Court and the public. Here is a young university, full of vigour and promise. It is growing: and it ought to grow. What it covets is not a lavish architecture, but roomy and convenient workshops in the simple style which has been tested and found good by our experience of the last twenty years. Can we not find helpers and benefactors once again? This at least is certain: the problem presses, it is likely to press more, and it must be dealt with if the University is not to be brought to a stand.

The University Halls

The University Halls are full. Many students whose homes are at a distance have no alternative but to live in licensed rooms. The residential Halls at Reading were one of the main factors which brought the University into being. They are also one of the main reasons why the University attracts students from the country at large. Reading was in this matter a pioneer: it set an example which has been widely followed by other universities and colleges. One modern university is now building a Hall for men students which will be as big as Wantage Hall and St Patrick's Hall together. Other instances could be quoted. One aspect, therefore, of this question is whether Reading is to preserve its lead and its reputation as a residential university. It must be obvious also that a university which requires students from a distance to live in Halls, but is in fact unable to provide enough Halls for them to live in, is com-

mitting itself to many difficulties of administration and control.
The University now possesses land at Whitley on which new Halls
could be raised if funds were forthcoming. This problem, like the
previous one, will force itself more and more upon the attention of
the University. It is satisfactory to be able to report the possibility
of an early extension of St Patrick's Hall owing to a special grant
for the purpose from the University Grants Committee. But valuable as this enlargement would be, it does not dispose of the general
problem which affects the residence of women students as well as
men students.[1]

Childs naturally did not set this lengthy plea against those arguments
which had buttressed the recent application for the Charter, nor did he
reflect on that unevenness which bedevils the development of academic
institutions. The plain fact was that Reading's distinction in teaching and
research, reinforced by his own insistent advocacy, had enabled it to
acquire its independence as a university earlier than its material resources
really warranted. It now had to bring them up to scratch.

There were other attendant problems. Much the most important was
the role played and to be played by the Faculty of Agriculture and Horticulture. In the *Proceedings 1925–6* the report from the Farm and Horticultural
Station was sufficient to indicate that Reading was to be no ordinary
university:

Reports from the Farm and Horticultural Station are satisfactory.
Cereal crops were good and were well harvested. Root crops suffered
from the drought at the end of the summer. In the Berkshire Milk
Recording Society's trials, the Farm herd was again placed second
in the small herd section, and it won the cup for grading-up. Grass-
fed sheep won the first prize at the Wokingham Agricultural Show:
a first prize was also won for table poultry. Professor Percival's
wheats ('Fox', 'Starling', and 'Blue Cone') have done well in numerous places. 'Fox' headed the list of trials at the Midland Agricultural College, with a yield of over 6 quarters an acre. From a York-
shire farm, a yield of $7\frac{1}{2}$ quarters is reported. This year the demand
for seed has outstripped the supply. Apples in 1925 were a record
crop. Newton Wonder yielded $13\frac{1}{2}$ tons from 100 trees occupying
less than an acre. The plum crop of 1926 was good: but weather
conditions here as elsewhere adversely affected the apple crop. The
University exhibit at the Royal Show held at Reading in July,
1926, included fruit trees (about 100), and flowers (about 1,500
plants). A feature was the exhibit showing the evolution of the
dahlia. Prizes for apples were won at the Imperial Fruit Show; a
gold medal was won for a non-competitive exhibit at the Reading
Horse and Agricultural Show; and a new dwarf dahlia received the

[1] *Proceedings 1925–6*, pp. 44–5.

Award of Merit at the trials of the Royal Horticultural Society.
Many lectures were given in the locality by members of the horticultural staff, who also acted as judges on many occasions. Advisory
work increases. Large totals were as usual recorded for the principal
crops of vegetables, fruit and flowers.

No one should be misled by the pleasantly bucolic tone of this note. In 1926
the Faculty was already the largest and most complex centre of agricultural teaching and research in the United Kingdom.

The development of agriculture and its associated subjects is the first
and probably the most striking example of a policy which Reading's
geographical location encouraged: development through association and
amalgamation, even annexation. Expansion had come from a coincidence
of interest in which men and institutions with practical requirements drew
on and in turn supported the growing expertise of the Faculty. It took place
at an opportune moment. Reading was establishing its resources in agriculture just as British farming, by transferring investment from arable to
meat and dairy production, was achieving some recovery from the de-
pressions of 1875–84 and 1891–9. The teaching of agricultural subjects
was founded in the first place on support from the newly revived Board
of Agriculture,[1] and the transfer from Aylesbury to Reading of the British
Dairy Institute.[2] In 1926 the Institute was still a highly active section of the
College:

The Manager of the British Dairy Institute reports a slight fall in
the number of long-course students last Session; but the entries for
the present Session are larger. The total number of students attending the Institute last year was 146. Nineteen students passed the
examination for the Diploma in Dairying granted by University
College and by the British Dairy Farmers' Association; 14 gained
the National Dairy Diploma; and 53 gained certificates for butter-
making or cheese-making granted by the British Dairy Farmers'
Association. During the year 44,565 gallons of milk were used in
the Institute; and 2,177 lb. of butter were made as well as a large
quantity of cheese of many varieties. The usual exhibit was arranged
for the Dairy Show.[3]

However, there were now other important links with government and
agricultural organizations. Before the First World War the Berkshire
County Council had placed its agricultural programme under the supervision of the College. In 1926 the Faculty was providing lectures, demonstrations and classes throughout the County in addition to testing samples

[1] The Board of Agriculture was refounded in 1889 on the model of the Board of Trade.
It retained that title until 1903 when it became the Board of Agriculture and Fisheries.
It was converted to a Ministry in 1919.
[2] See above, p. 7.
[3] *Proceedings 1925–6*, pp. 37–8.

in the laboratories. Scholarships were also provided for Berkshire students.[1] The College had also become the centre for the southern province of the Agricultural Advisory Service which the Board of Agriculture had established. In 1926 advisory officers were engaged in linking the research of the College with practical agricultural problems which ranged from field-plot trials of manures, the cost of producing TT milk, to the control of the mangold fly and the prevention of Bunt in wheat. Finally in 1912 the Board of Agriculture and Fisheries had given support to the establishment of a research institute which became the National Institute for Research in Dairying. In 1920 the Shinfield estate was acquired for the Institute, which moved there in 1924. In 1926 it was engaged in a wide variety of work on cattle foods, milk yields, cheese production, and, most important of all, the bacteriology of milk, especially of tuberculin infection. The work of the Director, Professor Stenhouse Williams, in this field was included by Childs in his list of research submitted in support of the petition for the Charter.[2]

These links brought in revenue.[3] In 1926 the Parliamentary grant-in-aid for the University of £26,500 was almost matched by the recurrent grants for agriculture. The Ministry of Agriculture and Fisheries provided £19,435 for the general work of the Faculty, the operation of the Farm, the advisory work and the National Institute for Research in Dairying.[4] It also provided a further £900 for the Dairy Institute, and the Berkshire County Council contributed £3,922 from its Agricultural Instruction Committee. The revenue went in part to the provision of staff. In 1926–7 the Dairy Institute had three academic staff. The work from Berkshire was in the hands of five instructors. The staff providing the Advisory Service totalled four. At the National Institute Stenhouse Williams was backed by seven lecturers, researchers and assistants, along with a librarian. Together, the staff in the various branches of agriculture was roughly equivalent in number to the whole of the Faculty of Science. At the National Institute there were more laboratory assistants, eleven in all, than in the whole of the rest of the University; there were also five office assistants, including a curator of farm records.

In 1926 the Faculty of Agriculture and Horticulture suffered from the disabilities of all other sections of the University. It was short of teaching accommodation and research facilities. But in terms of its total resources

---

[1] *Ibid.*, pp. 39–40.
[2] *Ibid.*, pp. 38–9, for the work in 1926 and Childs (1933), pp. 200–1, 251–2, for the earliest history. The notes on the work of Stenhouse Williams and other members of the Faculty are in Childs (1929), pp. 53–64 *passim*.
[3] In what follows all the information about income and expenditure and student statistics is taken from *Proceedings 1925–6*. The information about staff is taken from the *Calendar 1926–7*.
[4] £3,300 was granted for general purposes, £200 for the Farm, £3,696 for the advisory work and £12,239 for the National Institute for Research in Dairying.

it was in a much healthier and more confident condition than the rest. With all its ancillaries it accounted for approximately half the University's departmental expenditure. The departmental and laboratory budgets of the Faculty amounted to nearly twice those of the Faculty of Science. The budget for Agriculture and Dairying was higher than the total for the whole Faculty of Science.[1] The Faculty and its ancillaries also had an edge in its academic staff. The Faculty of Science numbered 29. The Faculty of Agriculture proper numbered 30, of whom two were shared with the National Institute. But with all the ancillaries added, the agriculturalists totalled 48 out of a total of 148 academic staff in the University.

The advantages of these arrangements were immense. The teaching in agriculture benefited enormously from the involvement in national and local responsibilities. Likewise the diversification of agriculture spread the involvement to departments in the Faculty of Science, especially to the biological sciences and geology; more generally also, the Faculty provided an example of a well supported range of subjects directed towards practical research. It set a standard, as yet distant and unattainable in other subjects, of the resources which might yet be accumulated for the proper pursuit of university work.

Against this the College passed on to the University a problem which was very apparent in its agricultural work but was by no means restricted thereto. Much of its teaching was not of university standard. At least, much of it did not involve work for a first degree or postgraduate qualification, whether certificate, diploma, master's degree or doctorate. The reasons for this went back to the College's foundation in which a University Extension College had been combined with local Schools of Science and Art. To this the developments in agriculture had added responsibilities which were not related to degree work. In pressing for the Charter, Childs and others had of course been acutely aware of the need to increase the numbers reading for degrees, and indeed the Privy Council had required this of them.[2] But when the College became a University there were no obvious alternative institutions to which the non-degree work might be transferred. Hence the work of the College passed *in toto* to the University.

The effect of this was marked. In 1926 fewer than half the total number of registered students were under tutorial supervision, receiving that pastoral care which Childs had imported with such pride from Oxford. Of those under tutorial supervision less than half were reading for degrees.

---

[1] In 1926 the Faculty absorbed £15,000 out of a total departmental expenditure of £50,000. To this £15,693 should be added for the National Institute for Research in Dairying and £4,927 for the Dairy Institute making a total of approximately £35,500, out of a total of approximately £71,500. The total of the maintenance votes of the Faculty (excluding the National Institute for Research in Dairying, the Dairy Institute and the Advisory Service) was £2,591. The total for the Faculty of Science was £1,005. The Department of Agriculture and Dairying had a vote of £1,112.
[2] See above, p. 12.

The total of 1,656 students was distributed as follows:

Day students under tutorial supervision
    reading for a degree   306
    reading for a diploma   247
    reading for a certificate   60
    reading other courses   58   671

Day students not under tutorial supervision   275

Evening students   710

                    Total   1656

A roughly similar distribution is revealed by the examination results reported for the same year. These were:

Degree examinations[1]

M.A.	1
B.A., B.Sc., Final Examination, Pass	82
or Honours, General or Special	
B.Sc. Part I	3
Intermediate	45
College diplomas	100
College certificates	75
Dairy Institute diplomas	36
Dairy Institute certificates	53
Other examinations	54

The diplomas, except for the one-year postgraduate Diploma in Education, were all awarded after courses of two years' duration. The certificates were a miscellaneous bag, some involving a year's course, some evening work over a longer period, one of them a 'ten weeks' course in poultry-keeping.

    This non-degree work was concentrated in a pattern largely determined by the evolution of the College. The Faculty of Agriculture with its ancillaries had the largest proportion of diplomas and certificates as against degrees, 175 compared with a mere 6 B.Sc.s.[2] It also had to contend with the most variegated demand for teaching. In 1926, Percival was Vice-President of the Linnean Society of London. A graduate student from Cracow had come to study under him. Both he and H. A. D. Neville were

---

[1] These were all external examinations of the University of London.
[2] These were B.Sc. (Agriculture) General Degrees. There were also three successful candidates in B.Sc. (Horticulture) Part I.

attracting research students who had graduated in pure science. At the same time, in its local training work in Berkshire, the Faculty was providing courses in hedging at nine different centres, one course in rick thatching and, at Abingdon, a course in horticulture, dairying, poultry and bee-keeping for the Women's Institutes.

The second concentration of such work arose from the College's origin in the local Schools of Science and Art. This left it with a foot in a wide range of technical, domestic and craft subjects. It provided a two-year Diploma in Domestic Subjects in a department which had more staff than any department in the Faculty of Science except Mathematics. In 1926 seven students received the Diploma, and a further eight the Certificate, in Domestic Subjects. The enormous number of 710 evening students was spread across all Faculties except Agriculture, 415 of them falling in the Faculty of Letters, where most of them were at work in the Department of Commerce and the School of Art. There were also more than a hundred engaged on Machine Construction and Building Construction in the Faculty of Science and twenty-one attending a new course instituted with the co-operation of the Reading Gas Company on Gas Fitting and Gas Supply; for this a teacher in Gas Fitting and Gas Supply figured in the Department of Chemistry. The College always reported the daily occupations of its evening students. This splendid source of local social history is in some ways predictable. In 1926 much the largest group, working it is to be presumed for commercial qualifications, was listed as 'clerks'. Teachers came next, numbering seventy-four, plus one solitary governess. The next largest total of thirty-five was described as 'persons engaged in household duties'. There was naturally a wide scatter of students employed in trades and industries. The College was also providing an educational diet of some kind for a number of apprentices and, among other oddities, for a soldier, a brewer and the manageress of a billiard hall. Some of this work was examined by other authorities. In 1926 there were two candidates in Builders' Quantities in the City and Guilds of London Institute examination, forty-five candidates in the examinations of the Royal Society of Arts, chiefly in Book-keeping, and six successful candidates in the examinations of the Institute of Certificated Grocers. Study was encouraged by numerous College prizes.

All this was separate from the Tutorial classes under the Joint Committee of the College and the Workers' Educational Association. In all, it amounted to a massive investment of time and resources. It was particularly worth-while in agricultural subjects where there was a continuous exchange of ideas and expertise between theory and practice. There were also other areas where there was a convenient mixture of the academic with the practical and the professional. The School of Music already had an established reputation. It provided no degree courses as yet, but it taught for a College Diploma and the various national examinations in the subject; it also provided instrumental and vocal tuition. The School of Art likewise provided practical training. In 1926 it had fifty-five students, fourteen of whom were awarded the Diploma in Fine Art. Finally the Department of Education provided various forms of teacher-training. These three branches of the College went back to its earliest days. The School of Art was the oldest of all, dating from 1860 and the original establishment in West Street. The School of Music had been established as a department of the College in 1897. The training of teachers had begun at Reading in 1892 and the College was recognized as a Day Training College in 1899.[1] The Department of Education had played a particularly important role in the College's early development. Its requirements as a training college ensured the survival in the early years of the Literary Department, from which the Faculty of Letters emerged, and hence it effectively ensured that the College would not become a purely technical or agricultural institution.[2] The Department had developed in a varied manner. It provided a post-graduate diploma for intending teachers with degrees. It also embraced students who were taking two-year courses of training as teachers. All equally attended degree classes. In 1926 eleven students obtained the Diploma in Education.

At its birth the University of Reading was committed by its history to extraordinarily diverse responsibilities. It had become a university, but it was also an agricultural college, a technical college, a teacher-training college, a college of art, a college of music, a college of further education and a centre for both the Workers' Educational Association and other extra-mural education. It will not be lost on the attentive reader that it was in fact a comprehensive institution of higher education. In later years this might have attracted the laudatory attention of the *avant-garde*. Reading might have been blessed by ministerial visits and sundry other uncovenanted benefits. It could even have been upheld as a shining example to the rest of the country, with its vital statistics displayed for others to copy. In 1926 these multifarious interests awoke no such responses. Instead the new University got down to defining and refining its proper function.

---

[1] The earliest history of the Department is summarized and discussed by various of its members in *The Education Department through fifty years*, ed. H. C. Barnard (Reading 1949).

[2] See Stenton's preface to the above, *ibid.*, pp. 4–6.

Chapter 3

Developments 1926–39

W. M. Childs retired as Vice-Chancellor in 1929, four years after the successful application for the Charter. He had dominated the College and the University by sheer force of personality. In his clarity of purpose, his energy, his effectiveness, he was a giant of a man, perhaps the only one in the whole of this story.

Throughout his life he showed a remarkable capacity to establish easy relations with the patrons of the College, above all with George William Palmer, Alfred Palmer and Lady Wantage. Without this relationship there would have been no University. Childs was able to encourage in them that same interest and concern which drove him on. He persuaded them to provide the land and the endowments on which the University was founded. Even more he was ready to visit local firms, cap in hand, in seeking contributions to the Reading Citizens' Endowment Fund.[1] This ability to get men of wealth behind him was one of his chief qualities. Yet he hated to beg for money.[2]

This was only one of several conflicting traits in an unusually complex character. Those who knew him as a colleague are at one in expressing surprise that a man who seemed austere and remote in his relations with the academic staff should have been able to develop such easy relationships with the Palmers, the Suttons and the county landowners. With them he seems to have established an understanding, trust and ready give-and-take in discussion which eluded him when dealing with all but the closest of his colleagues in the University. One of his few errors was to propose a form of University government which would have perpetuated this personal experience.

He was not just a fund raiser. From the moment in 1906 when he first announced it, he pursued the objective of university status with a methodical and relentless intent. He was personally responsible for some of the most characteristic features of the University College: the emphasis on residence and the importance of agriculture. He was the inspiration behind the movement for the Charter. Indeed he gave it his own ingenious touch by including in his final statement of the College's revenues all the special

[1] Childs (1933), pp. 249–50.
[2] That was the opinion of Miss Florence Maslen, Childs's secretary.

provisions which the government made for the National Institute for
Research in Dairying. Hence he achieved the target required by the Privy
Council through sums which the government itself provided.[1] His general
abilities were formidable. In marshalling an argument he was outstanding.
In pressing it to a conclusion he was ruthless. Yet, despite this relentlessness,
he knew when to hang back and allow time for a point to sink in. It took
him twenty years to found the University. He never lost sight of the ultimate
objective. His vision of a university was sharply focused. He saw the way
to it. He had little appreciation and less patience with what lay outside his
view. Everything on the periphery was ignored or simply swept into his own
discernment of what the University should be. He was a man to found a
university. He was not equally a man to develop one, once founded.

Some of this is revealed in his treatment of what came to be remembered
as the Great Row.[2] Occasionally the devotion of universities to the arts of
peace is interrupted by an internecine belligerence in the management of
their internal affairs. From 1913 to 1916 the University College was riven by
such an argument. It concerned the proposed constitution of the new
University. Childs, supported by a majority in the Academic Board and by
all the lay members of the responsible College committee,[3] wanted to
establish a unicameral system of government in which decisions on academic,
financial and administrative matters would all be taken in a single body, in
which lay members and members of academic staff would join. The scheme
also envisaged the establishment of a small powerful Finance Board on
which the Principal would be the only academic member. A majority of
the professors objected. Indeed they rebelled:

> Having met together they resolved unanimously to form themselves
> into a Committee, and to oppose by every legitimate means the
> incorporation of the official constitution in the University Charter.[4]

In February 1914 eight of them issued a splendidly printed *Appeal against
the form of constitution proposed for the University of Reading*.[5] They argued
vigorously for the more usual arrangement of Council and Senate, with

[1] Childs (1933), p. 258.
[2] The story is summarized, a little tendentiously, in Childs (1933), pp. 206–9.
It was also reviewed by Childs in two pamphlets written, but not circulated, in 1916.
On these see below pp. 30–1. The importance of the Great Row in the constitution of the
University is discussed further below pp. 266–8, 272.
[3] Childs (1933) gave the balance on the Committee as eight to two. He did not indicate
that the minority of two were academic members.
[4] See their *Appeal* (discussed in the following note), p. 3.
[5] The dissentients were Bassett (Chemistry), A. L. Bowley (formerly Professor of
Mathematics and now Lecturer in Economics), Cole (Zoology), R. Dewar (English
Literature), H. N. Dickson (Geography), W. G. Duffield (Physics), F. Keeble (Botany),
S. B. McClaren (Mathematics) and Edith J. Morley (English Language).
I am grateful to Professor Barnard for lending Cole's copy of the manifesto to me. This
copy also bears Sir Franklin Sibly's signature on the fly-leaf. It contains a few annotations
by Cole, on which see p. 29, note 1 below. It seems likely that the *Appeal*, which runs to
fourteen octavo pages and is printed on very high quality paper, was produced in the
School of Art.

the latter exercising immediate authority in all academic matters. They opposed the concentration of financial authority in a small committee which lacked professorial representation and went on to assert that 'the scheme gives excessive power to the Principal. Instead of being *primus inter pares*, he may easily become the dictator of the University'.[1] The details of the quarrel no longer matter. The objectors won. They gained support from responsible opinion outside the College.[2] Faced with such opposition the Council of the College did not press the scheme. When the University was established in 1926, it was given the usual constitution of Council and Senate.

Childs had been defeated. Yet when he wrote about these events in 1933 he scarcely allowed himself to say so. He was an effective exponent of the short, trenchant sentence. His admission on this occasion was obscure and convoluted:

> Quiescence came at last, and the final outcome of this episode of disunion, which remains the one cloud of its kind in a history of forty years, was the draft of a constitution which, except for a few particulars, such as the unusually large academic representation upon the Council, corresponds closely with the normal pattern.[3]

He was more concerned to emphasize the statesmanship of the defeated party:

> Deliberately, but without hesitation, the Council set itself to tread the path of compromise . . . . There were no martyrs. There was no public scandal. Constitutional authority emerged unscathed: it had kept its head in situations where there was some temptation to lose it.[4]

This was curiously insensitive. So also was his comment on the position of the Principal:

> Some persons, I believe, imagined that it must be inspired by visions of autocracy, or by transatlantic precedents.[5]

---

[1] *Appeal*, p. 10. Cole here pencilled in an 'a' to replace the somewhat accusatory definite article attached to the word 'Principal'. He also queried 'being' as if it were a little odd to suggest that the Principal was in fact a *primus inter pares*. Childs certainly was not.
[2] In 1933 Childs noted that the dissentients 'made their grievances known outside Reading' (*ibid.*, p. 207). He also sought views elsewhere. The surviving answers are uniformly against him. Sir Joseph Larmon, Lucasian Professor of Mathematics at Cambridge wrote 'I may say at once that if I had a responsibility in the matter I would be unhesitatingly on the side of the dissentients'; he suggested that Lord Haldane should be asked to arbitrate. Sir Walter Raleigh, Professor of English Literature at Oxford, apparently writing to one of the dissentients, perhaps Edith Morley, commented 'Thank you for the Appeal. I agree with every word of it. . . . If the constitution passes Reading will cease I think to be a serious rival to the other new universities'. Sir Henry Jones, Professor of Moral Philosophy at Glasgow, writing to Childs, commented on his proposed scheme – 'while one of its main purposes . . . is to overcome 'duality' and secure harmony, I should expect the very possibility of it to create dissension'. He was right. (URC, Registrar, box 219).
[3] Childs (1933), pp. 208–9.
[4] *Ibid.*
[5] *Ibid.*, p. 206.

That scarcely did justice to the straightforward and well founded objections which Cole and others had presented twenty years earlier.

The rift was serious. At one point Childs came close to widening it beyond repair. After his death in 1939 Mrs Childs deposited a sealed packet with the University library. This contained two pamphlets. On the cover of one Childs wrote:

Notes and instructions written October 1937 by William MacBride Childs, M.A., D. Litt., LL.D., first Vice-Chancellor of the University of Reading, with respect to (a) the custody of two pamphlets, namely (1) *University College, Reading; Its Aims and Character, 1916* and (2) *University College, Reading; The University Question, 1916*, and (b) the use and publicity to be accorded to them in the Library of the University of Reading.

The two pamphlets (one copy of each) will be handed to the Librarian by my executors in a sealed envelope, bearing upon it instructions that the envelope is not to be opened nor publicity given to any of its contents till 1 January 1970. These instructions will be authorized by me.

The pamphlets were written by me, paid for by Alfred Palmer, privately printed at the Clarendon Press, but were never circulated. So far as I know, no copy has ever passed into general circulation.

The pamphlets were written in order to state in a clear and exhaustive manner the circumstances which led to the dispute in the College on the subject of the new University constitution.

They were withdrawn when one or two persons consulted, notably Sir George Young, a member of the University College Council, conveyed to the writer of them, myself, that the general effect of the publication of the two pamphlets might be prejudicial to the good name of the College and the prospects of the University cause.

The pamphlets contain no scandals and nothing new. They are not likely to be read. Nevertheless they have a certain value as an exact and measured statement of the value of the kind of constitution which the University College Council and its Academic Board originally preferred.

William MacBride Childs
Oct. 29, 1937
Grimsbury Bank
Hermitage, Berks

The first of these pamphlets was a review of the distinctive character of Reading and what it had achieved so far. In a final section headed 'The Obligation' Childs concluded with a passionate plea that the new constitution should match the individual character of the place and should not be constricted by principles borrowed from outside. That was an understandable response in the circumstances. The second pamphlet was altogether different, for it amounted to a blow-by-blow account of the development of the controversy. In a prolonged exposé of more than forty pages no detail was apparently spared, and Childs's message was clear: he and the Council and the Academic Board had made every possible concession to the view of the dissidents, including the constitution of a Senate on the normal lines, only to be met with complete intransigence on their part. He now concluded that 'decisions by the constituted authorities of the College, which have been reached after proper deliberation, must be respected'. That came at the end of a long summary of the argument by one of the parties to it. In the circumstances the publication of the pamphlet could only have enraged tempers already overwrought. Sir George Young was right: it was best suppressed. The College Council had already cracked the whip by resolving on 26 October 1915, 'that these controversies should now cease, and that all members of the Academic Board should unite in furtherance of the university policy on the basis of the draft Charter and Statutes, as passed by the Academic Board and the Council'. It went on to record that it was 'in complete accord with the appeal for unity which was addressed to the Academic Board on 7 June 1915, by the Principal'. Although severely provoked by the continued opposition of the dissidents, Childs now threatened that unity for which he himself had appealed. It was well that the history of the College, to which he made such strong appeal, had conditioned him to heed the opinion of the lay members of the Council. It may also be that in writing it all down he purged himself of the urge to confront the dissidents on ground of principle. At all events he accepted Sir George Young's advice. The match was not applied to the explosives. Somewhere the match must have been put to a stock of pamphlets. It was characteristic of Childs that he wrote them; it was also characteristic that he ensured the survival, under strict terms of secrecy, of a copy of each. The pamphlets reveal his domineering quality. Their survival reveals his ingenuous candour. Their suppression had been a matter of tactics. He saw nothing to be ashamed of.

Of Reading's five vice-chancellors Childs is the only one to have provoked professorial rebellion. He revealed himself in small things as well as in major questions of policy. It was he who initiated the admirable Reading custom of abandoning professorial title in the Common Room. Once there, all were equal. But Childs retained a massive high chair at the centre of the long table in the dining room at which he usually took his lunch. The technique will not be lost on the careful student of Aristotle.[1] Such apparently contradictory qualities run through much of his work. He was shy and, to many, seemed remote. He took the trouble to give an annual address to the Common Room, in which he reviewed the problems of the current year in a lengthy talk which was usually pessimistic in tone.[2] Yet he could pass

[1] 'The story is that Periander, when the herald was sent to ask counsel of him, said nothing, but only cut off the tallest ears of corn till he had brought the field to a level.' (*Politics*, iii, 13, trans. Jowett, p. 130).
[2] Conversation with Ernest Smith.

colleagues in the cloisters without noticing them.[1] He allowed a certain amount of open banter from students at the annual ceremony for the conferment of the Associateship.[2] Yet he could address them on discipline in stentorian tones and with punitive intent. His view of the development of the University always tended towards the autobiographical. When in the early years of the College it was appreciated that there might be some rift between the College and the newly founded Wantage Hall his solution was thoroughly characteristic: there would be no problem if the Principal of the College himself lived at the Hall. And so it came about. The danger of a rift never materialized. In any case it was lessened when a second Hall, St Patrick's, was founded in 1913.[3] Nevertheless Childs stayed on. He finally moved from the Warden's lodgings in 1927, leaving behind a plaque, later regrettably removed, which read 'Between 1908 and 1927 this house was occupied by William MacBride Childs and Catherine his wife'.[4]

This imperious and insistent involvement remained with him to the end of his office and beyond.[5] He must be one of the few vice-chancellors to have attended the committee appointing his successor. The handwritten notes for the case he presented to justify this still survive.[6] After agreeing that the Vice-Chancellor was excluded by statute from such a committee he went on to argue that it was never intended that he should not be consulted or kept informed, still less that he should be superseded in his

[1] Conversation with Dr Nellie B. Eales.

[2] The *Reading Standard* (14 June 1924) reported on 'the students' "rag" which has now become what one might call a recognized feature in the otherwise dignified ceremony of the conferment of the Associateship . . . when Miss Hilda Beck was called for the same mysterious voice started a ditty about "A young lady named Hilda". "Remember where you are" was the advice humorously given to Principal W. M. Childs, and several lady students were told to "Kiss daddy, then".' According to the reporter this was before 'the real fun began'. This consisted of the erection of a Heath Robinson wireless set and the presentation of a bulletin on the affairs of the College.

[3] Childs (1933), pp. 91–2.

[4] Childs liked a resounding inscription. See the opening of his note to the pamphlets of 1916 quoted above, p. 30 and the provision in his will that 'my photographic portrait of the late Lady Wantage shall be given after my wife's death to the University of Reading with a request that it be placed in the Overstone Library with this inscription: "This framed photograph of herself was given by Lady Wantage in 1908 to William MacBride Childs, then Principal of University College, Reading, and was by him bequeathed to the University of Reading, with the suggestion that it might be hung in the Overstone Library"' (Mrs Childs in fact presented the photograph to the University in September 1939; see URC, Vice-Chancellor, box 42; it cannot now be traced).

[5] For an intervention with Sibly in November 1933, see below p. 43. This concerned student-entry and arose from Childs's presentation of the prizes at Ealing County Secondary School for boys. It begins: 'I am going to report to you some observations which I made yesterday and some notions arising. I am quite sure that you will not regard me as pushing or interfering or even as embarrassing. If you decide to take no action of any kind on the lines I suggest I shall not be hurt or even disappointed. Please be very sure of that. You have a view of what is possible and expedient which no outsider, whatever his goodwill, can possess. I thoroughly understand that.' There follow four closely written pages of information with suggestions on policy.

[6] URC, Registrar, box 219.

natural and proper functions, which, in his view, embraced all the communications, formal and informal, in which the Committee was engaged.
Attached to the notes is Childs's own schedule of the qualities desirable in
a Vice-Chancellor and a list of the 'great and the good' who, in his view,
ought to be consulted in seeking a suitable candidate.[1]

Such interference was in every way characteristic of the man. Reading
was his place and he was determined to have his say. But even more
revealing is the fact that the Committee accepted the argument. Indeed
it went further and invited him to every subsequent meeting.[2] That is one
measure of Childs's quality. And it was just recognition of the part he had
played in the development of the College and the University. If any one
man could claim to have made Reading it was he. Sibly summed this up
shortly after his arrival.

> I can still speak with detachment about Reading, and I consider
> that the building up of the University College and University
> under the shadow of Oxford (but with the powerful support of
> Oxford men), and within less than forty miles of London, and the
> successful establishment of a residential system, make by far the most
> notable contribution to university work in the history of the last
> thirty years or more in England. The thing would have been a failure
> had it not been for the extraordinary idealism, courage and strength
> of purpose of Childs himself and his chief supporters.[3]

Before his retirement Childs sought to perform one last great service for
the University. Already in 1926 he had added a special section to his annual
report in which he reviewed the inadequacy of the teaching and residential
accommodation.[4] Between then and 1929 he tried to ensure that something was done. In July 1927 the Council asked him to prepare a special
report. This he submitted in January 1928. It was the first thorough

[1] Childs's requirements included the following:
'(3) A scholar, but aptitude for government and rather a comprehensive and
sympathetic intelligence. e.g. (a) He need not be an agriculturalist, but he must be able
to understand and respect agriculture and to help to administer that side of the
University. If he does not, there will be trouble. A dreamer, a purely academic person
won't do. *Extreme importance of this.* . . . If he holds aloof or fails to get a good
understanding, there will be a rift; and a dualism of disastrous consequences. (b) He
must know how to manage students. Difference between Reading and all modern
universities. (c) He need not understand a balance sheet, but he must be an economist
[*sic*] and keep a firm watch over expenditure. Estimates.
(4) He must not be a crank. No political cranks, no enthusiast either for Fascism, or
Labour, or Socialism, or any other cause will keep this place together. . . .
(6) He must be prepared to attend to his job. He must be here constantly. The
"public man" V.C.'
[2] The Committee consisted of J. H. Benyon, the Chancellor, Sir William Mount, the
Treasurer, F. B. Malim, the Master of Wellington, as Council representatives; and the
three Deans as representatives of Senate, viz. de Burgh, Bassett and H. A. D. Neville.
[3] Sibly to George Glasgow, of the *Observer*, 7 November 1929 (URC, Vice-Chancellor,
box 44).
[4] See above, pp. 18–20.

review of the teaching accommodation on the London Road site. He ended it *con brio* in characteristic manner:

Clearly, therefore, the building problem before the University is formidable. Nothing is to be gained by minimizing it. The first thing to be grasped by all concerned is that if the University is to continue to advance, if it is to justify the status so recently won after more than twenty years of striving, it must now gird itself for a great effort. A great sum of money is wanted, not to lavish upon architectural display but to enable living and fruitful work to thrive and grow. The simplicity and economy which have marked all our buildings in the past will mark no less the new buildings that must now be undertaken. With a site like ours, endowed with wealth of lawns and trees and flowers, we can dare to erect the plainest type of building without fear of the resulting effect. What the University of Reading wants is not elaborate architecture but plain and roomy workshops, for all faculties and departments. It will be difficult to better the type of building represented by the cloister laboratories which has approved itself after twenty years of experience. Two pitfalls must be avoided. The first is to imagine that a little here and a little there constitutes a policy able to cope with a general and comprehensive shortage of room. Not 'tinkering' but 'thorough' is the word. The other is to suppose that the problem can be dealt with by erecting buildings of a 'temporary' character. The University has no desire to enlarge its painful and costly experience of this unsatisfactory type of structure.

The Council moved quickly. In March 1928 it established a New Buildings Committee and agreed to launch a Building Fund Appeal. The estimated cost was £200,000, of which £55,000 was required as an endowment for the maintenance of the new buildings.[1] That was equivalent, in real terms, to roughly 60 per cent of the University Endowment Fund which George William Palmer, Alfred Palmer and Lady Wantage had established in 1911. This time Childs's magic did not work. The Appeal Fund realized over £7,000 in the first year, over £9,000 in 1930 and over £8,000 both in 1931 and 1932. Thereafter it declined steadily. In July 1937 the total stood at just under £50,000.[2] The donations of that year amounted to £166. Launching a scheme for a university in the high tide of Edwardian England was one thing. Seeking private subscriptions to provide it with buildings during and after the slump of 1929–31 was quite another. Not even Childs's persuasive flair could alter that. When Sibly took over he did his best to ensure full publicity in the London press. A letter of appeal was published in *The Times*, *Telegraph* and *Morning Post* on 15 November 1929, but the *Sunday Times* could not find room for it, although it promised

---

[1] This was a revision of an initial estimate of £110,000 plus £27,500 as an endowment.
[2] There were also ear-marked donations totalling approximately £20,000.

a favourable notice, while at the *Observer*, where Garvin had proved unresponsive, George Glasgow undertook to provide a special feature which was replaced in the end by Sibly's appeal.[1] None of this yielded encouraging results. In 1930 Sibly reported realistically:

> The Appeal Fund, after a promising start, has made but slight progress during the past year; and although this may occasion little surprise, in view of the depressed state of national industry and the world-wide prevalence of financial difficulties, the authorities of the University cannot regard the situation without anxiety. The University stands in need of large benefactions, not only for additions to the buildings used for teaching and research, but also for the improvement and increase of residential accommodation for students, and the need does not arise in the slightest degree from ambitious plans for new departures; it relates solely to the improvement of existing accommodation within the range of our present activities.[2]

The appointment of the Secretary to the Appeal Fund ended in June 1930. It was not renewed, nor was he replaced.

Reading was now in difficulties. It had become a university and had to measure up to new standards. Its activities would become more costly. It could not expect to accumulate resources in the old way from benefactors. Yet there was no alternative, for governments were parsimonious. Much was still expected, in the official view, of private benefaction.

To say that Reading was stuck would be only partly true. The effect of the financial and economic crisis was not so much to cut off the flow of donations as to alter the form they took. Large sums of money for building were not easy to raise, but benefactors could still provide land and property. Moreover testamentary bequests were encouraged by the increasing impact of estate and death duties. Hence the fortunes of the University continued slowly to expand. Eustace Palmer provided land for the Boat House in 1928 and covered the cost of the building which was opened in 1930. When Alfred Palmer died in 1936 he not only bequeathed to the University the four houses in Portland Place, but also the properties which housed St Andrew's Hall, part of Wessex Hall and the headquarters of the Advisory Officers of the Southern Agricultural Province. In the same year R. H. Mardon gave Shiplake Court Farm, a property of 350 acres. There were also important donations for special purposes. In 1930 the Earl of Iveagh gave £15,000 in instalments and Sir George Watson bequeathed £10,000 for the National Institute for Research in Dairying. Scholarships were founded, in 1936 one in the memory of Leonard Sutton, and in 1938, one in the memory of William Haynes, a former member of Court and Council. Some of these grants had beneficial effects on the University's

---

[1] URC, Vice-Chancellor, box 44.
[2] *Proceedings 1929–30*, p. 34.

general income.[1] But they only contributed indirectly to its capacity to provide new buildings at London Road.

Yet Childs's plan was modest enough. It included proposals for a small hall adjacent to the Great Hall and a nearby chamber for Senate and Council. It also provided for a new main entrance between the Old Red Building and the Acacias. Thereafter it envisaged a series of departmental buildings, each lying east to west along the western boundary of the site.[2] This was the only part of the plan to be achieved, and that only partially and with increasing difficulty. The first flush of the Appeal Fund in 1930 paid for two new buildings, for the departments of Geography and Geology. The latter was provided by a large donation from Miss S. R. Courtauld.[3] In 1931–2 the Fund was further augmented by donations from the trustees of S. W. Farmer, H. R. Beeton, the Chairman of the Appeal Fund Committee, and Imperial Chemical Industries. This allowed the erection of a third new building, which housed the Department of Agricultural Chemistry and the offices of the Faculty of Agriculture and Horticulture. The next departmental building, designed for the departments of Psychology and Zoology, was not begun until July 1939. Work was suspended at the outbreak of the war and the building was not finally completed until January 1942. It still bears the marks of its completion during war-time. There were other smaller additions elsewhere. At the National Institute for Research in Dairying a Library was built as a memorial to Stenhouse Williams in 1935; this was provided through private subscriptions.[4] There were also additions to halls of residence.[5] But the total achievement was still very inadequate for the University's needs. The government had not provided much assistance. In 1931 the Ministry of Agriculture approved a matching grant for the building for Agricultural Chemistry, but the

---

[1] The University had hitherto paid a rent of £695 for the properties which Alfred Palmer bequeathed in 1936. In 1937 Sibly reported: 'The increase of the Treasury Grant from £35,000 to £42,000 as from the beginning of the financial year 1936–7, and the financial benefits resulting from Dr Alfred Palmer's bequest of properties and Mr R. H. Mardon's gift of Shiplake Court Farm, enabled the Council to meet some urgent needs. The salaries of many lecturers were raised; a number of new appointments to the academic staff were sanctioned; and provision was made for a pension scheme for University employees.' (*Proceedings 1936–7*, p. 31).
[2] The freehold of this part of the London Road site, originally leased by the College for horticultural purposes, was presented by Alfred Palmer in 1911. On the western boundary itself, the Gymnasium, presented by Dr J. B. and Mrs Hurry, was erected in 1914. Childs's ultimate intention was to link the western ends of the new buildings proposed in 1928 by wings running north and south, broken only in front of the Gymnasium. This was still the intention in 1943–4. However, the sites north and south of the Gymnasium were already occupied by 'temporary' rough-cast concrete buildings, running along the western boundary, which were erected during the First World War. These still remain in use, as unintended relics, in 1976. For a development plan of the site of 1943–4 see plate 25.
[3] Miss Courtauld added a further gift of £2,000 to cover the cost of equipping the new building. See URC, Vice-Chancellor, box 42.
[4] H. F. Burgess (1962), pp. 68–70.
[5] See below, pp. 58–9.

Treasury would not sanction it. In 1938, £5,000 was obtained through the University Grants Committee from the National Fitness Council. This provided for the erection of two squash courts and the pavilion on the Sports Ground and also for improvements to the Boat House. These were opened in the spring before the war.

These additions increased the space available to the Department of Agricultural Chemistry and the Faculty of Agriculture and Horticulture by roughly thirty per cent. It provided separate new buildings for Geology and Geography and a joint building for Psychology and Zoology, but really did no more than house these departments adequately for the first time. They were soon to experience overcrowding in their new homes. The space they evacuated created a little extra elbow-room for the departments left in the older buildings, but for some, especially in the Faculty of Letters, there was scarcely any improvement at all. The Old Red Building and the adjacent houses in Portland Place,[1] where they suffered the increasing noise of traffic in London Road, were still their only home. But building for teaching and research had come first. Nothing was done to provide the various University committee rooms which had been envisaged and nothing was done to improve the Main Entrance. When building development was again re-examined in the winter of 1943–4, with post-war requirements in mind, the Report of the Development Committee proposed little in this area which was not simply a reiteration or adjustment of the proposals which Childs had advanced in 1928.[2]

This limitation of its accommodation and hence of its growth was important in a negative sense in the development of the University. Those who visit the site in London Road today see the University not just as it was before the move to Whiteknights, but very largely as it was when it gained the Charter in 1926. The western cloister and the four buildings bounding it are the only major additions made since. The grounds have matured. The upper storey of the old Central Chemistry Building, which was incomplete in 1926, was finally completed in 1976. Greenhouses have been inserted here and there; improvements in heating arrangements have required small additions to some of the buildings; and there are scattered intrusions of 'temporary' buildings reminiscent of a dilapidated army camp. But the peculiar amalgam of intimacy and spaciousness, which Childs intended, is still the strongest impression of the place. That physical setting was as important to Reading as the Backs to Cambridge. It encouraged the continuation in the University of all those close associations which had been developed in the College. Childs summed it up almost mystically:

[1] Two of the houses in Portland Place (nos. 24 and 30) were rented from Alfred Palmer in 1918. These and a further two (nos. 26 and 28) were secured on a fourteen-year lease in 1922. Alfred Palmer bequeathed the University the freehold of all four houses, along with other properties, on his death in 1936. From 1922 they housed the departments of Classics, History, French and Education, along with St David's Hall.
[2] See below, pp. 134–6.

I find myself perpetually coming back to this view of our enterprise
as something social, something which means or should mean
fellowship, comradeship, friendship. I think that amongst us we have
succeeded in giving to our College and University something of this
attractive character.[1]

Sibly, too, was soon affected:

This little University is unique in its character, and you have to see
something of it to realize how much has been done in the way of
establishing corporate life in the best sense of the term. We have
nearly 500 students in residence in Halls out of less than 700
full-time students. If only you can come down I can shew you
pleasant buildings and beautiful gardens, and a Senior Common
Room which I find quite delightful.[2]

Reading had achieved this intimacy because the members of the University
met in the cloisters linking the low, inexpensively designed buildings.
Large buildings, which might have isolated separate sections of the University, could not be afforded. Up to the war there was only a very ineffective, battery operated telephone system. How else to deal with business
other than by a visit through the cloister or a conversation in the Common
Room?

Childs embodied this stage in the University's history. To his last annual
statement as Vice-Chancellor, presented to Court in January 1928, he
appended a long valedictory statement.[3] It was headed 'Remarks on
Policy'; it was in fact a review of the past; 'policy' was simply implied
in the unstated assumption that Reading would continue to grow in the
mould in which the College had developed into a University. The 'Remarks'
are the most succinct statement of Childs's view of the University. But if
they embody most of what Reading, under Childs's guidance, had come to
stand for, they also marked the end of an era. Indeed they pointed to an
impasse. That was represented physically by the site, even more by the site
as Childs had planned it, for the 'workshop-type' buildings, linked by
cloisters, were prodigal of space. The waste was acknowledged but not
repaired by the provision that all the single-storey buildings should be
designed to carry a second storey if necessary. Because of its site and the way
it was used Reading had to be a small university, and that conclusion was
reinforced by the intention to accommodate most students in Halls built
and owned by the University. But at the same time Childs still insisted that
in a town as small as Reading it was incumbent on the University to provide
all those services which might be expected in a larger city from a technical
college and allied institutions. Moreover, the University embodied within
itself, especially in the Faculty of Agriculture and Horticulture, institutions

[1] See Appendix 3, below, p. 339.
[2] Sibly to George Glasgow, 30 October 1929 (URC, Vice-Chancellor, box 44).
[3] This section of the statement is reproduced in Appendix 3, below, pp. 337–42.

which had teaching commitments which spread far beyond the work essential for degrees. How could a University of the size of Reading perform these multifarious tasks? His 'Remarks' lacked the essential element in policy: academic planning. Five years later, in the closing chapter of *Making a University*, he still had nothing to say on the direction Reading should take within the constraints which its site, its buildings and its history now imposed on it. Here he made room for a superb appreciation of Alfred Palmer and for some characteristically visionary rhetoric on the functions of a University;[1] for the rest he was more concerned to ensure that, in rounding off his work, due acknowledgement was made to those who had played their part in helping to establish the new university. Childs's silence was significant. The circumstances of the 1930s allowed no room for any broad reshaping of the University's academic functions. The same economic restrictions which limited new building also prevented any major increase in general resources.

In 1926 the University's gross recurrent income was £94,953. By 1929 it had risen to £102,963. During this period the grants from the Board of Education and the Ministry of Agriculture and Fisheries rose modestly,[2] but there was no increase in the Treasury recurrent grant of £26,500. The effects of the crisis were not immediate; on the contrary the Treasury increased the recurrent grant to £35,000 for 1930–1. But that was the last hint of optimism. In February 1931 Leonard Sutton, the Treasurer, reported that a bank overdraft of £15,485 would have exceeded £23,000 but for the inclusion of capital sums in the current account and that that sum represented less than half the total indebtedness of the University.[3] Both Sutton and his successor, Sir George Mowbray, in his reports of the following years, emphasized the paramount need to reduce this debt. In 1931 the Government's Economy Report proposed a reduction of £250,000 in the Treasury Grant to universities. Sibly feared that the recent increases in the recurrent grant would not be maintained.[4] By November, in answering an enquiry from Eustace Morgan of Hull, he reported that a number of local authorities had cut their grants to universities and colleges.[5] These worst fears proved groundless. The Treasury grant was maintained throughout the worst of the crisis and was raised to £42,000 in 1936–7. Only a few of the local authorities cut their contributions to Reading. In 1933 the total recurrent income stood at £115,804. It rose steadily to a total of £138,225 in 1939.

[1] Childs (1933), pp. 270–5.
[2] The grant from the Board of Education rose from £8,366 to £10,597 between 1926 and 1929, but this increase was largely offset by an increase in the remission of students' fees. In the same period the grant from the Ministry of Agriculture and Fisheries rose from £19,435 to £22,186.
[3] *Proceedings 1929–30*, p. 13.
[4] Sibly to Kenneth Vickers, Principal of University College, Southampton, 10 August 1931 (URC, Vice-Chancellor, box 48).
[5] Sibly to A. E. Morgan, 24 November 1931 (*ibid.*, box 45).

This allowed some gradual modest improvements, but it was no basis for enterprising experiment. As Childs remarked, overdrafts seemed 'to cling to life with almost feline tenacity',[1] and the University still remained unusually dependent on individual goodwill. When Alfred Palmer died in 1936 the University still benefited from a loan of £3,300 which he advanced in 1925.[2] Individual subscription, organized by H. R. Beeton, provided for the foundation of libraries in the halls of residence. The main University library enjoyed the benefit of some recurrent income from its original endowment. Thereafter it ran from year to year on an inadequate grant which was all that the University Council could manage,[3] eked out by occasional non-recurrent grants from the Treasury and private donations from interested individuals. R. H. Mardon was a regular benefactor, year after year. For many years also H. R. Beeton, A. T. Loyd, H. G. Willink and Eustace Palmer paid the subscriptions to a number of periodicals. In 1927 W. V. Rivers made a splendid donation of £1,040 for the purchase of books on medieval English history. In Oxford Sir Charles Firth was a regular benefactor, and his kindness was continued after his death by Lady Firth. The Library slowly gained the quality necessary in a university; it owed much to Cole, the Stentons, Wolters and de Burgh, all of whom garnered books from donors or fastened on bargains in second-hand catalogues. Throughout the University, in its departments and amenities as well as in the Library, much good work was channelled through the Friends of the University. Founded in 1927 as a continuation of the old subscribing membership of the College Court,[4] the Friends, on a basis of an annual individual subscription of £1, came to provide an important supplementary resource throughout the 1930s and beyond. From 1928 onwards scarcely a year passed without some kind of grant from the Friends to some specific cause in the University. By 1934 they had disbursed £1,218 for various purposes and in that year they found £750 to help in the building projects in the west cloisters. But if on the one hand this speaks for the concern and generosity of the Friends, on the other it reveals the extraordinarily parsimonious economy which the University's financial situation demanded. In 1929 the Friends provided £150 'for library purposes and in aid of the Physics Department' and for the Boat Club; in 1930, £330 for various departments and halls of residence; in 1931, £271 for the same purpose,

[1] Childs (1933), p. 275.
[2] URC, Vice-Chancellor, box 46.
[3] The grant from Council for books and periodicals in 1926–7 was £1,240. It was increased to £1,300 in 1927–8 and to £1,750 in 1930–1. It remained at that figure up to the war. Endowment and other ancillary income increased these resources. The total spent on books and periodicals in 1926–7 was £1,726. In 1938–9 it was £2,171 19s. 5d. In 1926–7 the total expenditure on the Library (including administration) amounted to £3,076, which was roughly 4.0 per cent of the University's total expenditure, excluding the National Institute for Research in Dairying. The average for English universities and colleges in that year was 3.1 per cent. See D. J. Hewlett (1970), pp. 63–82.
[4] See Childs (1933), pp. 279–81.

and in 1932, £187, of which £100 was for furnishing St David's Hall. In 1933 they were buying dictionaries for the Hall libraries, in 1939 a gramophone and records for the School of Music, and in 1940 a binocular microscope for the Department of Zoology and a set of the *Complete Peerage* for the Library. That such items were 'extras', provided from special funds, reflects the generally low level of the recurrent provision for the University. In the main the Friends and other patrons were paying for necessities, not frills.

Childs retired in 1929. His successor, Franklin Sibly, had been a Professor of Geology at University College, Cardiff, and Armstrong College, Newcastle. In 1920 he had become the first Principal of University College, Swansea, and in 1925–6 Vice-Chancellor of the University of Wales. In the latter year he moved to become Principal of the University of London. Hence he brought to Reading a remarkable range of academic experience. He took to his new post with enthusiasm and was soon at home. But from the start he was wary of Reading's readiness to undertake large enterprises with minimum resources[1] and was tolerantly amused by some of the inbred self-importance which survived from the time of Childs.[2] He quickly knew everyone at the University. He listened to them both for advice and through concern for their own problems. But he was tough. He was not shy of dressing down a member of staff when he thought it necessary. No one could close an unwanted interchange of letters more quickly.[3] He was con-

[1] See above, p. 8.
[2] He was somewhat bemused by Reading procedures for choosing a Vice-Chancellor: 'After a long talk here with Childs, this morning I am accepting a private invitation from him to spend next Friday night at his house; and certain persons will dine with us, but there is to be no mention of the V-C. ship in conversation. That is as far as I could go; but short of that it would have been a deadlock because of his position and the awkward way in which he opened the proceedings. Thereafter 'twill take them about a fortnight to go through laborious motions in accordance with an absurdly rigid ordinance before any final decision is reached. I feel very vexed about the position; but I'm not inclined to cut off my nose to spite my face.' (Sibly to A. E. Morgan, 14 May 1929, URC, box 256).
   He subsequently reported in a lighter vein: 'At tea-time and afterwards throughout a long evening on Friday I was studied closely, first by some Council fellows and afterwards by the Deans: and in the interval I explored miles of University quarter with Childs. Still later, when Childs had sped his last guest and returned to the fireside to express the opinion that it "was virtually settled", I yarned away till the small hours. So you will understand that I felt whacked yesterday. They behaved jolly well, however, and stuck scrupulously to the fiction that I was paying a chance visit to my host; it was not until Saturday morning, when old de Burgh blew in again for a private chat, that the cat came out: and then he begged the momentous question by telling me what I should find and how I should like it etc. etc., giving me some amusing sketches of some of his colleagues' (Sibly to A. E. Morgan, 19 May 1929, URC, box 256).
[3] For example he received a letter of 16 November 1932 from Henry S. L. Polek, Chairman of the Executive Committee of the Joint Council to promote understanding between White and Coloured People in Great Britain, alleging that coloured students were barred from residence in Halls. On 22 November 1932 Sibly replied: 'With all respect to your Council and yourself, I am unable to enter into a discussion on this question. The authorities of the University are fully alive to their responsibility for promoting the welfare of all students of the University.' (URC, Vice-Chancellor, box 42).

servative, but not distinguished from his peers in that respect.[1] His advice
was much sought and valued. He was a superb chairman and a wise and
effective administrator; from 1938 to 1943 he was Chairman of the Committee of Vice-Chancellors and Principals. The overwork into which his
sense of duty led him was largely responsible for his early retirement and
death. Childs is remembered as formidable; Sibly with respect and
affection. He had the knack of letting good men get on with the task in
hand. This fitted the situation at Reading exactly. Financial stringency
ruled out any large schemes. Willy-nilly Reading could do little more
than consolidate. That is what it needed most. That is what Sibly gave
it. Many of those who worked with him would still argue that this was the
best period in the history of the University.

The change was not marked simply by Sibly's arrival. The first Registrar, Francis Wright, had already retired in 1927. Even more than Childs
he embodied the history of the place, for he had been Secretary of the
School of Science and Art from 1887 and continued thereafter as Secretary
of the College. Wright was succeeded by Herbert Knapman who had
been appointed first as an Assistant Lecturer in Mathematics and had acted
as Tutorial Secretary since 1906. The continuity was broken by Knapman's
death in 1932. Ernest Smith succeeded him. Two years later de Burgh
retired. He had been associated with the College since 1896 and, with
Childs and Wright, had formed a kind of inner cabinet. Probably more than
the other members of the old guard de Burgh was able to adjust himself to
the changing problems facing the University. He had more time in which to
do so and was in closer touch with the academic staff. Stenton became the
new Deputy Vice-Chancellor. He too had been associated with Reading
over a long period. He was elected to a Research Fellowship in Local
History in 1908 and had been Professor of Modern History since 1912.[2]
He had a shrewd head for business and was wonderfully lucid in summing up
an argument. Above all he was respected for a quality which his surviving
colleagues sum up as 'wisdom'. But he was no administrative *dévot*. Once
away from the committee his mind reverted to the more delectable problems
of Anglo-Saxon England. Until the war he had no telephone at his home at
Whitley Park Farm. He was not always as accessible as his Vice-Chancellor
would have liked.

These changes coincided with the arrival of new men, many of whom
came to stay and to play a large role within the University. A. A. Miller, a
future Professor of Geography and Dean of the Faculty of Science, was
appointed in 1926. Edgar Thomas, who became the first Professor of

[1] See below, p. 279.
[2] Stenton's first link with Reading went back even earlier. He was a student of the
School of Music in 1897–9 and played Chopin's 'A Flat Ballade' at the Concert of 1898.
Under the guidance of Childs and de Burgh he then won a scholarship to Keble College,
Oxford, where he went in 1899. Childs was largely responsible for developing his
historical interests (Doris M. Stenton, 1968, pp. 330–9).

Agricultural Economics and a Dean of the Faculty of Agriculture, was appointed in 1927. H. A. Hodges, who succeeded de Burgh as Professor of Philosophy in 1934, came in 1928. Betts succeeded Seaby in the School of Art in 1933. In the Faculty of Agriculture W. B. Brierley came as Professor of Agricultural Botany and H. D. Kay became Director of the National Institute for Research in Dairying and Professor of Biochemistry in 1932, and in the following year R. H. Stoughton took over the Chair of Horticulture and R. Rae the Chair of Agriculture. These men naturally had their own views about the development of their subjects. Some of them, through skill and persistence and the sheer strength of the case they advocated, were able to steer the University along the route they wished to follow. But all of them had to accept and work within the practical limitations which old hands accepted as part of the air they breathed. Very soon the new men became old hands too.

The first of these limitations was one of size. From the granting of the Charter until after the war there was no significant change in overall numbers. In 1926 there were 671 students under tutorial supervision. In the following year the number rose to 738. It remained roughly at that level until 1946, never falling below 660, even in the war years, and never rising above 750. The number of academic staff likewise varied very little. There were 148 in 1926. The number never fell below 140 or rose above 155 until 1947–8. Some efforts were made from time to time to increase the number of students reading for degrees, thereby altering the balance within the total. In 1926 Childs organized a three-day conference for headmasters and headmistresses in order to advertise Reading's new status and forge fresh links with public and secondary schools. The number reading for degrees rose from 306 in 1925–6 to 374 in 1927–8. Childs felt some natural and justifiable satisfaction.[1] However, from 1928 onwards the number reading for degrees scarcely altered at all. It never fell below 349 or rose above 398 until the war. In April 1933 Sibly held a similar conference. This had no effect upon the totals. In November Childs wrote in. He had met some of his old pupils among the headmasters in Middlesex and suggested that it might be a good idea to entertain all the headmasters and headmistresses in Middlesex for a day in the hope that they would provide Reading with more and better pupils. Indefatigable, he had also caught a far-off scent of money.[2] Nothing came of his intervention. It probably came too soon after Sibly's effort in April. The total again remained unaffected. For the first twenty years Reading remained a small, settled institution.

---

[1] Childs (1933), pp. 267–9. Compare his annual statement in *Proceedings 1927–8*, p. 30.
[2] Childs to Sibly, 12 November 1933 (URC, Vice-Chancellor, box 42). 'The chairman of the meeting was Alderman Fuller, chairman of the Middlesex County Council Education Committee. He impressed me very favourably. . . . He told me that his County Council are about to give £100,000 to the London University Building fund. Now this set me thinking. This County Council is very rich: the only rich one that Reading is connected with. . . .'

However, it was no longer a college. The increase in the number reading for degrees in 1927 was maintained; by and large, the students under tutorial supervision held their numbers while other categories declined. This was despite the fact that the University still carried most of the old commitments of the College as a local centre of higher and further education. Hence although degree-work was still only a proportion of the total it formed a steadily increasing proportion. The student statistics of 1937, set against those of 1926, record this unmistakably:

Day students under tutorial supervision
reading for a degree	379	(306)
reading for a diploma		
postgraduate	46	(—)
other	184	(247)
reading for a certificate	30	(60)
reading other courses	57	(58)
	696	(671)

Day students not under tutorial
supervision	62	(275)
Evening students	656	(710)
Total	1414	(1656)

The degree students in 1937 formed 54 per cent of the total under tutorial supervision as against 46 per cent at the earlier date. They formed 27 per cent of the total students as against 18 per cent earlier. During the first eleven years of the University's existence the number of students reading for degrees increased by 24 per cent while the evening students decreased by 8 per cent and the day students not under tutorial supervision dropped from 275 to 62, a decrease of 77 per cent. Some of these shifts and changes were the result of deliberate policy; others were consequential. As the number of degree students increased, the resources and energies available for other categories, now a smaller proportion of the total, declined; and some of these categories were abandoned. Reading was beginning to change in function and character. It was becoming more of a university, less of a college.

A comparison of the examination results of 1937 and 1926 tells the same story:[1]

[1] These figures are based on the examination results, not on the list of degrees conferred. In the Faculty of Science it was possible to achieve Honours in the General Degree. Such results have been included in the Honours total, as have cases where Honours were awarded in the Special, but not in the General section of the examination. It should be noted that the large increase in postgraduate diplomas in both this and the preceding table simply reflects a change in the status of the Diploma in Education. On this see below, p. 50.

Degree examinations

Ph.D., M.A., M.Sc.	11	(1)
B.A., B.Sc., Final Examination, Pass or Honours, General or Special	107	(82)
B.Sc. Parts I, II	31	(3)
Intermediate	77	(45)
College diplomas		
postgraduate	44	(—)
others	63	(100)
College certificates	33	(75)
Dairy Institute diplomas	17	(36)
Dairy Institute certificates	41	(53)
Other examinations	60	(54)

But these figures also reveal how slow and difficult the change proved to be. In 1937, eleven years after its foundation, the University awarded only 107 first degrees. Against that there were 63 successful candidates for Reading diplomas, 33 for Reading certificates, 23 for diplomas of the National Agriculture and National Dairy Examination Boards, 41 for certificates in cheese-making or butter-making of the Dairy Farmers' Association, 27 for the examinations of the City and Guilds of London Institute,[1] 18 for the examinations of the Royal Society of Arts[2] and nine other miscellaneous examinations and certificates.[3] In the Faculty of Agriculture and Horticulture in that year there was one successful candidate for the degree of Ph.D., four for the M.Sc., and three for the Postgraduate Diploma in General Bacteriology. Two obtained a B.Sc. with Honours, and 32 a Pass Degree. There were then 62 students who obtained diplomas and 53 who obtained certificates either of Reading or of other examining bodies. Such a distribution between degree and other work was typical of the years before the Second World War. It is fundamental to the understanding of the University in these years. If, on the one hand, it meant that much time, energy and resources had to go into teaching of less than degree standard and into subjects which could not possibly be fitted into a university curriculum, it meant, on the other, that a great deal of individual attention could be given to the small numbers reading for an Honours Degree. In 1937, for example, there were only five successful Honours students reading

---

[1] These were for qualifications in Builders' Quantities, Electricity and Magnetism, and Telephony.
[2] These were chiefly for Book-keeping but also included qualifications in French, German and Spanish.
[3] These were for the Licentiate Diploma of the Institute of Builders, the National Certificate in Building, the National Certificate in Mechanical Engineering and the Preliminary Scientific Examination of the Pharmaceutical Society of Great Britain.

English, four reading History and six French. In the Faculty of Science there were two successful candidates in Mathematics, six in Physics, four in Chemistry and one each in Geography and Geology. The two successful Honours students in the Faculty of Agriculture fell between Agricultural Chemistry and Agricultural Botany. Throughout the University no Honours group in its final year exceeded ten; most were less than five. Honours graduates at Reading were hand made. This was one cause of the friendly intimacy which developed between teacher and pupil. It contributed directly to the quality of the place.

However, if the University remained small, it was also undergoing a change which was not immediately revealed in the overall statistics. The most important consequence of the conferment of the Charter was that the University gained control of its own curriculum. In his statements to Council in 1927 and 1928 Childs gave great emphasis to this new academic independence. The increase in the number of degree students in the two years immediately following the granting of the Charter may have led him into exaggerating the extent of the achievement, but he never tired of pointing out what the new independence meant:

> University independence was sought for many reasons, and of these reasons perhaps the most potent was that it would confer upon us freedom to plan our own curriculum, and to use our ideas and resources in obedience not to the requirements of external syllabuses, but to our own will and judgement. The conviction that such freedom is an essential condition of effective teaching has not been shaken; and the remarks of one of my senior colleagues upon this point will be read with interest. 'I wish to say', writes Professor Stenton, 'that the change to university status has been a cause of great relief. It is now possible to give due attention to aspects of history which in the hurry of the congested London course have hitherto out of fairness to our students been treated in a very summary manner. Lecturing is no longer merely the dictation of facts sufficient to appease an external examiner: it is becoming possible to use our own researches for the benefit of students, knowing that special information will have a value in examination for them. Of all the changes of the last two years, this is by far the most important for daily work. The destiny of the History School is now in our own hands.' There would be no difficulty in procuring endorsements of this testimony from other quarters. In every Faculty there has been a release of ideas, a quickening of mind, which can never be found save when men are working in responsible independence.[1]

That was an enthusiastic review of the change to University status. The facts were more humdrum. The new syllabuses were worked out rapidly in the winter of 1925–6 in time to appear in the first University *Calendar* of

[1] *Proceedings 1926–7*, pp. 29–30.

1926–7. Within each faculty committees were responsible for designing the syllabuses, subject by subject. It may seem to have been a rushed job, but departments were well enough aware of the pattern of the courses in other universities, and in science departments, in particular, the syllabus turned on the straightforward notion that there was a clearly defined ground which the undergraduate had to cover in studying for a first degree. Hence the syllabus for the B.Sc. course in Physics could be splendidly brief:

Final B.Sc. (General) Course (Two Years).
General properties of Matter and Mechanics. Heat. Light. Sound. Magnetism and Electricity.

Final B.Sc. (Special) Course.
The syllabus is the same as for the Final B.Sc. (General) Examination, but is treated more fully.

That remained in successive *Calendars* unaltered in any respect until 1946. In Chemistry likewise no distinction was made between the General and Special courses other than by noting that 'The standard required in the Final Examination (Special) will be considerably higher than in the Final Examination (General).' This pattern was followed, perhaps not quite so tidily, by all the departments in the Faculty of Science. In Zoology, as was common in many universities at the time, provision was made for a special paper on a subject or group selected by the student and approved by the Board of the Faculty. Only perhaps in one general respect did the Reading Science syllabuses follow an individual line. All of them, with the exception of Physics, included the history of the subject in the General or the Special degree, or in both.

In the Faculty of Letters from the start the syllabuses contained features which have remained with the Faculty ever since. The various departments, living cheek by jowl in cramped accommodation, came to co-operate almost automatically. The Political Thought course in the Department of Philosophy was also used in the Department of History. Conversely those reading medieval philosophy in the Department of Philosophy were advised to attend certain classes in medieval history. The course on Modern Philosophy was also used by the Department of Psychology, which in turn provided optional papers within the Philosophy course. In two Departments, English and French, students were required to take one or more special subject papers in other disciplines. New arrangements for the Pass Degree were concluded less easily. The old London B.A. Pass Degree involved four subjects, of which one had to be a classical language, and another selected from a group which included Philosophy, Psychology, Economics and Mathematics. The Faculty based its Pass Degree on three subjects and the language requirement was abandoned. However, the specially selected group of subjects, consisting of Greek, Philosophy, Psychology, Pure Mathematics and Economics remained and this soon became a battleground between conservatives and radicals. De Burgh, with a mixture of frankness and ambivalence, urged the retention of the select group as a means of preserving those departments which taught 'non-school' subjects, in particular his own:

> The maintenance of the small Pass group is of vital concern to the department. Mr Wolters, Mr Ward and I believe that the course of study furnished the students with a discipline in philosophical thinking that is of real value. Were the group to disappear, the department would be left in a very precarious condition. I naturally view with serious concern any proposed changes in the Pass curriculum that might result in this disappearance. . . . I would deprecate our approaching this question as if it were one of 'protecting' certain subjects in the Faculty. It is rather a question of maintaining in existence certain subjects which have hitherto proved a living influence in our university teaching, and which are recognized throughout the academic world as essential constituents of an Arts Faculty. I feel that the present issue is crucial in the interest not merely of these subjects, but of the whole of the University.[1]

This readiness to generalize and base the argument on academic principle was fully matched on the other side where Edith Morley provided a passionate assertion of the student's right to a free choice:

> I am in favour of free choice of subjects for the final degree examination because I believe, after long experience of compulsory subjects, that undergraduates at this stage are competent, with advice, to choose for themselves; that such freedom in itself is part of their education and that only if it is accorded them, will they produce the best work of which they are capable. In my opinion the division into so-called school and non-school subjects is indefensible, undignified and unnecessary. . . . I cannot voluntarily accept any proposals for a final degree curriculum which, whether deliberately or unintentionally, draw a distinction between the educational and academic value of the various subjects taught in the Faculty. . . . It is necessary to realize and to accept that, for good or for evil, according to one's point of view, the modern subjects claim the equal place in the new universities which they have now obtained in the old; absence of such acceptance can result only in discontent among teachers and taught. . . . Finally there is the argument that the newest and smallest university cannot venture on the innovation of free choice in addition to the reduction of subjects. To that the answer seems to be that this University has

[1] Senate Reports, I, 22 November 1926. Memorandum of Dean of Faculty of Letters, 17 November 1926.

come into being precisely because it has dared to make 'impossible' innovations – about compulsory residence, about the introduction of technical studies, (even of 'degrees in dairying') or of fine art and music on equal terms with other subjects. The Faculty of Letters, in spite of attractions and new studies in other departments, still holds its own in both the number and quality of its students. It is un-necessarily sceptical, if not worse, to believe that such subjects as Philosophy and Greek have ultimately anything to fear from competition within the Faculty.[1]

The concerns, the attitudes and the arguments are not unfamiliar.[2] Nor is the ultimate outcome of the argument in a compromise. The radicals won on principle. In 1928 the grouping of subjects for the Pass Degree was abandoned. However, the conservatives were allowed some protection against dire calamity in the provision that 'a candidate who desires to confine his choice to modern languages (including English), Modern History and Geography must apply in writing for the permission of the Board of the Faculty of Letters to do so.' With that awkward regulation, which remained in force until 1946, the matter rested.

This scarcely hindered the increasingly close co-operation between departments, which soon led to the development of a number of Combined Honours courses. The first of these, introduced in 1930, was in Philosophy and English Literature. It was a product of the close friendship and almost daily interchange of argument between Hodges in the Philosophy Depart-ment and H.V.D. Dyson in the Department of English Literature. By 1939 fifteen students had read this course; in the same period only seven chose to read Philosophy as a single subject.[3] This course was the first of many, perhaps in the end of too many. By 1939 Greek and English Literature, Latin and English Literature, Economics and Social Psychology, and Philosophy and Economics had been added to a modest but interesting list.[4]

There was one other important innovation. In the Honours course in both French and German, students were required to spend a year abroad, either in a university or *lycée* in France, or in a German, Austrian or Swiss University. Desseignet, the Professor of French, himself a Frenchman, was the originator of this. The practice had to be suspended during the war, and since 1974 it has encountered a more insidious threat from the depreci-ation of sterling and other financial difficulties. However, it became and

[1] *Ibid.* Memorandum of Edith Morley, 19 November 1926.
[2] De Burgh's concern is underscored by the fact that there were only eleven Honours graduates in Philosophy between 1927 and 1934, when he retired.
[3] In the same period fifty students took the English Honours examination.
[4] At this stage Economics was only studied in these combined subject courses at Honours Degree level. There was only one lecturer in the subject in the Faculty, Dr Mabel Buer. The Librarian, S. A. Peyton, was a lecturer in the Department of Modern History, where he taught Economic History. This figured as one of the papers in the course.

has remained an essential feature of the language teaching at Reading. It has been followed, sometimes directly copied, many times elsewhere.

Finally the Faculty benefited directly from the changes in the arrangements concerning the training of teachers. Up to 1926–7 Reading still accepted a mixed bag of students as intending teachers. Some entered to read for a degree followed by the Diploma in Education. Others still came under the old College regulations which allowed them to study for the two-year Diploma in Letters or Educational Handicrafts. After an initial period following the First World War, in which the shorter courses were popular with ex-servicemen seeking qualifications, there was a steady drift towards the Honours Degree course. The establishment of the University had a decisive effect. The Diploma in Education in the University became available only to graduates. The Diploma in Letters wasted away. There were sixty students reading for it in 1925–6, but only nine in 1927–8 and none at all in the following year. It was removed from the *Calendar 1930–1*, along with the Diploma in Educational Handicrafts. The University had sucessfully sloughed off one of the multifarious functions it had inherited from the College. It was no longer trying to serve as a training college. Instead from 1926 onwards it came to play a very important role under the new arrangements devised by the Board of Education whereby the work of training colleges was supervised by the local university.[1] Both the Colleges and the University benefited: the colleges through the development of a very close link with the University, the University from the clearer definition of its own immediate role in the training of teachers.[2] Henceforth the teachers it trained were graduates.

The curriculum of the Faculty of Agriculture and Horticulture was the most complicated of all. Departments in other faculties might co-operate and interchange courses. In this Faculty the close integration of the work of different departments and individual teachers was essential. Its syllabuses called on a wide variety of disciplines, brought together to serve the practical objectives of agricultural and horticultural studies. The Faculty designed

[1] From 1926–7 six colleges were associated with Reading: the Diocesan Training College, Brighton, the Municipal Training College, Brighton, Bishop Otter College, Chichester, Culham College, Abingdon, the Training College, Portsmouth, and the Diocesan Training College, Salisbury.

[2] Childs reported very fully on the arrangements made for the supervision of the Colleges in the *Proceedings 1926–7*. A Joint Committee was established, along with boards of studies under the chairmanship of a professor or head of department of the University. He commented: 'The scheme was intended to be no mere piece of educational mechanism, but to be human, friendly and helpful.' Sibly reported further in 1928–9: 'From the beginning co-operation between the University and the associated colleges, as apart from that involved in examinations was regarded as a vital part of the scheme. In pursuance of this policy, numerous lectures and demonstrations have been given by professors and lecturers of the University to students in the training colleges.' In 1928–9, the first year in which the University supervised the Certificate Examination, Dewar, Professor of English Literature, chaired the board of examiners in each of the colleges in order to ensure uniformity of standard. There were 430 candidates.

three Pass Degrees, in Agriculture, Horticulture and Dairying. They included a wide range of practical subjects including building construction, book-keeping, the design and management of dairies and greenhouses, and the design and operation of agricultural and dairying machinery. They brought in the study of agricultural history and agricultural economics. But they also sought to link the practical work with the study of basic sciences. Hence the agriculture course included papers and practical examinations in agricultural botany and agricultural chemistry. The course in Dairying included three papers and practical examinations in Bacteriology and Mycology and one paper and practical examination in Chemistry; and the course in Horticulture included papers and practicals in Chemistry, Entomology and Botany. Two Honours courses were provided in Agricultural Chemistry and Agricultural Botany. These linked the more theoretical studies provided in the Faculty with some of the Intermediate and General Degree examinations in the Faculty of Science; Agricultural Chemistry with Geology or Physics, and Chemistry, Agricultural Botany with Geology or Physics, and Botany. In this the Faculty was seeking some kind of balance between applied and theoretical studies. It was not easy to achieve. Repeatedly on the side of the Faculty it raised the problem of the usefulness of the courses provided in the Faculty of Science. Increasingly on the side of the Faculty of Science it raised questions about the depth of the courses in the sister Faculty. The difficulties stemmed from the fact that the two Faculties were primarily concerned with different objectives: the one with developing each discipline in depth within each Honours course, the other, even in its Honours courses, with providing its students with a broad experience which they could use in the field. This was summed up well by the Dean of the Faculty of Agriculture and Horticulture, H. A. D. Neville:

> In the Faculty of Agriculture we are continually telling students that they are not to consider their training complete when they leave the University. We tell them, and I believe we are right, that they are here to get hold of the fundamental principles of their profession, but that immediately they are through their degree examination they must get out into the industry, in order to familiarize themselves with practical conditions and problems. In fact, I look upon a man who has just graduated as one who, under the old apprenticeship system, would be called an 'improver'.[1]

Even so, in this Faculty, as in Letters and Science, the drift was away from the lower towards the higher qualification, from the less towards the more academic. Between 1927 and 1937 the number reading for first degrees more than doubled while the number reading for diplomas and certificates fell by

---

[1] H. A. D. Neville to Sibly, 21 January 1931, supplying information in reply to an enquiry from the D.S.I.R. (URC, Vice-Chancellor, box 43).

a quarter.[1] In 1936 the old Certificate in Dairying was abandoned. In the
last year of peace the diploma courses in the Faculty were still being actively
followed,[2] but the number of Certificate students had dropped to twelve,
six in Agriculture and six in Horticulture; in 1940 these certificates also
were abandoned.

These developments in the courses and syllabuses of the University
provide one illustration of the steady and deliberate movement towards an
improvement in its academic quality. There are others. The academic staff
received scarcely any of the encouragement which has since come to be
regarded as essential to its well-being. Numbers were static. No new departments were founded. There was little hope of promotion. Yet there was a
very strong sense of participating in a growing University which was
designing its own lines of development. There was a sense of joint achievement which is still recalled with zest by those who participated in it. And
there was a real possibility that individuals, with ingenuity and determination, could build something out of all proportion to the limited resources
available. One illustration of that must suffice.

When Betts arrived to take charge of the School of Art in 1933 he was
informed by Sibly that he could expect 'a very humble start'. The point
was emphasized by the meagre material resources.[3] But there was worse
to come as Betts himself recalled:

> I had come from a much wider world into an enclosed community
> which contained a School of Fine Art which many of my painter
> friends looked upon as an artistic backwater and far too sheltered and
> cosy for a person of my temperament. It is true that on taking up my
> appointment I was very conscious of an air of leisurely inactivity in
> the School; the tempo (as one of my new colleagues informed me)
> was distinctly and happily *andante*. There was a prevailing sense of an
> arty-crafty attitude and there were far too many middle-aged women
> weaving indifferently designed and badly woven fabrics on rickety
> handlooms, and many students working at various kinds of handi-
> crafts. The so-called Fine Arts were distinctly limited. I could not
> accept any of these activities as being work of the kind one should
> expect from a university School of Fine Art and I knew that if the
> School were to survive I had to change it.[4]

In short, the conditions, the resources and the staff were quite inadequate
for the proper tasks of a university school. It was still financed partly by

[1] The examination results for 1937 (1927) were:

Ph.D., M.Sc. or Postgraduate Diploma	8	(1)
B.Sc.	34	(13)
Intermediate	39	(16)
Diplomas and Certificates	117	(155)

[2] In 1938–9 there were 17 students reading for the Diploma in Agriculture, 40 for the
Diploma in Dairying and 29 for the Diploma in Horticulture.
[3] See above, p. 17.
[4] Conversations with J. A. Betts, May 1972, August 1975.

the town and the Ministry of Education as well as the University; all three, Betts felt, were parsimonious. He sensed a real possibility that the School might drift slowly away from its attachment to the University, and even a threat that it might be abolished altogether.[1] Undismayed he set out to establish the School properly within the Faculty of Letters. He redrafted the syllabus and introduced a well founded course in the History of Art. He exploited Reading's proximity to London by persuading scholars and artists to come to give lectures or classes; Leopold Ettlinger, from the Warburg Institute, provided the first course in the History of Art and helped Betts to start the 'autumn' lectures in art history in the Faculty of Letters. Meanwhile, under Sibly's careful guidance, he was able to persuade some of the teachers in handicrafts to take due retirement. He brought in men from London to reinforce the teaching of drawing, painting and sculpture. He began to attract good students seeking to follow a properly based course in Fine Art. This influenced the Faculty of Letters and attracted support from Stenton, Dyson and others. In 1937, only four years after Betts's arrival, the Faculty recommended the introduction of an Honours Degree in Fine Art. By this time Betts had also recruited Robert Gibbings who had been forced to sell the Golden Cockerel Press in 1933. Betts was able to persuade Sibly to find a salary for Gibbings 'ostensibly to teach'. He and Gibbings searched London for a second-hand press and scraped together type and other items. Gibbings came in 1936. Betts had recruited a superb craftsman and designer who contributed immediately to the new degree course. Gibbings also began an advanced course in Design applied to Typography and Book Production. He was given a Lecturership in 1937 and remained at Reading until 1942. For six years limited editions, elegantly produced and beautifully illustrated, some with his own engravings, emerged from his second-hand press.[2] Already before the war the School had built a national reputation as a centre of design and typography.[3]

[1] The situation was not as black as it seemed to Betts. Before the retirement of Betts's predecessor, Seaby, Sibly commented 'The local School of Science and Art was one of the essential elements upon which the University Extension College was originally based in 1892, and a School of Art has always been an integral part of the University College and University of Reading. . . . In view of the impending retirement of the present Professor, we have been considering very carefully the possible future of the School of Art in relation to our Faculty of Letters, and especially the question whether a place can usefully be found for the History of Art as a subject for the B.A. Pass Degree. The matter is not yet settled, but it seems likely that we shall decide that the inclusion of the History of Art is desirable and practical.' (Sibly to Hugh Stewart, Principal of University College, Nottingham, 13 June 1932; URC, Vice-Chancellor, box 45).
[2] Some of the items are listed in *Four aspects of the work of Robert Gibbings* (University of Reading, 1975), p. 19. For a more complete list see A. Mary Kirkus, *Robert Gibbings: a bibliography*, ed. Patience Empson and J. Harris, London 1962. *Lashly's Diary*, a log of Scott's antarctic expedition of 1911–12, of which only seventy-five copies were printed, was a particularly prized item. See URC, Vice-Chancellor, box 45.
[3] The British Federation of Master Printers held a summer school for Young Master Printers at Reading in 1937. It returned both in 1938 and 1939 and regularly since then, See URC, Vice-Chancellor, box 46.

This was a result of Betts's inspired opportunism. Sibly also contributed for he knew and backed a good man when he saw one. In 1938 he commented on the achievement:

Our B.A. degree in Fine Art is a very recent development, the current session being the first year of the degree course. We have great hopes of this course, but it remains to be seen whether they are well founded. You will see that we provide an Honours course only, and that it extends over four years. We attach great importance to the fact that the degree course provides a technical training fully equal to that given by the Diploma course. The students who take the degree will be fully equipped as executive artists. . . .

My experience at Reading has convinced me that a School of Art can be a most valuable element in a university, provided that the students do not form a class apart. In Reading, the residential system is our safeguard in this respect, and the day students conform to the practice of the residential students.

It seems to be an essential condition of success that our standards of teaching (including specialized teaching in some but not all branches) should be equal to those of the Royal School of Art in London. Our proximity to London is an important factor in this respect. Our staff is composed partly of full-time teachers and partly of part-time specialists (all of whom are practising artists) who come down from London on one, two or three days a week. The fact that we have to fulfil the function of a municipal School is also very important. It enables us to provide a sufficient number of students and an adequate range of studies to carry a large staff.

We were most fortunate six years ago to secure a man of outstanding qualifications as the new Head of our School. He has put new life into the place. It was he who introduced the part-time specialists from London. . . .[1]

That omitted one essential detail. Throughout these formative years Betts taught for thirty hours a week. He always lunched and dined in the Senior Common Room. He ate at home only at the weekend. In recollection he enjoyed every minute of it.

[1] Sibly to J. W. Ogilvie, Vice-Chancellor of The Queen's University, Belfast, 24 May 1938 (URC, Vice-Chancellor, box 45).

Chapter 4

The University community 1926–39

Buildings and revenue, syllabuses and student-places, form but the context of a university. The university itself, its life, its quality, is compounded of what men and women, teachers, scholars, researchers and pupils, do within it. It is perhaps best described by the German term *Genossenschaft*.[1] To ask those who were at Reading what it was like is to uncover memories and impressions of a community. That was the word to which Stenton turned in writing of Reading to Pollard.[2] That community might be defined or described in a number of ways. Some, the members of staff, may talk in the first place of their research and teaching, of shared endeavour in mustering resources for their departments or for the Library, or for performances in music or drama. Some dwell affectionately on the Senior Common Room in the Acacias. Many, both staff and students, recollect the close intimacy between teacher and pupil which was easily encouraged in an institution which contained roughly 700 students. Some old students talk about their departments; most recall the 'characters', the inspiring lecturers or the oddities among their teachers and other members of the academic and administrative staff. All of them, all that is of the resident students, retain an abiding memory of their Halls, of the students whom they met in Halls, and of their wardens. Ask a Reading student of the thirties what it was like and he is likely to talk first of Wantage or 'Pats', or she of St Andrew's, Wessex or St George's. They will then talk of university societies, of the Gild of the Red Rose and Jantaculum, of games and of the river. But they will not recall the Students' Union. Nor do they have memories of long journeys by bus or tram across a large industrial town to catch the first of the morning's lectures. Essentially Reading for them was the small,

---

[1] 'The English translation must carefully avoid Partnership; perhaps in our modern usage Company has become too specific and technical; Society also is dangerous; Fellowship with its slight flavour of an old England may be our least inadequate word' – F. W. Maitland's comment in his edition of part of Gierke's *Das deutsche Genossenschaftsrecht* (1868–81) as *Political Theories of the Middle Age* (Cambridge, 1900), p. xxv. It is noteworthy that Childs's comments on the University frequently seem to reveal a strong influence of Gierke, direct or indirect. For an example see above p. 38. Childs attached strong moral overtones to the notions of Fellowship. Maitland was seeking for legal and political definition, as indeed I am; he made light of an impossible task of translation. He did not, however, consider what is perhaps an even better word – community.

[2] See above, p. 3.

compact community centred on the site in London Road and the Halls clustered around it. There were outliers, the University Farm in Sonning and the National Institute for Research in Dairying in Shinfield, but the 'agrics' like other students had their home in the Halls and the National Institute was neither so distant nor so dwarfed by the parent body as to feel cut off or overwhelmed.

The picture, as it survives, is doubtless distorted. It is painted largely by those who have remained within, or in close touch with, the University; by those who fitted easily into the pattern and achieved success within it. But there were others who questioned the objectives and methods which Reading had adopted. There must have been a few who hated it, who were revolted by the heartiness of Hall and embarrassed by the determination of their wardens to 'bring them out'. These voices are not so easily heard. But that they were there, that differences of view were possible is apparent even in so simple and elementary a matter as the aspect of the site at London Road. To Childs this seemed so comely that he looked upon his charge of it as a trust almost moral in its binding quality.[1] Sibly found it pleasant and charming.[2] There were students too who were greatly impressed by the beauty of the gardens: 'money could not be afforded for imposing buildings, but the site was beautified by the gardeners and the planning of the buildings round the cloisters gave it a working intimacy.'[3] But much of this was in the eye of the beholder. Elspeth Huxley, who came to Reading from Kenya in 1925 and measured Reading by the standard of Oxford, gained a very different impression:

London Road was not as squalid as many of the neighbouring streets consisting of squashed-together little dwellings dark with grime, and all alike. It had a number of detached three-storeyed houses possessed of basements and a patch of garden enclosed by laurel hedges; some respectable pubs; and it had the Royal Berkshire Hospital, which looked much more like a university than that establishment itself. Nearby, a narrow wooden porch abutted on to the road, and if you turned into this, you found yourself in a lobby with notice-boards and an office or two, much less imposing than the booking hall of any small country station. Beyond this lay the university: a red brick library with an ugly clock tower, a sort of outsize garden shed where examinations, dances and assemblies were held; and a straggle of low buildings, all of a temporary looking nature, which embraced lecture rooms and laboratories, linked by what were known as cloisters but were merely brick-floored pathways roofed by corrugated iron. The whole place had a newly

[1] Childs (1933), pp. 50–1.
[2] See above, p. 38.
[3] Conversation with Professor P. Allen, November 1969.

spawned and makeshift appearance and lacked dignity, coherence or style.[1]

That is a critical view which cannot be ignored or dismissed. An objective assessment of the site is impossible. Perhaps its chief importance in this story is that it did inspire affection in some. *Sub specie eternitatis*, as it were, it must be counted null; neither the gardens nor the buildings are mentioned in Nikolaus Pevsner's *Berkshire*.[2]

Such differences in opinion extended into much of the University's work. There were conflicts, sometimes sharp, on the merits of academic proposals or achievements. Students expressed concern about the general objectives of university education. Increasingly in the 1930s political questions produced more and more debate. As always in enclosed communities there were gossip, rivalry and petty jealousies or irritations which the passage of time has sometimes magnified. All this was natural enough. In the long run much of it did not matter. It still has to be borne in mind. The University was variegated not uniform in pattern. Almost any view of the quality of life therein can be countered by its opposite. Most of the Reading shibboleths were criticized or mocked at some time by some one. Nevertheless there was character in the place and that derived in part from an accepted pattern and standard of behaviour. It tolerated variety, and applauded eccentricity; in some ways it was liberal beyond the conventions of the time; but the pattern was ever present nevertheless.

Undoubtedly the fact that Reading was a provincial university which was also residential was the most important element in that pattern. In establishing a tutorial and a residential system, Childs set out to copy one of the most important features of Oxford. He could see at once that this was beyond complete realization, and in one respect he did not want to realize it, for he determined from the start that the halls of residence should be subordinated to the University and should not acquire a teaching role.[3] Nevertheless the Halls expressed the firm intention of the College and then the University to take responsibility for the moral and physical welfare of its students. In the development of such Halls Reading gave a lead. The first of them to be fully established, Wantage Hall, which was founded through the benefaction of Lady Wantage in 1908, became a model. Before the First World War it was a show place, visited by representatives from other educational institutions and authorities. By the 1930s, when Wantage had been joined by other Halls, Reading had become the prototype of the modern residential University, and Sibly a source of information and advice

[1] Elspeth Huxley, *Love among the Daughters* (London, 1968), p. 47. On the Entrance compare Edith Morley's comment that it was 'more reminiscent of an underground railway station.' ('Reminiscences', URC, MS 528, p. 112).
[2] Pevsner discussed the buildings in Whiteknights and also mentioned St Andrew's Hall, the oldest part of which, formerly East Thorpe, was built for Alfred Palmer by Waterhouse in 1880 (*Berkshire*, 1966, pp. 203, 207).
[3] Childs (1933), pp. 89–90.

on questions of Halls, residence and related questions to other vice-chancellors and principals of colleges.[1]

Wantage Hall originated in a single benefaction and was constructed on the model of an Oxford college building. The other Halls had multifarious origins and varied histories. St Patrick's was started as a private hostel by R. L. Pearson in 1908 to accommodate students who could not gain places in Wantage. It was taken over by the College in 1909, with Pearson continuing as Warden, and was established in newly-built accommodation as a second men's Hall in 1913.[2] It received several additions and extensions between the Wars: in 1927–8 further student accommodation along with common rooms and a library, provided by the University Grants Committee; in 1934 a warden's lodging and more student accommodation provided by a donation from Miss Edith Knapman; and in 1936 further rooms for students in a neighbouring house which the University leased. St Andrew's was also started as a private venture in 1900 by Miss Mary Bolam, who was to play a dominating role in the development of the women's Halls. In 1911, as a College Hall with Miss Bolam as Warden, it moved into Alfred Palmer's old house, East Thorpe. The house was provided on a beneficial lease and Alfred Palmer added a new wing which accommodated forty students.[3] Thereafter, St Andrew's expanded through the acquisition, either by gift or purchase, of neighbouring houses in Redlands Road. St George's like St Andrew's began as a private venture at the beginning of the century. It was housed in specially designed accommodation at Christchurch Green in 1905, but was not taken over by the College until 1918. By 1925 an annexe to it had been established in Lynwood, a house in Redlands Road, and in 1929–30 it was joined in a single unit by Ashdown Hall, which as Cintra Lodge, had originated in 1917 in a private house provided by Leonard Sutton.[4] Of all the Halls, St George's was the most scattered and least economic to manage. In 1934 the University bought a new site for it in Elmhurst Road. Sibly appealed for benefactions and despite the aftermath of the Slump met a ready response.[5] A matching grant was given by the University Grants Committee and building was completed on its new site at the outbreak of the Second World War.[6] It was not, however, until 1940 that the Hall finally gained its new accom-

---

[1] See the inquiries which came to him from Kenneth Vickers (Southampton), Maxwell Garnett (Oxford), B. Mowat Jones (Leeds), T. Loveday (Bristol), Geoffrey H. Thomson (Edinburgh) and H. A. Fyfe (Aberdeen) in URC, Vice-Chancellor, boxes 44, 45. It was rarely noted at Reading that Durham provided yet another variant of residential development in colleges.

[2] Childs (1933), pp. 169–76. The building was financed by a long-term loan.

[3] Childs (1933), pp. 176–7.

[4] *Ibid.*, pp. 81, 176; *Calendar 1925-6*, p. 6.

[5] By 1938 private donations amounted to £11,655. Lord Iliffe provided £5,000 and Miss Beeton, Miss Courtauld, Mrs Eustace Palmer and Dr Gerald Palmer all made major contributions.

[6] The original plan envisaged 99 study bedrooms and cost an estimated £54,000. It was reduced to 55 places and a cost of £33,000. The UGC provided £12,500.

modation.[1] Wessex Hall had a less confused history and a harder fate. It was opened in October 1913 in Lower Redlands, a property which had belonged to Herbert Sutton. Adjoining houses were added in the 1920s so that it developed as separate buildings set in pleasant gardens around the central dining and common rooms. In many ways it was the most distinctive and attractive of all the Halls for women; it was certainly Childs's favourite.[2] Since the war it has been completely destroyed to make way for the expansion of the Royal Berkshire Hospital.

These Halls together could accommodate a very considerable proportion of the students under tutorial supervision. In 1925–6 Wantage and St Patrick's provided for 78 and 70 men respectively. For the women St Andrew's could provide 127 places, St George's 58, Cintra Lodge 31 and Wessex 65.[3] There were 429 students in Hall out of a total of 671 under tutorial supervision. By 1938–9 the extension to St Patrick's had added a further 50 places, bringing the total to 480 against 698 students then under tutorial supervision. At any one time in the 1930s roughly two-thirds of the students under supervision were living in a hall of residence. The remainder were not forgotten. In 1920–1 they were organized in an association under the name of St David's Hall, and provided with a common room and a warden, who, with interested members of the academic staff, did their best to develop some kind of community among those not in a residential hall.[4] Some of the staff, J. W. Dodgson, R. Bowen and Mabel Buer, were devoted to it. Some of the students shunned it:

> Occupants of 'approved lodgings', such as myself, were loosely banded together, mainly for purposes of sport, in a non-existent Hall called St David's, whose only physical presence was a room in a dark and rather smelly house off the London Road which had a metered gas fire and a ping-pong table and where, on certain evenings of the week, between five and ten, we were entitled to forgather. Very few of us did.[5]

The Hall's reports to the University magazine are zestful and possess a curiously modern ring:

> St David's Hall is a mixed Hall. It is therefore empty in the summer term. For those who must work – work, and those who would play – play. . . . There is now both an atmosphere and a history about David's. It was never apologetic, and it is always friendly. The only distinctive things about it are that it is the only mixed Hall, the only

[1] In 1939 Wantage Hall was commandeered for the Royal Air Force and in the emergency the Wantage men were placed in the new building for St George's. St George's therefore had to remain in its old accommodation and in Ashdown Hall, neither of which had the University intended to retain. In 1940 the men and women were switched round.
[2] Childs (1933), pp. 177–9.
[3] I have taken these figures from the *Calendar 1925–6*, p. 6. They differ slightly from those given by Childs.
[4] Childs (1933), p. 252.
[5] Elspeth Huxley, *op. cit.*, pp. 49–50.

non-residential Hall, and the only completely happy Hall. It is, of
course, the best Hall.[1]

In 1927, the year of that report, the Hall won the Rowing Shield and Hockey
Cup for women, the Ladies Cup (awarded to the men) for rifle shooting,
and the inter-Hall tennis tournament.

The Halls did not lie entirely easily within the framework of the University. The wardens exercised much day-to-day responsibility for the students
in residence. To them their role seemed large. To members of University
departments, in contrast, it could appear more domestic. Wardens sought
a status within the University which acknowledged their special role. The
academic staff thought of that role as something less than their own. The
differences came to a head in the discussions surrounding Statutes and
Ordinances. As these took shape in the course of 1925–6, wardens were
given a place *ex officio* on the Court of the University, but received no other
special recognition. In July 1925 all wardens wrote a joint letter to Childs
requesting representation on Council, Senate, boards of faculties and the
committees for the management of Halls. Childs pointed out that such an
amendment to the proposed constitution could not be introduced during
the final consideration of the Charter and Statutes by the Privy Council; it
would rather be a matter for the University, once founded. The wardens
persisted and asked that their case should be considered by Council with
their own representatives present. On 23 October 1925 Council ruled that,
without prejudice to the principle of the matter, it could not now alter the
submission to the Privy Council. It did not admit wardens to the discussion.
The wardens were interviewed by Childs and agreed not to rock the boat.
With that submission Childs promised 'to bring the question of the wardens'
claims before the governing bodies of the University, and to recommend that
those claims should receive practical recognition in whatever way might
seem best'.

The matter was soon resolved. On 3 December 1926 the Senate recommended regulations to Council for the definition of the academic staff under
the new Statutes. Wardens of Halls were included. But beyond that the
Senate would not go. At its next meeting of 20 January 1927 Childs fulfilled
his promise to the wardens by presenting a long memorandum which
recounted the history of the affair. He scented difficulties ahead:

> The offer thus made was personal; it was limited; and it in no way
> compromised the discretion or freedom of the Council and Senate.
> That there may be no misconception on this point, I append to this
> memorandum the passage in my letter relating to it.

Nevertheless his memorandum was a paean in praise of the hall of residence.
He came down firmly on the wardens' side:

> The function which the Halls fulfil in the life of this University is vital,
> whether it is viewed in retrospect, or in its present or future activity.

[1] *Tamesis*, xxv (1927), p. 224.

Without the Halls there would not be a University now; and without
the Halls the University could neither flourish nor survive. There can
be no grasp of policy for this University which does not appreciate
them as one of the principal factors to be dealt with. We have set a
lead which is being vigorously copied; and one of the fundamentals in
our policy must be to keep that lead and to make the growth of our
Halls keep pace with the requirements of the University. The question
now is whether this vital factor in the life and well-being of the
University is to have adequate recognition in University government.
And here, I think, is a choice between policy and impolicy. . . . A
faculty board is concerned with purely academic matters, but the
responsibilities of the Senate in administration extend to the University
as a whole. They include many matters, prominent among which are
teaching, research, standards of examinations, staffing, and the
discipline and welfare of students. The Senate is constituted with
reference to these responsibilities, but in one respect, I venture to
suggest, inadequately. Since the residence of students in Halls is the
predominant fact in the life and character of our University, I find
myself unable to defend the exclusion of wardens from the Senate, and
unable to doubt that the Senate would be strengthened by their
presence. Every warden is of necessity an officer of discipline; the
views of such officers on all regulations affecting discipline and
questions arising can never be negligible. Further, from the nature of
their post, wardens have an intimate knowledge of many things
affecting students, apart from purely disciplinary questions, which
often gives to their opinions a special value. I submit, therefore, that
the Senate would gain particularly in certain parts of its work, if
representative wardens shared in its deliberations and decisions; and
I am confident that the effect of such recognition of the warden's
office would enhance the prestige of wardens among the students in
Halls, would deepen the warden's sense of responsibility, would prove
a stimulus and encouragement to them, would make for the solidarity
which is vital to the successful advance of a small university, and
would remove the sense of exclusion and isolation which is undoubtedly felt under the present conditions.[1]

This exhaustive presentation of the case was to no avail. By a vote of fifteen
to two it was resolved at once that wardens had no claim to representation
on the Senate. Other matters were referred to a committee which when it
reported at the next meeting of the Senate recommended 'that the existing
practice whereby the wardens are not members of the Halls' Committees

---

[1] This and other evidence above is taken from Childs's memorandum of 6 December
1926 attached to the Report of the Senate Committee on the Status of Wardens of
15 February 1927 (Senate Reports, i).

but attend by invitations should be maintained'.[1] The only concession made to meet the wardens' case was to give them *ex officio* status on a newly constituted Consultative Committee on Discipline which the report recommended. For the next ten years the *Calendar* noted that wardens attended the Committees for the management of Halls by invitation. It was not until 1938 that they were finally accorded full membership.[2]

This argument was a symptom of a deeper unease which was probably inherent in the development of Halls at Reading. With the foundation of Wantage Hall, the simple notion of providing for lodgings for students in hostels, managed either directly or by private individuals, came to be blended with something much larger, namely an Oxford College with its dining hall, common rooms and library. Childs's main fear when Wantage was founded was that 'there might have been repeated in Reading, upon a petty and stultifying scale, the old story of collegiate usurpation at Oxford and Cambridge'.[3] Hence he saw to it that the Halls should have no teaching function and this was reiterated in the Ordinances of the University. Whether it was a real risk when Wantage was founded may be doubted. The new Hall still had far to go before it had the resources to provide for teaching Fellowships, and neither Wantage nor any other Hall had any corporate capacity to acquire and retain endowments except through the College and University. Certainly by 1926 there was no real likelihood of Halls usurping the University's teaching function. Meanwhile a companion problem had not been given the attention it deserved. In developing the hostels into Halls which were pale reflections of an Oxford College, Reading was in fact requiring its wardens to act at one and the same time as heads of houses; as deans responsible for discipline; to some degree as moral tutors with an intimate knowledge of, and responsibility for, the students in their Halls; and finally as domestic bursars immediately responsible for the day-to-day running of institutions, some of which served more than a hundred students.

---

[1] The Committee consisted of Childs, Cole, Crowther, Edith Morley, H. A. D. Neville, Knapman, who was then Censor of Discipline as well as Registrar and Tutorial Secretary, and H. H. Nicholson, a lecturer in the Department of Agricultural Chemistry who was a resident of Wantage Hall.

[2] The note in the *Calendar* referring to attendance by invitation can scarcely have been other than a permanent irritant. It was dropped in 1937–8. On 12 May 1938 the wardens wrote to Sibly requesting representation on the Committees for the management of Halls. He referred the matter to Council and a committee appointed by Council reported in December 1938 in favour of their inclusion (Council Reports, vii; Council Minutes, i). This settled the matter. However there was still a residual trace of subordination. Hitherto there had been two committees, one for men's Halls and one for women's, with responsibility for St David's divided, by sex, between them. In 1938 the Council committee recommended that there should be a committee for each Hall. This, however, was met by using the two existing committees. Hence, apart from the wardens, the committees of all the men's Halls had the same membership and so also had the committees of the women's Halls. Notionally each committee was separate. In fact there were still two committees which wardens attended, each for his or her own Hall. See *Calendar 1939-40*, p. 116.

[3] Childs (1933), p. 90.

It is true that the wardens had the guidance of the committees of management, that the University took ultimate responsibility for drafting rules of
discipline and that in financial matters they could call on the resources of
the University Bursar. But there was one essential difference from Oxford or
Cambridge on which no one seems to have commented at the time. There
was no governing body of Fellows. There were senior common rooms and
resident members of academic staff in most of the Halls, but they shared no
collective responsibility. The tasks which fell on several individual Fellows
in a College were all concentrated at Reading in the person of the warden.
So also was the responsibility. In advocating the wardens' case in December
1926 Childs disclosed the consequences:

> No one who has been concerned with the selection of a warden will
> make light of the difficulty of securing a candidate with requisite
> qualifications. It is agreed that these qualifications should include (a)
> a sufficient academic status; (b) a personality fitted to exercise a
> beneficent personal influence over the individual members of that
> community; and (c) a competent ability to manage or supervise from
> day to day the business and administrative side of a large institution
> under the general direction of the University.[1]

He failed to note the really essential qualification – a strong constitution.

To seek such a combination of talents was to restrict the field of search. It
was further reduced in the case of women by the many obstacles which still
lay in the way of those who looked for a career in teaching or administration
within a university. Hence the wardens formed a highly selected group,
made up of determined and able people who knew that they were placed in
positions of responsibility and influence and were ready to exercise both.
They directed the affairs of their Halls as a matter of personal pride. When
Evelyn Wiseman arrived to take charge of Cintra Lodge in 1926, she was
advised by Mary Bolam, Warden of St Andrew's and doyenne of the women
wardens – 'Do not let the Committee know what you are doing, my dear, the
Hall is yours'.[2] St Andrew's was certainly Miss Bolam's. She had been a
member of Somerville College before women were accepted to a degree at
Oxford; like others of her generation she held her first degree of the University of Dublin. She arrived in Reading to join the Department of Education
in 1900 after a period as an assistant at Cheltenham under Miss Beale.
Childs relates the outcome:

> She came into a young and rapidly growing College: and she was not
> long a member of it before she saw what she ought to do. She ought
> to do something for the residence and care of women students. The
> College blessed the idea, and she went to work. From that moment her
> work never paused or looked back. Her mind was full of what she
> wanted to do; she saw visions, and she saw no less clearly what had to

[1] Senate Reports, i.
[2] Conversation with Miss Wiseman, 2 November 1969.

be done in order to bring them to pass. She proved herself to be intensely practical, a marvellous contriver, a born manager. Yet whoever had to do with her had always to reckon with something else much less easy to describe. It was clear that Miss Bolam lived and worked for an idea. She went her way and held her course in pursuit of it with north-country tenacity and unconquerable perseverance. She was not trying to make a fortune: money has little power over people of her kind. She was not trying to achieve fame, to use the College as a stepping stone to something better, or to make herself a power in the College. Her concentration upon her own purpose was too great to allow of any secondary ambitions. Her aim was to make the best women's Hall in the country. Her way of explaining her ideas did not always appeal to everybody. Occasionally she trod upon people's toes, but I do not think that Miss Bolam, kind-hearted as she is, greatly cared or even noticed. She was full of her purpose; and always her purpose has possessed her to the full.[1]

It was that kind of devotion which attracted Alfred Palmer when he provided East Thorpe for the establishment of St Andrew's Hall. It was not Miss Bolam's only quality. When the Senate was constituted in 1926 she was appointed to it. In that year, apart from the Lecturer in Education, who was present *ex officio*, she was the only non-professorial member.

Miss Bolam was succeeded at St Andrew's in 1927 by Eleanor Plumer who moved to Oxford in 1931 to take charge of home students and ultimately found St Anne's College. She was in turn replaced by Dorothy Mack Smith. At St Patrick's, Pearson continued as warden up to 1949. Evelyn Wiseman moved to Wessex in 1929 and remained there until 1954. Isobel Turner succeeded Miss Wiseman at Ashdown Hall in 1929 and then replaced Emily Little at St George's in 1931, where she stayed until 1952. Wantage, after Childs's long sojourn there passed in 1930 to J. B. Passmore and then in 1938 to J. S. L. Waldie. In pressing their demands for recognition on the University the wardens acted as a small tightly-knit group. But they managed their Halls each in relative independence, one or two, the less successful, in increasing isolation. They could be prickly, competitive and critical of each other. Evelyn Wiseman recalled that Winifred Britton, her predecessor at Wessex, suffered from the fact that she had no degree, simply the associateship of the old University College.[2] Miss Wiseman herself in later years was known to take a pointedly comparative interest in the tidiness of Hall gardens, which other wardens might satisfy by leaving areas of untidiness for her critical attention and comment. Wardens lived in a pernickety world.

However, it was a world which they shared closely with the academic

[1] *Tamesis*, xxv (1927), p. 209.
[2] Winifred Britton failed to get on with Childs and resigned in 1929. She was touchy about her lack of a degree, which Eleanor Plumer, on occasion, rubbed in (Conversation with Miss Wiseman, 2 November 1969).

staff. Some of them, Emily Little, Passmore and Waldie, like Mary Bolam, were members of the academic staff before becoming wardens. Many of them, with the permission of the Hall committees, did some teaching as sessional lecturers or tutors. Unmarried members of staff lived in Hall. At Wantage and St Patrick's especially, they soon established traditions as small, closely-knit, senior common rooms. Some were prepared to act as temporary wardens during a vacancy. H. A. D. Neville, though Head of the Department of Agricultural Chemistry and Dean of the Faculty of Agriculture and Horticulture, could still find time to act as Warden of Wantage in 1928–9. Already by 1926 Reading had established a pattern which has changed very little since.[1]

Halls were for students to live in. At the same time they were one of the main features and attractions of Reading to the world outside. The warden was placed very much *in loco parentis*. The Halls were moulds in which young men and women grew to maturity. The social assumptions of the day left room for jests, or for calculated misbehaviour which amounted to fun or 'ragging'. It was agreed that youth would, indeed should, express itself. But at the same time this was allowed within regulations which the student had to obey and social conventions to which he or she was expected to conform. The wardens maintained orderly behaviour and sought to ensure that their charges developed as young gentlemen and young ladies, especially young ladies.

In this the Halls at Reading were little different from other similar institutions of the time. It may be that the small size of Reading encouraged an ingrown concern for the detail of rules and regulations. There can have been few other universities where a student required the permission of the Vice-Chancellor to be absent from Hall overnight.[2] Within the Halls the warden was the dominating influence. Childs summed up Miss Bolam in emphatic terms worthy of an emphatic character:

> Miss Bolam was the merciless enemy of the slovenly. She exorcised
> from her Hall that unpleasing forlornness and shabbiness of demeanour
> which so often clings about such places like a mildew. The orderliness
> and trimness of St Andrew's, from attic to cellar, might well remind
> the visitor of a first-class battleship.[3]

The simile is not calculated to endear her to later generations. But her own students adored her. Of all the wardens her memory is the most cherished. She was indefatigable and she was a Tartar:

> She very quickly knew all her students and she had such a
> pigeon-hole type of memory that she soon knew each student's

[1] Separate Hall committees, each with its own discrete membership, were established in 1967. From 1969 to 1976 wardens were appointed simultaneously to wardenships and lecturerships, with the heads of the appropriate departments exercising a voice in the selection.
[2] Regulations for Discipline 1926–7. See Appendix 7, below, p. 357.
[3] Childs (1933), p. 182.

table-napkin ring as well. This was important, for she arranged the seating for lunch and dinner and she carefully mixed the students to avoid the formation of cliques and to broaden their educational interest. Thus she would place an Agricultural or Horticultural student next to a Classics or Fine Art student. . . . Also she rang the changes of students sitting at the high table. . . . Students had to be in St Andrew's Hall by 6.0 pm. in the winter and 7.0 pm. in the summer, unless they had permission to attend lectures or meetings of societies or other approved functions. The doors of the Hall were locked and a late-comer had to ring the front door bell for admittance and was met on the mat by 'Ma'. . . . To the dance at the end of the summer term each student had to invite a man and moreover had to tell Miss Bolam the name of the man she wished to invite. Her first question on hearing the name of the proposed guest was sometimes, 'Is he a *gentleman*, my dear?', and the second question, 'Has he an evening suit?' If a woman student did not know a man whom she could invite, 'Ma' would be very helpful in providing one. . . . She would not countenance any unseemly behaviour and would not allow the men to swing the women off their feet when dancing the Lancers. . . . If a student wished to entertain a man in her room for tea she had to have a chaperone, or she might be allowed to entertain him in 'Ma's' private drawing room. . . .

That is recalled by a student who came to St Andrew's Hall in 1913.[1] By 1926 skirts were shorter, the Lancers had been replaced by the 'Fox-trot' and Hall rules had been relaxed a little.[2] But Miss Bolam in her last year had become a living legend. Had she not resisted the proposal to do away with open fires in St Andrew's with the devastating and incontro-vertible argument – 'What woman ever told her secrets to a radiator?'[3]

In all this Miss Bolam was simply expressing in a very individual way a tradition and an attitude to management which was common to all wardens. Some were kinder and gentler than others but all were clearly in charge. At St Patrick's Pearson exercised a similar influence and control. V. Mallinson watched him with respect in his last years as warden after the Second World War:

For a good many years I lived in St Patrick's Hall when Pearson was warden there. He was very much an ex-Army type. I had not been there very long when there was some sort of rampage of students

[1] Conversation with Dr Adela G. Erith, 21 March 1971.
[2] Compare the Rules of *c.* 1922 and 1932, Appendix 7, below, pp. 358–9.
[3] Conversation with Dr Erith as above and with Mrs Annie D. Ure, 19 March 1970. Mrs Ure, who entered St Andrew's in 1911, shared Dr Erith's recollections – 'Lights were out at 11.0 pm. Miss Bolam went all round the Hall in person turning off the switches on every landing. We used to watch the glass fanlights over our doors till the flash of her torch had passed and then we draped our gowns over the fanlights and got out our candles (a farthing each at Woolworth's) and settled down to work.'

shouting and singing round the quad late at night. I thought to
myself – well, I suppose I have to deal with this – and I climbed
out of bed. I had just got to the door when the lights suddenly and
strategically came on, and there, fully illuminated in pyjamas and
dressing gown stood Pearson. He just stood and the men silently
faded away. He was a very good warden indeed, very human, and he
cared deeply about students.[1]

When Professor Mallinson became Warden of Whiteknights Hall, the first
of the Halls to be built after the Second World War, he deliberately tried
to model himself as warden on Pearson. In like manner Miss Wiseman, in
her own way, created a legend somewhat similar to Miss Bolam's. She had
a firm view of discipline and a clear conception of acceptable behaviour.
Vera Willis recorded her only serious conflict with her Warden as follows:

It was indirectly *à propos* of Bryan that I had my first and only
conflict with the Warden. I had a troublous fortnight. I had been
reproved by authority for leaning my bicycle in a flowerbed (I
claimed it was a path, but half a dozen geraniums appeared next day
just to show that it was a flowerbed), for throwing onions at the
Library window, and for hanging my bathing dress out to dry on the
telegraph wires. On Whit Saturday I went to Oxford with Mac. We
explored colleges, had tea with Professor Powicke and supped with
Bryan. . . . We took the last train back to Reading, but being Bank
Holiday season it brought us back twenty minutes later than we had
bargained for. I had neither signed out nor asked permission to go
beyond cycling distance of Reading. I therefore deemed it expedient
to return by way of Sheldon's window. Miss Wiseman, however, by
means of that intuition which is given to wardens was aware that I
had been in Oxford. She told me with great eloquence that this was
not such as she expected from one of my pretensions. . . .[2]

Miss Willis added – 'the incident increased rather than diminished our
friendship'. Like Miss Bolam, Miss Wiseman became a powerful influence.
In her last years as warden it was alleged that members of Wessex could
always be identified anywhere in the University simply by their deportment
and mien. To one newly-arrived young professor, attending a social
engagement at the Hall for the first time, they all seemed to carry the
same expression.[3] On Wessex Day, the annual garden party at the Hall,
she would gently but firmly wave aside those of her charges who failed to
introduce their guests correctly so that they had to do another circuit of
the lawn and come in for a second landing.

Wardens varied in their attitudes and methods. Some, not many, were
remembered as gentle creatures.[4] All had to manage the lives of young

[1] Conversation with Professor V. Mallinson, 25 February 1971.
[2] Vera Willis, Diary 1931–4, pp. 29–31.
[3] Conversation with A. G. Lehmann, 6 August 1975.
[4] Miss Wiseman's comment on Miss Little.

people after organized working hours. Their guiding hand could gain no support from the need to discuss an essay or set about a laboratory practical. A warden who failed to lead by one method or another, was vulnerable. At Wantage the wardenship of Ward from 1927–9 was peppered with incident. He was a stickler for closing the Hall gates on time. On a night in November 1928, as a demonstration that locks did not a prison make, the sheep from the nearby Pigeon's Fields were driven into the quadrangle and left until morning. Wantage's first Sheep Night, celebrated annually ever since, was the work of Arnold Halliday, a philosophy student from Halifax, who made the happy discovery that the key to the garage which had been issued to him was in fact a master key to the Hall gates.[1] Worse was to follow in other incidents. Ashes were thrown at the Warden; perambulators were hoisted to the roof; ultimately superior authority had to intervene:

> I remember one very noisy night when for some reason or other some
> students came in rather late and rather drunk. They lit a bonfire
> outside the Warden's Lodging and danced round with tin trays and
> pokers asking for the Warden to come out and be burnt. Before long
> most of the members of the Hall were doing this. There was
> tremendous noise and then suddenly the clock struck twelve, but
> instead of being silent after the twelfth stroke, it went on striking
> up to sixty-six times, whereupon it got faster and faster. We thought
> it must be out of order until someone found the door to the clock
> tower open and a student up there hammering away at the clock
> for all he was worth. As a result of the noise and the light reflected
> in the sky from our bonfires, the neighbours sent for the fire brigade,
> but when it arrived the men of Wantage told it what it could do.
> Later we were all summoned to the Great Hall where Dr Childs
> read out letters from the local Member of Parliament, the chief of
> the Fire Brigade and the Chief Constable asking 'Were we all
> drunk?', and we had to pay a fine of ten shillings each.[2]

It seems to have been worth it.

That was simply to vent feelings. There were other more rational channels of communication. Every Hall had a Junior Common Room Committee which was given formal recognition in Hall rules as follows:

> The Common Room Committee, which is elected annually by the
> students of the Hall, is recognized as an essential part of the
> organization of the Hall. It possesses the right of approaching the
> Warden, either through its Chairman, or as a Committee, upon any
> matter affecting the welfare of the Hall, or the interests of its members.
> The Warden will expect that all such representations will be made to
> him through the agency of the Committee. He will himself consult

[1] Conversation with Sydney Taylor, 19 January 1971. See also plate 19.
[2] *Ibid.*

the Committee upon matters affecting the Hall, whenever he deems it necessary. The recognized status accorded to the Committee as an essential part of the organization of the Hall carries with it the obligation and understanding that the Committee will on all occasions exert itself to maintain the welfare and best standards of the Hall.[1]

Beyond that the University would not go. In 1938, while the wardens were successfully pressing their case for full membership of the Committees for the management of Halls, the students wrote, asking for representation. When Sibly reported the matter to Council it was turned down flat. When the President of the Students' Union renewed the request Council minuted a formal reply:

After full consideration of the points which you raised, the Council requested me to write to you in the following terms. In their opinion, student representation on the Committee for the management of halls of residence is undesirable. These Committees supervise the financial, administrative, and disciplinary management of the Halls, and are therefore concerned with many matters with which students, by reason of their standing in the University, are unqualified to deal. In each Hall there exists a Junior Common Room Committee, elected by the students, which possesses the right of discussing with the Warden any matter affecting the welfare of the students in residence. In exceptional cases, with the knowledge of the Warden, the Junior Common Room Committee has also the right of expressing the views of the student body to the Vice-Chancellor. These are important rights; and they place a definite responsibility for the maintenance of good standards within a Hall upon its students. In view of these facts, the Council sees no reason why there should be any room for misunderstanding. They do not feel that any useful purpose would be served by an interview with members of the Students' Representative Council.[2]

Occasionally protest went beyond the accepted limits of the day. On 8 February 1938 Sibly had to write to the parent of a student:

I regret to inform you that I have found it necessary to suspend your son . . . from attendance and residence at the University for two weeks. . . . Last night during dinner in [St Patrick's] Hall he walked up to the high table carrying a plate on his hand, and coming to a halt in front of the Warden, called out 'Will you please look at this meat and say whether it is fit to be served?' This was said in such a tone as to be heard by every one of the students and members of staff present. The Warden asked your son to return to his

---

[1] This is taken from Wantage Hall, Rules and Customs, January 1930 (Appendix 7, below, pp. 359–60). The same appeared in the Rules of St Patrick's and with a slight modification in the Rules for all the women's Halls.
[2] Council Minutes, i, 9 December 1938; Council Reports, vii.

seat, but he persisted for a time, eventually retiring. He was subsequently interviewed privately by the Warden, who pointed out that
he had committed a gross breach of discipline and good manners, but
he refused to recognize this, and argued that he had taken the only
possible course open to him, in view of complaints which had not
been attended to. In personal interview with me this afternoon,
your son has declined to admit that his conduct was reprehensible,
and has offered no apology. I am obliged, in the interests of discipline
and good behaviour, to make it clear beyond doubt to your son, and
to all his fellow students, that his conduct was inexcusable. . . .

Sibly followed with an ominous report from the student's dean which
recorded that he was slacking and wasting his time, a conclusion in which
the student himself concurred. Meanwhile his action in the Hall led to
a strike against attendance at Hall for dinner. On 9 February 1938 the
matter was given half a column in the *Reading Evening Gazette*. On the 10th
Sibly had the following notice posted in the Hall:

Any student who prevents or endeavours to prevent another from
entering the dining hall will render himself liable to expulsion from
the University.

That ended the affair.[1] To set it against the earlier events at Wantage
is to reveal something of the atmosphere of the time. For a near riot which
led to the intervention of the Fire Brigade and complaints from the Chief
Constable, a fine of ten shillings a head. For a challenge to authority,
rustication; for any attempt to enforce common action, expulsion. Buf-
foonery was tolerated; rebellion was suppressed. The distinction between
the two had long been accepted in English schools and universities.[2]

All this is a useful reminder that many of the issues which have arisen
in British universities in the last ten years are very far from new. Maurice
Barley, who came up to Wantage in 1928 and subsequently became the
first Professor of Archaeology in the University of Nottingham, remarked
'Looking back over my diaries, my strongest impression is of how *little*
universities have changed in forty years'.[3] That comment may be applied
not only to the substance of life in a university but also to the evidence
about it. In the nature of things the evidence is largely concerned with
the abnormal. Sibly had to write to the father of a peccant, lazy student
who challenged the authority of his warden. There was no need for him to
write to the parents of the hundreds of students whose behaviour required
no such intervention. The quality of their lives, therefore, is to that extent
lost to us. Likewise the students of Wantage in 1928 all remembered

[1] Registrar's Office. It is to be recorded that the menu of the objectionable meal was
soup, grilled chops and apricot flan. It had been preceded by a breakfast of bacon and
eggs and a lunch of fried fish and canary pudding.
[2] For a discussion of this at an earlier period see Keith Thomas, *Rule and Misrule in the
Schools of early modern England* (University of Reading, Stenton Lecture, 1976).
[3] URC, box 256.

Sheep Night and other riotous incidents of the time. Not so many recall the normal day-to-day routine and peaceful evenings of work or conversation. In peace or war, the dog days are unmemorable. Few have the capacity to recreate them in their minds. Still fewer regard their memory of an un-adventurous existence in which they were getting on with their work, establishing friendships with other students, relaxing by going to the cinema or walking down the river, as relevant historically. Yet that is what life at Reading was like for most students.

Occasionally this sense of the past is caught and held, especially perhaps by those who have remained within the university world.

> The great thing in those days was to come to a real university in the sense that it was the university that mattered. The Hall system really worked too. In Wantage, we lived in beautiful surroundings and we were thrown among students of other disciplines. It gave you an insight into studies other than your own and made you more tolerant. That was an important aspect of any university in 1936. It was an intimate university and one where you got to know teachers in other subjects as well as your own. . . . We felt identified with the University and were concerned about its future. There was a group of us at Wantage that used to discuss this at length. I can remember a fellow student (Arnold Martin, doing Agricultural Chemistry) and myself walking along the bridle path in Whiteknights Park, and even then – in the late thirties – we saw it (though despairingly) as the place where the future home of the University ought to be. We rather looked down on Oxford and Cambridge. We believed that Halls should not be any more independent than they were at Reading, otherwise the University could be too diffuse. We liked being in a small university in a small place, and we had no use for the 'day school' universities of the big cities. We believed that a student, for the few years that he was one, should *live* the life of a student, and we felt our residential system at Reading to be enormously important. We believed fiercely that Wantage Hall had not been accorded nearly enough recognition as the pioneer of the new residential system, although it had been taken as prototype by other univers-ities.[1]

That is peculiar in the extent to which it recalls a general concern for the well-being and future development of the University. Day-to-day life is reflected perhaps more immediately in the following:

> My recollection of Wantage at this time is of a strong social division between students with comfortable means – sometimes from public schools, and most of them reading agriculture – and those like myself

[1] Conversation with Professor P. Allen, 12 November 1969. Compare the comment on Whiteknights with below, pp. 137–8, 142.

from a working class background, with limited means and more serious intentions. To some extent this distinction pervaded the University as a whole. I at any rate became conscious of the superior social background of, for instance, women doing the dairying and domestic science courses. Among the men, drinking beer, singing dirty songs – a legacy, I suspect, particularly of men who came to the University after service in the 1914–18 war – and ragging freshers were all part of the manly tradition. In appearance, the manliness comprised wearing plus-fours of heavy light brown tweed, hanging well below the calves. . . . I can still see the porter of Wantage Hall – was he called Brett? – sitting in his lodge, beerily puffing at a pipe, or carrying his belly carefully and laboriously across the quad to the Warden's office. I fell with pleasure into the life-style of a student in Wantage; I soon bought a Rockingham-ware tobacco jar (which I still possess) for my mantelpiece. I can still see the crusty roll and ball of butter provided daily for tea; I can still visualize the two fire-lighters provided, with one bucket of coal each two days, for the evening fire. I do not recall that anyone actually sported his oak. The oak served as a screen round which senior students could tiptoe, in the night, to tip up the bed of a despised fresher and drop him in a clatter on to the floor.[1]

That, recalling 1928–32, is matched on the women's side:

Life in Hall was very like what I imagine a nice girls' boarding school would be in those days. All meals were eaten in the dining room at long tables – there was a system of signing out for dinner and we had to be in by 10.0 pm. Men friends were allowed in the common rooms, but certainly not in the bedrooms – and I have no recollection of this being questioned. Social life with fellow students consisted largely of going for walks and occasionally being taken out to tea. In my first year I was friendly with a German student and it seemed quite a daring adventure to go with him to a *thé dansant* at Maidenhead. Tea at the French Horn at Sonning was the conventional aftermath of Hall dances – the dance on Saturday night and the tea on Sunday afternoon. Mapledurham was another favourite place to visit and for whole day outings we used to go as far as the Berkshire Downs or Pangbourne and Streatley on the Thames.[2]

The men and women students mixed in university societies and at the dances which provided the main social occasions of the term. But the setting was formal and the students themselves shared in the defensive mechanisms which separated the sexes:

[1] M. W. Barley, URC, box 256.
[2] Diana Morgan (Mrs Barley), URC, box 256.

In those days there were very few student dances and we never
danced during Lent. All dances were formal, with programmes. The
Officers' Training Corps Dance was the great dance of the year.
Members of staff came and wardens, as chaperones. We rarely
invited a woman student into Hall; this was regarded as brazen. It
did happen occasionally in my day and then the students leant out
of the windows at St Patrick's to cheer. In the Buttery the sexes never
sat together for coffee and students of the opposite sex would never
dream of walking round the University arm in arm. If we invited
women out, we took them to tea at the Country Kitchen in Sonning.[1]

An invitation to tea in Sonning on the Sunday after a dance gave social
cachet. It was a preliminary declaration of interest.[2]

This settled world of the students had its own distinct hierarchical
arrangement:

I soon discovered that, as in all walks of English life, this unpretentious
university of some eight hundred lower middle-class students was
honeycombed with subtle snobberies. There was a pecking order
among studies as well as among people; agriculture ranked high,
not because farming was regarded as a snob pursuit – very few of the
'agri' students were likely to plough a furrow or hoe a field of roots,
and we had no sons of landowners – but because most of the graduates
would join the staff of some local authority or government department, the latter often in the Empire as it then was. They would go
forth to romantic sounding places like Nigeria and the Gold Coast,
Barbados and Fiji, Tanganyika and the Solomons, where they would
enjoy a most enviable status with bungalows, servants and sun-
downers, and become bronzed and manly in topees and shorts . . .

So to be an 'agri' was all right, and so was a 'horti'; pure scientists,
historians and classicists occupied a middle range, and at the bottom,
I regret to say, came the future teachers, who read for a two-years'
diploma instead of for a three- or four-years' degree. Why future
teachers should have been so poorly thought of, I do not know – I
suppose because they were so poorly paid. 'Edu's' tended to cluster
together looking earnest, pallid (probably from malnutrition) and
even more drearily dressed than the rest of us; to dodge coffees in the
Buttery because twopence was beyond their means; and, if girls, to
live at a remote Hall called St George's that no one else ever visited.
The smart hall was St Andrew's, just as among the men it was

---

[1] Conversation with Dr R. Bowen, 15 December 1969. Bowen came to Reading in 1928.
[2] The dances and tea in Sonning are recalled at length in Elspeth Huxley (1968),
pp. 51–65.

Wantage, with St Patrick's in second place.[1]

Each of these recollections casts a shaft of light on the students of Reading. Each picks out something of significance. But they leave out the questioning and the self-doubt. It would be unwise to accept editorials of student magazines as an unbiased historical source. No one cries 'apathy' sooner than a student editor short of copy. Even so, the editorials of the student magazine *Tamesis*, writings of far higher standard in style and intellectual content than is now the vogue in most student journals, should not be left out of the picture. They were of the Reading which has been sketched above, but they tried to stand outside it and assess it. At times they were solemn in their seriousness. But they are revealing evidence, both in what they say and in the targets they choose for criticism, perhaps above all in their consciousness of Reading as a new university.

Such an editor in Autumn term 1932 chose to comment first on the Halls and relations between the sexes:

> No other university has such a large proportion of its students in residence in Halls. The policy that begat the Halls was an under-standing, a far-sighted, and a very courageous policy. But have we deserved it? Have we achieved its aim of engendering one body politic and corporate? . . . There is a danger that the Hall system may defeat its own purpose by forming discrete elements within the University. Moreover, the Hall system inclines to segregate the sexes in a way that has unfortunate repercussions. . . . The relations between the sexes here are for the most part either relations of open or veiled hostility or of adolescence. . . . There is far too little of the frank cameraderie that should characterize the home of men and women who are credited with more than an average intelligence and who are supposed to have reached years of some discretion. . . . One day there will be a Union building and students who know it will not be able to see our present difficulties. But it is essential that we see them ourselves. We can do much. A building of itself is not a magical thing that will cause all shortcomings to vanish away. Its purpose must be appreciated and eagerly fulfilled. And we may fulfil that purpose if never a brick of the building be laid. For the barriers between the sexes and forgetfulness of the University as a whole through pre-occupation in the individual Hall are artificial mistakes;

---

[1] *Ibid.*, p. 49. The attitude towards 'Edu's' in this passage reflects the situation before the old diploma course was abandoned. On this see above, p. 50. Miss Wiseman provides a cross-bearing. When she arrived to take up the Wardenship of Cintra Lodge in 1926 she found that her predecessor H. S. Cooke, the Lecturer in charge of the Education Department had accepted only Education students. She suggested that vacant places should be filled by students from the different faculties, but Knapman, then Tutorial Secretary, told her that it was only fit for Education students. Elspeth Huxley is recalling a period when Cintra Lodge, as Ashdown Hall, had just been incorporated with St George's. It had been greatly improved, but its original association with Education students clearly remained and affected the reputation of its parent Hall.

they are not imposed upon us nor are they necessarily in the nature
of things here: they exist because we suffer them.

He framed this within a commentary on the University's Charter which
amounted to a passionate plea that students at Reading should consciously
set about creating their own ethos:

In the formal phrases of our Charter is enwrapped a tale unique in
the history of higher education, and it is a tale whose sequel is for
our making. To make it worthily we must learn of the past and
examine the present, with the same admirable far-sightedness that
was in the men and women who have guided our college to its present
stage. And our task is not so easy to grasp as was theirs. We seem to
have attained the position they desired; we are a university; what
else is there to do except to go on being a university? If we reason
so we are unjustifiably aping the older universities; we are putting
on airs and graces with our gown. We shall be able to assume the
University as an accomplished fact and to cease from self-consciousness
and self-examination only when we have become truly 'one body
politic and corporate'.

Some stand aloof who are too much engaged with the importance
of their own individuality. They are not conceited in the ordinary
sense. But they are convinced that their personal work and careers
matter so very very seriously. Let them reflect how much more
important a place is the University than they are individually. Let
them think somewhat of the world as a whole, for so may they
realize the insignificance of even the most prominent of them. Let
them think, who cram their heads with what in our ignorance we call
knowledge, of the progress yet to be made in surveying the vast
simplicity of the universe and the microscopic complexity of the
human mind – then, maybe, they will be more ready to help forward
the business of the University extraneous to their own immediate
courses of study, for they will realize that they only have significance
at all in so far as they are members of a society which will outlive
them but which will long be influenced by them if they wish it.

But threats are more potent than appeals. . . . In determining the
spirit that shall pervade this place hereafter, we shall determine
ourselves. And there shall be a Day of Reckoning. The Recording
Angel will say: 'What did you do at Reading University?' The
answer will come: 'I got a degree in ——.' 'Yes,' the R.A. will say
testily, 'but what did you DO?' Ah, so many ghostly limbs in woe
shall tremble, so many phantom knees in fear shall knock together.[1]

That was high idealism untainted and unsuppressed. A successor only two
years later wrote in a fashion more down to earth, but his message was the
same:

[1] *Tamesis*, xxxi (1932), pp. 5–6; edited by D. C. T. Sullivan.

Before coming up to Reading we were told by a gullible greybeard
that the greatest charm and glory of university life was that so many
young people were together, and nowhere else could youth have such
power to put into practice its wild and beautiful theories. After four
years at such a concentration point of burgeoning powers in body
and mind, we are as disillusioned as the rest. The representative
student would have us believe that he was dead before he was born.
Not blasé, sophisticated, jaded and satiated, as youth is accused so
often of being, but settled, be-paunched, middle-aged and mediaeval,
he sits securely on the fence awake only enough to prevent himself
from slipping off.

Generosity, spontaneity, are practically unknown, because the
whole of the commandments are for him summed up in the words
'Thou shalt not commit —— thyself'.

The root of the matter lies in the fact that most of the students are
not the cream of their age and rank. From their schools the best,
financially and in brains, went to the older universities, or had no
need of training to earn their living. We are the second class, the
fairly intelligent and poorer section whom economic pressure thrusts
out into the world where we must get a job or starve. The mistaken
idea has taken root, that the best way to succeed in life is to cram
in enough to get some certificate which will automatically supply a
post later. That this is mistaken becomes daily more apparent. The
enormous number of certificated teachers without posts proves that
either influence or special ability is needed for success in the world
of teaching at any rate. Turning Reading into a technical college or
a training college is useless to us as individuals. That argument
should appeal to those who would not listen to the second.

Reading was never meant to be a technical institute or a cramming
school. The other provincial universities were started by local enterprise, usually led by a business man interested in the scientific basis
of his trade. Reading was founded as an extension centre from
Christ Church, Oxford. Not even Cambridge, with her search for
'exact knowledge', gave us birth, but Oxford, standing for 'knowledge
of values'. Where then is the excuse that we, like all the provincial
universities, should follow the industrialist or the pedant in our
policy? Truly it is to the generosity and intellectual ideals of our
founders that we owe so much, not to their desire to know the inner
truth about biscuits or seeds.

Surely the cautious, matured, pennywise, long-headed student
will perhaps realize that he is violating all he holds sacred by turning
his university into an Observatory for the Main Chance.

We are not known. We have no tradition, complains someone. That
is the fault of our founders for not living several hundred years
earlier. . . . Tradition does not lie in age. A tradition can be built

up in a very short time, and we're building one up every day for
Reading University. Those who complain because we are the
youngest university are destroying our richest treasure. . . . Everyone
coming up to Reading has Reading's future in his hands every time
he discusses the age of the University. Let him then be proud to
belong to a university which should never be more than four or five
years old, never really more than a year old, because new life is
being born into it every year. Other universities have their tradition
of age, or size, or wealth. We have the greatest tradition of all –
Reading is the youngest university.[1]

Not all editors struck this high, enthusiastic note. One, stung by lack of
material, decided that assault was preferable to exhortation:

Nobody has that *urge* to write without which editorial promptings are
useless; and the grief which this causes us is the reason for the
renewed indictment which we propose to make upon that age-old
subject, student apathy (and the apathy, perhaps, of others besides
students). If the remarks which follow offend somebody, we shall be
delighted.

Considered in the light of its alarming failure to exert any cultural
influence upon the majority of its students, we are not sure that the
modern university is a good argument for popular education. A fair
proportion of those students come from classes to whom a university
education would not have been accessible much before the beginning
of the present century. They now come up to acquire a varying veneer
of specialized knowledge which has little visible influence upon their
general mental habits. We are not suggesting for a moment that a
university should turn them into snobs who speak as if they had been
educated at a bad public school, but need they be so ready to revert
to type? Take away one man's Physics, and another's History, and
another's English (yes, even the *literae humaniores* have precious little
effect) – and you have the original shopkeeper or bank clerk or bus
driver or whatnot, neither better nor worse than the original, and
retaining all those cultural and moral limitations which it should have
been the business of a university to remove. One finds their opinions
prematurely solidified (if not fossilized) and their minds invincibly
closed against argument – particularly political argument. Their
lack of intellectual resources is appalling; they have no interest in
their work (one could number on one's fingers the students at
Reading for whom it provides a sustaining intellectual interest);
'flicks' and shove ha'penny (or in more exalted cases, crosswords)
are the occupations of leisure.

Partly the economic situation is to blame for this. But a few short
years and one will be ejected into outer darkness, very probably into

[1] *Tamesis*, xxxii (1934), pp. 105–6; edited by E. M. Williams.

a job and an environment where the absence of any intellectual
growth during the previous four years will not be noticed. Perhaps
it is no wonder that we are unenterprising and afraid. But this is a
vicious circle. It is no excuse for the number who leave a university
as expert drudges, hating novelty and experiment, who have within
themselves neither the ideas nor the resources to avoid an early
falling into the rut.[1]

That was written in Autumn term 1937. The author did not envisage
the outer darkness which was to come as anything worse than a dull,
uninspiring job. He was an optimist. Nevertheless his comment contrasts
sharply in tone with the ingenuous zeal of his predecessors. Indeed it
matches a general change in *Tamesis*. Gradually the self-consciously
exuberant reports from the various Halls gave way to more general articles,
then to the familiar political debates of the 1930s. The cause of pacifism
surrendered to the certainty of war. The Labour Club and then the Political
Club came to a prominence earlier enjoyed by the British Universities'
League of Nations Society. In 1926 there were few who protested against
the students' reaction against the General Strike.[2] Now, Communists
wrote in to assert the ultimate triumph of the proletariat.[3] It was not that
the enthusiasm of the early thirties was dead; rather was it transferred to
other objectives. The same editor who challenged his fellows' view of their
purpose at the University in Autumn 1937 went on to urge them in the
summer of 1938:

It will be apparent, therefore, and it has become increasingly
apparent during the last few months, that the democratic states must
resist if they are to survive. It is not a question of Pacifism, because
the calculations in the minds of English statesmen and the vast
majority of their supporters are not pacifist at all. The sympathy
which we must all feel for an ill and ageing man in a difficult position
should not blind us to the fact that Mr Chamberlain's policy has
been bad; bad because unprincipled, short-sighted, and selfish in a
curiously unimaginative way. The complaint against him and his
colleagues, apart from all specific counts, must indeed be that they

---

[1] *Tamesis*, xxxvi (1937), pp. 3–4; edited by V. Barber.
[2] For an account of the University during the General Strike see Elspeth Huxley (1968),
pp. 138–45. She tells of an encounter with a 'proletarian revolutionary' student who
supported the strikers and used the Dramatic Society as an emotional and political
release – 'I want to put on *The Emperor Jones* next term' and 'D'you know what the Club's
putting on . . . Barrie! Sir James bloody Barrie! A play about a butler' (*ibid.*, p. 143).
[3] See 'Trova' in *Tamesis*, xxxii (1934), pp. 80–2. This was the second part of a debate,
Communism *v.* Fascism, of which the justification of Fascism appears *ibid.*, pp. 59–61.
'Trova' ended on a resounding note: 'It is not difficult to see why many students and
middle class people are joining the Communist Party. By associating themselves with the
working class movement they help to fulfil the evolution of society. By not doing so, without the least exaggeration, they are supporting reaction, starvation and war'. Editorial
wit presumably lies behind the juxtaposition of the immediately succeeding item – a short
elegant poem entitled 'Propaganda-Ridden'.

have lacked vision – the vision to see that if civilization is to survive, democracy must survive, and that democracy can only survive if, with its strength renewed by a purification of its affairs at home, it proclaims its principles in the world with a louder and stronger voice.

You cannot separate the inner nature or postulates of a state from its action in the world. If democracy believes in the necessity for international law, it must uphold international law or surrender some of its moral strength.[1]

In the same number a student writing under the name of Figo contributed a short article entitled 'We have been cheated'. This was in truth a passionate cry against the outer darkness:

Not to hope, not to plan, not to dream is our inheritance. We may not even enjoy what is given to us – who plans to marry, build, have children, change a law, sow a garden? These are idle and, to some, heart-breaking occupations. . . . Our only hope is in resentment which may spring even to rebellion and the repudiation of this curse which has been laid on us, the curse that we shall die young, shall know no maturity, raise no children, learn no wisdom, and die for no faith, that the history of mankind shall close with us, the castrated generation.[2]

This varied student community was matched by a much smaller community of staff. The academic staff numbered approximately 150; there were roughly a further 20 in senior administrative or similar posts who also formed part of the family. The staff tended to live concentrated in the neighbourhood of the University site. The University provided their social as well as their working life. New members of staff were introduced to it by a round of invitations and in their first formal dinner in the Senior Common Room. It was enclosed, concerned very much with the immediate problems and the gossip which a small university tended to generate, and perhaps not a little self-satisfied. Reading struck one new lecturer arriving in 1928 as a 'cosy, civilized, middle-class institution'. Another new arrival, a young professor arriving from a northern university after the Second World War, was surprised to find that some of the wardens kept horses and that bachelor dons breakfasted in some style in the Senior Common Room. In the 1920s and 30s, a small group of twelve, with Dyson the driving force, formed a dining club within the Common Room. They enjoyed good fellowship, good food and wine and the pleasure of inviting distinguished visitors as guests. The place as a whole was a little dressy. 'We wear evening dress, without academic robes for Jantaculum' wrote Sibly in reply to the Chancellor, Sir Samuel Hoare, who had inquired

---

[1] *Ibid.*, pp. 88–9.
[2] *Ibid.*, pp. 103–4.

whether he should wear a white tie, with or without medals.[1] Still after the War evening dress was expected of male guests who dined on high table in Wessex Hall. One professor recalls that the purchase of a new evening dress was the first thing he had to see to on arriving at Reading.[2] Socially the atmosphere was conservative. The wardens were by no means to the fore in the drafting of their regulations governing student behaviour. When Miss Wiseman relaxed to the extent of suggesting to Childs that women might perhaps be allowed to go on the river on Sundays, she received the daunting reply – 'No. That rule must stay. I tell you, there is gunpowder about'.[3] Childs's sense of the proper was not restricted to the students. Dyson recalled a walk on which he and his wife accompanied the Principal and Mrs Childs. To his suggestion on passing an inn – 'Principal, what about a drink?', he received the answer – 'But Dyson, the ladies are with us'.[4] Such a sense of the proper, languish though it might with the years, was slow to pass. The students helped it into oblivion. In answering an enquiry about academic dress from Richard Livingstone, Vice-Chancellor of The Queen's University of Belfast, Sibly commented:

> The wearing of caps is certainly required by the letter of the
> regulation. In practice, however, it has never been enforced.
> Repeated attempts were made to enforce it in the case of women
> students in the first year or two of the University, but they all failed
> because the women declined to be different from the men in this
> matter.[5]

That early blow for women's liberation was really directed against the memory of the heavy school velour which was standard headgear in girls' schools. To yet another enquiry from B. Mowat Jones, Vice-Chancellor of Leeds, Sibly wrote:

> A bar is allowed in the Buttery on the occasion of Students' Union
> dances, and no other occasion. An occasional licence is taken out
> for each dance by a reputable firm in the town, which assumes
> responsibility. The arrangement for a bar on the occasion of Union
> dances is less than a year old and it can be said still to be in the
> experimental stage. It is clearly understood by the Union that any
> abuse of the privilege in the way of unseemly conduct may lead to the
> withdrawal of the privilege at any time. In actual experience, the
> arrangement has worked very well indeed. In my personal view,
> young people expect to be able to get alcoholic refreshment at dances
> nowadays, and the feeling in favour of such an arrangement is so
> strong that it is wisest to allow a bar.[6]

[1] URC, Vice-Chancellor, box 42.
[2] Professor F. P. Pickering.
[3] Conversation with Miss Wiseman, 2 November 1969.
[4] Conversation with H. V. D. Dyson, 8 November 1970.
[5] URC, Vice-Chancellor, box 45.
[6] *Ibid.*

That letter was written in February 1940. The occasional bar to which Sibly referred was the only one available to students throughout the University. In all these matters change occurred as individuals among the staff no longer saw any point in preserving or trying to justify accepted convention. Here and there the sterner rock stood out against the tide. Lady Stenton did not retire from teaching until 1959; no woman student ever attended her tutorials wearing trousers.

In some respects Reading set out on its own tack. Under Childs's inspiration it sought to take care of the moral as well as the intellectual well-being of its students. As a residential College it had to look after their physical health, and Reading was one of the first to develop a full medical service for its students.[1] When it came to their spiritual welfare, however, it fought shy of denominational labels. The Charter of 1926, like that of other modern universities, forbade religious tests within the University. The old College *Calendar* announced that:

> The College is strictly undenominational, but the College authorities are prepared, at the request of parents or guardians, to introduce students in residence to a Minister of the religious body to which they belong.

There were daily prayers in Hall, and in 1926, on an endowment provided by Eleanor, widow of George William Palmer, a small Anglican centre, with a consecrated chapel, was established as St Augustine's House. However, as Childs insisted, St Augustine's was 'completely independent. The University had no responsibility for it. The University could not have prevented its establishment even if it had wished to do so.'[2] For Childs, it was partly an administrative matter. In 1931 an article in *The Times*, occasioned by a grant from the Central Board of Finance of the Church Assembly to support an extension to St Anselm's Hall, Manchester, implied misleadingly that there were similar Church hostels at Reading. Childs immediately wrote to Sibly:

> I don't know whether you will think it worth while to take any notice of a paragraph in today's *Times*, which clearly implies that there are Church of England 'hostels' at Reading. I am not sure that it *is* worth while. I myself regard this policy of developing sectarian hostels at modern Universities as a deplorable mistake. I know that Moberly and some of the northern VCs don't, and I admit that their circumstances may be different from ours. Not long before I left Reading I wrote a memorandum about this and circulated it to the VCs. Miss Maslen probably has a copy if you cared to see it. I think

[1] A sanatorium was established in Shinfield Road in 1916. It was extended on the same site in 1921. In 1935 it was moved to Bradfield House, Northcourt Avenue, which was given to the University by Miss Alice Constance Miller in memory of her brother. On the new site it provided beds for twenty students. For later developments, see below p. 261.
[2] Childs (1933), pp. 288–9.

the St Augustine's solution is incomparably better than cutting up a
university into sectarian cliques; nor do I think that the real interests
of religion or religious unity are best served by such a policy.
However, I imagine that if these ecclesiastical busybodies come fussing
around at Reading they will not find much opening. Quite apart
from the religious question, there is the question of control. I had to
deal with this many years ago, and we then laid it down that all our
Halls must be under the unfettered control of the Council. I feel
pretty sure that you would endorse this.

Sibly must have shared Childs's view, for Childs wrote again two days
later:

I think you are right to take no action. After all, if these people think
that there *are* Church hostels already at Reading, they are less likely
to trouble you.[1]

Reading was not the most fertile ground for the development of established
religion. George William and Alfred Palmer were brought up as Quakers.
There were men of deep Christian faith within the University, like de
Burgh and Hodges, but they tended to assume that religion was a highly
individual matter, to be discussed with, but not imposed on, students.
There were others who, whatever their faith, were unlikely to encourage
the development of the formal study of Theology. Doris Stenton regarded
Theology as an 'easy subject' and fought with vigour and success against the
introduction of Biblical Studies into the Faculty of Letters. Stenton, on one
occasion at least, read a famous passage from Bede at a secular funeral.[2]
There were others again who were plainly atheist or agnostic in outlook.
But there was little argument about policy. It was simply assumed that the
University was a secular, scholarly institution. It has so remained.[3]

There was another less usual feature for which Reading was known in
university circles. Its academic staff included a high proportion of women.

[1] The notice was in *The Times*, 12 November 1931. Childs's first letter to Sibly was of the
same date (URC, Vice-Chancellor, box 42).
[2] This was at the funeral of Mrs E. H. Neville. The passage in question is: This is how
the present life of man on earth, appears to me in comparison with that time which is
unknown to us. You are sitting feasting with your ealdormen and thegns in winter time;
the fire is burning on the hearth in the middle of the hall and all inside is warm, while
outside the wintry storms of rain and snow are raging; and a sparrow flies swiftly through
the hall. It enters in at one door and quickly flies out through the other. For the few
moments it is inside, the storm and wintry tempest cannot touch it, but after the briefest
moment of calm, it flits from your sight, out of the wintry storm and into it again. So this
life of man appears but for a moment; what follows or indeed what went before, we know
not at all. (*Ecclesiastical History*, ii. 13, ed. B. Colgrave and R. A. B. Mynors, Oxford, 1969,
pp. 183–5). I have used the editors' translation.
[3] St Augustine's House and the Chapel were on the corner of Redlands and Addington
Road. The Chapel became a pharmacy store when the buildings were taken over by the
Royal Berkshire Hospital in 1960. This led to the appointment of an Anglican Chaplain
to the University. Other churches followed suit. In 1974 a small chaplaincy centre was
established in the University Buttery.

They made up roughly a fifth of the full-time academic staff in the three faculties.[1] One, Edith Morley, was a professor. Some, a few, were married. On this, as on many other questions, Sibly was a source of information to other vice-chancellors. In 1933–4 Hector Hetherington, Vice-Chancellor of Liverpool, wrote to report and seek advice on affairs in his own university, where there was some discussion of the Council's right to review the contracts of women members of staff on marriage and where as a result he was under fire from the local branch of the British Federation of University Women and their supporters within the University. Sibly simply indicated the situation at Reading:

1. Independent Lecturer in Domestic Subjects, appointed in 1916, married in 1921 at age 48. No question raised.
2. Lecturer in History, appointed in 1917, married in 1920 at age 26. No question raised.
3. Sessional Lecturer in Psychology. The holder was married before appointment.
4. Teacher of Singing (School of Music), appointed in 1921 and married in 1931 at age 37. No question raised.
5. Honorary Research Fellow in Greek Archaeology.[2]

Reading had come quite easily to accept matters of which other universities made very heavy weather indeed.

The staff and the students formed a single community. This depended essentially on three facts. First, the University was relatively small. Secondly, it was housed on a compact site, with students accommodated in the Halls and many of the staff living locally in the immediate neighbourhood. Thirdly, the ratio of academic staff to students allowed the staff to pay a great deal of attention to individual students and involve themselves very thoroughly in the life which they and the students made for themselves. Up to the Second World War, the ratio of academic staff to all students was roughly 1:10. The ratio of academic staff to day-students under tutorial supervision was roughly 1:5.[3] The ratio of full-time assistant lecturers, lecturers and professors to the students under tutorial supervision was roughly 1:7.[4] The ratio of those teaching degree-subjects to those studying

[1] This count excludes the National Institute for Research in Dairying, the Schools of Art and Music, the Department of Domestic Subjects and the wardens of Halls. To include these would raise the proportion.
[2] URC, Vice-Chancellor, box 45.
[3] The figures for 1928–9 are 150 academic staff, 1498 students of whom 713 were under tutorial supervision. In 1938–9 there were 148 academic staff, 1406 students of whom 698 were under tutorial supervision. These are gross figures for the academic staff and include sessional lecturers and teachers, and also wardens of Halls.
[4] The calculation of this ratio is a little hazardous at the margin because of the dual status of some of the staff of the National Institute for Research in Dairying. The staff of all those departments or sections entered in the *Calendar* as part of the National Institute for Research in Dairying have been excluded from the count. The count also excludes the wardens of Halls.

for first degrees was roughly 1 : 4.5.[1] That was indeed a generous provision.

There were a number of societies which brought staff and students together. Foremost among these was the Gild of the Red Rose.[2] This was invented by Childs in one of his most Ruskinian moods in 1895. He implored the existing Literary and Historical Society 'to commit suicide', arguing that the 'sin of Literary Societies is to beget prigs', and in seeking to found some corporate sense among the students, turned to borrow the vows, titles and ceremonies from the Reading Gild Merchant of the fifteenth century. The result was a peculiar amalgam of a literary and dramatic society and a social club. It survived through periodic vicissitudes and the proliferation of other societies which took over part of its activities. Its fortnightly readings, or Morowspeches, were the chief literary meetings both for staff and students until after the Second World War. Its Easter play was the main dramatic production. Its Jantaculum, which from 1900 onwards was always held at the end of the Autumn term, was the University's Christmas feast. For this, in the first years of the University, the students and some of the staff still wrote, produced and acted their own plays. As time went on it became more formal and less home-made. The 1938 programme was summarized by Sibly:

> Jantaculum begins at 7 o'clock, and the first item is carol-singing,
> lasting about twenty minutes. This is followed by a light supper,
> served to members of the audience in their seats. After supper there
> will be a performance of A. A. Milne's 'The Ivory Door', which is
> expected to end at about 10.15 pm. Finally, there is dancing until
> 11.45 pm.[3]

The atmosphere was nevertheless still one of a party rather than a theatrical performance. The audience sat in three sides of a square with the acting taking place in the centre:

> One recollection remains of Passmore as Reeve carrying the boar's
> head high and leading a procession of all the officers through the
> Great Hall, singing in his splendid bass voice the wassail song.[4]

In the Gild and especially in Jantaculum Reading invented a form of association and entertainment all its own. The other societies in the University were more commonplace. 'Kosmos', founded in 1897, brought the scientists together and the Agricultural Club, founded in 1920, served a similar function on that side of the University. Its regular weekly meetings became part of the calendar of the Faculty. There were political clubs which

[1] Teachers in the Department of Education and wardens have been excluded from this count, which is subject to the same difficulty concerning the staff of the National Institute for Research in Dairying as the preceding one.
[2] The best account of the origin and development of the Gild of the Red Rose is by W. Lloyd-Davies, 'The Gild of the Red Rose 1897–1933', *Tamesis*, xxxi (1933), pp. 113–17. See also Childs (1933), pp. 30–2, and Edith J. Morley, 'Reminiscences' (URC, MS 528), pp. 103–6.
[3] Sibly to Sir Samuel Hoare (URC, Vice-Chancellor, box 42).
[4] Diana Morgan (URC, box 256).

waxed and waned in their fortunes: the Labour Club, the Political Club, the International Society and the British Universities' League of Nations Society. The Student Christian Movement provided yet another focus. The School of Music, the regular annual performances of the choir and orchestra, also provided circumstances in which staff and students mixed and worked readily together. And there were informal amateur groups emerging and fading with the enthusiasm of the moment:

> I joined, once only, what I imagine was a select group of amateur musicians in the Great Hall on a Wednesday afternoon. S. A. Peyton played the organ. I played the piano (Bach), and Stenton soon saw that I needed to improve my fingering and gently told me so. I cannot remember that he performed.[1]

Similar groups met under Betts's guidance in the School of Art. Such societies and groups constituted much of the social life and provided much of the extra-curricular intellectual interest and energy in the University throughout the first twenty years of its existence. Many survived the Second World War; Jantaculum is still one of the great events in the annual calendar. They owed some of their vitality, perhaps, to the fact the Students' Union could provide few comparable facilities. Indeed the Union played a very minor role, except in sporting matters, and even there much activity still centred on inter-Hall matches and competitions. There was no Union building, merely a room tucked away in the Old Red Building:

> We beg to call the attention of our readers, students, members of the staff and others to the parlous state of the Students' Union Common Room. What! You did not realize that such a room exists! Well, Well! And yet you may be forgiven for not knowing the whereabouts of this secret chamber that modestly hides itself away in a far corner of the second storey of the Old Red Building, remote from the track of the mere student-in-the-cloister. Few are they who mount to its aerial heights. Fewer still are they who remain longer than to scan the news, and idly turn the pages of contemporary magazines. The majority then . . . flee hastily to the warmth and companionship of the Buttery.[2]

In addition there was much informal interchange between students and staff. It was not simply that the staff had the leisure to entertain students at home, for that was likely to produce its own peculiar social stress and was in any case a blessing which was liable to fall unevenly and with uneven effect on different students. It was rather that some, the best of them, so blended their life at home, their participation in the social activities of the University and their formal teaching duties that it would have been difficult to say where one began and the other ended or that they ever ceased in their endeavour to interest, inform and inspire.

---

[1] Maurice Barley (URC, box 256).
[2] *Tamesis*, xxvii (1929), p. 75. The object of the exhortation was to appeal for contributions towards new furniture.

He loved Youth with a capital Y, and had his theories about us which
he was fond of reiterating. In brief, he admired us for our zest in living,
our vitality, but he censured us for our ignorance, our disinclination to
think and our lack of reverence for the things that are great and the
things that are eternal. But he did not stop at generalizations – he
cared for us as individuals too. A student was not merely something
to which he taught philosophy, but a whole person, an individual with
a background, interests and ambitions of his own. His breadth of
understanding gave us confidence, and we were never shy of getting
our problems explained or if the occasion demanded of talking about
ourselves. His interest made one want to do well.

I have heard it said that things that would have sounded 'pi' coming
from anyone else did not when they came from him. In a sense, he
was always preaching but it was so spontaneous and inevitable that one
never felt it intrusive. Who but Billy would have produced the remark:
'Humanism – to love a man just because he is a man – is one thing,
but to love him because he is part of the mystical body of Christ
incorporate – why, that's quite a different kettle of fish'.

All that Billy felt was lacking in our generation he had with
abundance in himself together with that for which he claimed to admire
us. With his knowledge, his power of clear and far-sighted thought, his
love of the great and good in achievement and in ideal, there went a
vigour and enthusiasm, a spontaneous and infectious happiness.

That is a pupil, Vera Willis, writing of her teacher, W. G. de Burgh, and
doing so not for some public valediction, but in her private diary.[1] Let no
one imagine that de Burgh behaved towards his students as a kind of
universal counsellor. Something of his style comes through in one of his last
speeches as a guest at Wessex Hall:

I suppose that you want me to talk about ancient history, but the fact
is that I am tired of ancient history. What I care about is the future.
A university could manage quite well without students, but since they
insist on coming they should take some responsibility for the university,
which *qua* university, is interested in nothing but their intelligence. A
place with hot and cold water laid on does not exist to train character.
If you want to be in a place that will give you that run away to sea or
go on the stage. Things that may matter infinitely to you as an individual,
like games, religion or friends, don't matter at all to the university.
The university is dependent on its members and the present lot of students
are a very poor lot by what they might be. . . . Beware of false prophets.
No one reads the Old Testament nowadays, but if any of you did, you
would know that the mark of a false prophet was that he said nice
things to the folk who entertained him. God bless you, my dears![2]

---

[1] Vera Willis, Diary 1931–4, pp. 46–8.
[2] As summarized *ibid.*, pp. 92–4.

De Burgh was archetypal Reading. He was imbued with the same kind of missionary zeal which had inspired Childs and others in the early days of the College and he carried this on into the early years of the University. He knew all the students in his faculty and was ready at all seasons of the year to lead those able to keep up with his rapid pace in long expeditions over the Downs in which he engaged all comers successively in conversation on almost any topic under the sun. Regularly on Thursdays during term he held a Philosophy Seminar in his study at 2 Southern Hill. The invitations have a nice businesslike ring to them:

> A meeting of the Philosophy Seminar will be held at 2 Southern Hill
> on Thursday next . . . for the discussion of the nature of 'Moral Evil'.
> Members' definitions are set forth below. Tea at 4.45 pm.

On this occasion de Burgh was almost the only one not to adopt a relativist view: 'Moral evil is the self-assertion of a finite will in conscious opposition to the universal principle of volition'.[1] By May 1921 the Seminar had met on 236 occasions and de Burgh continued with it up to his retirement. He also retained his capacity for provoking thought. His last address as Dean to the students of the Faculty of Letters in October 1933 was concerned like much of his thinking with the relationship between eternal truth and the fashions of the moment. 'I do not as a rule read contemporary literature,' he began, 'at a certain age I feel one may exercise privileges.' Then he tackled D. H. Lawrence – 'His gospel is, *live;* don't reflect about life. He is against all attempt at interpreting the world.' Then he challenged his audience – 'In revolting against the Victorian age, are you revolting against crinolines and bustles, or against Darwin's *Origin of species*?' And finally, after giving them a peculiar mixture of learning, perception, high principle and down-to-earth common sense he summarized it all:

> You have come to a university to have the opportunity of contact, not
> merely with direct living, but also with what is absolute and enduring
> in art, literature and the other things that have value. And you have
> the opportunity of avoiding the mistake of separating off the values
> and standards as something abstract and remote from the direct
> experience which you all want to enjoy.[2]

> Others carried on this tradition. In the Faculty of Letters, Hodges, Betts and Dyson came to form a trio devoted to the discussion of common academic interests:

> We organized evening meetings of the three departments. We would
> miss our dinner, meet in the Art School, take potato crisps and things
> and have an alfresco meal, and then one of us would hold forth on

[1] The minute book of the seminar was transferred to the author by Professor Hodges and is now in URC.
[2] *Tamesis*, xxxii (1934), p. 117. For further commentary on de Burgh see a memoir by one of his pupils, G. H. Langley, in *University of Reading, Old Students' Magazine*, no. 30 (1944), pp. 1–2.

some topic. A student audience from the three departments would
join in.[1]

That was the origin of an informal seminar which continued to meet for five
years up to the Second World War. It not only provided a forum in which
staff and students of different departments could talk seriously together; it
also contributed to the development of combined-subject degrees and the
whole scheme of interdisciplinary interchange. Hodges, like de Burgh,
approached his work in a missionary spirit:

> Having a university here was pioneer work. I was quite clear that I
> wanted to be a university teacher and I had wanted to be in Oxford,
> but as soon as I saw this place I felt the difference in atmosphere. We
> were teaching not the privileged élite, but people. . . . I was quite
> clear that my vocation lay in Reading or some place like it, and that
> this was where I belonged.[2]

In others enthusiasm for teaching and devotion to the subject went hand in
hand:

> As a teacher of the young and of the 'young in heart' (his phrase for
> the amateur) Hawkins excelled. He had a superb ability for winning
> over uncommitted students intent on reading other subjects. This
> accounted for the steady recruitment into the more advanced classes
> during those lean years. Some of his conversions would have been
> embarrassing today, for Hawkins did not discriminate. A dedicated
> convert with fervour but little ability was as welcome to geology as any
> other. Devotion to the subject, educative development of the whole
> man, were the things that mattered in those days.
>
> At any time he would stop what he was doing to help the serious
> student or the amateur, however trivial the request. No schoolboy
> ever brought the dullest flint in vain. Rather he went away inspired
> by it, or by Hawkins's intensely personal view thereof. Many a time-
> waster (as one has heard them called by others) subsequently con-
> tributed to science in his own right. Others merely led richer lives.
> Was that not, as Hawkins said, his main job of work? Happiest in the
> field, Hawkins spared no pains in the most unpromising terrain.
> Around Reading there were no 'gravel deserts' for him; only rivers
> mercilessly competing among themselves, hunters making do with
> berries and roots, lowering skies over the ice-fields beyond Oxford,
> sometimes perhaps as close as Goring?[3]

Such zest for the work took different forms in different individuals. Of all
the original staff at Reading Edith Morley is probably recalled as the least
comfortable by all colleagues. She was likely to subject even the most casual
of remarks about the weather to acid criticism. Her driving was memorable;

---

[1] Conversation with Professor H. A. Hodges, 9 February 1970.
[2] *Ibid.*
[3] P. Allen, 'Herbert Leader Hawkins', *Biographical Memoirs of Fellows of the Royal Society*,
xvi (1970), p. 323.

Dyson was heard to remark that he was glad to discover that accompanying
her was not one of the conditions of his appointment. And her driving was
a direct expression of her character. She was provocative, disturbing,
aggressive, intransigent; others kept their distance to avoid collision and
damage. One colleague recalls her as 'a robust Socialist and a Fenian who
tried to convert her students to it, and who pounded poor old Childs until
he made her a professor'; if she succeeded in that she was formidable
indeed.[1] Despite her offer to accept reduced remuneration which would
simply have covered her superannuation, the University refused to extend
her appointment beyond the age of sixty-five;[2] her colleague, Dewar, had
had enough. Characteristically, she later wrote to Sibly to indicate that she
was braving the war-time trains and the threat of air raids to accept an
invitation to teach in the University of Liverpool.[3] A Jewess and a resolute
representative of her sex, she was a very different type of person from de
Burgh or Hodges. Even Dyson, the most extrovert of men with a zest for
badinage, was frightened of her. De Burgh himself could not overbear her.[4]
Yet she loved humanity as much as he. She was ever ready to fight for the
oppressed, especially if feminine. She organized work in Reading to aid the
refugees from Germany.[5] She intervened with Sibly on behalf of poor
students, pleading that they might be relieved of payment of fees.[6] And she
was just as devoted as de Burgh to the welfare of the University. In 1937 she
offered to lend £10,000 to finance the building of the new St George's Hall.
Sibly felt that he had to decline the offer. Undeterred Edith Morley
promptly agreed to contribute £500 as a gift, £450 of which she asked to be
recorded anonymously. She continued to make contributions up to the war,
her intention being to donate approximately a quarter of her net salary each
year. When the new buildings were finally occupied in 1939 it was by the
students of Wantage whose own Hall had been commandeered. Edith
Morley left no doubt about her attitude:

> Dear Vice-Chancellor,
> I am writing to say that I am not sending my donation of £200 this
> year but I do not wish you to suppose this is on account of the war.
> I had put it on one side. But, speaking as a private donor not as a
> member of staff, I am very distressed at the decision about Elmhurst.
> If one of the women's Halls had to be taken for men, it seems to me it

[1] She became a professor in 1908, a year later than the other lecturers in charge of
courses in the College. The matter is discussed in her 'Reminiscences' (URC, MS 528,
pp. 114–7). Her account gives some substance to the comment given above.
[2] Sibly to Edith Morley, 7 February 1940 (URC, box 256). He softened the blow by
indicating that he considered that 'in view of the general circumstances of the University,
the Council would be well advised to discontinue the separate Professorship of English
Language after the end of the present session'.
[3] Edith Morley to Sibly, 21 March 1941 (URC, Vice-Chancellor, box 43).
[4] See above pp. 48–9.
[5] She was founder and Hon. Secretary of the Reading and District Refugee Committee.
[6] Edith Morley to Sibly, 30 September 1942 (URC, Vice-Chancellor, box 46).

need not have been this.

I am equally interested in men's Halls and in similar circumstances should have wished to help a new one for them. But that does not affect the present case.

Presumably when the Halls Committee meet we shall be able to discuss the matter in that capacity. Meanwhile I wanted you to know why my donation is not forthcoming.[1]

That had an ominous ring; a rough meeting lay ahead. Yet this woman of whom her colleagues went in irritated trepidation, attracted some kind of sympathetic affection in her students:

The Morley was really a very good natured old woman, she would do anything for her students. One admired her courage and energy, but she was rather a pathetic figure.[2]

Moreover, for all her irritating crankiness she shared with de Burgh the capacity to speak seriously and directly to her students. In 1940, she ended her farewell message in *Tamesis* as follows:

It does not matter what is the subject in which one specializes; at a university, if anywhere, one should realize that learning is one great whole and that all its branches are in living relation to one another. The pursuit of Truth includes all separate truths, and wisdom is the outcome of something more profound than mere knowledge of facts, though without such knowledge it may not be acquired.

Integrity of mind signifies the refusal to be satisfied with half-truths, shoddy make-shifts, anything short of honest, patient and independent, unravelling of difficulties and facing of fact. To try to see things as they are without shrinking, bias or pre-judgement, to see them in relation to other things as they are and to fundamental truth – this is the great task for which university education should fit us. If, as we hold, we are fighting today to maintain freedom of the mind and spiritual values, it is this kind of integrity which we must place in the forefront of our striving. So let my last exhortation to you be this – cultivate intellectual integrity, hate insincere processes of thought, seek honestly to 'know the truth' in order that the promise may be fulfilled 'and the truth shall make you free'.[3]

She and de Burgh would have not agreed on what Truth was for they were separated by their faith as well as by attitudes and character. But their concerns as university teachers were identical; and they could both preach.

In this last quality they were probably exceptional. In the thirties what they had to say about Truth or Beauty or Moral Good struck an answering

---

[1] Edith Morley to Sibly, 5 October 1939 (URC, box 256). The disenchantment was only temporary. Miss Morley had already made the University her residuary legatee and made testamentary arrangements for the establishment of what became the Morley Bursary for students reading English.
[2] Vera Willis, Diary 1931–4, p. 71.
[3] *Tamesis*, xxxix (1940), p. 5.

chord in some students, to judge from the solemn self-examination in which
various contributors to *Tamesis* indulged. But it was not the only effective
method, even of teaching Philosophy or English. If de Burgh swept his
students along with broad gestures Hodges patiently dissected and analysed,
and he was just as effective in a different style. Moreover there were others,
quietly at work in their own subjects, who disturbed the surface of the
waters less but were equally influential in informing the minds and arousing
the interests of their students. Indeed how far the students as a whole con-
formed to the tone of *Tamesis*, how far they even read *Tamesis*, how far de
Burgh or Edith Morley assessed their audiences accurately in talking as
they did, is in the last resort a matter of conjecture. But at least the evidence
stemming from the articulate and assertive tells a clear and reasonably consistent story. What the inarticulate thought about is less easy to describe.
Many, those whom an editor of *Tamesis* might denounce as apathetic or
selfishly concerned with obtaining the best degree they could, were probably
simply getting on with the task in hand.

That task was formed for them very largely in the lecture theatre and the
laboratory. Reading clung to the lecture as the main instrument of teaching
despite the advantageous staff/student ratio, partly perhaps because it was
inherited from the College, partly because it was the usual method of teaching in most comparable universities and colleges, and partly because it was
a convenient method for a miscellaneous audience which might include
diploma as well as degree students. The good lecture remains one of the
abiding memories of Reading students. Stenton had a remarkable gift of
exposition:

> He paced the platform of the History hall with measured tread and
> his eyes on the ground before him. He had the gift of arranging his
> matter systematically without taking from its accuracy by over-
> simplification, and he could make his facts interesting or amusing
> without digression or false emphasis. He had his phrases that we
> waited for: the 'sinister' and 'subnormal' kings of Spain, or 'Historians
> *used* to believe . . . you'll find in the textbooks that . . . But I say
> unto you . . .'[1]

Others were more dramatic in their attack:

> Of the English lectures we enjoyed Mr Dyson's most. One agreed that
> he was brilliant and stimulating but one argued as to whether he
> taught us anything. Personally I believe that he did. He wrapped his
> gown dramatically about him and threw his whole self into his oratory.
> His discourse usually defied summary but was full of *bons mots* and
> suggestion.[2]

De Burgh was a spell binder:

> We most of us heard him lecture on Logic and few of us evaded his

[1] Vera Willis, Diary 1931–4, p. 16. This refers to his lectures in the Intermediate course.
[2] *Ibid.*, p. 18.

famous 'Republic' lectures. . . . He lectured to us always in his own
room in the University. We sat about his fire and he sat in the biggest
armchair with his scrappy old notes in one hand and his spectacles in
the other. He thundered his stuff out at us and drove it in by repetition.
I cannot claim that his lectures were always interesting for they most
certainly were not, but I can claim that they could be just thrilling.
He always lectured as though he were interested. To describe his style
as 'vigorous' is a cliché but inevitable. When he digressed he was never
dull. He excelled in the serious treatment of the trivial or unexpected.
I can remember well his eloquence on the possibility of developing an
art of smell, or a projected life of Satan, best of all perhaps on 'Wash-
ing'. He treated the subject historically, geographically and personally
– how staying in Paris he was obliged to wash himself *en arrondissements.*
Lectures were a serious matter. He reproved you if you came without
a gown. If you omitted to come at all, however large the class, he was
apt to notice. 'Will you tell Miss Wratislaw that this is the way to
Death, Destruction and Damnation?' . . . Once he started a Plato
lecture – 'I am not speaking to those of you who are here, but to those
who are not . . .'. He expected us to be punctual and was always there
first himself.[1]

Hodges had a quite different gift, but was just as effective:

Hodges was no orator. He did not build up towers of words, deck out
his thoughts with example or contort it into paradox. He said what
he thought important about the subject in hand, and said it in the
simplest way possible. I think he would have called his lectures
introductory rather than expository, and certainly they had the effect
of making us want to go straight to the works of which he talked and
see for ourselves. Sometimes he had his notes open on the desk before
him and sometimes he had not – it made no difference to his fluency
or his systematic utterance. Clarity of thought and sympathy in
interpretation were the characteristics of his style. He stood well
behind the great men of whom he spoke and one could imagine that
here was a Berkeley, Bergson or Kant himself come to explain his
system. The most superficial of idealists was allowed a hearing before
his interpreter stepped aside to criticize. Even in his criticism he was
impersonal. Metaphysics is never easy and often we left his room in
a whirl, but even then one enjoyed it.[2]

Such gifts were not restricted to particular subjects or faculties. Cole also
had a great reputation as a lecturer:

The Zoology class was small, and we were left very much alone, but
the lectures were so exceptional that Professor Cole's students can
remember them to this day. He combined modern Zoology with a

[1] *Ibid.*, pp. 43–6.
[2] *Ibid.*, pp. 73–4.

knowledge of the history of the subject that not only made it more interesting, but fixed it in the memory of his hearers. He believed with de Quincey, that the lecturer should 'alleviate the tedium of instruction with an apt analogy or appropriate anecdote'.[1]

In Geology Hawkins played a similar role, although with mixed effects:

In formal lectures and on field classes Hawkins had, as Professor F. Hodson (one of his students) said, 'a profound ability to reduce the fundamentals of a subject to a few graphic words'. Many will recall his reduction of the structural pattern of Britain to a herring bone 'with' (as Hodson writes): 'the spine stretching from the Shetlands to the western Mendips, the ribs displaying a Caledonoid trend to the west and a Charnian pattern to the east.' Professor P. C. Sylvester-Bradley (another student) recalls that: 'His ability was to fire the imagination, and it was especially in the first year and in the field that he was so successful'. Mr R. V. Melville remembers fellow-students of widely diverse future careers lovingly reciting once-heard but un-forgettable passages from Hawkins's lectures. Professor E. A. Vincent and I, freshers straight from school in October 1936, were initiated into the mysteries of global petrology with: 'Would you assume, from pus in a boil on your skin, that your insides were made of the same material?' In November, sedimentary petrology was equally arresting: 'The Burning Cliff at Ringstead burns only in the rain. This is because the water gets at the sulphide of iron, forming sulphuric acid and green vitriol; and the heat produced, going beyond the flashpoint of the oil, lights it'. Thermodynamic analogies had no dangers: 'Perfection is death. Nothing happens'.

Hawkins's lectures to more advanced classes and his role as a research supervisor were not so successful. Having in principle planted the seeds of scepticism and free discussion, he was not adept at tending the delicate growths. Basically, his habits of oral argument through analogy, hyperbole, over-simplification, teleology and anthropo-morphism, his defence by rhetoric, and his authoritative approach through the 'sermon', failed. Except for the occasional use of an out-dated table of strata Hawkins never used notes. Advanced classes hungry for up-to-date news, views (with references) and injections of basic science felt they never really got them. Belonging to an older academic tradition, Hawkins was more concerned to preach human wisdom through geology than to produce students with a vocational title to a career in the subject such as the time demanded.

Field-classes were largely field demonstrations amplified by beautiful hand-drawn large-scale maps prepared by Hawkins before the party left Reading. Junior members of the staff assisted in these

[1] Dr Nellie B. Eales, January 1970 (URC, box 256). Her comments refer to the years 1907–10, when she was a student.

classes, which were largely run by 'the Prof.' himself. It was not until 1938 that Wager, of Greenland and Everest, was permitted to lead his own field 'expedition' [*sic*] to Arran. Some colleagues were able to loosen Hawkins up and evoke the superb best in him. One was Dr Gilbert Wilson of Imperial College, who deputized for Wager during his absence on Everest (1933) and in Greenland (1935–6). During the second period Wilson introduced the students to the principles of field mapping in the area around Osmington Mills. Equally matched in oratorical and dramatic skills, the two friends staged many a field 'performance' which, besides being a riot, had high teaching value. Wilson with his gusto and sketch-pad, Hawkins with his fiery imagination and eloquent persuasion, were complementary. Some field days and evening discourses were topped off by Hawkins's accomplished playing on the piano.[1]

The reputations of some spread beyond the limits of their own departments, either through the University societies or through the gossip and casual conversation among students in Hall. In the thirties Stenton still lectured over a wide range of English history, modern as well as medieval. For so mild and scholarly a man he had an astonishing taste for a good murder.[2] When he was approaching the unedifying fate of the men in the life of Mary, Queen of Scots, the word went round and his audience multiplied.

The lecture was not always so enthralling. It was assumed to be a necessary vehicle for the transfer of information from teacher to pupil, especially in subjects where knowledge and understanding were cumulative and especially where the class was largely made up of diploma students. Elspeth Huxley records a hard but rewarding grind:

> While we did our best to pursue, at a considerable distance, the Oxford tradition, we could not follow it all the way, for example to the extent of never going to lectures. In our case lectures were more or less compulsory, and so were 'practicals' in the laboratories. Our Dean, a small, squat, ugly, rather savage Midlander who taught biochemistry, spitting out the formulae as if they had been so many oaths, kept us under a discipline closer to that of school than university. I do not recall that anyone defied this. Dutifully, we carried our notebooks about and recorded the gist of our lectures; this amounted almost to dictation in some cases.
>
> Sidney Pennington, our Professor of Agriculture, made no bones about it and dispensed his wisdom at dictation speed, as if we had been children learning French; we could scarcely have departed farther from the tutorial system. It was in the labs more than in the

---

[1] P. Allen (1970), pp. 323–4. Hawkins's beautiful hand-drawn maps are now in the University Library.
[2] Stenton built up a splendid collection of crime fiction. This was dispersed to the local hospitals when the Stenton Library was established in the University.

lecture rooms that we acquired a smattering of the biological sciences. And very much a smattering it was, because our field was so wide. On the one hand were the basic sciences: chemistry, divided firmly down the middle into organic and inorganic, flanked on one side by physics and geology, and on the other by botany, zoology, entomology and bacteriology; on the other hand were non-scientific subjects such as agricultural history and economics, with a glance at accountancy, farm management and law. On top of all that we spent many wet, cold and inconclusive afternoons trudging round the university farm learning how to mark out a field for ploughing, to distinguish York-shire fog from cocksfoot and sainfoin from broad red clover, to master the show points of bulls, cows, pigs and fat bullocks, and to calculate the areas of fields.

Nevertheless it was a course that opened many windows, at least for me, to whom the whole field of natural sciences had hitherto lain in total darkness.[1]

By 1939 the system was under fire. An article entitled 'The Lecture System' appeared in *Tamesis* announcing that the students were under-taking a review of lecturing and other forms of teaching. The argument and method have since become familiar:

As we feel that facts are no longer the first essential we would suggest that all lectures of a factual nature be discontinued and that printed lecture notes be substituted for them. Such a measure would be a saving of time both for the lecturer and for the student and would prevent the tendency, which such lectures have, of destroying the student's interest in his subject. In conjunction with such notes we would suggest a reading list which would keep the student informed of literature available and of value to him.

In making this recommendation we do not deny the many benefits to be derived from lectures and we would not suggest that the human element should be removed from education methods. We do feel, however, that lectures should be designed to encourage the student to wider reading on his subject, to make him think about it and criticize the ideas of others intelligently. We urge, therefore, that lectures should be stimulating and not necessarily factual.

In connection with the desire to develop the student's power of intelligent criticism we feel that seminars are invaluable. At such meetings it is certain that many different points of view would be put forward on every subject and students would have to make use of the facts at their disposal to defend their own attitude. Here, we see an excellent method of ensuring that students learn how to use the facts when they have obtained them. At the same time students derive great personal benefit in so far as they are being trained to express their ideas

[1] Elspeth Huxley (1968), pp. 116–7. The Dean mentioned was H. A. D. Neville.

clearly and convincingly; a quality which cannot be developed if they merely sit and take notes from another person's lecture. Moreover, such a system enables students to obtain more frequently and more easily that intellectual intercourse which is vital to the development of mind and personality.

> We suggest that the system could be completed by tutorials in which the lecturer could give attention to the student's particular difficulties and could give him that personal guidance which is so valuable. There is no need to labour the value of tutorials and the disadvantages of introducing them will certainly not be educational, but there is a possibility that it would be impracticable under the present staffing conditions. This is a matter for investigation and it will be one of the tasks for the committees who are helping to draw up the memorandum.[1]

This failed to disturb the settled ways. The matter was not raised in Senate or Council, and then war intervened.

Perhaps for the best and most committed students more important than the immediate reaction to lectures and other forms of teaching was the sense of being among some of the great, among those who were in the forefront of the work in their subjects. All Stenton's pupils sensed this. It is still among Allen's most vivid memories of the Faculty of Science:

> As far as the staff was concerned, it was the time of giants: Wager, Hawkins, Harris, Brierley. They were national figures and they were an inspiration, even if they worked in fields other than your own. As a research student, I could potter along to other departments where staff and professors all knew you and spoke to you. . . . This was the time when 'Bill' Wager was going off on his great journeys and Tom Harris was a world figure in Palaeobotany. Harris and Wager appeared as men of determination, dedication and complete integrity; self-brutal integrity.[2]

Some inspired affection through the manner in which they combined devotion to their subjects with their own human frailty. Hawkins, imaginative though he might be as a teacher, was no administrator either of his department and faculty, or of his own research:

> He had the remarkable ability to occupy completely any space, no matter how large, in which he was currently working. The ultimate in occupation was his private room. When I first knew it, a narrow gangway led via his desk to the sink on one side of which was a huge cone of ash from knocking out his pipe and on the other an equally impressive structure of spent matchsticks. On the floor below the sink was a heap of clay – the elutriated residues from the Tertiaries of the Enborne Valley. Into this he had cut steps to provide access to the

[1] *Tamesis*, xxxvii (1939), pp. 53–4.
[2] Conversation with Professor P. Allen, 12 November 1969.

actual disposal unit. When the Enborne boreholes reached the Chalk, volumes of milky suspensions were poured down the sink which eventually obstructed it. Condescending to accept advice on its un-blocking and having hydrochloric acid suggested (by me), he inverted a winchester of concentrated HCl over the hole. The resulting chaos intrigued him enormously seeing, in the impressive upward splurge of acid and fizzing Chalk, a convincing demonstration of vulcanity and pointed proudly to the dripping ceiling. I forget whether the process actually unblocked the sink but in any case the original purpose of the operation had ceased to be relevant and provided only raw material for analogy, speculation and dramatic description.

As the years rolled on however all access to the sink became impossible and the desk became lost under debris. The 'Prof.' was reduced to writing his letters on the seat of his chair whilst kneeling on the floor. As the chair itself migrated doorwards, a position was reached when the 'Prof's' back was jammed against the door. Further work there became impossible so he locked the door and moved into another room never again visiting the old one. Miss Walder and I cleaned it out when he retired in 1952 – one of the most exciting jobs which I have ever done. It was a veritable treasure hunt, a copy of Murchinson's *Silurian System* (complete with map) and an enormous collection of farthings were amongst dozens of exciting finds. The farthings were given to the 'Rag' funds. We filled three collecting tins with them.[1]

Others were both scholars and men of action. Wager, member of Gino Watkins's Greenland expedition of 1931, of the Everest expedition of 1933 in which he was a member of one of the final assault parties, and leader of the East Greenland Expedition of 1935–6, was a legend in his own life-time:

Mr Wager came to the department on his great bedstead of a bicycle. This rusty steed was left in the entrance lobby during the day, leaning against the 'men's radiator'. His Intermediate lectures (later bequeathed to Miss Walder and recently, as 'Year 1', to Dr Bailey) were dreadful. But somehow we came away with the feeling that crystals were rather scrumptious. He'd stalk back to his room on the hour, slam the door, and get on with the Skaergaard struggle. Yet his second-year dis-courses were revelations – based on innumerable sheets of paper, blank except for a few pencilled words at the top. Fascinated, we couldn't wait to get to Scotland to see a living granite. Lifetimes of pleasure

[1] F. Hodson, 'Professor Hawkins: an appreciation', University of Reading, *Geology Newsletter*, no. 7 (1969), pp. 1–7. The example set seemed to be effective. Harris commented: 'I admired Hawkins very much. There was the loosest possible discipline in his department, but the students were always quietly working there at any hour of the day and no kind of pressure was exerted. Three-quarters of his students worked quietly, as real students should. Hawkins was the gentlest creature; and in examinations he never failed a soul.' (Conversation with Professor T. M. Harris, 21 January 1970).

date for many from those lectures and their field classes. . . . 'Bill' was
our most illustrious researcher, and one of the geological 'greats' of all
time. This is so whether you're thinking of adventures of the mind or
spirit. From his great Skaergaard 'bomb', where he interpreted planet-
sized experiments of mantle and crust, to 28,000 ft plus on Everest,
his intellect and personality shone forth to our generation.[1]

However, it would be invidious to imply that Reading's success and
advancing reputation were the work of only a few outstanding figures. Able
men in every faculty were adding to the strength and range of interest of
their departments and subjects. At the same time as Betts was establishing
Fine Art within the Faculty of Letters, Edgar Thomas was developing the
Economic Advisory Service as a department of Agricultural Economics
which by the mid-thirties had become a major centre of research.[2] Members
of staff were going on to distinguished careers elsewhere, Semple from
Classics to a Chair at Manchester, Gilbert from Geography to a Lectureship
and ultimately to a Chair at Oxford. Still, as in the days of the College,
Reading was producing among its pupils men and women who stayed or
returned to teach in the University or went on to distinguished careers in
other universities: Wainwright and Barley from the History department,
Allen from the Geology department, Baskett who took his degree in Agricultural Chemistry in 1930 and was already a Professor in The Queen's
University of Belfast in 1938, W. R. Trehane, who graduated in Agriculture
in 1934 and went on to become Chairman of the Milk Marketing Board in
1958, A. C. Fabergé who took a degree in Horticulture in 1933 and within
eight years had established a reputation as an experimentalist and inspired
'gadgeteer' at the Galton Institute of Genetics.

The advance was expressed in yet another fashion in the sheer bulk of
research which the University and its associated Institutes was encompas-
sing. Year by year the Research Board reported on the published work
which had come within its view. It carefully distinguished between books,
articles embodying results of original work, and other publications. In 1926
the list of the first two categories covered four pages, in 1935 six and a half,
in 1939 eight and a half. In 1926 the whole list extended to six pages, in 1939
to over eleven. The books included de Burgh's Giffard Lectures *From
Morality to Religion*, Stenton's classic Ford Lectures, *The First Century of
English Feudalism*, four volumes in the Place Name Society of which Stenton
was co-author, nine superbly edited pipe rolls and two volumes of eyre rolls
from Doris Stenton, six volumes from Edith Morley on Henry Crabbe
Robinson, three volumes from Aspinall of the correspondence of George IV,
A. A. Miller on *Climatology*, Cole on *Early Theories of Sexual Generation*, Nellie
Eales's *Littoral Fauna of Great Britain*, Wager on *The Petrology of the Skaergaard
Intrusion*, two volumes from Harris, one on *British Rhaetic Flora* and the other

[1] P. Allen, 'Professor L. R. Wager F.R.S.' (Reading, 1966), pp. 2–3.
[2] A. K. Giles (1973), pp. 12–14.

on *British Purbeck Charophyta*, the fourth edition of Crowther's *Manual of Physics* and the fifth and sixth editions of his *Ions, Electrons and ionising radiations*. The original papers reveal a wider spread of interests and activities. Guggenheim made a fleeting appearance, at work on liquid helium; Cole produced numerous papers on the history of natural sciences; Crowther was at work, in the late thirties with H. Liebmann, a refugee, on X-radiation of colloids; a wide range of work was coming in annually from the Faculty of Agriculture and Horticulture and the National Institute for Research in Dairying; at the Institute H. D. Kay and S. J. Folley had begun the studies of the biochemistry of milk and lactation physiology which led to their election as Fellows of the Royal Society. This increase in the output of original work is a good measure of the advance which the University was making. The outstanding figures gave the lead and set a standard. Thereafter it derived from an enthusiasm and a capacity for solid slog in which most members of staff shared. It was reflected in the advanced teaching. In 1925–6 there were seventeen students reading for Ph.D.s, M.A.s or M.Sc.s of the University of London. In 1929–30 there were twenty-four reading for similar degrees of the University of Reading. By 1938–9 the number had increased to forty-one. Throughout that period the number of staff had scarcely changed.[1]

In this too the small size of the University was important. All the members of the academic staff knew each other. They went out of their way to welcome new members and to introduce them to the academic family. They shared common interests which crossed subject-boundaries. Stenton and Cole came together partly as book collectors and partly through music, the one as a performer on the keyboard, the other as an expert on the pianola, each sharing equally in reverence for Bach. H. A. D. Neville and Robert Gibbings came together through a common love of the River Thames, which Gibbings was beginning to explore for *Sweet Thames run softly*. Everybody knew Gibbings and Gibbings talked to everybody, or played bowls with them or lured them into exercise with the medicine ball, for he was a mountain of a man. In all this the Common Room was the centre. The mid-morning break was signalled by the sound of the 'dairymaids' trooping to the Buttery. That was the social centre for the students. The staff gathered for coffee in the Acacias. Most of the great figures were regular attenders: Stenton, de Burgh, Hodges, Betts, Dewar, Crowther, Harris, Cole, Brierley and H. A. D. Neville. Sibly came in regularly if he was in Reading. The occasion was convenient for the interchange of business, but departmental 'shop' was discouraged. The atmosphere was that of an academic club. It was strictly non-political, even as the country moved from Munich into war. Coffee brought in the widest social gathering. Lunch on Saturday was another occasion when men stayed to gossip into the afternoon. Tea brought in a smaller group, mainly from the Faculty of Letters. In the memory of

[1] See above, p. 43.

those who can look back through the years of war to Reading as it was, perhaps the most poignant picture is of the Common Room, with de Burgh throwing out great intellectual challenges, or Dyson's dominating, husky voice launched on some flight of fancy, or Stenton looking rather like a figure from a medieval stained-glass window discussing his latest find with Cole, or Gibbings absorbing information and experience from all and sundry. For those who remained after 1945 it was never quite the same again.

For a small group, a very few, the last months of peace brought a moment of private hilarity. It had always been intended to record Childs's retirement in 1929 in the customary manner by the presentation of a portrait. The business had dragged; Childs became pressing; Sibly found the matter embarrassing and asked Betts to do something about it. In the summer of 1938 Betts was able to persuade Eric Kennington to undertake the picture; the sum available was quite inadequate as a fee for such an artist in ordinary circumstances, but Kennington respected Childs and was prepared to do it for a song. So the work began. But Kennington soon came to be involved in a number of War Office committees concerned with camouflage, and during the winter and spring of 1939 Childs became increasingly concerned and insistent. In the end Kennington agreed to three final sittings; the head was finished and he was left to complete the background on his own. For this he provided a splendid tapestry on which were portrayed three female figures representing the Graces. Childs characteristically provided the inscription himself. He came to look at the finished work at the end of April. The inspection was disastrous. He and his wife were of one mind: it was quite impossible to accept a portrait of the first Vice-Chancellor in which three women were portrayed behind him, especially since it was to hang in a men's hall of residence. Through a somewhat impatient Betts an even more impatient Kennington was asked to alter the background. With artistic prescience, he now produced something remarkably like the black-out.[1]

Childs, as so often, had the last word. It was perhaps the last word, or nearly so, of the old Reading. Neither in the next few years nor afterwards would men (or women) be worried by the presence of female figures as a backcloth to a Vice-Chancellor. But it was a tragi-comedy. The portrait is of a dying man, his earlier fires now only aglow. Childs never saw the war; he died on 21 June 1939. Sibly survived it, but worked himself to the verge of death.

[1] See plate 1. Copies of the letters from Kennington to Betts and Childs to Betts, along with Betts's own notes are in URC, box 256.

Chapter 5

The War 1939–45

The war was an experience in which all universities shared. They had to manage with reduced resources. Members of staff left to join the Forces or government services. Men students still came to study science courses which were useful to the war economy, but for most of them arts courses were truncated, a mere interval between school and active service. Women students likewise had to accept increasingly precise and detailed direction on the work to which they might turn once their courses were completed. All universities had to cope with the circumstances of war which affected the whole country; rationing, the black-out, fire-watching, service in the Home Guard, the vagaries and delays of war-time transport. Some suffered through enemy air attack. Reading escaped that. However, sited as it was in southern England, it found itself providing help and accommodation for other institutions which were more vulnerably placed. Some of its resources were commandeered by the Armed Forces or the Civil Service. The University involved itself very fully in the war. This was true of departments in all faculties. However, it was the Faculty of Agriculture which was able to make the greatest contribution. Other faculties contracted in the circumstances of war. The Faculty of Agriculture, like English farming itself, expanded. The war therefore had a direct effect on the internal balance of the University.

In 1939 the University lost accommodation immediately. Wantage Hall was commandeered by the Royal Air Force, which remained there throughout the war. A year later the Air Force also issued a requisition order for Elmhurst, the new building for St George's Hall, but appeals to the University Grants Committee and the Air Ministry averted this.[1] The Ministry of Supply took over the Central Chemistry Building in the autumn of 1940. It released its hold in 1941–2 after an awkward interval in which laboratory classes had either been duplicated or suspended. In the early months of the war especially the pressure on accommodation was increased by the evacuation of more vulnerable institutions. Immediately in 1939 the threat of air attack was exaggerated. As a result the Faculty of Agriculture was inflated by the arrival of over 100 students chiefly from Wye College and the Royal Veterinary College. This was only temporary; they returned to their

[1] URC, Vice-Chancellor, box 43.

own centres at Christmas 1939; but the Royal Veterinary College retained accommodation at Reading throughout the war, and in the summer and autumn of 1940, when Kent lay as it were in the front line, there was further talk that the students of Wye College might return. The British Institute of Physics likewise came to Reading in 1939 and remained in the accommodation of the Students' Union in the Old Red Building until 1945. Others came and went, like the British Institute in Paris which was housed in Chedworth, an annexe of St Patrick's Hall, between 1939 and 1941. Throughout the war Sibly did his best to help other institutions, especially those in London, by providing temporary accommodation for the administration of examinations and other purposes.[1] Regularly, Sir George Mowbray, as President of Council, reported on the occasions on which the University buildings had been used by other organizations. Once, in September 1940, refugees from the London bombing found a temporary home in the University: women and children used the Senior Common Room as a dormitory.[2]

The effect of the war on the students of the University varied from faculty to faculty. The National Service Act allowed students who were called up for service to obtain postponement for varying periods and for different purposes. The Joint Recruiting Boards which were set up by the Ministry of Labour and National Service to administer the Act had a number of initial objectives. They permitted postponement to students who were due to take examinations within a limited period on the condition that they joined the Officers' Training Corps or the Air Squadron.[3] At the same time they allowed students who were reading scientific or technical subjects to continue with the full degree course so that they were professionally trained for the technical branches of the Forces or for work in industry or government departments. The time allowed to the students reading arts subjects was steadily reduced. In 1941 and 1942 a few of the younger men remained for longer than a year while they completed both Certificate A and Certificate B in the Training Corps for direct entry into Officer Cadet Training Units. In 1942 the period was reduced to a year, thereby lowering the average age of entry into the University, and in 1943 the scheme for deferring service was terminated altogether. Over the same period the Ministry insisted on the reduction of the period allowed for the completion of degree and diploma courses. As a result the University had to introduce a fourth term in the Long Vacation in 1944 and 1945. It created considerable com-

---

[1] In September 1939 Reading was established as one of the local centres for the examination of the external B.A. and B.Sc. General Degrees of the University of London (URC, Vice-Chancellor, box 43).

[2] J. W. Dodgson, Diary, v, 6 (University of Reading Library, MS 1170). Dodgson was a lecturer in the Department of Chemistry 1904–34 and 1941–5. He left a diary, in seventeen volumes, covering the years 1939–50.

[3] The Air Squadron was established in 1940 and was closed down in the summer of 1943. It had produced insufficient numbers for aircrew duties to prove worthwhile.

plications, both in teaching and administration, especially in the organization of examinations. Women also were allowed fewer and fewer exemptions under the National Service Acts. From April 1942 onwards they were subjected to the same regulation and direction as the men. However, subject to satisfactory progress, they were allowed in effect to complete their courses before going into industry, government, the Forces, or the teaching profession.[1]

The effects on the balance of the student population are apparent. Between 1940 and 1944 139 women graduated with degrees in the Faculty of Letters, but only 20 men. In 1943, 43 women graduated in the Faculty and no men; in 1944, 22 women and 2 men. In the Department of Education the decline in numbers was even more dramatic. In 1940 Sibly reported as follows:

> The Professor of Education reports a great reduction in the number of students. In the Session 1938–9, the figure was 62; it fell to 45 in the Session under review; and in the current Session the number is only 22, of whom 2 are men. It is inevitable that a department which provides a postgraduate course should, under existing conditions, be deprived of practically all its men students; and some of the women who might normally have been reading for the Diploma in Education have taken up national service work instead. It is becoming increasingly difficult to provide adequate teaching practice for the students. In spite of all the handicaps, however, work is being carried on successfully; and students are giving freely of their spare time in order to help local schools which are short-staffed or overcrowded, and to take part in other forms of social work. It has been necessary to dispense with many of the usual educational visits and external lectures.[2]

It was not until 1942–3 that the numbers taking the postgraduate Diploma in the Department increased, probably as a result of the increasingly strict direction of women, which had the effect of increasing the numbers of those who took up school-teaching. In other spheres also the war had results which few would have predicted in 1939. Immediately, the uncertainty and the inexperience of war conditions caused a drastic reduction in the number of evening students. It fell from 652 to 356. However, in 1941–2 the number rose to 649 and by the last year of the war it had risen to 751. Peace in fact brought a reduction to 641 in 1945–6. The war produced a demand for educational qualifications. In the military establishments around Reading it brought together men and women for whom evening classes were a welcome change and relaxation. In 1942–3, of the 677 evening students 194 were serving members of the Forces. There was one other curious effect

[1] The specific rule was that women were allowed to complete the academic year in which they reached the age of twenty if in that year they could qualify for a degree or diploma.
[2] *Proceedings 1939–40*, p.37.

which is not easy to diagnose. In many belligerent countries, Germany just as much as England, men and women found some refreshment or solace in great music. Reading was no exception to the trend. Between 1939 and 1941 the number of students in the School of Music nearly doubled; and the School, like the National Gallery in London, was a centre for lunch-time concerts.[1]

The effects of the war on the staff were more diverse than on the students. In the first year the younger members who were not reserved as teachers or scientists or technicians joined the Forces. Some of the older ones went too; Desseignet sailed for France in October 1939 to join the French army, only to be returned in May 1940 with the firm instruction that his work as a Frenchman in England was more important than anything he could achieve in battle.[2] More and more of those who remained were involved in war work of one kind or another. When J. W. Dodgson returned to the Chemistry Department in January 1941 to replace A. K. Mills who had left for the Ministry of Aircraft Production, he noted that the staff at lunch were almost all women and opined that before long the staff would consist almost entirely of 'charming ladies and aged veterans'.[3] That was misleading. The plain fact was that by 1941 many of the staff were far too busy elsewhere to appear at lunch with any regularity. The younger members were enrolled in the Home Guard.[4] Others were involved in the supervision of fire-watching. Cyril Tyler was one of the Gas Identification Officers in the Air Raid Precaution Service. H. A. D. Neville and Robert Gibbings managed to combine personal enthusiasm with the defence of the realm as part of the Thames river patrol. In retrospect and even at the time some of this had a lighter aspect. It was noticeable that members of the Home Guard were quicker in resorting to the prone firing position than they were in recovering afterwards, and there were moments to savour, as when Harris, Professor of Botany, learned from the sergeant of the Training Corps that there were two kinds of trees, pine trees and bushy-topped trees. But in the long run it was wearying, all the more so because it intruded into academic duties which were themselves rendered more difficult and tiresome by the war. In all departments members of staff had to make necessary adjustments to the courses they provided in order to match the changing demands of national service on their students. In the science departments they had to fight off threats to the supply of necessary chemicals and apparatus which

[1] See plate 23.
[2] J. W. Dodgson, Diary, i, 138; v, 259.
[3] *Ibid.*, viii, 108.
[4] I have not been able to trace the complete membership of the Home Guard contingent. Sibly's files still include instructions from the Ministry of Labour and National Service for the enrolment of several members of staff in 1942–3 (URC, Vice-Chancellor, box 44). However, this was preceded by the formation in 1940 of a body of volunteer irregulars from 'a group in the Senior Common Room who decided to know something about arms-drill and got the Sergeant Instructor of the OTC to give rifle drill and explain the workings of a Lewis gun'. This included Harris and Ian Crichton.

the conflicting demands of different government departments and the plethora of regulations sometimes produced.[1] The general load of work increased as the University sought more and more to provide a service for the surrounding community both civil and military. In December 1939 Reading accepted an invitation to join forces with Oxford in providing educational facilities for the Forces.[2] By 1941 the staff of the University was providing roughly forty lectures a month. A year later Sibly reported:

> In 1942, 1,151 lectures were given to the Army, and, in growing proportion, to the RAF and to Canadian units, many by members of the University staff, others by outside experts at the invitation of the University. Many more lectures were arranged than given, cancellations due to troop movements being inevitably frequent. In addition, the University has on several occasions helped with courses for training officers in giving ABCA talks.[3]

That was no mean burden.

On two occasions in 1941 Sibly tried to summarize a view of the University in war time. The first was in February in answer to a request from the *Times Educational Supplement*. He sought aid in preparing it and the result is curiously stilted and formal:

---

[1] The following correspondence reveals one occasion of difficulty. On 27 September 1940 H. A. D. Neville reported to Sibly as follows:

> I have heard from Mr S. L. Turner, the representative of Messrs Gallenkamp in this area, that there is likely to be serious difficulty in the future in connection with the supply of chemical apparatus and perhaps other chemicals. Mr Turner tells me that the difficulty arises in two ways. In the first case, his firm has received orders that they are not to supply apparatus without either
>
> > (a) A contract number being quoted, which, I gather, means ordering through the Ministry of Supply, or
> > (b) The production of a priority certificate, or
> > (c) The production of an export reference.
>
> It is obvious that (a) and (c) are impossible for a university and that (b) is the only line of procedure.
>
> Secondly, he tells me that, even if his firm obtained and packed the goods, the railway companies would not transport them without the production of a priority certificate.
>
> The matter happens to have arisen in connection with the Agricultural Chemistry Department but it will affect all departments in the Faculties of Science and Agriculture. Fortunately, in my department, we have sufficient stock to carry on for some time but eventually all practical teaching will cease, if the present ruling holds.
>
> It might be possible to obtain, through the Ministry of Agriculture, a priority certificate for the apparatus and chemicals required for the Advisory Service but I doubt whether we could get such a certificate for our teaching activities. In fact, I would not care to raise the point.
>
> As the difficulty will affect all universities, I suggest the matter might be brought to the notice of the University Grants Committee....

Sibly circulated vice-chancellors on the matter to collect information. However within a fortnight Neville was able to report that the matter had been settled satisfactorily through the intervention of Oxford University (URC, Vice-Chancellor, box 42).

[2] Sibly, Ernest Smith and Dyson represented the University on the Regional Committee on Education for H.M. Forces. Much of the work ultimately fell to Dyson.

[3] *Proceedings 1941–2*, p.30. ABCA stood for the Army Bureau of Current Affairs.

After seventeen months of war, it can be said that none of the
essential activities of the University has been destroyed, and that few
of them have been seriously weakened. After a considerable increase
at the beginning of the war – mainly due to the closure of certain
agricultural colleges, many of which were re-opened – the number of
students now in residence is not far below its pre-war level. The space
at the disposal of the University has been reduced by the accommodation which it has given to the Royal Veterinary College, to the
Institute of Physics, and to a group of Government workers. There is
much congestion in a number of laboratories, but it cannot be said
that there has been any serious dislocation of the arrangements for
teaching and research.

It would be idle to pretend that the students have not felt the strain
of war conditions. Many of them come from districts which have
suffered heavily from enemy action. All men students are naturally to
some extent preoccupied with the prospect of military service. But the
result has been less serious than might have been expected. Students
have kept their sense of proportion, academic routine has been maintained, and there has never been any thought of lowering the standard
of the work required for University examinations. In this respect, both
the University and the students have been greatly helped by the
operation of the Joint Recruiting Board scheme and by the application
of those provisions of the Armed Forces Act which enable students to
obtain postponements of military service when a critical examination
is to be taken within a reasonable time. The one piece of academic
readjustment directly caused by the war has been the reorganization
of a number of courses and examinations in order to secure that a
student who is unable to complete the three years of residence needed
for a degree shall be able to take an examination in a definite and
coherent part of his studies at the end of each year.

It should be added that the student body has been remarkably
successful in maintaining the corporate activities of peacetime under
war conditions. The Students' Union has continued to function. Teams
have been arranged, and matches played. It has been difficult for
students' societies to carry out their normal activities, but many evening meetings have been held, and the members of these societies have
done much to make good from their own resources the scarcity of
available speakers from outside the University. Although one of the
two University halls of residence for men students has been requisitioned by a Government department, its members, in temporary
quarters, are maintaining in full the traditions of their community.
The response of the students and members of the staff to the circumstances of the time has taken many forms, but special reference may
be made to the successful experiment of the School of Music in the
institution of midday concerts, and to the lectures given by various

members of the Faculty of Letters in order to meet the desire of
students for information about the problems of the contemporary
world.

Within the sphere of research, the lines of work which are normally
followed in the Faculties of Science and Agriculture have been
adapted to the necessities of the present time. The departure of a
number of young lecturers and postgraduate students has meant the
interruption of many pieces of work begun in previous years. But in
the University as a whole, the continuity of research has not been
broken; contact with other workers, though difficult, has not been
impossible, but in some faculties obstacles have arisen to hinder the
publication of results. . . .[1]

The editor had asked him to review the prospects of the University. In
sending the article he wrote somewhat bleakly that 'we have not found it
possible to review the prospects of the University at a time of such great
uncertainty.'[2] Eight months later in September he wrote less formally to
Sir Samuel Hoare the Chancellor of the University. Now with Russia in the
war and with the grim winter of 1940–1 behind him he was more assured,
though not yet perhaps completely optimistic:

The University came through the second session of the war very
successfully, and we were fortunate in escaping all air attack. One or
two more members of the scientific staff were released to take up special
war work – one of them has been appointed Scientific Adviser to the
Air Officer Commanding-in-Chief, Middle East – but we have reached
the limit of possible releases from the scientific staff if we are to carry
on our work efficiently. A few members of staff on the arts and administrative side have joined the Forces on dereservation. The number of
undergraduates fell a good deal below the exceptionally high total of
the first year of the war (when we received large numbers of agricultural students from other centres), but still remained higher than
we had expected. The number of women undergraduates has actually
increased, and nearly all of them are qualifying for really useful work.
The number of men has fallen considerably, but is unlikely to decrease
any further, in view of the great need of young men trained in
scientific and technical subjects.

The Joint Recruiting Board scheme, under which men pursuing
scientific courses are virtually reserved so long as they make satisfactory progress, and are then assigned to technical positions in the
Forces or in industry on the completion of their courses, has worked
extremely well at Reading, and indeed in all the universities in the
kingdom. I have seen a great deal of the development of this scheme

[1] URC, Vice-Chancellor, box 48.
[2] *Ibid.*

in my capacity as Chairman of the Committee of Vice-Chancellors, and have taken part in all the negotiations with Government departments.

We are all agreed that the undergraduates have never worked better than during the past year. They have risen to the occasion not only in application to their studies but also in their work in the Senior Training Corps, the University Air Squadron, and, in the case of women, in social service in the town.

There can be no doubt whatever about the way in which the universities generally are standing up to the war. Great difficulties have befallen the large colleges of London University, nearly all of which are exiled in the provinces. Oxford and Cambridge have sustained a large fall of numbers – about one-third or more – but the provincial universities of England and Wales and the Scottish universities are carrying on in full vigour, and all the universities are making their contribution to the war effort without dropping the torch of learning and scholarship.

Inevitably, the calling up of young men at nineteen is depleting the faculties of arts; but arrangements have been made with the Service Departments, under which promising students of the humanities can come up to the universities for a year at least, and carry on their studies concurrently with part-time training in Senior Training Corps or Air Squadrons, and then pass direct to Officer Cadet Training Units. My Chairmanship of the Committee of Vice-Chancellors has given me a good opportunity of estimating the position as a whole, and I am sure that, despite mistakes in the early days, the general position is thoroughly healthy today. I succeeded to the Chair two months before Munich, that is, in July, 1938, and now I cannot get released from it.

At Reading our Schools of Agriculture and Dairying are very flourishing, and in the Faculty of Science we are making a modest but useful contribution to the Radio Training Scheme, in which the universities have a vital part to play. We have been allowed to continue the erection of our new building for Zoology and Psychology, in view of our very urgent need of increased accommodation, and although progress has been very slow, we hope to bring the whole building into use early in the new year.[1]

Much the most important sections of Sibly's reports were those in which he referred to the changes in the Faculties of Science and Agriculture. In the early years of the war especially the British proved superior to the German Government in ensuring the effective direction of material re-

[1] URC, Vice-Chancellor, box 44.

sources, including labour.[1] One effect on universities can be traced in the direction of women into war work or other essential employment.[2] Another is to be found in the relative ease with which universities involved themselves in the war effort, either in research, or by providing the kind of training which the war required, or through direct involvement in war-time administration. Peace-time institutions were adapted easily to war. The University Grants Committee lay to hand as an effective channel of communication. The system of State Scholarships provided a pattern for the establishment of State Bursaries in science and technology which ensured the supply of the necessary number of graduates in these fields. War-time co-operation grew naturally from the close and easy peace-time relationships in which government ministries had financed the work of university departments. In Germany, by contrast, the Nazi party was an artificial intrusion and a severe administrative disadvantage.

This affected the various faculties at Reading in different ways. There was little which the Faculty of Letters could contribute except to provide the time for the one or two days' training which students had to undertake in the Officers' Training Corps or the Air Squadron. Research in the Faculty continued, hampered increasingly by the difficulty of publishing finished work. The School of Art tried to make a more direct contribution to the war:

> Robert Gibbings was very interested in the way different animals, birds and butterflies took protective covering from their environment, and in 1939–40, when it looked as if the Germans were coming to this country, we decided we would like to put up some kind of fight, and I invented a sniping suit. The whole idea was that you could adapt the suit to any environment. You put it on like a night shirt and it was painted in different strips, some the colour of green grass, some of bricks, some of concrete, and so on, and you could turn it round so that the strip in front conformed in colour with the place where you found yourself. But how to launch this thing? The Reading Defence Committee had arranged that certain parts of the town should be tank barriers (one at Cemetery Junction, one at the Roebuck, one by Suttons Garden Centre and one in Tilehurst). I was working with the Committee to camouflage these tank traps and the Committee felt that the sniping suit would be very useful for the men who manned them. But how were we to get in touch with the War Office? Eventually I went to see Sibly who said: 'I will write to General Auchinleck of the Southern Command' – but first he wanted a demonstration so that he should know how to describe the thing he was writing about. So I got

---

[1] For the British side see W. K. Hancock and M. M. Gowing, *British War Economy* (London, 1949), pp. 101–2, 312–4, 456–62; and M. M. Postan, *British War Production* (London, 1952), pp. 86–102, 145–63, 217–27. For the German side, see Albert Speer, *Inside the Third Reich*, Eng. trans. (London, 1970), pp. 300–20.

[2] See above p. 103.

three men, with rifles, and I camouflaged them myself, and at
11 o'clock on a certain day Sibly was to be at his window with the
Bursar and Registrar. At precisely 11 o'clock on the day, I blew my
whistle and they all looked out; but they were under fire for three or
four seconds before they discovered the whereabouts of my men. Sibly
wrote his letter and eventually I was summoned to Wilton House,
Headquarters of Southern Command, where I was received by
General Ritchie, at that time Auchinleck's chief of staff. The result of
the whole operation was an order for 100 sniping suits. It all goes to
show, too, that Sibly was not a man who turned things down – he took
trouble and he acted.

   There was also the camouflaging of the tank traps to be looked after,
and I went to the University Gardening Committee to ask if I could
borrow plants – geraniums and the like. The tank barrier at Cemetery
Junction was a little difficult because of the awful lavatory buildings
and the machine guns. But I bought some cheap trellis work, and with
the aid of this and some plants I disguised the immediate surface.
I wanted to give the whole thing an air of dignity by placing a statue
of Venus on top of the lavatories. The School of Art would not lend me
theirs, so I bought a smaller one from a breakdown yard for £1, and
I got Carter to make a base for it. I was hoping that the Germans
would be too interested in the Venus to notice the trap until it was
too late.[1]

From such whimsical activities the University was saved by the other
faculties. By 1940 the main lines of research which had been in progress
in the Faculties of Science and Agriculture before the war were largely
in abeyance. Some departments turned deliberately to war-work. Up to
the war, for example, the Department of Physics had concentrated its
research on the X-radiation of colloids. Crowther, the Head of Department,
had served as a conscientious objector in an X-ray unit in the First World
War. By 1939 he had collected a small team in which H. Liebmann, a
German refugee, was doing the chemistry and Paul White was providing
the mathematics. They were developing an interest in the effects of X-rays
on cancer. With the Second World War all that was dropped. The Central
(Technical and Scientific) Register required men for radar. Under the
urging of C. P. Snow, the Department of Physics introduced a two-year
course in radio in 1941. In the Long Vacations of 1941 and 1942 it also
provided eight-week conversion or revision courses in radio for graduates.
Initially all this was done on pathetically inadequate resources; T. B.
Rymer had to go out to buy valves and other materials at radio and
second-hand shops in Reading.[2] Moreover, as in other universities concerned in similar training courses, the Department was steered away from

[1] Conversation with Frank Ormrod, 14 June 1971.
[2] Conversation with T. B. Rymer, 3 September 1975.

the immediate war-time application of its teaching.[1] It was required simply to provide the basic training on which Government establishments and the Services could subsequently build. Nevertheless, it greatly increased the work of the Department.[2] It had to make new temporary appointments in 1941 and 1942. There was nothing comparable in other departments of the Faculty. In the Department of Geology Hawkins was involved in work on the supply of scarce minerals on behalf of the Ministry of Supply, but on the whole the science departments at Reading were too small to attract much contract work from the Government. They lacked the necessary resources in material and personnel.

In the Faculty of Agriculture the matter was very different. It was much larger. It was accustomed to rely on the Ministry of Agriculture, and its work was closely integrated with practical farming and its administration. It was admirably adapted to assist in all the varied concerns which centred during the war on increasing the output of English farming. It was directly involved in a vital part of the war effort.

By 1939 Reading had become one of the foremost centres in the United Kingdom for the study of agriculture and related subjects. Its advance to this position had been marked in several ways. As H. A. D. Neville was never tired of pointing out in his annual reports as Dean, it attracted an increasing number of students, and of that increasing number, year by year, a smaller proportion read for certificates and diplomas and a larger proportion for first and second degrees.[3] Since 1926 the resources of the Faculty had expanded considerably. In 1933 Robert Rae was appointed to the Chair of Agriculture. Within a year he had persuaded the University that the existing farm at Shinfield was too small. In 1934 the University bought Sonning Farm; this gave the Faculty a working farm of 380 acres

[1] The following was sent from the Wireless Personnel Joint Sub-Committee, 17 December 1942:

Instructions on Ultra short-wave technique in civilian establishments

I am directed to refer to the desirability of introducing instruction on ultra short wave wireless technique in certain establishments, as detailed in the Appendix to this letter, in order that students taking Bursary Courses in Physics and Electrical Engineering may be given a broad outline of development in radio technique during the last five years.

It has been decided that a wavelength of the order of 12 or 12.5 centimetres is suitable and for this purpose magnetron valves type E.1210 may be used for generating ultra short waves of low power by the colleges detailed in the Appendix. The colleges will only concern themselves with short wave developments such as have appeared in technical publications from time to time. They are not required to teach anything on service equipment and it is highly undesirable that they should go into any details whatsoever of wavelengths or circuit arrangements on service equipments. In fact they should be discouraged from making enquiries in respect of these equipments.

[2] The vacation course was attended by 35 students in the summer of 1941. The two-year course accounted for the increase in the number of students reading for the B.Sc. General Degree from 61 in 1940–1 to 86 in 1942–3.

[3] For details of this process see above pp. 51–2.

against the 145 acres hitherto available at Shinfield[1] and enabled it to acquaint students with the capital and labour involved in a greater variety of farming methods.[2] At London Road new buildings had become available;[3] H. A. D. Neville still complained of the shortage of accommodation and the unavoidable duplication of classes; but by 1939 the Faculty was far better housed than in 1926. Moreover it had been reinforced in senior staff. H. D. Kay, Stenhouse Williams's successor as Director of the National Institute for Research in Dairying, was appointed to a Research Professorship in Biochemistry in 1932, R. H. Stoughton to a newly-established Chair of Horticulture in 1933, and E. Capstick to a newly-established Chair of Dairying in 1938. By 1939 the Faculty, along with the National Institute for Research in Dairying, the British Dairy Institute and the Agricultural Advisory Service, had become the largest organization of its kind in the country. It was attracting other institutions. When the British Commonwealth Scientific Conference of 1936 recommended the establishment of an Imperial Bureau of Dairy Science, the National Institute was chosen as the natural home for it; Kay was its first Director.[4] The research of the Faculty and the associated institutes covered an extraordinarily wide range of agricultural topics: soil survey, crop diseases, economic and accountancy studies, animal genetics and physiology, food chemistry, lactation physiology and the biochemistry of milk. Those involved kept a close eye on practical issues and responded to the needs of the industry. The National Institute devoted both its theoretical and immediately practical work to improvement in the quantity and quality of milk production. It was also one of the centres for the Machinery Testing Scheme of the Ministry of Agriculture.[5] At the Dairy Institute every effort was made, first under A. Todd and then under Capstick, to adjust the work to the changes in the industry away from farm to factory production. As Todd remarked in 1935, 'employers were asking for technologists and managers instead of cheesemakers'.[6] The Institute was re-equipped to deal with these changes. In the Advisory Service Edgar Thomas changed the

[1] The purchase price of Sonning Farm was £14,500. It was met through the sale of investments held in a number of endowment funds, the income on which was made good by charging rent on the farm accounts. It was decided to sell the Shinfield Farm except for fifteen acres which were retained for the Horticultural Station. However the Farm failed to reach the reserve price at a public auction on 1 December 1934, and it proved impossible to sell it in separate lots. It was subsequently leased to a tenant and returned to the University's direct management in 1950. The acquisition of Sonning Farm was followed in 1936 by R. H. Mardon's gift of Shiplake Court. However, the University simply received the freehold; the tenant of the land remained *in situ* at Mr Mardon's wish.
[2] Record of conversation with Sir Robert Rae, 17 July 1970.
[3] See above, pp. 35–7.
[4] H. F. Burgess (1962), p. 71.
[5] *Ibid.*, p. 53.
[6] E. L. Crossley, 'The British Dairy Institute and the University of Reading', *Journal of the British Dairy Farmers' Association*, lxii (1958), pp. 5–8.

emphasis of the economists so that to the work on cost-accounting was added a series of regional and special studies, beginning with the first of the series of *Financial Results of Dairy Farming in the Blackmore Vale*, published in 1932.[1] The National Institute and the Advisory Service were largely dependent on the Ministry of Agriculture and Fisheries. The Dairy Institute and the Faculty also drew on it for resources. They were all involved in the teaching work of the Faculty. At Reading a complex had been created in which the funds and effort of the University, the allocations of the Ministry and the donations both of land and money from private benefactors were all combined, if not inextricably mixed. Much of this was the work of H. A. D. Neville who held all the various institutions in close combination and had a masterly expertise in pressing forward their interests both within the University and with the Ministry.[2] At the Ministry Reading's skill in pressing its claims became famous. H. G. Richardson, who took a kindly interest in the estimates of the National Institute and for whom, as a distinguished expert on the workings of the medieval Exchequer, modern accounts held few terrors, commented: 'We don't mind how you do us, so long as you always do it in the same way'.[3]

At the outbreak of war the Faculty and the associated institutes were plunged immediately into the affairs of war-time agriculture. Long-term research plans were dropped in favour of solving some of the immediate problems of increasing food supply, making do with less adequate food stuffs, and extending the range and output of English farming. The professors and directors were involved immediately in committee work. Some were lost to the University; Capstick joined the Ministry of Food in 1939 and Rae, after serving on numerous committees, took up a post as Agricultural Attaché at the British Embassy in Washington and Agricultural Adviser to the High Commissioner in Ottawa in April 1943. The Advisory Officers were involved at once in the ploughing-up campaign which the Ministry organized through County Committees. The survey work which Edgar Thomas had pressed on before the war now qualified him for service as the Ministry's Intelligence Officer reporting on the campaign for food production in the Southern Province. In May 1941 his department was made responsible for assembling and filing farm records collected by the War Agricultural Executive Committees in the Province. This involved 23,000 farms. At the National Institute researchers turned to investigating the nutritive values of dried skim milk and the vitamin content of various foods. The cow, as Kay remarked, had become 'farm

---

[1] A. K. Giles (1973), pp. 12–14.
[2] See the short but telling tribute by Crossley (1958), pp. 3–4: 'The year 1919 saw the arrival of H. A. D. Neville as Professor of Agricultural Chemistry; he was destined to exercise an outstanding influence upon agricultural and dairy production for the next quarter of a century'.
[3] H. F. Burgess (1962), p. 54.

animal number one.'[1] At the Dairy Institute the staff turned to help with cheese-making in quantities which the equipment and the space were not designed to take. In all these sections new staff was added to cope with the extra work. This was true also of the Faculty. It was booming. Qualified graduates in Agriculture were now in high demand. The Dean reported in 1942 that 'it had been impossible to satisfy the demand for qualified men and women'. Classes were duplicated and then triplicated. There was no aspect of the agricultural work of the University which remained un-affected. In 1940, for the first time, the University Treasurer was able to report a net profit on the Farm account. It continued to show a profit throughout the war.

The effects of this were to be important within the University. The Agriculture Faculty expanded while the other faculties contracted or at best remained unchanged. The staff of the National Institute numbered 50 in 1929, 68 in 1933–4, 72 in 1939 and well over 100 in 1946.[2] The support which the University received respectively from the Treasury and from the Ministry of Agriculture and Fisheries grew in a roughly constant proportion throughout the 1930s. The Parliamentary grant recommended by the Treasury increased by roughly 60 per cent[3] and so also did the grant from the Ministry.[4] However, from 1939 to 1945, while the Parliamentary grant remained unchanged, the grant from the Ministry doubled.[5] It amounted to three-quarters of the Parliamentary grant in 1939. In 1945, in contrast, the Parliamentary grant was two-thirds of the grant from the Ministry. Much of the additional expenditure on agriculture was directed to the Advisory Service and the National Institute for Research in Dairying. But the increasing shift to agricultural studies was not restricted to finance. There was a similar shift in student numbers. The main effect of the war on Reading was to alter the internal distribution of its total resources and the general balance of its work. The first task facing those who planned for the future after the war was to decide whether to continue or restrict that change.[6]

The general planning for the future began remarkably early. In October 1941 R. A. Butler, as President of the Board of Education, appointed a committee to consider the curriculum in secondary schools and the related examinations. The result was the Norwood Report of June 1943. In March 1942 he appointed another committee to investigate the supply and methods of recruitment of teachers and youth leaders. That led to the McNair Report of 1944. Most important of all for Reading, R. S. Hudson, Minister of Agriculture and Fisheries, appointed a committee which in

[1] *Ibid.*, p. 75.
[2] *Ibid.*, pp. 60, 70, 76.
[3] The Parliamentary grant was £26,500 in 1927 and £42,000 in 1939.
[4] The Ministry grant was £20,557 in 1927 and £32,935 in 1939.
[5] The figure for 1944–5 was £64,848.
[6] See below, pp. 120–3.

1943 presented the Luxmoore Report on Agricultural Education in England and Wales. The Faculty of Agriculture and Horticulture at Reading was the only university faculty or department to appear among the witnesses.[1] Neville's evidence to the committee was generally recognized as masterly. In its discussion of university departments of agriculture the committee recommended the type of course which Reading was providing. It also proposed the introduction of graduate courses in agricultural studies for students who had taken their first degree in some branch of the natural sciences. But it insisted that the work should be done in a practical context: 'No university course in agriculture, whether it be practical or academic, can be complete without practical experience'.[2] It envisaged extra expenditure:

> So far as agricultural education is concerned, the position of the universities has been, still is, and must continue to be of the utmost national importance. It is no doubt for this reason that the Ministry of Agriculture has in the past provided, and still provides, financial assistance for their services. If the suggestions we make below are accepted, the financial assistance provided in the future must necessarily be increased. . . .
>
> It is as essential in a university department of agriculture as in any other university department that each member of the teaching staff should be free to devote some part of his time to research work without which his teaching is bound to become uninspired and stereotyped. Provision for this must necessarily postulate a larger teaching staff, and this must be recognized in the future in fixing the grants to university departments of agriculture.[3]

That was a natural enough line for the committee to take nationally. Locally at Reading it threatened to accentuate the imbalance which the war had caused.

The war had one other effect which was individual but more than personal. At the outbreak Sibly was already Chairman of the Committee of Vice-Chancellors and Principals, and, as he wrote to Sir Samuel Hoare, he found it impossible to quit the office. This left him as the main intermediary between the Government and the universities. It was an unenviable, onerous task, involving him in committees, discussion, correspondence on all those questions where the conduct of the war and the establishment of a war economy impinged on the work of universities: the call-up and its deferment for students, reserved occupations, the training of scientists and technicians, the supply of teachers, the provision of equipment and chemicals, the requisitioning of accommodation, the

[1] The Oxford University School of Rural Economy submitted a memorandum, as also did Reading. Several professors at other universities submitted memoranda or appeared as witnesses in an individual capacity (Luxmoore Report, pp. 84–7).
[2] *Ibid.*, p. 54.
[3] *Ibid.*, pp. 53–4.

provision of special courses. With all this he had to contend not just once in the initial negotiations with the relevant Ministries, but many times over as other Vice-Chancellors and Principals wrote in for advice or merely to compare notes.[1] Understandably his letters occasionally reveal the onset of a weary but still deliberately polite impatience. This was only part of the burden. Many turned to him for personal advice or assistance. Sometimes it was a pleasure to provide it, as when he was able to rescue Fabergé from a Training Regiment in the Royal Armoured Corps and arrange his return to the Galton Institute of Genetics at Rothamsted.[2] But on many occasions his view was sought or his intervention required on matters on which he should not have been troubled: the provision of subsistence allowances for firewatchers sleeping in university buildings, the provision of army, as opposed to civilian, rations for the Officers' Training Corps in their summer camps, the possibility of obtaining equipment for the Training Corps from the local Home Guard, the question of whether honorary degree cere- monies should be continued during the war. All this and much else of a similar sort was the subject of solemn interchanges or enquiries from other vice-chancellors and principals. That is quite apart from the occasions on which he had to smooth the ruffled feathers of principals who felt that they were being left out of consultations, and quite apart again from all the local problems affecting his own university and other institutions in Reading which arose from war-time regulations. By the autumn of 1943 the burden had become too much. In November he was ordered to take a complete rest for two months and had to resign his Chairmanship. He never fully recovered. He was one of Reading's war casualties.

[1] It should be noted that the Sibly papers in URC, Vice-Chancellor, boxes 42–8, contain a considerable number of interchanges with other vice-chancellors which provide comment on the management of the universities during the war. This source has not previously been used.

[2] URC Vice-Chancellor, box 43. Sibly wrote as follows to C. P. Snow: 'I shall be very grateful if you can dig out of the Army a brilliant young fellow, named Fabergé, lately a member of the staff of the Galton Institute of Genetics (formerly at University College, London, but now at Rothamsted). He would surely be very valuble in radio-work or some other scientific field, and he is certainly unfitted by constitution and temperament for a hard life in the Armoured Corps. My personal interest arises from the fact that he was a student of Horticulture here some nine years ago. He made his way into genetic research by sheer ability of the highest order. He is a gifted experimentalist, capable of handling the most delicate instruments. His tale of woe is contained in a letter – copy of which I enclose – written to my colleague, Brierley, who has appealed to me. Professor Fisher of the Galton laboratory is incapable of helping him in present circumstances.'

1 W.M. Childs: portrait by Eric Kennington

2 Alfred Palmer, Hon.D.Sc., 1927: portrait by Sir Arthur Cope

3 Sir Franklin Sibly: portrait by William Dring, 1947

4 Gerald Palmer, 1957

5 The announcement of the Charter: Childs chaired by students 30 May 1925

6 Graduation procession, 6 July 1929 (from left to right, H.A.D. Neville, Knapman, Leonard Sutton, De Burgh, Alfred Palmer, Macebearer, Childs)

7 Old Red Buildings, *c.* 1911

8 The Library, London Road, Degree Day 1975

9 Great Hall and Memorial Tower, London Road, August, 1939, with the turf cut for the Zoology building

10 Physics Research Laboratories, London Road, August 1939

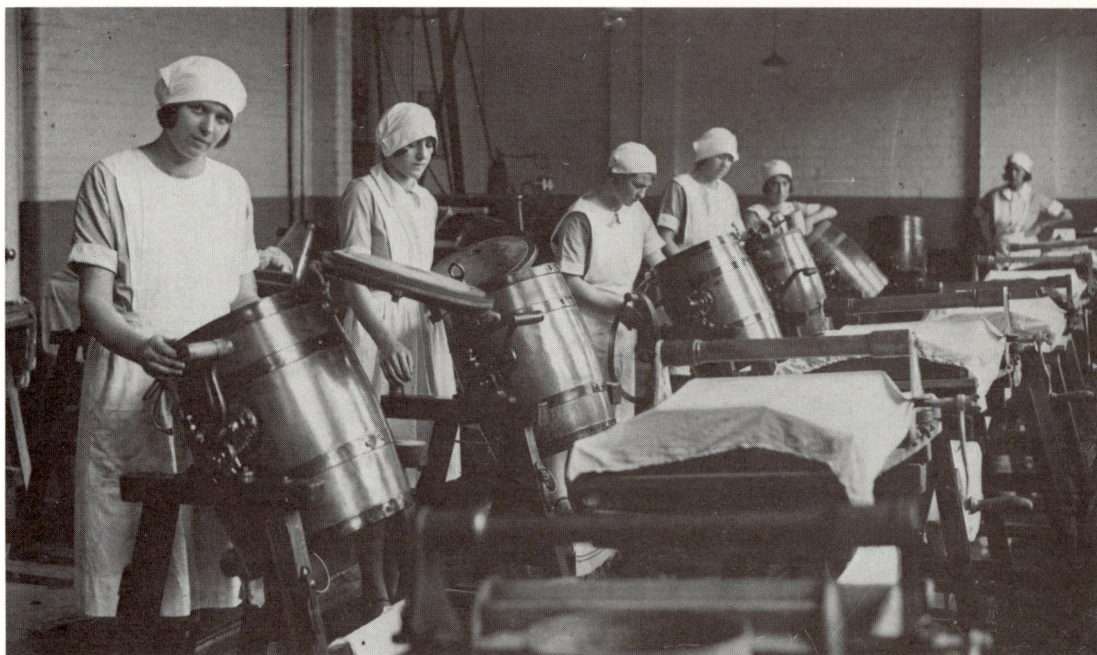

11 Butter making, the Dairy, London Road, *c.* 1927

12 'Agrics', *c.* 1933

13 Sonning Farm, 1975

14 The National Institute for Research in Dairying

15 Cintra Lodge/Ashdown Hall

16 Old Wessex Hall

17 St Patrick's Hall

18 St Andrew's Hall

19 The first Sheep Night, 1928

20 Ashdown Hall, 1929

21 Wantage Hall: the dining hall

22 Wantage Hall

23 The University Orchestra, conducted by Thornton Lofthouse, playing in the air-raid shelters beneath the cloisters, London Road, 1941. Painting by Frank Ormrod

24 Short course on farming for American servicemen, 1943

25 The development plan for London Road, 1944

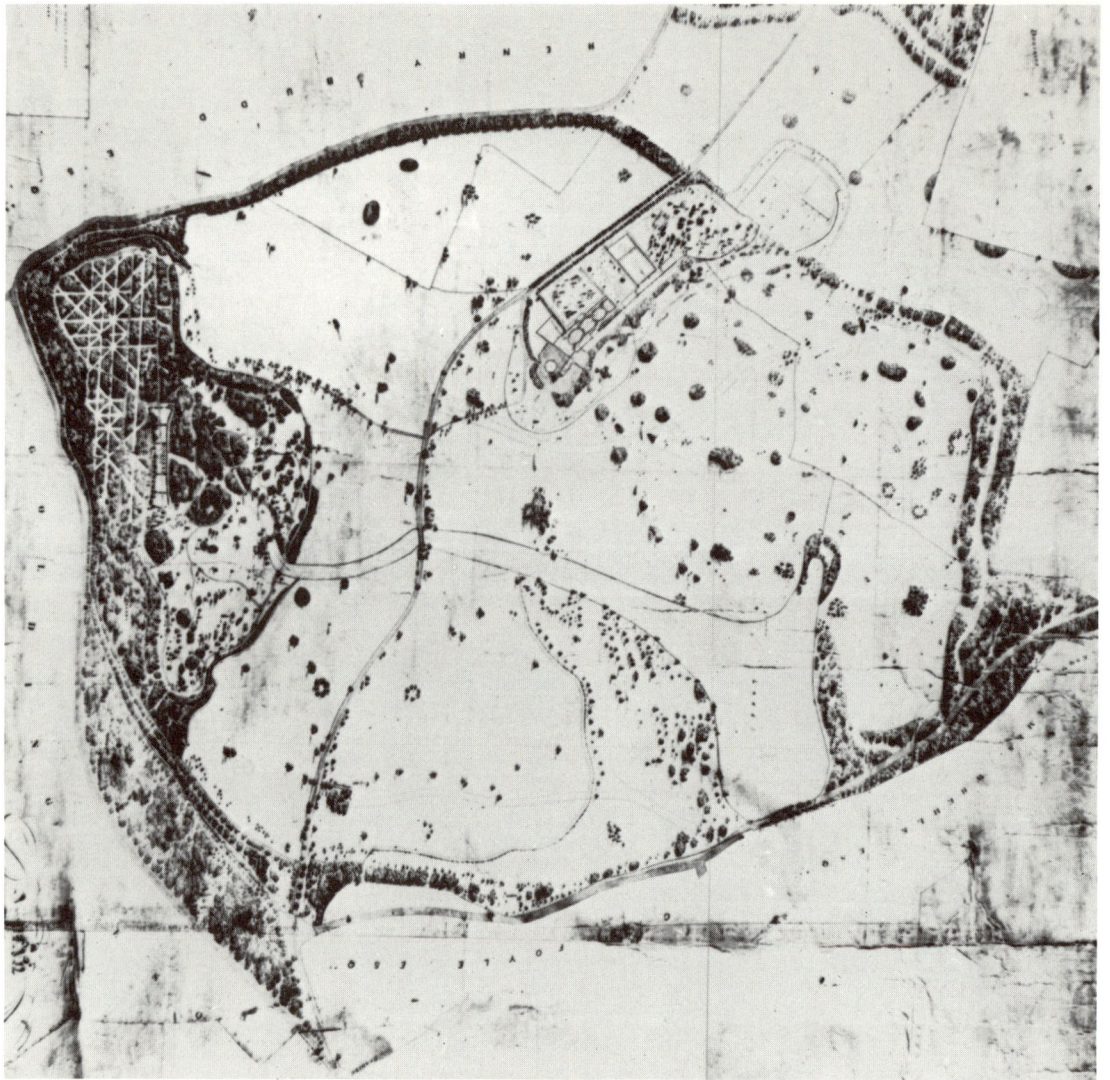

26 Whiteknights, plan of 1844

27 Whiteknights, *c.* 1950, looking west

28 Stenton at work, 1946

29 Stenton at work, 1946

30 Whiteknights, Park House

31 Whiteknights, the Lake

32 Whiteknights, cutting the first turf for the Faculty of Letters: Stenton speaks (from left to right, Stenton, F.L.Preston, Lord Templewood, Howard Robertson, Wolfenden)

33 Whiteknights, cutting the first turf for the Faculty of Letters: Stenton digs

34 Whiteknights, 1966, looking south-east

35 Whiteknights, 1976, looking north-east

36 The opening of the Faculty of Letters by H.M. the Queen, 22 March 1957

37 Fiftieth Anniversary celebrations, 1976: H.R. Pitt and Lord Wolfenden

38 The Faculty of Letters, 1956

39 The Library, Whiteknights, 1964

40 The Palmer Building, 1968

41 The main staircase, Department of
Chemistry

42 Faculty of Urban and Regional Studies, 1973

43 Visitors on the campus, demonstration against the Vice-Chancellor, 13 June 1973

44 Summer term, Whiteknights

45 Wessex Hall, Whiteknights, 1966

46 Netherfield Hall, National College of Food Technology, Weybridge

47 Mrs Annie Ure, student 1911–14, assistant librarian 1917, research fellow in Greek Archaeology 1922–76, Honorary D. Litt. 1976

Prospects 1943-4

In the winter of 1943 the University began to think about its future. There was no great movement of reforming zeal. No one looked ahead to some utopian institution. It was rather that shrewd men of business in the University, as in the rest of the community, saw that the war would be won, and that they would have to try to envisage and plan for what the universities would do on the return of peace. They worked with limited information and with only a hazy view of what the future might hold. A few scientists saw further, but detailed knowledge and experience of the enormous resources and skilled direction which had been applied to their subjects during the war, came chiefly to those whose main effort for the time being lay outside the universities. Moreover, those who sensed most deeply that the post-war world would be different and had to be different, those indeed who would make it different, were in the forces. Not many of those who planned the future of the universities in 1943 later created it. Not many of those who rebuilt or founded universities after the war took part in the planning at this stage. Partly because of this, partly because of the intrinsic difficulty of the task, carried out as it was with little accurate information about objectives and available resources, the planning was ineffectual. Some of it was quaint. At Reading it was done without the benefit of guidelines from the University Grants Committee or any government department. The University simply tried to state what it would like to become.

The game was begun in the Committee of Vice-Chancellors and Principals. Sibly as Chairman of the Committee was the driving force. On 11 June 1943 he wrote to the Chairman of the University Grants Committee, Sir Walter Moberly:

We are aware that HM Government now have under consideration the future of education in Great Britain as a whole. In that future the universities are anxious to play their full part; and we therefore venture to draw attention both to the duties which the public may expect them to perform and the present inadequacy of their means of performance.

Their duties will fall under the two heads of education and research. Under the first head, the universities will be called upon to deal, not only with a great number, but also with a greater variety of students. . . . Under the second head, fundamental research has always been a charge upon university resources, and its importance has been emphasized by the experience of the war and by the many schemes now under discussion for extending the application of science to the whole field of social and industrial reconstruction. But it has not, perhaps, been sufficiently realized how greatly this charge upon university resources has been increased . . . by the growing expense of pure research itself . . . and by the demands made on universities for the postgraduate training of research workers.

We invite therefore a review of the financial implications of the expansion which national policy will require the universities to undertake, both in the immediate future and over the next ten or twenty years. We submit that this review should be specially directed (1) to the capital and maintenance costs of new lands and buildings, (2) to the cost of maintaining adequate teaching establishments adequately paid (the problem of university teachers' salaries, already acute is likely to become more so after this war), and (3) to the cost of maintaining and developing fundamental research.

He ended the letter with a statement of faith which came more easily and was accepted more readily then than now, but which is still true both in principle and detail:

We are very conscious of the responsibilities of the universities in the building of the future. To a great extent the successful development of a stable democracy depends on the advancement of knowledge and the power to reason and make judgments. If the universities are to carry out their mission it is imperative that the importance of their work should be more widely recognized. This can only be achieved if they are freed from the constant anxieties of finance and if, in addition, adequate funds are provided to enable all those who would profit by the education which the universities can give, to have the opportunity of receiving it.[1]

In his own university Sibly did not wait for a reply from the Grants Committee.[2] On 1 July 1943 the Senate elected a committee to consider the post-war development of the University. It met for the first time on 22 October and completed its work on 10 April 1944 when, in its thirteenth meeting, it approved a draft report to Senate. The committee was composed of the Vice-Chancellor, the Deputy Vice-Chancellor, Stenton, the three Deans of the Faculties, Dewar, Miller and H. A. D. Neville, and Betts, Crowther, Hodges and Rae.

Sibly was anxious to ensure that the issues were debated as generally as

---

[1] URC Registrar, box 70. This contains copies of correspondence on post-war development and the Registrar's set of working papers of the Development Committee. All references to external and internal correspondence are from this file except for the submissions by heads of department. On these see below, p. 119, n. 2.
[2] Letters from the UGC requesting details and costs of proposals for post-war development were not sent out until 8 November.

possible. He sought the opinions of all heads of department, emphasizing that they should express 'whatever opinions they had formed on the general problem of university development . . . not only with immediate reference to the post-war years but also with the ulterior development of the University in constant view'.[1] Throughout the summer he received memoranda from faculties and departments. He circulated copies or summaries of these on 28 September in time for the first meeting of the committee, and the committee used them as a basis for its work.

These memoranda and the subsequent papers and minutes of the committee lay bare the University's view of its future as it saw it in the winter of 1943–4.[2] It was impossible, as indeed Sibly put it to the Registrar, 'to forecast the exact nature of the problems by which universities will be confronted when the war is over'.[3] In writing to the Chairman of the University Grants Committee Sibly had written prophetically of enabling all those who could profit by it to enjoy a university education. Within his own university he was only too conscious of the constraints on such a policy:

> There are two considerations which, in my own mind, are fundamental to the inquiry. The first is the question of the maximum extent to which the number of students can be increased without detriment to the character and well-being of the University. I do not feel that a policy of unlimited expansion, even if it were practicable, would be desirable for a university which has acquired the characteristics imposed on Reading by its history and geographical position. My second point is that unless the population in and around the town of Reading increases beyond any probable estimate, any considerable expansion of the University must depend on the provision of more halls of residence.[4]

The second consideration has affected the development of the University throughout its history. It is still the most important single constraint on its expansion. But the first is altogether different. It was, as Sibly saw, an expression of all that Reading had stood for hitherto. It had been a small university. Sibly did not see that it could be otherwise. This view was shared by a majority of his colleagues. As discussion advanced during the summer and autumn the target became clearly defined: Reading should not go beyond a maximum of 1,000 students.

---

[1] Vice-Chancellor to Registrar, 20 July 1943.
[2] The committee papers in URC Registrar, box 70, include a set of submissions from heads of department and others, but many of these are in summary form as prepared for the Committee. The original submissions, with covering letters, and draft summaries, still survive in URC Registrar, box 219. Quotations below have been taken from the originals. The original submissions which were circulated to the committee complete, or nearly so, were those of Stenton, H. A. D. Neville, Edgar Thomas, Capstick and Kay, and Peyton, the Librarian. The summaries are not completely reliable.
[3] Vice-Chancellor to Registrar, 20 July 1943.
[4] *Ibid.*

The matter was summarized succinctly in the first item recorded in the business of the Committee at its first meeting of 22 October:

> The University should be kept relatively small, for any large increase would destroy its present corporate character. It could never become a regional university. The optimum number of 1,000 students represents an increase of more than 30 per cent over the average of approximately 700 during the last fifteen years. Such increase is dependent on the provision of new halls of residence, owing to the limitations of local supply of students.[1]

This was a clear guide-line. Those conversant with such minutes may detect a slight note of unease. The addition of 300 students is noted and magnified as a 30 per cent increase; the case stated depends essentially on accommodation; in the record 'could' is amended from 'should'. Moreover as Sibly indicated in introducing the matter the point was one of several which had 'general but not necessarily universal agreement'. Perhaps even more important was that all those who submitted memoranda as heads of department stated desiderata and objectives which *in toto* were quite inconsistent with the proposed limitation on size. All except a few agreed that Reading should remain small. Yet almost to a man they wanted developments which in sum could be supported only by a far larger institution. The satisfaction they derived from membership of a small community and the apparent strength of the case for remaining small were in conflict with their academic dreams.

The case for a larger future was argued mainly by the Faculty of Agriculture. Most of the Faculty's activities had continued to develop during the war. Between 1929 and 1932 it had numbered on average 225 full-time and postgraduate students, 32 per cent of a total of 706. It comprised 276, 41 per cent of a total of 698, in 1938–9.[2] In 1943–4 it had expanded to 353 full-time students constituting 52 per cent of a total of 683. H. A. D. Neville, as Dean, tried hard to justify and extend this in his letter to the Vice-Chancellor of 18 August:

> The one point of general policy on which I must ask a question is whether there is, or is not, to be any artificial restriction on the growth of the Faculty of Agriculture. Is it to be allowed to expand as the demand for its services increases and every effort be made to meet its financial and other needs, or is it to be argued that its growth must be kept in step with that of other faculties lest the University, as a whole, becomes too lop-sided? I have noticed a recent tendency in some quarters to take the latter view and I should have been more concerned about it than I have been, if I had believed that this is a policy which can ultimately prevail. The growth of the agricultural

---

[1] Minutes of Committee, 22 October 1943.
[2] These figures and percentages are contained in a table on student numbers included with the Registrar's minutes of the first meeting of the Committee.

work of the University has been a natural one from the start. It took root here from the beginning and has grown without any artificial stimulus. In fact, during a considerable period, it grew in face of considerable discouragement. Even within my time it was allowed, for example, two professorships only and was consequently a negligible factor in all decisions of the old Academic Board. There were other general restrictions of a similar kind. . . . Your letter does not require me to rake up past history but the general point is important. If absolutely no general restrictions – financial, residential accommodation, etc. – are placed on the Faculty's growth, I believe it will double its present size in the next twenty years.

That may seem a small statistical conclusion to a somewhat rhetorical exordium. But Neville was clear enough on where it would lead in practice:

If I am right in all this, the mere quantitative adjustment of Faculty facilities to meet the public demand becomes a very big matter, in fact so big that I doubt whether anyone would dare put even the most general kind of plan on paper. For it would lead, in my opinion, to the establishment of a School of Agriculture on some other than the main University site. . . . The natural thing would be for the Faculty of Agriculture to move out, so that it might not only have room to grow itself but also that it might leave room for the growth of other faculties.

The argument did not gain support. There were some others, especially among the scientists, who were ready to advocate or accept some expansion. E. H. Neville and Crowther were ready to envisage an increase in numbers in the hope of improving the academic quality of their students. Bassett maintained that the present number of students was:

too small to support properly all the activities, academic and otherwise which (the University) endeavours to perform. It seems to me that a minimum of 1,000 to 1,500 full-time day students should be arrived at and that a proportionate increase in halls of residence and other accommodation is called for. Such an increase in student numbers should be possible, and indeed might be greatly exceeded, should the new ideas about a later school leaving age and post-school education fully materialize.

But there was little in this to give support to the Faculty of Agriculture. Furthermore the Faculty was vulnerable: one-third of its students were reading, not for a degree, but for a diploma. Neville's letter of 18 August indicated that the Faculty was trying to get rid of such courses, but he did not make a major point of it.[1] Others did. From Chemistry Bassett argued that the University:

---

[1] Indeed, in considering the Faculty's possible commitments to the Intermediate Examination he included the diploma-work in his estimate of staffing requirements. Moreover he discussed the possibility of providing a further course of this kind in Rural Domestic Science.

should refuse to accept the large proportion of agricultural students
which is far more fitted for the farm institute type of training than for
the university type. Students in this category simply clog our
machinery.

Moreover, Bassett and others showed deeply felt concern about the balance
between faculties and subjects. Bassett was trenchant:

In name we are a university, but I think it fair to say that we are
scarcely regarded as such, either by our peers, the other modern
universities, or by the ordinary intelligent person. Many of the people
one meets, who take an interest in higher education, think of Reading
either as an agricultural college or as some queer kind of university
which teaches only agriculture. Some drastic steps will need to be
taken to get our reputation firmly established on the university level.
The first and most important is to establish a proper balance between
the three faculties.

Betts maintained that 'an increase in the number of university students is
necessary but should be controlled in relation to the balance between different departments'.[1] Miller, as Dean of the Faculty of Science, was emphatic:
'Expansion should be encouraged especially in Letters, and to a less extent
in Science (up to the limit of our laboratory accommodation when fully
expanded). The present predominance of Agriculture destroys the balance
of university life'.

The policy which Neville feared prevailed. At its first meeting on 22 October the Committee was presented with student numbers which clearly indicated the increasing proportion of agricultural students. It noted:

Restriction on the growth of the Faculty of Agriculture.
Accommodation will control growth, unless Agriculture is to expand
at the expense of Letters and Science, and at the possible price of
their ultimate extinction. It might be necessary to adopt a deliberate
policy of preserving a reasonable balance between the numbers in
the three faculties within the University.

One curious feature of this discussion is that Neville's case was founded on
an argument which was later to determine the whole course of university
development: the demand for student places. But the Robbins Report was
still in the future, and Neville failed to disturb the general view that Reading
should remain relatively small. This was held across the whole spectrum of
the University; by Miller who as Dean of the Faculty of Science noted
'1,000, not more, as the optimum size of a university such as Reading', by
O'Donoghue who submitted that 'a marked increase would destroy one of
the most desirable features of our university life, namely, the possibility of
close contact between members of the staff and students and between students pursuing different courses of study', within Neville's own Faculty by

[1] This is taken from the summary and not from Betts's submission, which is not
included in box 219.

Rae who suggested that 'a student body of not more than 1,000 would appear to be the optimum', and by Brierley of Agricultural Botany who maintained that 'any increase in student numbers or increase or dispersal of departments should be watched with jealous care. Perhaps student numbers could increase by 10–15 per cent with safety'. To Wolters of Psychology it was a matter not simply of tradition, convenience or feasibility, but of the known distribution of academic ability within the population:

> From 3 to 4 per cent of the population are sufficiently endowed with intelligence to succeed on a degree course. From this number of potential undergraduates there must be deducted (a) those absorbed by other types of high grade training, (b) the temperamentally or physically unfit, (c) those who choose not to attend universities and (d) the wastage of the social and educational systems. Collating these points with the census returns and the university statistics it became clear to me a few years ago that British universities were moving towards a crisis, disguised for the moment by the impact of the 'post-war bulge'. The birth rate has been falling for many years, and this fact will shortly affect universities. It is important that those who stimulate university policy should be aware of population trends and the now ascertained distribution of intelligence. . . . I am certain that our optimum size would be 1,000 students. To go beyond this is to destroy the essential character of the university we have built. . . . I would rather a lower number than 1,000 than a higher.

Stenton's argument was the most coherent of all:

> The fact which governs all speculation about the future of the University is the absence of any large centre of population from which it can draw students. . . . It is improbable that Reading itself will ever increase materially beyond the level of 100–120,000 individuals. . . . Reading can never become a regional university. This is its good fortune, for a type of university instruction based on and conditioned by the interests of a definite area would limit the range of experiment in a manner fatal to the vitality of higher studies. . . . It is doubtful whether it would be wise to plan for the expansion of Reading into a large university – that is, a university of more than in round numbers 1,000 students working for degrees. A small university has obvious weaknesses, but at least it provides a quiet setting for the kind of individual capable of intellectual activity. There is a real danger to the higher developments of university work in conditions determined by the mass-production of graduates. The number of persons capable of profiting from university work is by no means unlimited, and it would probably be wise to aim at the development of a comparatively small undergraduate community, of which the standard was so far as possible controlled by entrance and scholarship examinations of a type which looked for intellectual quality rather than proficiency in school exercises.

Stenton's policy was: 'keep it small and keep it good'.[1] In his submission to
the Vice-Chancellor this was developed by linking his analysis of resources
and practical possibilities to his insistence on academic excellence and the
need to build on Reading's established strengths:

> If Reading is to be small it is important that it should at least aim
> at distinction. . . . It may be suggested that in the future the claim of
> Reading to a respectable place in the university world may be best
> founded on the quality of the research that is carried out there – not
> in competition with other places, but by taking advantage of its
> fortunate local situation. For research in any Letters subject, the
> geographical advantages of Reading are unique, or at least are only
> equalled by those possessed by colleges situated in London. In so far
> as the materials for research are laid up in Oxford, Reading is un-
> rivalled in this respect by London itself. . . . An increase in the num-
> ber of professorships and lectureships in charge is clearly desirable.
> There are many subjects which have so developed in the past genera-
> tion that their control is beyond the effective power of a single
> professor. A fully developed university ought for instance to have
> professors of both Modern and Medieval History. It is an open
> question whether expansion at Reading should run along this line,
> or take the form of the institution of chairs or senior lectureships in
> subjects as yet unrepresented here. In the Faculty of Letters, the
> question is affected by the uncertainty as to the demand for 'Modern
> Studies' which do not give any particular teaching qualification, but
> are useful for social workers and as a preparation for secretarial posts.
> It is perhaps doubtful how far the university would be wise to spend
> on these less co-ordinated studies money otherwise available for the
> fundamental Letters subjects which provide a basis for research.

Stenton's vision was clear but sharply focused both by his own profession
and his experience as Deputy Vice-Chancellor. The future it envisaged
would be adequate for most historians. It was probably all that was feasible
within any reasonable estimate of future resources. Whether the intellectual
excellence which was Stenton's chief objective could be achieved in the pure
and applied sciences without the exploration of new fields of study, without
the development of completely new subjects and degree courses, without
the diversification and accompanying increase in numbers which he wished
to limit, were questions which no one as yet could frame or answer.

Yet in a sense the submissions from heads of department provided the
material for an answer. Each one of them, often in a modest way, wanted to
add to and round off the work in his subject. Typical of some was the firmly
held assertion of Ure:

> In England the basis of humane studies is the literature and cultural

---

[1] Conversation with the author, 1966. The remark concerned the Graduate Centre
for Medieval Studies. Compare below pp. 147–9.

achievements of England, France, Greece and Rome, and the first
requisite is the establishment of separate chairs of Greek and Latin.
The professor of Greek, besides being in charge of his part of the
Classical curricula, should have the important duty of seeing that
students of Latin and English literature have the kind and quantity
of Greek essential for their studies.

Others were ready to introduce major university subjects simply to provide
a service for established courses. Dewar wanted a lecturership in Law and
Public Administration as 'the most urgent need' in Social Sciences; Rae
argued that some such provision was also desirable for the agricultural degrees. Others again wanted larger developments which would add to the
work of their faculties. Some expressed concerns which could only be met by
a significant increase in the size and diversity of the University. There was a
wondrous variety of opinion.

First, in the Faculty of Letters, it was generally held that language studies
should be extended to include Italian and Spanish; Ure and Hodges also
wanted Russian, and Ure included Scandinavian languages as a fourth area
of expansion. Dewar also wanted Hellenistic and modern Greek, medieval
and Renaissance Latin, and a lecturer in phonetics to serve all the language
departments. It is clear that some development within these fields had wide
support. Secondly, some members of the Faculty were concerned for social
sciences. At Reading these were still in an embryonic state. They still passed
under the generic title of Political Economy or, more mysteriously, Modern
Studies. The basic elements of the case were put forward by Budden, the
Lecturer in Charge:

> In this University, a course in Political Economy, or for a degree in
> which the subject is studied jointly with others, should be modest in
> pretensions, realistic, and aimed at enlarging the student's power of
> understanding and expression by presenting him with problems which
> only clear-headed and systematic analysis can comprehend and by
> requiring him to read, above all, those classics of governmental, legal
> and economic science whose abundance makes the subject so emin-
> ently suitable a study for the growing mind. . . . There should be an
> Honours Degree in Political Economy. . . . A department of Political
> Economy should be encouraged to *grow* in this University. It needs
> only two staff members at first, though if the number of students
> quickly grows, more help would be needed.

This was a very modest assertion. It was supported by Wolters who wanted
to see Modern Studies 'developed with a view to openings not only in the
civil and colonial service, but also in industry and commerce'. But it was
Hodges who argued the point with vision and real passion:

> Our starting-point should be our social task. Learning pure for its
> own sake is today an indefensible frivolity. Economic, social and
> perhaps political changes are coming which will make the impact of
> social responsibility upon educated people stronger than it was at

any time in the liberal era. Increasing numbers will be directly
employed in social services. All will have to become actively interested
in social affairs if the concentration of power in the hands of a planning bureaucracy is to be balanced as it should be by an effective
public opinion. The educational system and in particular the universities have the task of launching people into the world with the
right kind of awareness, the right kind of knowledge and wisdom for
this. . . . It is not enough (though it is not a bad thing in itself) to
put students through special courses in 'civics' or 'citizenship' devoted
mainly to the descriptive study of economic and political institutions.
The information so gained is necessary, but equally necessary is an
appreciation of the quality of the human life that runs through this
institutional framework, and a knowledge of the psychological, social
and cultural forces which make it what it is.

He went on to urge that the curriculum should include a course devoted to
the study of current economic and political institutions along with recent
history of the last twenty-five years and a general course in world history
'to make clear the main cultural centres and creative periods'. He hoped
that it was 'common ground that the social sciences need to be more fully
represented in the University. The place is intellectually unbalanced
without them.'

In the Faculty of Science expansion was envisaged in a much less dramatic fashion. In Physics Crowther urged the need to establish electronics
as a postgraduate course; he also wanted a Chair in Mathematical Physics
or Applied Mathematics. In Chemistry Bassett envisaged expansion but
did not emphasize any new field of work. But E. H. Neville in Mathematics,
Harris in Botany and O'Donoghue in Zoology all had new proposals for
statistics, ecology and entomology respectively. However, the most
interesting aspect of the Faculty's response lay not in its new proposals but
in its general concern for the standing of science, especially physical science,
at Reading. E. H. Neville asserted:

The Honours School of Mathematics is too small to be healthy for
either students or staff. . . . The problem is insoluble so long as
Cambridge and Oxford are in a different education universe from
the other universities of the country. . . . Meanwhile, the only hope
of amelioration lies in emphasizing quality rather than quantity in
plans for expansion of the University. For general stability it is
probably sufficient to double the size of the University . . . if more
halls of residence are provided and the expansion is differentiated in
favour . . . of subjects proper to a university and against commerce
and the most elementary courses in domestic subjects. But for
intellectual prosperity it is essential to provide a stable student
nucleus in every honours school, and the only hope of doing this is to
multiply the number of attractive scholarships by ten or twelve.

To buttress his plaint he instanced as 'proper subjects' not sciences, but fine art, psychology and modern languages. Crowther of Physics pursued the argument more consistently:

> I anticipate, according to the best information I have been able to collect that the output of graduates in physics, throughout the country, may require to be doubled, to meet forseeable demands.
> It does not follow that each university will participate *pro rata* in the increase. The Norwood Report recommends that government grants to students should cover all necessary expenses, and that the system of allocating the grants to specific universities (as is done with the present State Bursaries) should be established. The modern universities will therefore have to be content with the residue which is unable to get into Oxford or Cambridge, since, as expense will no longer be any deterrent, most students will for obvious reasons try to get places in the older universities. If England really requires more than two real universities this policy is unfortunate. Nothing would more quickly and surely raise the status of the modern universities than the allocation to each of them of a fair proportion of first class student material.

Bassett's views were roughly similar:

> The judgment passed upon a university by other universities depends (i) upon the quality and success of its graduates, (ii) upon the reputation of its staff as teachers and (iii) upon the research work it produces. I do not propose to say anything about (i) and (ii) as I believe that these two factors are reasonably satisfactory. This does not apply to (iii) and I consider that the most important step which must be taken to improve our post-war position and reputation is to tackle seriously this factor. The poor output of research work of an academic standard appears to arise from three main causes: first, an unfortunately considerable number of the members of the university staff – both senior and junior – take little or no real interest in such matters; secondly the lack of postgraduate students to assist in such work; and thirdly the many calls of domestic, administrative and teaching duties on the time and energy of those members of staff who are interested in research work. . . . An endeavour should be made to secure money for a large number of postgraduate scholarships and fellowships, and by large I mean not less than twenty new appointments per annum in each of the three Faculties. I consider that, with a few exceptions perhaps, this is far more important than founding new professorships or appointing more lecturers. . . . It need scarcely be pointed out that the creation of a body of senior students . . . should be of great value in giving balance to our student body. This has suffered much from its immaturity and from the very small proportion of academically minded students which it contains.

In these views there was real unease, deepened perhaps by the primitive state of national planning for the universities. For the physical scientists above all this crystallized into a problem of equipment. The quandary was fairly put by Crowther:

> A considerable capital sum will be required to re-equip the
> Department, as purchases have been practically impossible to make
> during the last four years, and increased numbers will demand
> considerable reduplication of apparatus. A largely increased annual
> laboratory grant will be required for upkeep, and special grants for
> research apparatus. . . . At the end of the war, a very large amount
> of valuable apparatus will become available ex-government stores.
> It would be most helpful, if, instead of selling this off at knock-down
> prices as after the last war, the government would transfer it to some
> suitable body . . . for distribution to university departments.

No one as yet could do more than guess where the necessary resources were to come from.

This was very different in the Faculty of Agriculture. Here there was a well used channel to government resources and the Faculty as a whole was ready to plan for the future with confidence. The Dean wanted to see a properly established Department of Bacteriology and a total reorganization of the School of Dairying. The latter point was urged again by Capstick and Kay from the National Institute for Research in Dairying. All three emphasized the need to recast both teaching and research in dairying in a form suitable to a large-scale science-based industry. That the Ministry of Agriculture was apparently willing to provide assistance gave strength to the case. They wanted nothing less than a newly built 'technological institute of adequate size and scope to act as a national centre for advanced dairy education, particularly applied to the distribution and manufacturing industries'. They were ready to envisage capital expenditure of £100,000. Kay in particular was more generally sanguine:

> It would seem that a combination of circumstances now brings to
> Reading University the opportunity of developing into a great
> national and Empire centre for agricultural, animal husbandry,
> dairying and veterinary medical training, research and advisory
> work, with a postgraduate school which would attract promising
> young graduates from all over the world.

Others carried the argument further. Both Rae and Stoughton looked to a future in which the University would revolve round agricultural studies. For Rae:

> Reading could, if it wished, develop into the recognized University
> of Rural Culture. This would mean that much of the major activities
> of the University, not only in science but also in the humanities,
> would be directed to the study of rural and agrarian problems in all
> their various aspects – scientific, technical, economic, sociological,
> political, historical etc. If this development was accepted it would
> mean that the hallmark of everyone of our alumni would be that he

or she had an awareness of, and some familiarity with, the rural
problem both in its absolute state and in its relationship to national
and international well being.

For Stoughton:

A realization of the history and geographical associations of Reading
leads one to the conclusion that its future must lie in the direction
of the rural, rather than the industrial or purely academic aspects
of teaching and research. While the arts and the pure sciences should
in any university be unfettered and unbiased in development, a closer
degree of integration with the agricultural sciences in this University
would lead, not to any loss, but to a great gain in the status of the
University as a whole. As Birmingham, again for historical and
geographical reasons, has become identified with the industrial aspect
of university training, so Reading might become the recognized
centre for rural culture.

It is clear that some of the arguments advanced by the Faculty were not
such as to command ready acceptance in other quarters. There were serious
problems of demarcation and co-operation between Science and Agriculture. The most rudimentary and basic was one of space. After reviewing
the total exhaustion of laboratory space in his department of Agricultural
Chemistry Neville went on:

I cannot urge that another large laboratory for undergraduate
students should be provided when the Central Chemistry Laboratory
is not fully used. Some of our larger classes will have to be moved
to there but, if this has to be a permanent arrangement, and I
believe it will prove to be so, alterations in the Central Laboratory
arrangements will be necessary. The equipment there is not suitable
for agricultural work; there are no accurate balances and no balance
room to put them in, if they are provided. This limits the use of this
laboratory to qualitative, or the roughest kind of quantitative, work
and makes it available for elementary classes only. Full use can only
be made of the Central Laboratory if at least one of the rooms
occupied by lecturers of the Pure Chemistry Department, is converted
into a balance room. No doubt the Pure Chemistry Department
would want compensation elsewhere.

No doubt indeed. Meanwhile Bassett, of Chemistry, apparently unaware
of the proposed invasion, was himself asking for a considerable increase in
the number of lecturers and the amount of laboratory space including the
doubling of the floor space of the East Chemistry block. There were further
difficulties where departments in the two faculties overlapped in their
work. H. A. D. Neville was plainly dissatisfied with the provision made
for the Intermediate course for his students in the Faculty of Science:

There is one other matter which might, or might not, necessitate
additional expenditure in the Faculty of Agriculture. I refer to the
teaching of chemistry and botany to Intermediate students. In my

opinion, this teaching will have to be removed sooner or later, from
the Faculty of Science. At present, students arrive in the Faculty
of Agriculture, in the first year of their final work, with the wrong
kind of preparation for their course. An obvious question in connection with this suggestion is whether, if this change were made for
chemistry and botany, it would also be demanded for physics,
zoology and geology. I think no such demand could be put forward
within the period under consideration.

At this point the two faculties were already very involved in the difficult
and perennial problem of the provision of service courses for non-specialists.

It would be wrong to leave the impression that the boundary between
Science and Agriculture was marked by conflict, actual or potential. On
the contrary, it is very obvious in the submissions to the Vice-Chancellor
that many science departments welcomed and benefited from co-operative
effort with the Faculty of Agriculture. In Zoology O'Donoghue shared the
Faculty of Agriculture's interest in the development of physiology and
entomology; he also hinted at a possible development of veterinary studies,
as did H. A. D. Neville. In Geology Hawkins wanted to provide an introductory course distinct from the normal Intermediate course, specifically
for students in the Faculty of Agriculture. In Mathematics E. H. Neville
wanted to appoint a statistician who would serve the Faculty of Agriculture
as well as his own department. Although none of the scientists was ready to
concur in the numerical preponderance of the Faculty of Agriculture, there
were few who did not envisage some advantage in extending their own
co-operation with it.

In the development of economics the Faculty undoubtedly led the way
for the whole University. The pleas for the development of social sciences
advanced from the Faculty of Letters left economics out of the scheme.[1]
The subject figured in the course in Political Economy and in non-degree
courses in the Commerce Department, but it also played an important role
in the Faculty of Agriculture, where Agricultural Economics was an essential component of the degree course. H. A. D. Neville now wanted to
established a department of agricultural economics:

> I do not believe that the study of agriculture itself can be advanced
> without the participation of an active Department of Agricultural
> Economics. It is the only science, if science it be, which can give any
> rational explanation of the great mass of material now taught as
> husbandry. Further, it must be a main prop in any Honours degree
> in agriculture. If any Honours degree in that subject were merely a
> question of knowing twice as much husbandry as is required for a
> Pass degree, it would be a failure. The difference should be one of
> kind not of magnitude.

[1] The old Department of Economics in the Faculty of Letters was renamed
Political Economy in 1944.

That had the root of the matter in it, and it was supported by a cogently argued statement from Edgar Thomas, at this time Lecturer in Charge:

The most important point which I wish to make is the undesirability of considering the future of Agricultural Economics in this University apart from the future of Political Economy. A Department of Political Economy is an essential part of our University. But there are reasons for the view that the development of such a department in Reading can be only on a modest scale. An integration of the department of Political Economy with that of Agricultural Economics opens out, however, a much more ambitious prospect of development. Two obvious benefits would be the following. First, it would avoid any needless duplication and dissipation of resources both in staff and in equipment. Second, it would provide a splendid opportunity for co-operation between two faculties which at present have hardly any point of contact. . . .

There remains the question of research. I may perhaps be permitted to state, without being misunderstood, that the record of our Faculty of Agriculture in the field of research does not compare with its reputation in teaching. So far as the past is concerned this is understandable and the reasons are not far to seek. But it seems to me that the development of fundamental research must figure more prominently in the future if we are to maintain our position in the agricultural sphere. I feel confident that a well-equipped Department of Economics has a real part to play in any such development. I also feel that consideration of research activities strengthens the case for the integration of the two departments of economics in this University. In most of the provincial universities research work in economics is concentrated on and inspired by the problems of their industrial and urban hinterlands. In Reading our hinterland is farming and the countryside. I would urge that a concentration of our economic research work on the rural problem provides one opportunity for making an important contribution to 'the essential part [we have] to play in the national work of post-war reconstruction' mentioned in the first sentence of the Vice-Chancellor's letter.

Thomas wanted to go well beyond this limited statement. He noted that the University had submitted to the Luxmoore Committee the suggestion that agriculture might be included as a subject for non-agricultural students:

Such a suggestion should have a special appeal to our University which is so vitally concerned with the existence of an intelligent public opinion on agriculture. In later life many of our students will find it useful to have an understanding of agriculture and its problems even though they themselves will have no direct connection with the farming industry. It seems to me that for this purpose the economic and social approach is the one most suitable to the non-agricultural student. Furthermore, agricultural

economics can be made to provide a practical link between the social
and the other sciences, and this should be of special significance in
our University where agriculture is firmly established and where the
social sciences are attempting to break new ground.

Thomas was not alone in thinking that something should be done to
erode the divisions between accepted disciplines. Hodges wanted to give
arts students a year on a natural-science subject. Wolters wanted a degree
course in psychology in the Faculty of Science. Miller thought that more
general courses were desirable and that 'there should be more interdepartmental co-operation between departments for students pursuing
specialised courses.' Harris wanted a further broadening of the B.Sc.
General course so that the first year should include biology, physics and
chemistry, geology and geography. Hawkins was ready to provide a
short course on 'some civil engineering aspects of geology . . . for advanced
students of the Faculty of Agriculture and others'. He also thought that a
short course on geological principles and philosophy should be arranged,
'especially for students in the Faculty of Letters. This would be the most
valuable contribution that the Department could make to the cultural life
of the University'.

This was one point where the varied submissions from departments came
together to reflect a common experience. There were others. Almost every
submission insisted on the need for academic excellence. Almost everyone
maintained that more scholarships, studentships and fellowships should be
made available, that more funds should be provided to reinforce research.
Many emphasized the urgency of establishing adequate salaries for university lecturers. Some wanted proper arrangements for sabbatical leave.
All wanted proper facilities for research: for the Library, for laboratories
and for the essential equipment. Some, Hodges and Miller, wanted a
four-year degree course. Others, in particular Dewar and Stenton, wanted
to terminate evening classes and non-degree work and limit extra-mural
classes to the immediate locality of Reading. All were conscious of the
overriding considerations of cost and limited accommodation.

The Committee had to lick all this into shape. In its first meeting it
not only accepted the limit of 1,000 students[1] but also agreed that courses
of 'sub-university' standard should as far as possible be eliminated. Thereafter it had to fit its proposals within a clearly defined limit. It also recognized that the ultimate outcome would be a set of practical proposals
submitted to the University Grants Committee. It had no indication of what
might be available as new capital or recurrent grants. Hence it set out to
err, if at all, on the side of moderation. It also sought to distinguish between
urgent developments envisaged for the first five years after the war and
longer-term projects. In a very practical way it postponed larger, more

[1] This figure included those reading for first degrees, post-graduate diplomas,
diplomas in Fine Art and Social Studies and research students.

debatable schemes to a more distant, less certain, future.

The resulting proposals were modest. In its sixth meeting, on 17 December 1943, after considering priorities submitted by boards of faculties it drew up a list of desirable academic appointments. This included one new Professorship: in either Latin or Greek.[1] The Faculty of Letters had asked for four new lecturers, the Faculty of Science for six and the Faculty of Agriculture for an unspecified number which it costed at £3,000 per annum. Under the heading of new developments the Faculty of Letters sought lecturerships in Spanish and Italian, the Faculty of Agriculture and Horticulture a Lecturer in Law, and the Faculty of Science nothing at all. The total under the heading of expansion, along with demonstratorships and other ancillary appointments came to £12,125, with the new developments estimated at a further £1,550. It was noted that £12,125 represented approximately 20 per cent of the salary bill of 1938–9. These proposals were subsequently rearranged between expansion and new developments. At the next meeting of the Committee on 7 January 1944 Crowther provided a new development in the Faculty of Science in the form of a Chair of Mathematical Physics. This was ultimately included as an independent Lecturership in Applied Mathematics. With that addition the proposals were embodied in the final report to Senate and Council.[2]

The Committee was also very concerned that university work should be properly done. It met the many expressions of concern from departments by proposing an established scale of salaries and grading.[3] Once again it was moving, if not in the dark, at least in the gloaming. The Vice-Chancellor wrote to other universities, Manchester and Bristol, to discover what was done there. It also tackled the problem of the Library. Here it recommended a capital grant of £7,000 to cover deficiencies and new developments, and an increase in annual grant of roughly 50 per cent to a total of £3,000 per annum. It also proposed that the total staff of six,[4] should be increased by two assistant librarians.[5] It attempted to meet some of the ancillary requirements in the Faculties of Science and Agriculture by proposing the establishment of senior scholarships for research students who would also act as part-time demonstrators. But it had no recommendations at all on the provision of equipment and running expenses for the science departments. In the original submissions from departments, Crowther alone had emphasized that special steps would be necessary to meet these needs. The question was not minuted at a meeting of heads of

[1] The intention was to establish Chairs of both Latin and Greek. The proposal took this form because Ure, the Professor of Classics, could occupy either.
[2] The Report is reproduced below, Appendix 5, pp. 347–52.
[3] Minutes of eighth meeting, 21 January 1944, and twelfth meeting, 14 March 1944. Specific recommendations were included in the Report to Council but not to Senate. See below, Appendix 5, pp. 348–9.
[4] The staff was the Librarian, two senior assistant librarians, one full-time clerk and two attendants. See Lady Stenton's comments below, Appendix 4, p. 345.
[5] Minutes of seventh meeting, 7 January 1944.

department of the Faculty of Science on 26 October 1943; this was concerned with requirements for space and clerical assistance. Equipment
never figured in the business of any of the Committee's meetings and there
was no reference to it in the final report.

Accommodation overshadowed everything else. No one doubted and
many stressed that the University could scarcely expand at all unless
residential places were increased. Old halls of residence would have to be
extended and new ones would have to be built. In its first meeting the Committee estimated that the increase to 1,000 students would necessitate
additions to Wessex, St Andrew's, St George's and possibly Wantage, along
with the construction of a completely new men's Hall.[1] However, it soon
became more cautious. Subsequent discussions of accommodation steered
away from residence and in the final report only very minor recommendations for temporary buildings at Wessex were included as immediate
requirements. There was no site available for a new Hall. Furthermore, the
Committee was by no means certain that the post-war increase in numbers
would be permanent. It turned away from the financial risks involved in
establishing a new Hall and recommended an increase in the number of
licensed lodgings.

One reason for this is that there were many more obvious and urgent
concerns. During the summer department after department had submitted
that its existing accommodation was unsatisfactory or inadequate. Stenton
stated the case in measured phrases:

> The noise of the traffic on the London Road frontage is a serious
> hindrance to the use of the Old Red Building for teaching purposes.
> In many departments of the Faculty of Letters, work is being carried
> on under conditions which, though by no means intolerable, are
> inconvenient and tiring both to lecturers and students. The so-called
> 'History Room', for instance, which opens directly on the main
> university entrance, is singularly ill-fitted to be a place of serious
> study or instruction.

Thornton Lofthouse of the School of Music drew attention to even more
primitive circumstances:

> The building should be installed with electric light. Power is already
> laid on for the use of the radiogram. One of the rooms in the music
> school should be made usable for exclusive use as a gramophone
> room. It should be made as sound-proof as possible.

Wolters summed it all up without mincing words. 'The Faculty [of Letters]
should not be expected to continue indefinitely as slum-dwellers'.

In the Faculty of Science a meeting of heads of departments was called to
discuss accommodation and other matters on 26 October 1943. The Department of Geography alone was satisfied with its existing allotment and could

[1] The Committee considered that the optimum size of a Hall was 120–150 (Minutes
of meeting of 22 October 1943).

even manage some expansion. The Department of Mathematics asserted that its lecture rooms were quite unsuitable. All the laboratory departments reported serious overcrowding, especially in the Intermediate laboratories; they required 50 to 100 per cent more space to do their job properly. The Department of Zoology stated that its present accommodation was already inadequate for its present numbers; it regarded 'with dismay' the possibility of any increase in numbers beyond those at present in attendance. The story was the same in the Faculty of Agriculture and Horticulture. Here every department asked for a new building or extended accommodation. In addition to all this men scattered widely across the University felt that the Library required more space. The Librarian submitted requirements, the most important element in which was the establishment of a stack which had been approved by Council in 1936. Some again were concerned for the general running and appearance of the University. H. A. D. Neville summed this up in drawing attention to:

the complete unsuitability of our present administrative offices,
the lack of a Council and Senate Chamber and the handicap we are
under owing to the appearance of the University from the main road
. . . . Of these I would merely say that I think we sometimes forget
how much we lose through the dreadful external appearance we
present to the general public.

Yet amidst all these requirements the *genius loci* still cast its spell. The first principle laid down in the Committee's final report was 'if possible no encroachment should be made upon the area at present under grass on the main University site'.

The Committee sought the professional advice of the London architect, Verner O. Rees, and was soon involved in the minutiae of planning. The search for economy and the desire to preserve the appearance of the site encouraged notions of adding storeys to, or excavating cellars under, existing buildings. These now leave a piquant trail in the records:

Dear Mr Rees,

Professor Stenton agrees to your asking Mr MacCarthy Fitt to
report to you on the thickness of the walls etc. of the Chemistry block,
in order that you may have the advance information you require.

Neither the Controller of Works nor Collier and Catley's (the
builders) can give with sufficient accuracy the depth of the Library
foundations at the desired point. Please ask Mr Fitt to dig the hole
you wish. I think the hole should be at the S.W. corner, not the S.E.
corner as stated in your letter.

Messrs Collier and Catley report that the ground floor of the
Library is a Kleine floor made of interlocking blocks and reinforced,
but will not state specifically whether or not the floor is independent
of earth support.[1]

[1] Letter of Registrar, 25 November 1943.

In the end the Committee proposed a building programme which was as modest as its proposals for staff: a Senate and Council Chamber, which would release the west wing of the Library, hitherto used for meetings, for a book stack; new buildings for Education, languages, the biological departments and the Faculty of Agriculture, and a modest reconstruction of the unquestionably modest main entrance.[1] All could be achieved without destroying the character of the site. Verner Rees fitted the mood. In February 1944 he came to inspect the Old Red Building and recommended its retention:

> Whilst the building has no great architectural interest, it has, nevertheless, a pleasant air and a modest dignity, and if the University were satisfied with the usefulness of its rooms, its permanent retention might be considered. . . . Succeeding generations, surfeited with modern building, may indeed be pleased to have what may then be a rare specimen of the late eighteenth century.

The Final Report of the Committee was presented to Senate on 17 April and to Council on 5 May. Both approved it without amendment. Many, indeed most, of its recommendations never came about. None of the building was ever put in hand; when Verner Rees wrote to enquire about progress in the summer of 1946 he was informed that the building programme had been held up, partly because of the retirement of Sibly, partly because the University did not know its 'position with regard to views expressed in Government quarters about university expansion'.[2] By then an inner circle in the University knew that Whiteknights was available.[3] The problem of accommodating an expanding university on an inadequate site vanished overnight. But much of the thinking induced by the old site remained. When Wolfenden took up office as Vice-Chancellor in April 1950 the maximum of 1,000 students still stood as a target for expansion. He never even knew how it had come to be established.[4] By then it had been re-examined on several occasions and once at least Senate had agreed to go beyond it.[5] But it died hard. It was a considered assessment of all that Reading had stood for: the intimacy, the familiar contact between teacher and pupil, the shared concern for the University as a whole. To exceed this figure, almost mystic in the spell it cast, was to risk a future uncertain, uncongenial, beyond contemplation.

---

[1] See plate 25.
[2] Letter of Registrar, 10 August 1946.
[3] The first news of Whiteknights came in July 1946. Verner Rees wrote later in March 1947 when it became obvious that his plans for London Road had been overtaken (URC, box 70). He later acted as consultant architect for an extension to St George's Hall.
[4] Conversation with Lord Wolfenden, 22 March 1975.
[5] See below, pp. 147–9.

Chapter 7

Whiteknights 1946 [1]

The consideration of the future of the University in 1943–4 was over-shadowed by the limitations of the site in London Road. Amounting to just over nine acres, it was totally inadequate for all the development envisaged. Moreover the University possessed no suitable alternative. [2] This apparent dead-end helps to explain why, in planning for the future, desirable ideals and realistic limitations were so often in conflict. In their submissions to the Development Committee one or two let their thoughts range over surrounding property. Wolters ended his discussion of the ex-tension of existing Halls by wondering whether a new hall of residence for men could be placed in Whiteknights Park, and Miller took the same line. H. A. D. Neville had argued vigorously for the establishment of the Faculty of Agriculture on a new site [3] and he returned to the need for more land at the end of his submission:

> The question of playing fields also requires consideration. Again the growth of the town may play a big part in the matter. Playing fields at a considerable distance from the University and Halls are not desirable and the acquisition of suitable land, as it becomes available, is very necessary. I believe the Town Council are interested in some way in the future of Whiteknights Park, possibly only in its

[1] Except where otherwise noted this chapter is based on Bursar's Office, files 28/10, 1 & 2 ('Whiteknights Park Estate, General', two files) and 28/18 ('Park House, Upper Redlands Road'); also on URC, Registrar, box 70 (Whiteknights Park Estate, one file). This last is in fact a collection of correspondence and notes of the Vice-Chancellor. Since it includes some of Stenton's drafts it is a very valuable remnant from a crucial period in the University's history.
[2] A note in URC, Registrar, box 70, in the hand of Carpenter, lists the properties in 1946 as:

Main University site	9 acres	Wantage Hall and	
St Andrew's Hall	2 acres	adjoining field	6½ acres
Wessex Hall and		Whitley Park	22 acres
neighbouring properties	7 acres	University Athletic Ground	12 acres
St George's Hall and		University Farm, Sonning	400 acres
neighbouring properties	5½ acres	Horticultural Station	45 acres
Mansfield Hall	1½ acres		
St Patrick's Hall and			
neighbouring properties	7½ acres		

[3] See above, p. 121.

> preservation as an open space. Is any arrangement possible with
> them, so that our present playing fields can be extended?

Stenton above all saw clearly what had to be done. In reviewing the
'chief immediate needs' of the University he placed second only to the
provision of a new hall of residence for men 'the acquisition of every
available site in the neighbourhood and to the south of the present University quadrilateral':[1]

> It is already plain that the latter site is too small for the demands
> which are certain to be made upon it. Apart from demands for
> better accommodation which are certain in time to come from
> the Faculty of Letters, there is an imperative need for a room or
> rooms in which the Council, Senate and Faculties can meet, for a
> Students' Union House and for a building to take the place of the
> present inadequate 'St David's Hall'. Buildings to serve these
> purposes cannot be planted on the present university site without
> changing its character and destroying the sense of space which is
> the principal of all the amenities offered by the University. It
> would probably be wise, even at the present time, to make plans
> for the building of a new St Andrew's Hall on a new site towards
> the south, for the enlargement of the St Andrew's site, and for
> its development so as to serve general university purposes. But
> the history of the University has shown the many disadvantages of
> sporadic action, and the present seems a good opportunity for a
> movement towards the acquisition of whatever land lies between the
> Hospital and Addington Road on one side and between St Andrew's
> Hall and Morgan Road, if not Southern Hill, on the other. In
> fact, the general drift both of policy and of events seems to be
> towards the creation of a university quarter in Reading covering
> the whole district between London Road and the falling ground
> behind St Patrick's Hall and Whitley Park Farm.[2]

Stenton's proposal was one followed by many of the great civic universities both before and after the war. At Reading such serious and prolonged
interference in the life of the local community was to a great extent avoided.
The purchase of Whiteknights Park solved the problem. But if Stenton
was slightly wrong about the site, he was absolutely right about the scale.
Instead of a large campus he had imagined an enormous university precinct.

Whiteknights Park is the remnant of the medieval manor of Earley.[3]
This was held directly of the Crown by a family which took its name from
this seat. One member of the family, a John of Earley who probably
flourished in the early fourteenth century, was nicknamed 'Whiteknight',
and by the beginning of the fifteenth century the manor itself was described

[1] URC, Registrar, box 219.
[2] *Ibid.*
[3] For an elegant and scholarly account of Whiteknights, see Ernest Smith, *A History of Whiteknights* (University of Reading, 1957), on which the following summary is based.

familiarly as 'Whiteknight's'.[1] The name stuck. On the last occasion of the session of the court of the manor in 1840 it was described as the 'manor of Early Regis otherwise Earley Whiteknights';[2] in the passage of time only the original possessive sense of Whiteknight's had been lost. The Earleys sold the manor in 1362. It passed through various families in the later middle ages and in 1606 was bought by Francis Englefield. His descendant, Sir Henry Charles Englefield, sold it to George, Marquis of Blandford, in 1798. The Marquis, who succeeded as fifth Duke of Marlborough in 1817, created the park, laid out the ornamental gardens, including the Wilderness, and planted many of the surviving trees. He also established a lavish library and collection of manuscripts at the house. In 1819, loaded with debt, he had to sell the collection and abandon the house and the park. In 1840 the house was pulled down[3] and in 1849 the estate passed to Sir Isaac Lyon Goldsmid, a member of a firm of London bullion brokers, who played an important part both in the establishment of University College London and in the movement for the political emancipation of the Jews. In 1946 the estate was still in the hands of his descendant, Sir Henry J. D'Avigdor-Goldsmid. In 1867 the park had been divided into six leaseholds on which houses had been built. The estate had thus been preserved from other forms of development. The leases were due to expire by 1958. The total area of the park was nearly 300 acres.

The purchase of Whiteknights was the work of three men: Stenton, Ernest Smith and E. H. Carpenter. All three recognized the opportunity and had the vision and decisiveness necessary to seize it. They were re-inforced by three members of Council: Sir George Mowbray, President of Council, Sir William Mount, Treasurer, and Arthur West, Vice-President of Council and Chairman of the Finance Committee. The surviving records leave no trace at all of any doubt or hesitation on the part of any one of them. To those who have benefited from their work the move to Whiteknights may seem to proceed from an inevitable logic. In fact, it is the result of the opportunism and energy of this small group.

Stenton was the central figure in this. Sibly had fallen gravely ill in January 1946 and tendered his resignation to Council in March. Stenton, who had been Deputy since 1934, took over as acting Vice-Chancellor and succeeded to the office in September. He took responsibility for all the negotiations.[4] By instinct and training he knew what he was about. The

---

[1] The earliest reference to it I have found is of 1401–2: 'in manerio de Erlee vocato Whitknythes' (*Feudal Aids*, i.56). For other early references see E. Smith, *op. cit.*, p. 6.
[2] E. Smith, *op. cit.*, p. 1.
[3] The old house, which stood near the end of Chancellor's Way, was built early in the eighteenth century. It is illustrated in Smith, *op. cit.*, facing pp. 5, 21.
[4] Sibly played no part. On 17 September Carpenter wrote to Stenton in a letter concerned with planning negotiations for Whiteknights: 'A call came through on Saturday [14 September] in regard to this matter, and in the absence of Smith and myself it was taken by Sibly, and if he had a shock at the time he has certainly recovered by this time.' (Bursar, 28/10, 1).

descendant of a country family of small landowners and the son of a lawyer, he still held property in the family home of Southwell and in the open fields of Eakring, Nottinghamshire.[1] A large property transaction came easily to a medieval historian who, to his peers, seemed to be 'grabbing land like a medieval abbot'.[2]

But if Stenton was the central figure, the real initiative came from the Bursar, E. H. Carpenter. Carpenter was one of the most interesting and enigmatic figures at Reading. He husbanded the revenues of the University carefully and strictly. Frequently he would cloak the rigour of his principles in obscure and complex sentences whereby he sought to hide confidential matters or, in kindly manner, to say 'no' in as gentle a fashion as possible. But when necessary he could speak with unusual force and clarity. Moreover, his cautious management of the University's annual accounts was balanced by a remarkable flair in the acquisition and management of property. He had a nose for information, scented opportunity afar off, and was both persuasive in advancing his schemes and practical in achieving them. Working very frequently behind the scenes, he was one of the founders of the University's fortunes.

So it was on this occasion. The game began in the winter of 1945–6 when Carpenter found himself seated next to Sir Henry D'Avigdor-Goldsmid at a dinner of one of the Livery Companies.[3] There was some discussion of the Whiteknights estate, in particular of an outlying property, Park House in Upper Redlands Road. Sir Henry referred to the increasing difficulty of maintaining such estates, and Carpenter indicated that if at any time the trustees of the Whiteknights estate thought of disposing of any of their interests, then he hoped that they would consider giving the University first refusal. At the time he was following the lines discussed in the Committee on post-war development; the primary aim was to obtain land which could be used for an extension or annexe to St George's Hall. Early in April 1946 he seems to have visited Sir Henry's solicitors, Waterhouse and Co. of London, to discuss the question more formally. These conversations soon bore fruit. On 23 April Arthur West called on Waterhouse and Co. Carpenter was informed by telephone that the leasehold interest in Park House was for sale.[4] On the 29th he wrote asking for first refusal for the University.

The transaction was not a simple one. The leasehold was on the market because the current holder, Mr Audley Sutton, had given notice of termination. The house had been requisitioned by the Ministry of Works and

[1] Doris M. Stenton, *op. cit.*, pp. 316–30.
[2] The comment of Sir Maurice Powicke at the annual dinner of the Stubbs Society, Oxford, 1948, at which the Stentons were guests of honour.
[3] The detail of the following account is based in part on conversations with Carpenter and on the recollections of Mrs Carpenter, Miss Barbara Meade (Bursar's Secretary) and the Registrar.
[4] Bursar 28/18 contains notes of the telephone call.

was occupied by the National Savings Committee; the Ministry was ready to extend its tenure for at least three years. Despite these difficulties, Carpenter persisted. On 15 May he wrote asking whether the freehold was for sale. The reply on the 21st seemed to indicate a dead end. The University was offered the lease at an annual rent of £200; it would have to make its own arrangements with the Ministry; the lease could not be extended beyond 1958, when the other Whiteknights leases fell in. On 29 May Carpenter visited Waterhouse and Co. in London. He must have been both persistent and persuasive. On 2 July he wrote again asking whether their client was able to 'arrange for the University to acquire his interest' in the property. On the following day, 3 July, the solicitors wrote saying that Sir Henry had instructed them to offer the property to the University 'for outright purchase'. Carpenter reached agreement on a price of £11,750 on a visit to Waterhouse and Co. on 25 July. The conveyance was completed on 27 September.

It was during these negotiations for the sale of a relatively small property of 7¼ acres that the possible purchase of the whole estate arose. On his first visit to Waterhouse and Co., probably in April, Carpenter indicated that the University would be interested in land and properties in Whiteknights, should they become available. After receiving the letter of 3 July concerning Park House he must have had some informal communication with the solicitors. At all events he interrupted the meeting of Senate on the evening of 4 July and asked both the Vice-Chancellor and the Registrar to withdraw to deal with a matter of urgent business.[1] He had received a telephone call enquiring whether the University was interested in the whole estate. There and then the three men agreed to follow it up. The question was put more formally when Carpenter visited Waterhouse and Co. on the 25th:

> During the course of our interview Brigadier Crewsdon of Waterhouse and Co. asked whether the University would be interested in negotiations for the acquisition of the whole of the Goldsmid settled estates in Whiteknights, an area of some 230 acres. I was not able to call you on the telephone this morning, but I have had an opportunity of discussing the matter with Professor Stenton, Sir George Mowbray and Mr West, and they have all agreed that we should ask for details of the estate and a note of the asking price. I understand that it is the intention of the vendors to make an offer to the University and they do not propose to make a general offer of the property at the present time.[2]

---

[1] The incident has accumulated legend around it. Ernest Smith remembered it as the only occasion on which he was 'dragged' out of Senate – 'and it took the Bursar to do it'.
In conversation with the author, none of the participants recalled the precise date. The meeting of Senate of 4 July is the only possible occasion. However, it is not until 25/26 July that the purchase of Whiteknights appears in the correspondence, and 25 July is given as the starting-point in Smith, *op. cit.*, p. 30.
[2] Bursar, 28/18. Carpenter to Sir William Mount, 26 July 1946. The area given of 230 acres was an error or an underestimate.

Carpenter wasted no time. On the following day, 26 July, he wrote to
Waterhouse and Co.:

> With reference to my call at your office yesterday afternoon, I have
> had an opportunity of discussing the matters raised by you with
> members of the University Finance Committee and also with
> certain of my colleagues. I have pleasure in informing you that the
> University is interested in your proposition and I should be glad if
> you would kindly let me have a note of the extent of the estate and
> also your asking price.[1]

It is given to few university bursars to initiate a coup of such dimensions.
Up to this point it was all his own work. Childs, de Burgh and Stenton
had dreamed long before that Whiteknights might house the University.[2]
But Stenton did not move in circles in which he could realize that dream;
his milieu was academic. It was Carpenter who made it practicable.

The decision taken on 25/26 July was only the beginning of a long
haul. On 30 August Waterhouse and Co. wrote indicating that their
client would be ready to sell for £150,000; they also supplied the boundaries of the estate and a schedule of the leases. On 17 September Carpenter
visited the County Planning Officer for preliminary discussions of the sale
and immediately encountered an unexpected emergency: the Ministry of
Works had already presented proposals for the extensions of its buildings
on the site; if the University were to make reservations they would have to
be made soon. Once again the Bursar worked fast and effectively. On the
advice of Thomas Houghton, the County Planning Officer, he agreed that
the University's case should be presented to a joint meeting of the local
authorities on 30 September. All this he relayed to Stenton by letter in
which he indicated that the local authorities were likely to react favourably.[3] Even so, the meeting was critical. Stenton attended with the three
Deans, Dewar, O'Donoghue and Neville, the Registrar, and the Bursar.
Looking back in later years Ernest Smith recalled that he had never known
Stenton so persuasive. Stenton was not a born administrator; he used to

---

[1] Bursar, 28/10, 1.

[2] See Lady Stenton's comment: 'He looked back over a lifetime to early days when he
often as a boy walked in Whiteknights with de Burgh and Childs and someone nearly
always said, wistfully, but without hope, that it would be an ideal site for the future
university.' (*op. cit.*, p. 406).

[3] Bursar, 28/10, 1. Carpenter to Stenton, 17 September 1946. 'In the circumstances I
agreed to Houghton calling a meeting of the appropriate authorities on the 30th – the
matter could no longer be kept on a purely confidential basis, but it does not necessarily
mean that there will be a great deal of publicity. You may be interested to know that
Oldershaw [representative of Berkshire County Council on the University Council] is to
be in the chair and that the county officials are more than helpful. I enclose a copy of a
letter which I have sent to Houghton; this was approved in principle by the three Deans
and the Registrar who have been kept informed of the negotiations. I think it would be a
good thing if we were to entertain Houghton to lunch on say the 26th to run over tactics
in presenting our case'. This letter, which reveals so many of the facets of Carpenter's
character, suggests that the Ministry of Works did not stand much of a chance.

refer to his departmental administration as the 'bits and pieces' or the 'odd jobs'; Lady Stenton said that she and Frank settled them as they made the bed in the morning.[1] But in a meeting he was in his element. Both within the University and outside in the world of historical scholarship he was respected, even revered, for his chairmanship and the cool, shrewd, long-headed manner in which he marshalled arguments eloquently expressed. He could speak with a kind of controlled passion which was almost incandescent. By all accounts the meeting of 30 September was a triumph. After reviewing the needs of an expanding university and emphasizing the overriding need for land, he was able to persuade the representatives of all the local authorities to give preliminary approval to the scheme. There was only one condition: the park had hitherto been zoned as a public open space; Stenton now gave assurances that the parkland would be preserved, that the siting of buildings would be submitted to the local authorities for approval and that the public would have access to the park.[2] He 'carried all parties with him and came away tired but jubilant'.[3]

The general assurance which Stenton obtained from the representatives of the local authorities on 30 September was the signal for even more urgent activity. On the very next day Carpenter wrote to the District Valuer seeking a valuation of the whole estate. This had now been calculated accurately as amounting to 281 acres, of which over $14\frac{1}{2}$ had been reserved for temporary office accommodation by the Ministry of Works. Carpenter now asked that the work of valuation should be done urgently; he pointed out that the University would be seeking a grant-in-aid from the Treasury and that universities had been asked to submit all such proposals by 31 October. It was only a month since the detailed offer had been received from Waterhouse and Co. On 7 October Stenton met the University Grants Committee in London and submitted carefully prepared notes on the scheme.[4] Two days later Smith sent a characteristically modest note to all members of Senate:

> After the conclusion of the ordinary business of the Senate on
> October 14th the Senate will adjourn for 30 minutes and then return
> to receive and consider a statement by the Vice-Chancellor on the
> present state of the negotiations for the acquisition of the White-
> knights Park Estate.

The Senate was in no doubt; Stenton noted the resolution on his own copy of the notice:

---

[1] For the 'odd jobs' see Joan Wake on Stenton in *Northamptonshire Past and Present*, iv (1968–9), p. 183. The rest comes from conversations with the author.
[2] Bursar, 28/10, contains minutes of the meeting.
[3] Doris M. Stenton, *op. cit.*, p. 407. The minutes of the meeting do not contain any reference to any possible surrender of existing property, although Lady Stenton included in her summary of the speech: 'It would be possible to release the present main University site in London Road and the Wessex Hall site in Redlands Road would be available for the Hospital'. On this see below, pp. 146–7.
[4] See Appendix 6, p. 353.

> In the opinion of the Senate the acquisition of the Whiteknights
> Park Estate is desirable in the interests of the University.[1]

Within the space of a long vacation Carpenter, Smith and the new Vice-Chancellor, reinforced by an inner group of the Council and Finance Committee, had presented to the University a splendid revision of its future.

All this was done without any real assurance that there would be money for the purchase. The University Grants Committee could not authorize or meet expenditure of this size from its own resources. Accordingly Stenton carried the matter to the Treasury, where he saw Sir Edward Bridges.[2] The Secretary of the University Grants Committee, H. A. de Montmorency, also referred to the Treasury for a decision. The answer came in a letter of 23 October: the Treasury would provide the money so long as the District Valuer reported favourably on the price. In 1946 there was still some hope that private benefactors would provide for a great deal of university development. Hence the Treasury was cautious in its support:

> In view of the possible effect on private munificence of making an
> outright grant of 100 per cent at this stage, we think that the assist-
> ance should take the form of a loan. The loan would be free of
> interest.[3]

It was not until March 1955 that the loan was converted into an outright grant.[4] Nevertheless, the Treasury's proposals solved the financial problem. During the course of the winter the remaining arrangements were completed. In January 1947 Stenton was able to write to Sir Walter Moberly, Chairman of the University Grants Committee, to report that the final price of £105,000 had been agreed between the owners and the District Valuer. Formal agreement was obtained from the planning authorities for re-zoning the park as 'land reserved for educational purposes.'[5] Towards the end of February the purchase was reported to the University Court and thereafter it was announced in the press and became fully public. The purchase was completed on 25 March. From first to last there was scarcely a hitch. Indeed, the difficulties that were encountered, the interest of the Ministry of Works and the urgent requirement of the University Grants Committee for details of proposals for capital expenditure, had the effect of hastening the transaction.

That the purchase was executed so quickly was partly a matter of luck. On 10 May, after the negotiation for Park House had begun, the Finance Committee appointed a small sub-committee, consisting of Stenton, Sir

---

[1] URC, Registrar, box 70.

[2] Doris M. Stenton, *op. cit.*, p. 407.

[3] E. Hale to H. A. de Montmorency, 23 October 1946. Copies of the letter were subsequently forwarded to the University.

[4] Bursar, 28/10, 1.

[5] This was complicated by the fact that three authorities were involved: Reading, Berkshire, and Wokingham Rural District Council. The joint view expressed in the meeting of 30 September had to go to all three authorities for approval.

George Mowbray, Sir William Mount and West, to 'consider and report on all matters affecting the purchase of land and buildings on behalf of the University under the Town Planning Scheme'. As a result, when the offer of Whiteknights was made, there was a committee in being with authority to deal with preliminaries.[1] Its members, supported by the Bursar and Registrar, went ahead untrammelled by any machinery for official consultation. Partly through instinct and experience, partly because Waterhouse and Co. asked for the least possible publicity,[2] they held their cards very close to their chests. No major meetings had been arranged for the long vacation. The Finance Committee of Council held a special meeting on 6 September; by then the preliminary price of £150,000 had been received; but no discussion of the purchase was minuted. The matter was reported to Senate on 14 October, formally to the Finance Committee on 18 October and to the Council on 1 November. By then it was well on the way to a successful conclusion; Stenton had already made his approach to the University Grants Committee. The small inner group acted with complete confidence: Stenton, Carpenter and Smith in the knowledge that they had the backing of the three members of Council whom they consulted; and those three, Sir George Mowbray, Sir William Mount and Arthur West representing that element in the Council, the country gentlemen, the 'barts', which assumed that if the University needed land then it was natural that it should have it; hence action first, and the means and the constitutional blessing second.[3] This came the easier from the certain knowledge that the purchase would solve all those difficulties which the discussion of the development of the University had emphasized. The approval of Council and Senate would not be withheld. The easy informality, the excitement of the period, were later recalled by Lady Stenton:

> Occasionally I was pressed into help in the Vice-Chancellor's office.
> I vividly remember one Saturday afternoon when Frank had to
> interview the University Grants Committee on Monday morning
> and needed enough typed copies of his statement for each member of
> the committee to have one before him. Frank, a practised typist of
> historical works, the Bursar and I worked hard typing out the copies.
> The Registrar, a less practised typist, was kept busy looking up

[1] The committee also included H. A. D. Neville, but he does not figure in the correspondence of the summer. In his letters to Waterhouse and Co. the Bursar dignified the body with the title of 'University Properties Committee'. Its authority was in effect renewed on 18 October, when the Finance Committee delegated the business of the purchase of Whiteknights to a new committee. This was the same as the earlier committee except that Sir George Mowbray dropped out and the Registrar and Bursar were added as members.

[2] Waterhouse and Co. to Bursar, 30 August 1946 (Bursar, 28/10, 1).

[3] The purchase of Park House, Upper Redlands Road, provides a parallel. This was presented to the Finance Committee as a *fait accompli* on 18 October, when the action taken was approved. It was only in August 1947 that the purchase price of £11,750 was met by a grant from the Treasury.

points and helping generally, so that we could get the envelopes in the post in good time.[1]

That portrays the middle ages of university government. It worked. Amidst the committees, reports and statistics of a later age something may have been lost, not least the calm assumption that a Vice-Chancellor might interview the University Grants Committee.

The acquisition of Whiteknights was the most important single event in the history of the University. Hitherto the development and expansion could only be imagined as involving the slow and painful acquisition of property in what might have become a precinct: the addition to a hall of residence here, the establishment of teaching departments in large private houses there, perhaps ultimately the building of multi-storey blocks on the old site in London Road. Throughout such a development the need to provide suitable residence for students would have been an abiding difficulty and concern; the whole process would have been intricate, cumbersome and expensive. Suddenly, all these difficulties were swept away. The University now had land, more than enough to meet its teaching and residential needs for years to come. Relief and satisfaction may have come all the easier because the old University College had already moved once, from Valpy Street to London Road. And these feelings seem to have overwhelmed all else. No one seems to have wondered how the move would affect the old intimate comfort which the University had inherited from the College. Whiteknights would be a campus. Quite apart from any change in the size of the University, the new site was bound to affect the quality of life. No one at this stage settled down to study how far the ethos of Reading depended on the relatively enclosed communities created by the London Road site and the existing halls of residence, or how far this could be preserved in Whiteknights, or what measures might be necessary to preserve it, if that were to be the aim. This was put together slowly and pragmatically over the next two decades. Immediately, in the enthusiasm of the moment, men raced ahead, more relieved at jettisoning old problems than conscious of acquiring new ones.

There is no doubt that at first the difficulties of exploiting the new site were gravely underestimated. It was obvious that the move would take a long time to complete, but less clear that there would be many delays before it could even begin. In February the Treasurer, writing to the tenant of one of the leaseholds, stated that the University intended to start the move in 1950.[2] In fact the first building, the Faculty of Letters, was ready for occupation in 1957. Local interests also seem to have assumed that the start would not be long delayed. At his meeting with the local authorities on

---

[1] Doris M. Stenton, *op. cit.*, p. 409. The reference to Stenton's typing is of interest. Both he and his wife transcribed medieval documents, where possible, directly on the typewriter, on the argument that by eliminating intermediate stages in transcription the possibility of error is reduced.

[2] Sir William Mount to Mrs Gamage, 17 February 1947 (URC, Registrar, box 70).

30 September Stenton had indicated that if planning permission were granted for Whiteknights then the University would be ready to release the old site in London Road and make Wessex Hall in Redlands Road available for the Royal Berkshire Hospital.[1] In January and February both the Borough and the Hospital wrote to stake their claims. Meanwhile within the University, in the euphoria created by the new opportunity, enthusiastic schemes began to flourish. Already on 6 October Wolters wrote to Stenton:

> In its licensing programme for universities the Ministry of Works at present puts us at £350,000. This may be whittled down owing to the strong competition of Oxford. You must regard this as secret information improperly obtained.
>
> You would do well to start petting the Regional Licensing Officer, Mr House. He likes being associated with universities, and I understand that Oxford found him very malleable. When he is roped in you proceed to the Regional Officer above him.
>
> Obviously much expert advice will be needed before proceeding to plan the lay-out, including a civil engineer. But for the general development I suggest that we should not rely exclusively upon the architect employed to design the buildings. Since men of the order of Abercrombie are probably fully occupied, you might care to consider Jellicoe, who once did some part-time teaching for us. He is now thoroughly established, his present mission being to make cement works look like corners of Eden. You could be sure of his enthusiasm, but Betts would be a better adviser than myself on this point.[2]

Stenton proceeded more cautiously. Very soon he, Smith and Carpenter recognized that the move to Whiteknights could come only after careful consideration of the difficulties. Some thought that he was too slow;[3] but he himself recognized that he would have to leave the detailed planning of Whiteknights to his successors:

> As Moses stood supported on the one side by Aaron and on the other by Hur to view the promised land and keep the battle against the Amalekites going, so he could only stand supported on one side by the Registrar and on the other by the Bursar to look in imagination on the University which would in time be built.[4]

Nevertheless in the autumn of 1946 his mind was ranging ahead, planning the general development of the University. The University's target of 1,000 students had already been reviewed on two occasions. On 31 May 1945 de Montmorency wrote from the University Grants Committee that

[1] Doris M. Stenton, *op. cit.*, p. 407.
[2] URC, Registrar, box 70.
[3] It was felt in particular that he was dilatory in the choice of an architect. He was intentionally Fabian over this.
[4] A characteristic note struck in his farewell speech (Doris M. Stenton, *op. cit.*, p. 408).

the submissions received from British universities contemplated an increase of rather less than 20 per cent; the latest official prediction was that an increase of 50 per cent would be required. On this occasion Reading reaffirmed its earlier submission:

> If the present character of the University is to be maintained it is the considered opinion of the Council and the Senate that the number of students should not exceed 1,000.

Indeed it added that even an increase of 120 students above the present total of 698 would require a new hall of residence. In May 1946 the University Grants Committee returned to the charge, reinforced by the Barlow Report on Scientific Manpower of April, which recommended doubling the output of scientists. On 29 May de Montmorency wrote indicating that 'the national interest will require the doubling of the pre-war student population within the next ten years':

> In these circumstances, I am writing to ask that the Committee may be supplied with figures, revised if necessary, of the maximum number of full-time students for which the University expects to be able to make permanent and satisfactory educational provision by the end of the first decade after the war.

He invited an answer by 22 June. On the 19th Stenton replied. After indicating that the figure of 1,000 already submitted amounted to an increase of 43 per cent above 1938–9, he reasserted that the Council and Senate were still 'anxious to maintain the present character of the University, based on a series of halls of residence in the setting provided by a country town of moderate size'. However, he bowed to national requirements and reported that 'after such enquiry as has been possible' the University should be able to accommodate 1,300 by 1955; it would require two new halls of residence, the extension of others, and action on the building plan which the University had already submitted.[1] His sounding of departments had not been reassuring; most saw real difficulty in taking an increased number within their existing accommodation.

The possibility of acquiring Whiteknights put all this in a new light. The matter was discussed at a special meeting of Senate on 12 November. Stenton's notes for the occasion include carefully calculated estimates of the distribution of increased numbers among the existing Halls, some of which would have to be enlarged, and two new Halls which would be essential to complete the accommodation. His notes put the new total at 1,300. On his agenda paper he noted that this was to be achieved in five years instead of ten. More important still, he noted that the ultimate size of the University would be approximately 2,000.[2] All this was agreed by Senate. Its recommendation, though guarded and conditional, marked the first break in the

[1] The whole of this correspondence is in URC, Registrar, box 219. Stenton's letter of 19 June was discussed with and 'vetted' by Carpenter.
[2] URC, Registrar, box 70. See plates 28, 29.

doctrine that the University should not increase beyond 1,000 students.[1] Senate was now ready to envisage an ultimate size which was twice the optimum on which so many had insisted in 1944. Stenton may have seen himself as Moses, never to occupy the promised land, but he ensured that the University would occupy it in force. Quicker than any, he had appreciated that Reading could no longer be a small university.

However, the road towards this objective was strewn with obstacles. The six leaseholds which encumbered the estate were the most obvious. These were centred on six substantial houses: Whiteknights (House), Whiteknights Park (House), Blandford Lodge, Foxhill, Erlegh Park and the Wilderness. Negotiations for the purchase of the leaseholds could not begin until the purchase of the freehold was certain. The leases of Whiteknights House and Blandford Lodge were acquired late in 1947. Whiteknights Park House followed in 1948, but the rest only fell in at intervals in the following years. Some of the leaseholds were further encumbered: both Whiteknights House and Blandford Lodge had been requisitioned by the Ministry of Works for the Ministry of Labour and the Royal Air Force respectively, and the Wilderness was occupied by the Army. Moreover some of the land in the park was let on agricultural tenancies. The first problem therefore was to acquire enough immediate control to begin practical planning. Although the University Grants Committee persuaded the Treasury to help in the purchase of the leaseholds, more and more irritating complexities were encountered:

> We have reached the stage of draft contracts in the case of White-knights House, and our solicitors are making preliminary enquiries in regard to Blandford Lodge. We consider that it is essential that some considerable part of the Estate should be freehold and under the absolute control of the University, notwithstanding that development may well be postponed. It is particularly important in view of the attitude of the Ministry of Works, who appear to be anxious to secure their hold of a considerable area of the Estate and, in fact, have asked for what amounts to a 25 years' lease.
>
> We are proposing to use part of the Whiteknights House land for playing fields in the immediate future and arrangements have already been made to prepare pitches for rugby and association football as well as hockey. This has been made possible by the sublessee of the ground retiring from the holding on 29 September next. Although we should have no immediate user of the house

[1] The Senate minute was as follows: 'It was agreed that, provided it should be found possible to have moved one complete Faculty from the London Road site by the end of five years from the present date the University could plan to receive not less than 1,200 (maximum 1,300) students during the Session 1951–2. It was generally agreed that ultimately the University might hope to provide accommodation for not less than 2,000 students'.

itself, it was necessary to acquire the lease as a whole in order to
provide athletic facilities which are much overdue.[1]

Even when a leasehold was acquired, the University was still bound by the
Deed of Covenant governing the leases. This restricted the use of the proper-
ties as private dwellings; it had already prevented an attempt to turn
Blandford Lodge into a school.[2]

Of all the obstacles, the Ministry of Works was much the most obdurate.
It was already negotiating for the leases of Whiteknights and Blandford
Lodge. The Ministry's District Surveyor informed Carpenter of his moves
in November 1946. However, he does not seem to have realized the full
extent of the University's intentions and his reaction when he learned of
them was somewhat tart:

> I am informed by the District Valuer that he has completed arrange-
> ments to purchase the whole of the Whiteknights Park Estate,
> including the land upon which the Temporary Office Buildings have
> been and are being erected by this Department.
>
> This is rather an unfortunate development and one of which my
> Headquarters will probably take a serious view, but I have no doubt
> that some mutually satisfactory settlement can be reached in due
> course.[3]

As his letter revealed, the real issue was not the Ministry's interest in the
leaseholds, which was not pressed, but its continued interest in the temporary buildings which it had erected in the eastern corner of the park. The
Ministry had acquired the lease of this site in 1942 and subsequently
extended it to $14\frac{1}{2}$ acres. By the end of the war it had erected two blocks of
temporary buildings for use as office or emergency wartime hospital accommodation. A third block was under construction in 1946 and the Ministry
was seeking permission to build a fourth. The officials of the Ministry were
quite determined to go ahead and a tetchy argument developed. Ultimately
Lewis Silkin, the Minister of Town and Country Planning, was brought in
and visited Reading. He had a rough ride, as Stenton related to Sir George
Mowbray:

> In my talks with Mr Silkin, I deliberately kept the discussion to facts
> and firm proposals. It seemed to me that our case would be weak-
> ened by any expression of resentment at the action taken by the
> Ministry of Works. But without any motion of mine, he was told in
> the most uncompromising terms what is felt locally about this mis-
> use of Whiteknights Park. On Monday evening, after our talk, he
> was driven out to the site, and there met a representative company –
> including Oldershaw, Thomas, Saunders, the Mayor, and prominent
> officials. This discussion did not produce any new concrete facts, but

---

[1] Carpenter to W. C. Chesterman, UGC, 10 September 1947.
[2] See the correspondence between Waterhouse and Co. and Brain and Brain, acting for
the University, of February 1947 (Bursar, 28/10, 1).
[3] R. E. Robson to E. H. Carpenter, 6 February 1947 (*ibid.*).

it demonstrated the strength of local, non-party feeling about the encroachments in progress on Whiteknights. Before the end, it had resolved itself into a series of acrid exchanges between the Mayor and Saunders on one side and Mr Silkin on the other. Our friends of the Town Council were less strong than could be wished on details, but they made it abundantly clear that the high-handed, and what they called 'undemocratic' action of the Ministry was intensely resented in the neighbourhood. I said little at this stage, except to emphasize, at the end, to Mr Silkin that this feeling was a reality in the borough and county. But I am sure that he must have realized that the opposition was based on something wider than the mere resistance of a university to interference with its plans.[1]

A compromise was reached in October. A site for the fourth block of Ministry buildings was found near the Wilderness, and the University agreed to withdraw its objections on the understanding that the Ministry would not occupy the new building for longer than ten years and that it would accept an absolute limit of twenty years on its occupancy of the other temporary accommodation. The Ministry was effectively sealed off in a corner of the park, where it would not impede the main development of the University. It even agreed that '. . . the lease of the necessary land will provide that on the determination of the lease, the Ministry will demolish the buildings and leave the site tidy.'[2]

In fact the temporary buildings still stand. They were transferred from the Ministry to the University between 1965 and 1969. The structure of the first temporary block betrays its origin, for it was designed to be blast-proof. The later additions are less forbidding and now stand in orderly manner in pleasant lawns. With their wide corridors designed for hospital use, the standard of these buildings can no longer be matched by the University Grants Committee. Departments now hang on tenaciously to accommodation which their predecessors would not have admitted to the park in 1947.

This was local skirmishing. At the centre much more ominous difficulties were being spelled out. The University was planning to move at a time when all the essential resources were under intense pressure. Steel, building materials and labour resources were all in short supply and subject to government regulation. It was the era of austerity. De Montmorency sketched the situation for Stenton in a letter of 8 November 1946:

The Ministry of Works have made a preliminary survey of the prospects of such a programme of expansion in the regions in which universities are situated. The position of building labour is not unfavourable in some regions, but in others it is very difficult. There are large requirements for domestic housing everywhere, and there

[1] Stenton to Sir George Mowbray, 22 July 1947.
[2] T. Wells to Carpenter, 7 October 1947, summarizing a meeting with the Vice-Chancellor, Registrar and Bursar on 2 October (URC, Registrar, box 70).

are also heavy building programmes for urgent industrial buildings which in certain special areas have high priority. It may therefore happen that progress with urgent university building schemes will be less rapid in some areas than in others. As regards the supply of the chief building materials, we hope soon to circulate to universities a statement from the Ministry of Works describing the situation.

A year later the picture was even gloomier:

The University Grants Committee have been in communication with the Ministry of Works about the building programme of the universities. While it is the general policy of the Government to do everything possible to secure the carrying out of the programmes already contemplated, the limitation of supplies of steel for building must inevitably cause some retardation of progress for the next year or so. There is also a probability that the amount of labour at the disposal of universities will not be able to be increased at so early a date as had been hoped.[1]

In these competitive circumstances Reading was a weak contender. The need for residential accommodation which had run through all its thinking since the last years of the war made development at Reading expensive. Other claims would be met first if Reading's involved the provision of teaching and residential buildings at one and the same time. Perhaps also the sheer size of a scheme for transplanting an established university to a new site was a deterrent. At all events, feeling spread at the headquarters of the University Grants Committee that Reading had bitten off more than it could chew. De Montmorency, the Secretary, would on occasion refer to 'White Elephant's Park'. Stenton had to contend not only with local obstacles but also with official disenchantment.

So it remained to the end of his term of office. The essence of the difficulty was that governmental good intentions, limited resources, and other competing claims had not been resolved into a coherent national policy within which the University could seek to realize its aspirations. The resulting confusion was still profound when Wolfenden succeeded. On 1 June 1950 he met de Montmorency to discuss the future; by now there was some hope that the University Grants Committee would provide the funds for the construction of a new hall of residence; beyond that there lay a fog of contingencies and doubt:

We then extended our discussion over the whole future financial prospect. De Montmorency said (though I think that none of these opinions ought to be pinned on him officially):

1. That there was a body of opinion in the UGC Office which thought that the purchase of Whiteknights Park had been a mistake. I replied that neither they nor we could get out of that, even if anybody wanted to, because they had provided an interest-free loan for

---

[1] Letters of de Montmorency to Stenton, 8 November 1946, 21 November 1947 (*ibid.*).

its acquisition and it would be merely stupid to abandon the purpose for which that money had been advanced, namely the eventual transfer to that site of the University of Reading. His reply was that since 1946 two important changes in the general situation had occurred, (a) the very stringent restrictions on building, (b) the general deterioration in the national financial position.

2. That it would be unwise to envisage any substantial expansion in undergraduate numbers, because many people thought that saturation point in student numbers had just about been reached. I replied that I was very glad to hear him say that, because my disposition was to base our claims for money for Whiteknights Park not primarily on expansion for student numbers, but rather on replacement of obsolete plant on the present site; that the real question was whether it was more economical to rebuild the Old Red Building and Wantage Hutted Site in their present position or to put up in their places new buildings on Whiteknights Park; that some of our buildings were slums which would simply have to be dealt with soon anyhow; and that I would very much rather not put too much weight on the expansion plank of our platform.

3. That the UGC's total annual allocation of building expenditure at the present time, to be spread over seventeen universities and four university colleges, was £4,000,000. (Professor Sanders tells me that for this year it is £3,500,000.) I made no comment on this except to point out that we were already committed and so were they to £350,000, either next year or the year after, for the new hall of residence.

4. (This was obviously speculation on his part, but it is an indication of the way in which their minds are working) that if there should be a change of Government in the near future the policy with regard to university building might well be that universities were free to build as much as they liked, provided that they themselves produced the money.

5. That he was supposing that our total expenditure on Whiteknights Park would be of the order of two or three million pounds. I told him that it would be a great deal more than this, if only on the basis of £350,000 for one hall of residence. He said that it would be well to bear in mind what the UGC's annual allocation was, as mentioned earlier.

My general impression was that we shall have to start almost at the beginning in convincing them to give us any money for Whiteknights Park. I say 'almost at the beginning' because they are committed to the hall of residence and I doubt if there will be much argument about that. But it is pretty clear, though I can only report this as an impression, that they are not disposed either to throw money about or to undertake commitments for any length of time

ahead. In fact, there is no ground for easy optimism, but there is
every indication that we shall have to fight all the way. . . .

As I left Mr de Montmorency I was reminded that the University
of Birmingham began its move to Edgbaston in 1910 and has so far,
by 1950, transported about three-fifths of itself to its new site.[1]

This marked the beginning of a new phase of more realistic and closer
argued planning. But even Wolfenden's grim assessment proved to be
optimistic. The commitment to the hall of residence, which he assumed
would be firm, was to be delayed. The concluding interchange between him
and de Montmorency was perhaps the most significant. In this matter
Reading is well on the way to rivalling Birmingham.

[1] Wolfenden to President, Vice-President of Council, Treasurer, Registrar and Bursar
(Bursar, 20/4).

Chapter 8

New environment 1947–76

In 1946 Reading committed itself to a very modest programme of expansion. It was carefully considered. Those responsible were well aware that an increase of roughly 400 students, small enough in absolute terms, was large in relation to the total of 943 students under tutorial supervision in 1946–7. Moreover they had insisted throughout their discussions, as had Stenton in his communications with the University Grants Committee, that the character of the University should not be changed.[1] That was reinforced by practical considerations, for it seemed impossible to increase numbers unless additions were made to residential and other accommodation. In the event this proved correct. The University agreed to aim at a target of 1,300 students by 1955. Even that proved beyond its means. There were still only 1,192 students under tutorial supervision at the beginning of the year 1955–6; even a year later the total of 1,267 still fell short. For ten years therefore the University talked of and planned for expansion, but there was no great upheaval of its settled ways. It was not until 1957 that the annual increase in the number of students was greater than 100.[2] Only in 1948, 1952 and 1956 was it greater than 50. Between 1952 and 1955 numbers were almost static.[3]

By contrast the fourteen years following 1957 were cataclysmic. In 1957-8 there were 1,432 students under tutorial supervision. By 1965-6 the number had doubled to 2,835. By 1972-3 it had doubled yet again to 5,741.[4] Between 1962 and 1969 the annual increase in numbers never fell below 100. In 1965 and 1966 it was over 500. In 1967 it was over 1,000. In that year the increase in numbers was roughly equivalent to what had been envisaged in 1943 as the optimum total.

The change was therefore concentrated within a period of little more than ten years. It was not just a matter of numbers. Expansion meant migration. The first new building in Whiteknights, the Faculty of Letters, came into use in 1957. Within ten years Whiteknights became the centre of the University. In 1968 the administrative offices were established in Whiteknights House. Thereafter to refer to London Road as 'main site'

[1] See above, p. 148.
[2] 1,423 against 1,267 in 1956–7.
[3] The totals in these three years were 1,154, 1,161, 1,161.
[4] The numbers were 5,822 in 1974–5.

soon became a quaint archaism. In some ways the development of the University in Whiteknights was like that of new universities first established in the 1960s. There was elbow-room to build. Expansion was marked by new buildings, new roads and paths. Staff and students lived with the mud and noise inseparable from a construction site. But in other ways it was different. It was more haphazard and spasmodic. It began nearly ten years before Sussex, York, Lancaster and the other new universities were founded, at a time when there was no firm prediction of its ultimate size. It could not therefore be designed as a whole. Until experience inculcated wariness each stage was planned as though it might be the last. Furthermore, while the new universities founded a decade later were based on staff who were committed to experiment and expansion in university education, at Reading there was still a hard core of opinion which stood for the old ways and the old days of the small familiar institution in London Road. Some accepted expansion only with great reluctance. A few fought a prolonged Fabian campaign against it, which ended only with their retirement.

It is pointless to speculate how men at Reading would have reacted in 1946 if, in a University of less than 1,000, they had appreciated that expansion would entail six-fold growth to nearly 6,000 within thirty years. They were never allowed such a choice. Instead they accepted, or were brought to accept, expansion in stages, so that the experience of the gradual inured or attracted them to the precipitate. Willy-nilly Reading became a far larger university than the founding fathers could ever have imagined. The tale can be presented baldly in tabular form:[1]

	Date	Actual numbers	Planned expansion	Expansion achieved by planned date
1.	1946	793	1,300 by 1955	1,161
2.	1956	1,192	1,500 by 1962	1,765 (amended by 3)
3.	1957	1,267	2,000 by 1964	2,003 (amended by 4)
4.	1960	1,537	3,000 by 1970	5,318 (amended by 5)
5.	1963	1,818	3,700 by 1967–8	4,525 (amended by 6)
6.	1966	3,452	5,000 by 1971–2	5,612 (amended by 7)
7.	1969	4,996	8,000 by 1977	(amended by 8)
8.	1971	5,403	6,500 by 1977	

It will be observed that the target only stayed reasonably still during the first decade of expansion. Thereafter it receded rapidly until it was checked by economic considerations in the 1970s. Its movement was not even easily predictable. Between 1957 and 1977 there were four quin-

[1] All the figures in columns 2 and 4 are for the years ending in the date given.

quennia on which the planning of universities nationally was based. So far there have been seven agreed targets for expansion. All but one of the target-figures agreed between 1956 and 1966 for the quinquennia ending between 1962 and 1972 were changed before they were achieved. Only in 1964 among the target-years listed above was the university roughly where it had planned to be when the target for the year was first determined.

At first the policy of expansion was vigorously discussed and fought. Some, the unofficial custodians of the Reading *Penates*, were unwilling to budge beyond the target to which Stenton had agreed in 1946. Allowing for graduates, this meant a maximum of 1,200 undergraduates, and for ten years this figure assumed an almost mystic importance, as though Reading's very being depended on it. A few felt that any move to Whiteknights would be a mistake and that sufficient accommodation could be found for the modest scale of expansion which they envisaged on the London Road site and in the area immediately to the south. Of these Aspinall, who succeeded Stenton as Professor of Modern History in 1946, was perhaps the most persistent. He and others relied on the view expressed in the Development Committee's report in 1944; expansion should not be so great as to affect the essential character of the University. The argument was summed up in the oft repeated assertion that in an expanded University, especially one split between Whiteknights and London Road, 'we shan't know each other any more'.

This gradually lost its force. It was undermined by the experience of the first ten post-war years in which numbers gradually advanced without any obvious upset of the intimate atmosphere of the University.[1] It was further enfeebled by the retirement of many of those who had taken part in the discussions of 1943-4 in which the desirable maximum was established at 1,000. Between 1946 and 1954 no less than thirteen professors resigned or retired, including practically all the senior men: Basset, Capstick, Crowther and Ure in 1946; H. A. D. Neville in 1947; Dewar in 1949; Wolters in 1950; Barnard and Desseignet in 1951; Hawkins and O'Donoghue in 1952; Brierley and E. H. Neville in 1954. Of the old pre-war group only two, Harris and Hodges, still remained in post. They were accompanied by another small group of professors who had held junior appointments before the war: Aspinall, Betts, A. A. Miller, Edgar Thomas and C. Tyler. Some of these were already influential; some were to become so. But they were not numerous and none was as intractable as Aspinall in defending the concept of a small university. They had to work alongside new professors coming to Reading from very different environments, some of whom took Reading's view of itself with a large pinch of salt. Ditchburn in Physics and Guggenheim in Chemistry, who arrived together in 1946 fought, each in his different way, for a university which could sustain properly established

[1] The numbers under tutorial supervision were 698 in 1938-9, 793 in 1945-6, 1,161 in 1953-4.

studies in the physical sciences. Ditchburn became one of the most persist-
ent and determined advocates of greater expansion. A. G. Lehmann who
became Professor of French in 1951 after lecturing at Manchester, and
A. Graham who came to the Department of Zoology in the same year from
Birkbeck College, London, both felt that they were entering a small, enclosed self-satisfied community which would benefit from a shake-up. F. P.
Pickering, who became the first Professor of German in 1953, and, like
Lehmann, had taught at Manchester, was perhaps the bluntest of all in his
assessment. He roundly asserted that no self-respecting university should
number less than 3,000. That was a new voice and a fresh view.

However, it would be inaccurate to suggest that there was a sharp clear-
cut division between the old staff and the newcomers. Not all the older
hands were opposed to expansion; not all the newcomers were avidly for it.
There were enough men, both old and new, who lay between the extremes
or who held no firm view. Some of the newcomers moved almost at once
into representative office. H. G. Sanders became Professor of Agriculture in
1945, Dean of his Faculty in 1947 and Deputy Vice-Chancellor in 1952.
J. M. R. Cormack became Professor of Classics in 1946, Dean of his Faculty
in 1948 and Deputy Vice-Chancellor in succession to Sanders. Reading
welcomed new men. There was no rift. Instead, through their experience
and interests, they provided a wider framework for the discussion of
Reading's future.

The most important of the new men was John Wolfenden. He succeeded
Stenton as Vice-Chancellor in April 1950 and directed Reading's fortunes
throughout the debate about expansion. When he left to become Chairman
of the University Grants Committee in 1963 the University was already
committed to a target of 3,000 students; the decision to expand had been
taken; subsequent increases in the target-figure merely spelled out the
implications of that decision. It is true that in 1946 Stenton had shown
surprising readiness to consider a target of 1,300 and an ultimate size of
2,000, but this had been in response to the promptings of the Grants
Committee.[1] It reflected Stenton's practical wisdom rather than his
instincts, which were all for maintaining the old Reading atmosphere. By
contrast, Wolfenden brought to the problem a fresh mind untrammelled by
all those ties which long association with the place created. To be sure, he
was attracted by the relatively small scale of Reading, but this was partly
because he saw that it would be possible for one man, as Vice-Chancellor, to
'make something of it'. He was wary of Reading's cosiness and alert to the
possibilities of the move to Whiteknights.[2] He was not prepared simply to
preside over a prolonged discussion of how Reading might preserve what it
chose to regard as its essential character. He had not come to Reading, as
he put it, to manage a university in the third division.[3] If expansion were to

[1] See above, pp. 147–9.
[2] Conversation with Lord Wolfenden, 5 July 1975.
[3] Conversation with Professor A. Graham, 20 July 1975.

be national policy, then, shrewdly and carefully, seeking always to preserve the efficient working of the University, he would guide Reading towards expansion.

Wolfenden's Vice-Chancellorship was critical. His appointment reflected the feeling of Sir George Mowbray and other influential members of the Council that Reading should not lag behind in the coming expansion which could plainly be predicted. Moreover, it was clear that the University would require a cool head and a fresh mind in control of the move to Whiteknights. In Wolfenden it got both. More, it got an administrator of real flair, this perhaps less predictably, for as Headmaster of Uppingham and then Shrewsbury, he had scarcely encountered problems of the size and complexity which a university would present. He came to Reading when it was still possible for a Vice-Chancellor personally to supervise and direct much of the administrative and committee work of the University. To some he seemed distinctly headmasterly, an assessment which overlooked his earlier career as a Fellow of Magdalen. Others felt that he became too involved in broadcasting and in the various national and governmental committees on which he served. But the plain fact was that in any debate in the University, in Council or Senate, faculty or committee, he was likely to know the facts better than anyone else, to see the way forward more clearly than anyone else, and to cut through the fog of debate with an illuminating summary more incisively than anyone else. That earned respect. The Registrar, Ernest Smith, shrewd, wise, methodical and beloved of all, occasionally talked of keeping Stenton on the rails,[1] for Stenton's administrative methods sometimes reflected the inclinations and needs of the moment. Smith never talked like that of Wolfenden. Indeed, Wolfenden's quick-silver mind and Smith's prudent and sagacious caution blended in an easy and effective working relationship. Above all, Wolfenden brought a vivacity, a sense that the development of the University was exciting, a fondness for the precise, well chosen word, a wit and sense of humour which were themselves refreshing. He enjoyed it. Others shared in his enjoyment.[2]

[1] Conversation with Miss Anne Gooch, 13 August 1975.
[2] The following note in Wolfenden's hand still remains attached to the minutes of the Whiteknights Park Steering Committee of 18 September 1956: 'A quite different solution has just occurred to me. Put the Park House girls in my house – and we go somewhere else. And anyhow it could be argued that *some* day perhaps the Vice-Chancellor ought to live in Whiteknights Park! [? or in (a) the Gamage's, (b) Blandford Lodge, (c) the Museum, (d) the Lake, (e) the overhead duct carrier, (f) the boiler house.]' Suggestion (e) was contributed by Gerald Palmer who was in the chair; the Gamage's refers to Foxhill, one of the Whiteknights lease-holds; the overhead heating ducts and the boiler house were *ardua negotia* of the Committee.
It is difficult to imagine Stenton enlivening his chairman with such a note. His humour took a different form – 'I remember meeting Stenton in the cloisters on the morning of a grey, cold, drizzling November day when he was looking very starved and as miserable as the day itself. He stopped me and said in a doleful voice: "My dear Betts, do please recollect that it was on such a day as this that they hanged the last Abbot of Reading – a sorrowful occasion, supported fittingly by a chilly, drizzling day".' (Conversation with Professor J. A. Betts, May 1972).

The inner group in Council knew that the University would be unlikely to hold him until retirement. This reflected qualities which some condemned as careerist. But he felt genuinely that to remain too long was to encourage staleness. Stale he never was. Disturbing he could be, intentionally so. He came to Reading at just the right time.

It is important not to oversimplify the new Vice-Chancellor's role within the University. Wolfenden was not an evangelist for expansion. Reading was by no means dormant. It was rather that Wolfenden directed the fortunes of the University during the years when development was prescribed by the simple need to increase student numbers. In 1950 this was not yet the determining, and at times disturbing, element which it was to become in the next twenty-five years. Hence the change was not one from quiescence to ebullition, but from development based on academic ambitions and considerations, to development in which the demand for student places, actual or potential, real or alleged, played a major part. Each type of development involved difficulties, even inconsistencies. The first encouraged expansion on grounds quite independent of student numbers. At Reading it placed academic desiderata in conflict with limitations on overall size, both theoretical and practical. The second assumed that courses would be provided which would match the interests of the increasing flood of students; that supply and demand would neatly coincide. It soon became apparent that that could only be achieved through an imbalance between subjects which was academically unacceptable.

When Wolfenden arrived, the University was already at work preparing the ground for the Quinquennium 1952–7. A committee of Senate had been established in June 1949 to consider plans from faculties. Men were already looking ahead with hope and optimism. Typical was the report from the Faculty of Letters:

> Members of the Board are probably aware that, except for the
> separation of Psychology from Philosophy and the institution of
> Political Economy, there have been no subjects added to the Faculty
> programme for the past forty years. In our opinion the time has come
> when it is necessary to extend the range of our teaching and research.
> We think it now essential that certain subjects, commonly included
> in the courses of arts faculties, should be added, not only on account
> of their intrinsic importance, but also to enrich the studies already in
> the Faculty, while other subjects now deserve to be raised in status.
> We welcome the initiative of the Senate in taking in hand the
> question of the development of the School of Music, and we should
> be glad if the outcome were the institution of a Professorship of
> Music, and the development of the School of Music on lines
> parallel to those of the School of Fine Art. If the Faculty is to
> achieve the proper balance, we believe that certain departments
> should be raised in status and certain new ones created.

It went on to recommend the establishment of Chairs of German and

Political Economy, of Readerships in Italian and Spanish and of a Lecturer-ship in Phonetics. It also asked that special consideration should be given to the improvement of facilities for Medieval History, English Language and Applied Mathematics.[1] The Faculty of Science was in a similar mood. It asked for three new readerships and three new lecturerships and, as soon as the necessary accommodation could be provided through the move to Whiteknights, the establishment of a Department of Physiology and Biochemistry with two Professors and a Reader.[2] Not to be outdone the Faculty of Agriculture recommended the division of the Chair of Agricultural Chemistry into Chairs of Soil Science and Physiology and Biochemistry, and the foundation of Chairs in Microbiology and Animal Genetics, along with five new readerships or senior lecturerships and two new lecturerships. It recommended the establishment of eight further readerships or senior lecturerships as soon as the move to Whiteknights made further expansion possible.[3] The recommendations of all three faculties included the establishment of eight new chairs, twenty new readerships or senior lecturerships and six new lecturerships, along with an unspecified number of staff to support the established activities in the Faculty of Letters. No faculty report turned to the problem of student numbers. No faculty report discussed the emphasis placed on senior appointments. On at least one important matter, the Reports of the Faculties of Science and Agriculture were mutually inconsistent.[4]

These Reports clearly reveal the quandary in which Reading was placed. All faculties had proposals for development. Development meant expansion, but no faculty seemed ready to envisage, still less accept, the consequences of expansion. The Faculty of Letters wanted to establish a Chair of German, the Faculty of Science a Chair of Microbiology, the Faculty of Agriculture a Chair of Soil Science, but none was ready to face the dramatic increase in the overall size of the University which would

[1] Record of informal discussion by the professors in the Faculty, 9 March 1949, accepted by the Board and forwarded to Senate, 2 May 1949 (Senate Reports, ix).
[2] Report of the Board of the Faculty of Science, 24 May 1949, submitted to Senate, 13 June 1949 (Senate Reports, ix). The readerships were to be in Organic Chemistry, Theoretical Physics and Applied Mathematics; the lecturerships in Statistics, Genetics and Meteorology. The Faculty also proposed that as soon as the move to Whiteknights allowed, separate Chairs should be established in Organic and Physical Chemistry and that a Readership in Petrology should be founded.
[3] Report of the Board of the Faculty of Agriculture and Horticulture, 25 May 1949, submitted to Senate 13 June 1949 (Senate Reports, ix). The five immediate readerships or senior lecturerships were to be in Horticultural Botany, Animal Husbandry, Landscape Gardening, Agricultural History, and the Ecology of Crop Plants. The eight later proposals, to be implemented 'about the time of the move to Whiteknights' were for Agricultural Physiology, Chemical Protectants, Dairy Chemistry, Farm Management, Mechanization, Plant Genetics, Plant Pathology, and Pomology.
[4] This was the proposed development of Physiology and Biochemistry. On this prolonged wrangle, which concerned the fate of H. A. D. Neville's old Department of Agricultural Chemistry, see below, pp. 216–19.

necessarily follow if all such proposals were accepted. The desiderata seen by the faculties no longer matched the overall development approved by the Senate and Council. The difficulty implicit in much of the evidence received by the Development Committee in 1943–4 was now much more overt. Nevertheless, as yet, the limitation agreed on overall size was not seriously questioned, still less challenged.

On 27 February 1950 the Committee of Senate reported on these proposals. The Committee had been made up very much of the old hands.[1] It was the last important policy committee to sit under the chairmanship of Stenton. It now imposed some order and restraint on the divergent enthusiasm of the faculties:

> Your committee has reviewed, from the standpoint of the University, the proposals put forward by the boards of the faculties. At an early stage it became evident that questions relating to fundamental principles were involved and we therefore state our view on these before proceeding to present our detailed recommendations for academic developments.
>
> (1) The interests of the University override those of its parts and its internal organization must not be permitted to create any divisions within it which might impair its unity or prevent the fullest utilization of its resources. Only the University can exercise ultimate authority.
>
> (2) The organization of the University into faculties is for administrative convenience. The faculties should not be regarded as self-contained and semi-independent bodies, nor should they in any way set up artificial barriers within the University.
>
> (3) Consequently, the responsibility of any department is primarily to the University as a whole. The rights and duties of departments are not restricted to the faculties to which the departments are assigned . . .
>
> (6) We are of the opinion that in a university of the size of Reading it is undesirable to divide existing departments by the creation of new professorships.

After that sharp remonstration the Committee went on to limit its recommendations to those proposals which in its view required 'consideration and sanction at the highest level'. It left other proposals for heads of departments to make 'in the customary way'. It also categorized its proposals, distinguishing between those which could be accommodated forthwith and those which would require additional accommodation. In the first category it placed two professorships and five lecturerships in the Faculty of Letters, one professorship and four lecturerships in the Faculty

---

[1] The membership was Stenton, Wolters, who was Deputy Vice-Chancellor, the three Deans (Cormack, Harris, Sanders), Barnard, Ditchburn, Kay, Miller, E. H. Neville, Stoughton and Thomas.

of Science and three lecturerships in the Faculty of Agriculture.[1] This was a very truncated programme. The dreams of numerous senior appointments were swept aside. The Report also included one detailed change of direction which seemed to characterize its approach: the proposals for the Faculty of Science now included a lecturership in the History of Science which had not been included in the proposals originally submitted by the Board.

The Report then went on to emphasize the need to support existing departments, especially in those fields of study where Reading had already established some reputation:

> There are important branches of university study which from their nature fall within the province of large departments but are themselves highly specialized in content and methods. As we have already said we do not at present recommend the division of existing departments. We recommend that the University should be careful at all times to make adequate provision for teaching and research in these specialities. In many cases, some provision is in fact already made, but we consider it important that the University should explicitly accept responsibility for maintaining and developing these studies. Here, the initiative rests with the heads of departments, but the Senate has duties and authority with respect to all academic matters and its approval is essential before any proposals of this type can be carried into effect. We recommend, therefore, that the following special studies should be safeguarded by the employment of adequate staff, and by the supply of accommodation and equipment. The list, which is clearly related to the present organization of the University, need not be regarded as exhaustive.

This showed a sensible concern that the expansion of existing departments should not be sacrificed to the establishment of new subjects or fields of study. It was conservative in its effect; the specialities named in the Faculty of Letters for example, were Ancient History, Medieval History, Latin and English Language; but it added a further thirteen possible appointments to the shopping list.[2] Senate and Council accepted the Report.[3]

All this occurred before Wolfenden took over. Its effect and importance were considerable. First, when he arrived, a major debate on development

[1] The proposals were:
   Faculty of Letters: professorships of German, Political Economy; lecturerships in Italian Studies, Phonetics, History of Art, Landscape Architecture, Spanish Studies.
   Faculty of Science: professorship of Physiology; lecturerships in Statistics, Genetics, Theoretical Physics, History of Science.
   Faculty of Agriculture and Horticulture: lecturerships in Animal Genetics, Ecology of Crop Plants, History of Agriculture.
[2] The Committee proposed that appointments should be made in the four subjects named above in the Faculty of Letters; and also in the Faculty of Science in Organic Chemistry, Meteorology and Climatology, Applied Mathematics, and Petrology; and in the Faculty of Agriculture and Horticulture in Animal Husbandry, Farm Management, Mechanization, Soil Science, and Landscape Gardening.
[3] Council Reports, xii, 17 March 1950.

and expansion had already taken place. The Faculties of Science and Agriculture had planned to go much further than the final recommendations agreed by Senate allowed. The discussion had extended to the role of faculties and the subordination of departments to the University. The debate had not always been comfortable. It had certainly not been resolved, for scientists, conscious of the increasingly rapid development and diversification of their subjects, could scarcely be expected to accept the protective barrier which the Report erected around some of the established subjects in the Faculty of Letters. In this the Report underlined, rather than solved, the problems which the University faced. Nevertheless the Report was used as the basis for the academic development envisaged for the Quinquennium 1952–7. The quinquennial estimates drawn up in August 1951 proposed two chairs, in German and Political Economy, two independent lecturerships in Italian and Spanish, six grade I lecturerships of which three were to be in the School of Art, ten grade II lecturerships of which five were to be in the Faculty of Letters, and four assistant lecturerships, all of which were to be in the Faculty of Letters. The plain fact was that proper development in the Faculties of Science and Agriculture was hindered and held up by the lack of adequate accommodation. The Quinquennial Estimates noted the need for:

> . . . new laboratories for various departments on the existing site. Chemistry and Microbiology, in particular, have outgrown their present buildings; and the appropriate amount of higher degree work and research investigation cannot be carried on without additional laboratory accommodation. The departments of the Faculty of Science have been building up the numbers of their Honours Degree students during the current quinquennium, and the logical consequence is an increased demand for research space.[1]

Largely because of this the full interest in expansion was not brought to bear in the discussion. Scientists especially might favour it, but they could not achieve it simply because there was no accommodation into which their departments could expand. This made any debate unreal. The expansion which was possible immediately was so small that it was unobjectionable even to the most conservative. The ultimate objectives seemed so distant and unattainable that they provoked neither support nor opposition. On overall numbers the Quinquennial Estimates were almost apologetic:

> It is intended that student numbers should be increased, in the course of the first three years of the Quinquennium, by about 180. Such an increase would serve a double purpose: (i) it would bring the halls of residence nearer to an economically self-supporting position, (ii) it would provide a slight increase in numbers for those departments which can carry such an increase without a corresponding increase in overhead costs. On both counts the University might

[1] Council Reports, xiii, 9 November 1951.

well be thought to be at present of an uneconomic size, and the
estimated increase mentioned above should be regarded as a step
towards stabilization at a figure between 1,500 and 2,000. We
believe that the increase at present intended can be achieved mainly
by an increased use of lodgings for third-year and (especially) fourth-
year students, and partly, as opportunity arises, by the acquisition
of houses for use as annexes to the existing halls of residence.[1]

The figures given for stabilization were distant visions. Practicable expansion was represented by the increase of 180. That would have left the
University in 1955 just slightly below the total which had been intended
for that year in 1946. In the event it fell short even of this.[2]

The most immediate limitation on these discussions was a practical one:
the stark lack of resources. This affected all aspects of the University's
plans: for new posts, for teaching accommodation both at London Road
and Whiteknights, and for residential places in both old Halls and new. The
financial difficulties were brought home doubly in 1950–2. At this time the
University Grants Committee still considered that much of the capital
expenditure of universities might be met through private endowment.
When the Committee visited Reading in November 1950 it suggested that
the University should consider launching an appeal for funds. This was a
bleak proposal, coming as it did from the body responsible for the distribution of available public money. It met an equally bleak response:

Council has considered seriously and sympathetically the suggestion
made on the occasion of the Committee's visit in November last, that
a public appeal for funds should be launched. Council came to the
conclusion that the spring of 1951 would not be a propitious time
for an appeal, but resolved that the question should be raised again
in the autumn of 1951 and that in the meantime unofficial soundings
should be taken to discover what would be the reaction of individuals
and of industrial bodies to such an appeal. These enquiries are
proceeding, especially with the intention of tapping some of the
financial resources of the farming industry. It must be recorded that
opinions hitherto have not been very encouraging.[3]

Another difficulty was more immediate and pressing. In 1951–2 the
University went ahead with developments which were linked with the
coming Quinquennium. It established two new professorships, in Music
and Microbiology, and eight other new teaching appointments. It had now
made arrangements for the promotion of a limited number of academic
staff to senior appointments; it was attempting to put the laboratory
expenses of science departments on a better footing; it was facing in-

[1] *Ibid.*
[2] In 1946 the numbers intended in 1955 were 1,300. In 1951 the addition of 180 to the
current year in which the total was 1,090 would have produced 1,270 in 1955. The
actual numbers in that year were 1,162.
[3] Quinquennial Estimates, August 1951, p. 42 (Council Reports, xiii).

creasingly heavy expenditure in maintaining the University farms and the Horticultural Station; and for the first time it was trying to create a proper establishment for secretarial posts in all the larger departments throughout all faculties. These plans marked the point at which the University, under the leadership of Wolfenden, sought to repair some of the defects of the years before and during the War. However, the programme involved a budgetary deficit of £37,508 and the report of the Finance Committee in recommending the proposals, included a firm warning:

> It is clear that the annual rate of expenditure has now reached a level substantially above the foreseeable annual income, and a deficit of this magnitude cannot be contemplated as an annually recurring feature of the University's finances. It may therefore be necessary, in relation to the next Quinquennium and to the present national situation, to review, among other items, the fees charged to students for tuition and maintenance, the trading activities of the University, and the extent to which further expansion of departments will be possible.[1]

This was reiterated by Sir George Mowbray in his report as President of Council in January 1952:

> The present financial position of the University must cause serious concern, though to a great extent it arises from circumstances beyond our control. Last year I said that we should be confronted by many problems and meet with many disappointments. Those problems and disappointments have grown in number and size and I have no doubt that more lie ahead of us. I am equally convinced, however, that we shall overcome them, for the University is lively and vigorous, able to face its tasks and difficulties with confidence in its own strength.[2]

The deficit was partially met by transferring the greater part of it to the Capital Account. Even so over £12,000 remained to be funded in the new Quinquennium.[3] The experience was chastening. A modest attempt to establish a few new posts and give the academic staff reasonable support and encouragement had led to a disturbing financial problem. This was bound to dampen any ardour for expansion, and although an increase in the grant received through the University Grants Committee helped to repair matters in 1952–3 and thereafter,[4] it left Wolfenden in particular very conscious of the practical difficulties. There was a distinct aroma of burnt fingers.[5] In the course of 1952 the University Grants Committee

---

[1] Report of Finance Committee to Council, 25 May 1951 (Council Reports, xiii).
[2] *Proceedings 1950–1*, p. 6.
[3] *Proceedings 1952–3*, p. 7.
[4] The Parliamentary recurrent grant was increased from £251,510 in 1951–2 to £300,625 in 1952–3.
[5] Conversation with A. G. Lehmann, 6 August 1975.

placed an embargo on further new appointments. Some proposals were suspended.[1]

Underlying these difficulties was the much more serious problem of student residence. The University had always put residential requirements in the forefront of its plans. New Halls and extensions to old Halls seemed to be the first essential step in any development, and this impression was strengthened rather than weakened by the acquisition of Whiteknights. Sir George Mowbray summed this up in his Report of 1948:

> The present student population of approximately 1,000 is maintained by the presence of a high proportion of older ex-service men, many of them married, who are responsible for finding their own accommodation during their courses at the University. With the departure of these men there is reason to anticipate a serious fall in the total number of students during the next few years unless the University is able to provide an additional hall of residence for men students and to increase the number of lodgings at present available.[2]

He returned to the point a year later:

> Further expansion of the number of students is dependent on the provision of additional residential facilities, and, even so, any such expansion will be confined to a limited number of departments whose classroom and laboratory accommodation still permits an increased intake of students. In my report of a year ago I stated that there was reason to anticipate a fall in the total number of students during the next few years with the departure of the older ex-servicemen who have been responsible for finding their own accommodation, unless the University is able to make additional residential provision for men students. That this factor has already begun to operate will be appreciated when it is realized that notwithstanding the purchase of additional houses providing 40 extra residential places . . . the total number of students who were in the University at the beginning of the autumn term 1949 rose by only 22.[3]

Initially this emphasis on residence informed the policy of Wolfenden as much as that of Stenton. Indeed Wolfenden pressed on with the proposals for a new hall of residence in 1950 despite the increasingly emphatic

[1] This is apparent from a report submitted to Senate on 5 December 1952 on the establishment of the Professorship of German. The recommendation to proceed was made after notification of the recurrent grant for 1953–4 and on Wolfenden's advice that 'the ruling of the University Grants Committee that there should be no appointments to new posts would not be rigidly applied'. Senate also expressed concern about other effects of the UGC's intervention. It recommended to Council that 'steps be taken . . . to cancel the suspension, caused by the action of the University Grants Committee in 1952, of an appointment to the post in the Department of Mathematics for which provision was made in the Estimates for 1951–2.' (Senate Minutes, iii). The UGC ruling forbade the establishment of new posts if it resulted in creating or increasing a deficit on the current account.

[2] *Proceedings 1947–8*, p. 5.

[3] *Proceedings 1948–9*, p. 5.

negative response which Stenton had first reported in 1949.[1] Expansion and residence had to go hand in hand; without the first the second was impossible; that was the essence of the argument.

This seemed a powerful case at Reading. However, it encountered formidable obstacles in the University Grants Committee. First, it looked like special pleading, increasingly so in the late 40s and early 50s as provincial university colleges gained university status. Many of these could place a similar emphasis on student accommodation; some indeed had followed Reading in establishing halls of residence. Hence Reading seemed less and less exceptional and its argument for residential accommodation less and less convincing. Secondly, the more seriously the argument was taken the more it told against any significant expansion at Reading at all. If development there entailed the provision of residential accommodation then it was far better to direct the limited resources under the control of the Grants Committee to other universities where advances could be made without such extra costs.[2] That put Reading at a disadvantage. It was only removed by the increasingly rapid expansion in the university system as a whole. Once it became clear that civic universities sited near town-centres could only expand through the purchase and clearance of expensive municipal sites, once expansion was envisaged on so large a scale that all universities had to make claims for residential accommodation, then Reading's disadvantage became its opportunity. With Whiteknights available and long delayed schemes for development still in suspense, it suddenly seemed a much more fertile field for investment. This change did not begin until the mid 1950s. It reached its full effect after the publication of the Robbins Report in 1963.

However, at Reading the real debate about expansion took place much earlier. The expansion of numbers in the 1960s flowed from policies decided between 1956 and 1963. Participants recall some discussion and debate in these years, but in so far as it centred on the desire to preserve a small intimate university it was little more than a rearguard action fought by a diminishing minority. The matter was in fact settled in principle between 1951 and 1956, and it is the argument of this earlier period which still survives in the memory of the participants as the crucial turning point. As the rate of expansion increased so the debate about it diminished. From arguing whether the University should expand men turned to discuss how it should expand. Sometimes there was no less heat in that, but issues of principle were not perhaps so obvious.

Different individuals recall different incidents within this, the critical period, between 1951 and 1956. For Wolfenden the crisis came in 1951–2 in the discussion of the apparently minuscule increase of roughly 200 included

---

[1] URC, Registrar, box 70. For further discussion of the proposal for a new hall of residence, see below, pp. 186, 193–4.

[2] Conversation with Sir Harold Sanders, 12 August 1975.

in the Quinquennial Estimates:

> In retrospect the watershed was when the momentous decision was
> taken, laughable as it must now seem, to increase student numbers
> up to 1,200. That, of course, meant a corresponding increase in the
> size of the academic staff and the consequence of that would be, as
> somebody plaintively protested, 'But Vice-Chancellor, that will
> mean that there will be people coming into the Senior Common
> Room whom we don't know by sight'. But it was either that or stagna-
> tion and the Council, expertly handled by Sir George Mowbray,
> was emphatically not in favour of stagnation.[1]

For Lehmann also 'things began to warm up with a great debate in Senate
on the prospective size of the University which was held in 1952'; for him
the discussion turned on an increase to a total of 1,500.[2] That total, however, was not accepted until 1956. Once again there was a great debate.
Gerald Palmer, then Vice-President of Council and Chairman of the
Finance Committee and of the Whiteknights Development Committee,
recalls that it was still very conservative in flavour: 1,500 was accepted, but
2,000 'was considered outrageous, not to be discussed at all seriously'.[3]
Some, however, took such a possibility in earnest. Ditchburn argued
persistently for a target of 2,000.[4] In 1956 he and his supporters lost the
battle. The course on which the University settled is well defined in the
Quinquennial Estimates submitted for 1957–62:

> In the course of the quinquennium there has been a slight increase in
> student numbers made possible chiefly by minor additions to the
> amount of residential accommodation. The policy of extending
> halls of residence by the acquisition of houses for use as annexes has
> reached its limit; and it is impossible to find additional lodgings of a
> suitable kind. Careful and anxious consideration has been, and is
> being, given to the related problems of (i) the present size of the
> University and (ii) the provision which the University ought to make
> for the prospective increase in the number of applicants:
>
> (i) In many ways the present size of the University is satisfactory.
> Our numbers are manageable, and there is a pleasant feeling of
> intimacy, both in the academic staff and among the student body.
> On the other hand, from some points of view the present number is
> inconvenient. We are just too big for an entirely centralized and
> personal form of administration, but not quite big enough to justify
> a thoroughgoing system of delegation and devolution. Also our size
> is in some ways uneconomic; for instance, in some departments more
> students could be taught with little or no increase in the size of the

[1] J. F. Wolfenden, *Turning Points* (London, 1976), p. 114.
[2] Conversation with A. G. Lehmann, 6 August 1975.
[3] Conversation with G. E. H. Palmer, 12 August 1975.
[4] Conversation with Professor R. W. Ditchburn, 11 August 1975.

teaching staff. However this may be, we are not in a position to increase our numbers with the existing residential accommodation.

(ii) Some of these points have a bearing on our possibilities of expansion to meet the expected increase in total University numbers over the next ten years. We have based our plans for the Whiteknights Park development on an ultimate population of 1,500, a substantial proportionate increase in our present size; for instance we have planned the new Faculty of Letters building for 500. The crux is residential accommodation. This University, unlike those modern universities which are situated in large cities, has no substantial population round it from which to draw a body of 'day-school' students. If it is to exist at all Reading must be a residential university. And if its size is to increase there must be an increase in the residential accommodation available inside the University. It is accepted that residence is desirable in all universities; for us it is not merely desirable but essential. We are therefore in this position. We wish to play our part in providing for the expected total increase in university population. To do that we contemplate increasing our numbers from just over 1,100 to 1,500. To do that two additional halls of residence are necessary. One of these we now expect to start building in 1958. But another will be necessary within the quin-quennium if the total number of students is to reach 1,500.[1]

The discussion and the settlement of policy between 1952 and 1956 presents several peculiar features. First, the argument was decidedly vigorous for a planned expansion which was really so small. To some the expansion was envisaged, not as an addition of a few hundred students, 200 in 1952 and a further 300 in 1956, but as a proportionate increase of 50 per cent which was bound to affect the character of a small institution numbering little more than 1,000 at the start of the process. Some too thought that Reading was treading on a slippery slope of unfathomable depth, and this view gained strength from the readiness of others to go well beyond 1,500. Secondly the argument took place without any reference at all to the discussions and decisions of 1949 which had envisaged a short-term expansion to 1,300 and an ultimate size of 2,000.[2] None of the participants now recalled those earlier debates which would greatly have strengthened the case for expansion. Nor did the Registrar remind the Senate that it had already agreed to advance to those very targets which were now under discussion. This omission is at first sight surprising, for Ernest Smith was the most meticulous of men. It points to the changed terms of the debate. In 1949 the expansion was hypothetical; it was assumed and indeed stated that it depended on the provision of resources and in particular on an increase in residential accommodation. In 1952, this no

---

[1] Council Reports, xvi.
[2] See above, pp. 148–9, 164–5.

longer held good. The University now knew that the University Grants Committee did not accept the priority which had been given hitherto to the building of a new hall of residence. It was now resigned to extending residential accommodation by buying houses as annexes to existing halls.[1] Hence expansion in 1952 was a much more immediate and practical question than it had been earlier. Small as the proposed numerical increase was, it embodied a much more direct threat to the traditional atmosphere of Reading. It is probably for this reason that the case was argued *de novo*, without reference to earlier discussions, and with much greater seriousness and a sharper edge than the earlier hypothetical schemes had required.

Thirdly, and perhaps most important of all, the terms of the debate altered. It began as a discussion of principle, of the possible effects on Reading of any sizeable expansion, of the gains and losses which expansion would bring to the University. It became, increasingly, a debate about ways and means, about where new appointments should be made, about what new departments should be established, above all about priorities for the new buildings envisaged in Whiteknights. This change was already far advanced by 1956 when the plan for the coming quinquennium of 1957–62 was drafted. A year later the policies which Reading would follow were settled beyond recall. By November 1956 the government had already determined on a policy of expansion which went beyond the total increases envisaged in the quinquennial submissions. In January 1957 Sir Keith Murray, Chairman of the University Grants Committee, wrote to all universities seeking their support for such a policy. For Reading the proposals were indeed considerable:

> The quinquennial estimates which you have submitted to the
> Committee indicate that your University appears to expect student
> numbers to reach about 1,500 by 1961–2 and the Committee would
> like me to discuss with you the possibility of your envisaging a
> further expansion to 2,000 . . .[2]

This plea was backed by reference to national needs measured in the currently fashionable jargon of the 'plateau' which was supposed to represent the level at which the consequences of a rising birth rate and an increased demand for university education would settle. But essentially the request was for Reading to advance to a maximum number which not many within the university had so far advocated and which had not merited serious discussion six months earlier.[3] Reading accepted the invitation. On 21 January Senate minuted:

> The Senate considered a letter from the University Grants Com-
> mittee, dated 11 January 1957, suggesting that the University should

[1] Quinquennial Estimates 1952–7, pp. 33–4 (Council Reports, xiii). For further discussion, see below, pp. 186, 193–4.
[2] Sir Keith Murray to Sir John Wolfenden, 11 January 1957 (Senate Reports, xiii).
[3] See above, p. 169.

consider the possibility of increasing its student numbers to 2,000 by the mid-1960s.

After full discussion it was agreed to inform the Council that

(a) it was clear to the Senate that the University was under an obligation to meet as far as it could the national need for an increase in the numbers following university courses, and ought therefore to attempt to reach the suggested total of 2,000;

(b) it would be possible for the University to undertake such an expansion and still retain its present character only if sufficient residential accommodation were provided in addition to the necessary teaching buildings; and

(c) the Senate would discuss at their next meeting the academic and numerical considerations which would determine the direction of this expansion.[1]

Subsequent discussion revealed no further difficulty. All faculties were agreed that the expansion to 2,000 could take place without any lowering in admission standards. The scientists staked out a claim for more laboratory space; with that they concluded 'the Faculty could be reasonably expected to double its size'. Senate indicated that its agreement was based on the assumption that provision would be made for 'the necessary residential accommodation, the additional staff which would be required and the necessary additional accommodation for the Library'. Given that, 'it seemed that the University could hope to comply with the suggestion of the University Grants Committee that an increase in numbers be made by the mid 1960s to something like 1,850 to 2,000'.[2]

The difficulties all came later. One was general to all universities: they were being asked to expand in a year in which the current provision of money and the estimated provision for the coming Quinquennium seemed quite inadequate. In notifying the quinquennial allocations the University Grants Committee admitted as much:

As regards new developments, while the Committee recognize that the grants for the year 1957–8 cannot in general provide any appreciable margin for increased activity, they hope that in the later years of the Quinquennium it will be possible to undertake some of the developments which universities have proposed.[3]

That bland note scarcely did justice to the fact that it was the Committee itself which, only four months earlier, had invited these proposals. In October Wolfenden reported to Senate that the Committee of Vice-Chancellors and Principals intended to make a united approach to the University Grants Committee:

Among the points he had put forward to the Committee of Vice-

---

[1] Senate Minutes, iii, 2820, 21 January 1957.
[2] Senate Minutes, iii, 2835, 25 February 1957.
[3] Letter of 29 April 1957: Council Reports, xvii, 24 May 1957.

Chancellors and Principals were that the allocation of the grant for the current year would make it difficult for this University to maintain its present services at a time when it should be expanding its facilities, and that if the number of students in residence were to be raised to 2,000 by 1967 it was essential that facilities be provided so that the necessary teachers could be trained immediately.[1]

This represented only a pause in the onward march. By 1959 it had been agreed that the total of 2,000 would be attained by 1964.[2]

Another difficulty was centred on the problem of residential accommodation. At its meeting on 6 May 1957 Wolfenden warned Senate that the building programme would contain proposals on residence which were 'in a sense, revolutionary' and would raise 'entirely fresh problems'. These stemmed from the University Grants Committee:

> The Chairman of the University Grants Committee has suggested that consideration be given to the possibility of Halls having two sittings for meals; also that when new Halls are to be built, the feasibility of planning central feeding facilities for dormitory blocks or for more scattered units be borne in mind.

The Building Development Committee proposed just such a programme: the erection of a second new men's Hall which would share all central facilities with one already planned to start in 1958; the erection of dormitory blocks at St Patrick's, Wessex, St George's and Mansfield; and the acceptance of double sittings for meals at Mansfield and St George's. Senate accepted the scheme only grudgingly; adding the rider that:

> ... they felt that the scheme was not necessarily the one which the University would or should have adopted had it been free to plan without consideration of initial capital cost. (Some members dissociated themselves from this rider on the ground that the word 'necessarily' should have been omitted.)[3]

The Building Development Committee and the Council took note. The scheme for a double Hall was abandoned. Instead, a new court, dining room and kitchen was planned for St Patrick's; this, along with extensions to other Halls and a new Hall of ordinary proportions, was sufficient to accommodate the projected increase in numbers. There the argument rested and that was the extent of the debate. Within a year of agreeing to a total of 1,500 for the new Quinquennium, the University was set on a course for 2,000. In its intentions at any rate, if not yet in its achievement, it had passed through a size barrier.

That pattern was repeated three years later in the discussion of the Quinquennium 1962–7. Once again, in a letter of 8 January 1960, the Chairman of the University Grants Committee asked universities to

[1] Senate Minutes, iii, 2912, 14 October 1957.
[2] *Proceedings 1958–9*, p. 9.
[3] Senate Minutes, iii, 2856, 13 May 1957.

reconsider their schemes for expansion on the ground that the future demand for university education would be greater than had been envisaged hitherto.[1] Once again Reading responded, this time with a suggested target of 3,000 by 1970. A committee of Senate reported that both the Faculty of Science and the Faculty of Agriculture might find it difficult to match the increased intake planned for the Faculty of Letters, and it noted that it would be necessary to abandon the principle of parity in faculty numbers. Nevertheless, Senate accepted that the target of 3,000 could be achieved.[2] As in 1957 residential accommodation seemed to be the overriding difficulty. Once again a committee proposed a possible solution: that students should spend only two years in Hall but should remain as members of Hall during their year in lodgings. Once again Senate expressed its doubt and recommended that the provision of residential accommodation should 'allow for all members of a Hall to remain in residence for the whole of their university career'.[3] This, the residential question, was the residue of the more generalized argument about the ultimate size of the University. The core of the argument had been left aside. The principle had been settled by a discussion of the practicalities. And the principle of a small restricted university was no longer defensible. When expansion was next discussed in 1963, Senate recommended that 'a considerable increase to at least a student number between 4,000 and 5,000' was not merely practicable or acceptable, but desirable. This was on 14 October, ten days before the government's announcement accepting the Robbins Report.[4] Some still had doubts; Edgar Thomas was still ready to argue that the advantages of size were all quantitative and the disadvantages all qualitative; but the battle was over. Even Aspinall, who had persistently abstained in all the earlier votes recommending expansion, now acquiesced in a unanimous decision. The matter was aptly summarized by Ernest Smith's successor, J. F. Johnson, in the papers he prepared for Senate's discussion in the course of the summer:

The signs are, therefore, that the 3,000 target should be reached fairly

[1] Senate Reports, xvi, 18 January 1960.
[2] Senate Reports, xvii, 11 March 1960. The prognosis at Reading on the balance between faculties should be contrasted with the view of the University Grants Committee, expressed in the letter of 8 January 1960: 'So far as the division of the expansion between Pure Science and Technology on the one hand and Arts, Medicine, Agriculture and Veterinary Science on the other hand is concerned, the Committee see no reason to depart from their previous assumption that the additional numbers will be divided, among the Universities as a whole, in the proportion of 2:1.' (Senate Reports, xvi, 18 January 1960).
[3] Senate Minute 3226, 11 March 1960. Senate's objection to the Committee's proposal was on the ground that 'it would not be possible to find the number of lodgings that would be required'. It accepted that some students might wish to leave Hall in their third year and it recommended that the new Halls should include dining and common-room facilities for such students.
[4] Senate Minutes, iv, 3731, 14 October 1963.

comfortably by 1970, though perhaps not in exactly the ways envisaged in 1960.

The arguments for the University's aiming at a greater number – say perhaps 4,000 – are convincing, assuming always, of course, that the necessary buildings and finance are made available at the right time. The main points are, briefly:

(a) By the time the University numbers 3,000 much of the intimacy which characterized it when it was smaller will have disappeared, and a further increase in numbers will have little additional effect in this direction. Indeed, the 'point of no return' in this respect has probably been passed already.

(b) Unless the University grows, it will be in danger of becoming and remaining a 'minor' university in comparison with others.

(c) Some departments could, with profit, be bigger, and would become more effective and efficient if they were.

(d) It would be possible to have more 'peripheral' departments or sub-departments which, although they would not produce dramatic increases in numbers, would be of great benefit and stimulus to the principal departments in each faculty.

(e) The introduction of new subjects of study . . . would give a fillip to the whole tone and atmosphere of the University which in some sectors is feeling the disadvantage of having been restricted for a very long period to a comparatively small range of departments.[1]

That predicted too modest a future. Once the Robbins Report had gained government approval sights were raised even higher. On 20 November, Cormack as acting Vice-Chancellor and the three Deans reported that:

. . . it could be said with confidence that a target of 3,000 can be achieved by 1967–8; indeed, the figure of 3,000 seems well below the probable undergraduate population, and, as there is every reason to expect that the number of postgraduate students will also rise, the total population may well be 5,000 . . . .

It is perhaps sufficient to say here that a target of at least 5,000 by 1973–4 should, all other things being equal, be assured; and that the figure might well be considerably in excess of that. Consideration should be given, as soon as it is possible, to the assessment of the figure for 1980–1; and it should be borne in mind that the Robbins Report mentions some existing smaller universities as becoming 8,000–10,000 in size by that time.[2]

This ran ahead too far and too fast. Reading was not alone in its reaction. On 23 December 1963 Wolfenden, as Chairman of the University Grants Committee, wrote to say that the response of universities to the Robbins Report amounted to a higher aggregate of places than even Robbins had

---

[1] Senate Reports, xxi, 14 October 1963.
[2] Senate Reports, xxii, 20 November 1963.

envisaged in the immediate future. 'A degree of scaling down, or spreading over' was necessary. After discussions in January Reading's immediate contribution was reduced to 3,700 in 1967–8. In earlier years this news might have been received with sighs of relief. Now it was noted for Senate that 'in broad terms this means that the proposed rate of expansion will be delayed by about one year'.[1]

This marked a further important change in attitude at Reading. Hitherto expansion had come at the instigation of the University Grants Committee, which itself had but responded to national needs and available resources as envisaged, at times not entirely clearly or consistently, at the Ministry of Education and in the government of the day. Stenton's first essay beyond the original Development Plan of 1943–4 was a direct response to the urgings of the University Grants Committee in 1945 and 1946 following its first appreciation of post-war needs for students and the publication of the Barlow Report.[2] The raising of the current target from 1,500 to 2,000 in 1957 was again a response to the initiative of the University Grants Committee; the Committee itself proposed the new figure.[3] Yet again it was the Chairman of the University Grants Committee who in 1960 asked universities to reconsider their plans for expansion in the light of a future demand for places which was likely to be greater than hitherto envisaged; at Reading that led to an upward revision from 2,000 to 3,000.[4] Up to the publication of the Robbins Report, in short, the University Grants Committee had provided the stimulus; Reading had responded. That was made perfectly clear, without any fuss or comment, in the reports of Sir George Mowbray as Chairman of Council:

> Council and Senate have had under consideration the question of long-term development following the Government's announcement of its policy of making greatly increased provision for University education . . . . In a letter, dated 29 May 1946, the University Grants Committee invited the University to consider how far it would be possible to go in ten years towards achieving this aim.[5]

> In my last report I mentioned the possibility of increasing our numbers to 1,500 by 1962; since then the University Grants Committee has suggested a target figure of 2,000 for the middle of the 1960s.[6]

> Last year in my Report I referred to our plans for development based on the assumption that our numbers will rise to 2,000 by 1964 . . . . Meanwhile we have been asked to consider a rise to 3,000 by 1970.[7]

[1] Senate Reports, xxii, 20 January 1964: Senate Reports, xxiii, 4 May 1964.
[2] See above, pp. 147–9.
[3] See above, pp. 171–2.
[4] See above, pp. 173-4.
[5] *Proceedings 1945–6*, p. 6.
[6] *Proceedings 1956–7*, p. 3.
[7] *Proceedings 1959–60*, p. 9.

Sir George was nobody's fool, least of all in matters which concerned the financial relations of local and central government. His reports lay bare a reality which sensitive denials of intervention in the affairs of the University scarcely veiled. The University Grants Committee was effectively determining the future size of the University, sometimes directly, sometimes by inviting bids for increased targets, always after discussion and consultation. The University could not object; it was financially dependent on the Committee. Indeed it would not object for the simple reason that men at Reading just as in the University Grants Committee, the government or the country at large, could appreciate the need for expansion. This again was emphasized repeatedly in Mowbray's Reports. In 1957:

> There is no sign of slackening in the rate of increase. Indeed, the pressure on places is such that we are able to take one in every seven of our qualified applicants. And this at a time when those born in the peak years of high birth-rate have not yet reached university age. There can be no doubt that there are problems awaiting us over the next ten years. At the heart of them is the determination both to play our part in attaining a national objective and to ensure that this University loses nothing of the distinctiveness of the contribution which it has now for thirty years made to the education of young men and women.[1]

And in 1958:

> Our commitments are rapidly increasing and will continue to increase; so will our needs. The problem of providing education at the university level, never more acute than it is today, must be viewed from the national standpoint and must be seen as an investment in our future as a nation. To do otherwise would be not only to lose an opportunity but to starve ourselves of the trained leadership which we shall need so urgently in the future.[2]

In considering the development of Reading, therefore, there is no justification for pussy-footed concealment of the leading role which was played by the University Grants Committee. But it would be equally wrong to suggest that there was some kind of conflict of authority; the Committee simply beckoned along a road which the University was ready to travel. Discussion centred not on the development of Reading into a larger institution, nor even on the speed with which that development might ideally take place. It centred on the provision of the men and women, buildings and equipment, without which the agreed development could not take place. On the one side was the Grants Committee disbursing all too limited funds; on the other the University insisting that it could only expand if adequate provision were made. Once again the problem was summed up

---

[1] *Proceedings 1956–7*, p. 8.
[2] *Proceedings 1957–8*, p. 9. Compare *Proceedings 1960–1*, p. 11.

by Sir George Mowbray in commenting on the increased target of 2,000 agreed in 1957:

> It is quite startling to realize that if this target is reached we shall have increased our numbers threefold in thirty years; but we shall not be able to achieve this unless money is forthcoming for a considerable amount of new accommodation, for both residence and teaching . . . . As members will understand, the cost of such expansion and development for this University alone will not be small. Each of the twenty-one universities of the United Kingdom is facing similar problems, making similar plans and proffering similar financial requests. If the total university population of the country is to be increased to the extent which is at present envisaged a great deal of money will be needed. We await the outcome of our submissions.[1]

At the end of the Quinquennium of 1957–62 his view was much the same:

> The year under review, which marks the end of the Quinquennium 1957–62, saw the University trying hard to continue its expansion towards the target of 3,000 students by the early 1970s, albeit with some doubts whether recurrent grants or money for buildings would be sufficient to enable it to reach that target. One might think that merely to double the size of an existing institution was a straight-forward operation. This is far from the fact; and the creation of new universities has in many ways complicated the issue. We can all accept the need for new universities and yet feel that, with so many being founded so soon, added difficulties have been imposed upon existing institutions who have, after all, willingly accepted the University Grants Committee's requests for rapid expansion.
>
> Undeniably, much has been achieved during the Quinquennium 1957–62. We have increased our numbers substantially, and might have done even better had we been able to improve our facilities and increase our staff as we had wished. By this I do not mean that we expected to have a free hand, so much as that grants have not matched our legitimate needs.[2]

That statement was made in the knowledge that the Robbins Committee was at work and was due to report in the following year. The effect of the Report was summarized brusquely by Sir George in his next statement to the University Court:

> We were thus presented with a problem of a quite different order from the earlier one, the solution of which is immensely more difficult. The immediate need is to effect a large increase in student numbers in the period up to 1967–8, and the Council and Senate have therefore agreed not only to attempt to achieve our target of

[1] *Proceedings 1956–7*, pp. 3–4.
[2] *Proceedings 1961–2*, pp. 10–11.

3,000 by then but to go well beyond it, to a figure of some 5,000. Broadly speaking, this means more than doubling our present student numbers in four years. This bald statement alone will serve to point the magnitude of our task.[1]

Great though the task might be, the University took to it readily. Sir George went on to remark:

Many who were convinced that the earlier targets for expansion were too conservative and the financial provision too low are not surprised that a proper assessment of the national need should place such a heavy burden on the universities. I have been impressed by the good will and keenness with which all concerned in the University are approaching this considerable task. It has already meant extra work for the academic staff, particularly those members of it concerned with administration, and undoubtedly, it will involve a great deal more. I am convinced that we shall not fail through lack of enthusiasm here.[2]

The Robbins Report brought two important changes in its train. These are not easy to describe or date with precision; they were very probably unintended and were certainly unavowed; they stand quite apart from the straightforward increase in numbers which was the Report's chief intent, yet they followed from both the size of the intended increase and the Committee's proposals for achieving it. The first involved the relationship of the University to the University Grants Committee. Up to the Robbins Report the University Grants Committee had played the role of a petitioner, asking the University to consider increasing numbers. In response to the Robbins Report, Reading, like other universities, offered more than the Committee wanted. Moreover in the ten years of extraordinarily rapid expansion which followed the Report, the University, once again like other universities, continued to bid high, to offer, whenever the discussions with the University Grants Committee allowed, a higher rather than a lower target for development; and it persisted in this even when in 1974–5 it had become obvious that economic reality was reducing the planning of continued expansion to a mere paper exercise, unreal and unconvincing.[3] The information available at Reading suggested that in bidding for resources in this way it was not departing from the lines followed by other universities. Inevitably in such a situation the University Grants Committee became less of a petitioner, requesting the University to consider an increase in numbers, and more of an arbitrator, adjudicating between the

[1] *Proceedings 1962–3*, p. 11.
[2] *Ibid.*
[3] On 24 April 1975 the Chairman of the UGC notified all universities of a reduction in the projected expansion for 1981–2. His letter suggested that Reading's new target should be within the range 5,900–7,200 (Committee of Deans, 12 May 1975). The University returned a total of 7,200 (Vice-Chancellor to Deans, 7 July 1975). The previous target, submitted by the University, 10 July 1973, had been 8,500.

proposals and plans of all the universities by reducing the bids for expansion
to acceptable proportions overall. As Sir George Mowbray hinted in his
Report of 1962 the difficulty of planning within a single university had been
increased by the establishment of new universities. It was now compounded
by the even newer universities founded on the recommendation of the
Robbins Committee. There were now more bids from more institutions,
some of which had to be tended from foundation. Much more than previously developments at Reading depended on the specific approval of the
University Grants Committee. The rules governing the relationship
between the Committee and the University had not been changed. The
University still had formal control of the resources made available to it. It
was rather that as the schemes submitted by universities multiplied, and as
the schemes themselves became more costly, so the Committee necessarily
came to exercise a directing choice. This was not intervention in any literal
sense; the Committee was simply choosing whether or not to back proposals
which universities had themselves advanced. Nevertheless this had an
important effect. At Reading the Department of Law could not have
been established without the provision of special resources by the Committee. Once that provision had been made there was no going back.[1] Even
where there was no such special provision, the Committee's response to the
University's proposals was important. In discussions within the University
even the briefest approval of a particular proposal by the Committee was
sufficient to provide its advocates with a powerful weapon in debate. This
certainly contributed to the establishment of a Chair of Planning in the
adverse financial circumstances of 1976. The University Grants Committee
had perhaps become more powerful than it knew.

These developments were intimately related to a second change heralded
by the Robbins Report. Up to 1962 the University experienced little real
difficulty in envisaging its expansion as an organic development of its
existing subjects and departments. If the numbers of students were assured,
if 2,000, even 3,000 could be accommodated in lecture rooms, laboratories,
libraries and halls of residence, then their academic needs could be met by
expanding existing departments and developing new subjects around the
established courses. The whole development could be envisaged as a
necessary and welcome rounding-off of the University's existing arrangements. The expansion envisaged in the Robbins Report no longer permitted
such assumptions. If, as Sir George Mowbray summed it up, the University
was to double in size in a space of four years, then it would have to teach new
subjects and found new departments. Hitherto diversification had arisen

---

[1] The establishment of Law at Reading was advanced as an instance of direct
intervention on the part of the University Grants Committee by Lord Crowther Hunt in
the *Times Higher Education Supplement*, no. 240 (28 May 1976), p. 15. He did not note that
Reading had included Law in its quinquennial proposals for 1972–7. This submission in
turn was based on the work of an earlier University working party which reported on the
possibility of establishing the subject in 1963–4.

from academic desiderata. Now it was a consequence of the proposed in-crease in numbers. Up to 1963 Reading had sought resources to maintain a steadily increasing flow into its existing departments. After 1963 it also had to seek for courses towards which the vastly increased flood of new students might be directed. Hence the changes of the next decade cannot be mea-sured purely in terms of size. In 1962–3 there were 27 departments, in-cluding the Institute of Education and the Schools of Fine Art and Music, and 27 established professorships. Ten years later there were 38 depart-ments and 59 established professorships.[1]

The onset of these changes in 1962 and 1963 is perhaps best illustrated by two documents. The first comes from Professor A. G. Lehmann, Dean of the Faculty of Letters. It is dated 4 October 1962, over a year before the publication of the Robbins Report, but it attacked the problem which the Report was to present.[2] Lehmann pointed out that the completion, between 1963 and 1965, of halls of residence which were already under construction would inevitably add to the total number of students in his faculty. Assuming that the increased intake could scarcely be less than fifty, he went on to review the resources available:

> Expansion of existing departments to meet apparent demand is indicated positively only in the cases of English, French and Geography . . . . The capacity of these three departments to expand significantly, however, is limited by the fact that their present size is either near or at the optimum in terms of their structure, and further that major expansion by them would lead to a change of balance within the Faculty . . . . Clearly therefore any increase in student numbers in the Letters Faculty beyond an annual intake of about 290 (which represents a total undergraduate population of about 900) cannot be achieved without new developments. The proposals embodied in the Quinquennial Estimates 1962–7 suggest only one already considered field in which rapid expansion would be possible, and that is Sociology . . . . The real problem is of course that this extra resource is required by next October (1963), but the orthodox process of recruiting a professor and staff could not be followed through in the time available. A similar difficulty would arise if it were decided to pursue any of the other proposals approved for the present Quinquennium, such as Spanish or Russian, though early action upon these proposals is obviously desirable.

> At this stage therefore all that can usefully be said is that the need for urgent discussion of and action on the issues raised by the

[1] These developments are discussed below, pp. 223–36.
[2] Lehmann's prescience came in part from his membership of the Hale Committee on University Teaching Methods. The Hale Committee shared its statistical services with the Robbins Committee, and its members had sources of information, informal but informed, on the direction the Robbins Report was to take (Conversation with A. G. Lehmann, 6 August 1975).

> Hall building programme and the policy of expanding student
> numbers, is clearly imperative.[1]

This certainly, and understandably, underestimated the expansion which
could be achieved in the larger established departments in the Faculty.
Nevertheless, Lehmann had put his finger on the crucial problem in expansion: the difficulty of relating academic development to the building programme, and especially, at Reading, to the programme for the provision of
residential places. The same point was made by Sir George Mowbray in his
Report to Council in the year following the Robbins Report – 'The great
problem is, and will continue to be, the marrying of the building programme with academic expansion and development'.[2]

A second document of the period illustrates the consequences of the new
rate of expansion for the building programme. On 3 September 1963
Gerald Palmer, chairman since 1948 of the committees which had directed
the development of Whiteknights and the building programme of the
University, drafted a paper entitled 'First thoughts on the proposed further
expansion of Reading University':

> The question of the expansion of student numbers has arisen again
> and, in particular, is referred to in the letter dated 24 July 1963,
> from the Chairman of the UGC to the Vice-Chancellor and the
> memorandum dated September 1963, by the Registrar for submission
> to the Senate on the 14 October 1963.[3]
>
> I do not wish to comment on the broader background issues
> involved, for example those arising in connection with such matters
> as national or political party policy, or whether greater numbers
> are essential for the recognizably high quality which must clearly be
> the aim of the University. There are, however, some practical
> considerations to which attention will need to be given in arriving at
> decisions about further expansion, and it seems worth while to
> mention them at this stage.
>
> The post-war history of this, and other universities, has been
> dominated by the fact of having been presented with a series of targets
> which are always revised upwards before they are attained. It has
> been possible at Reading to cope with this situation to some extent
> owing to two factors: (a) a considerable surplus of land available for
> building, and (b) the fact that a considerable proportion of the
> building programme was still only in the form of projects for the
> future.
>
> The time has now arrived, however, when (a) the capacity of avail-
> able land has got to be looked at much more closely; the area of
> Whiteknights which is unusable either for building or playing fields is

[1] URC, Vice-Chancellor, Wolfenden papers (unsorted).
[2] *Proceedings 1963–4*, p. 12.
[3] See above, pp. 174–5.

New environment 1947-76 183

probably greater than is usually realized: and (b) the rigidities introduced by existing buildings or by buildings now in course of construction or planning have also got to be taken into account.

The purpose of these notes is not to solve these problems but to draw attention to the need for designing some procedure for examining them concurrently with the consideration of the purely academic aspects of the question. With this in view, the following examples are mentioned and it may well be that others would appear from a close look at the conditions.

(a) An additional 1,000 students would mean the construction of the equivalent of five additional new halls of residence (of an average of 200 students) none of which have hitherto been visualized. It is doubtful whether the periphery of Whiteknights Park will be adequate for this purpose.

(b) It will also involve a considerable additional demand on space for new teaching buildings and/or the extension of existing ones. One of the features that would almost certainly have to be faced would be a large scale or even total re-development of the London Road site, and its *permanent* acceptance as part of the University.

(c) Is the new Library on an adequate scale to provide for a 33 per cent increase over the target of 1960? Equally, will the new Departments of Physics and Chemistry need early extension?

(d) Will the scale of planning of [the] Botany, Zoology, Physiology and Microbiology [building] have to be stepped up and, if so, will this mean a further postponement of the starting date with the consequent effect on the current expansion target, i.e. could the building still be completed by 1968?

(e) Communal facilities will all have to be expanded in scale: for example [the] Administration Building, Senior Common Room, Students' Union, Buttery complex, car parks, perhaps the boiler house.

(f) It is almost certain that there will be little, if anything, left of playing field accommodation on Whiteknights.

As has already been stated, the purpose of these notes is not to offer solutions to these problems but to draw attention to the need for providing for their consideration in such a way that the purely academic aspects of the problem can be given a correct perspective.

There is one further suggestion which inevitably comes to mind and that is that a serious attempt should be made now to foresee the ultimate limit of expansion so that the wastefulness of having constantly shifting targets should be brought to an end.[1]

That final *cri du cœur* was answered. In the spring of 1964 it was finally agreed, at the request of the Building Development Committee, that the

[1] URC, Vice-Chancellor, Wolfenden papers (unsorted).

planning of layout and buildings should provide for a possible development up to 8,000 to 10,000 students.[1] But whereas in academic matters it was easy to overlay the smaller assumptions and more modest projections of earlier years, this was not so in the case of buildings. Let the visitor to Whiteknights leave the north side of the Faculty of Letters and cross the pleasant valley towards Childs Hall. If then he looks back to the Faculty buildings he will see all the planning tribulations of the University laid out before him, from the plain modest façade of the first Faculty building through the even plainer, projecting frontage of the first extension, to the grotesquely piled blocks of the second extension. Perhaps Reading might have done better. Reading probably would have done better if it had known at the beginning where it was going to end. It may not be too fanciful for the visitor to see in that prolonged, ill-balanced, ascending skyline some representation of the repeatedly revised targets of which Gerald Palmer complained. These repeated revisions form the essential background to the story of the development of Whiteknights. At first it was planned for a small university. Later, it had to accommodate a far larger university.

Originally, however, it was very difficult to plan at all. Whiteknights required a sudden switch in thinking. Hitherto Reading had concentrated on the difficulties of developing the small compact site in London Road. Now, suddenly, there seemed to be wide open spaces, and over these imaginations roamed in a state of innocence. The one immediate practical job was done by Hawkins. In the winter of 1946–7 he provided a plan of the geological drift for the whole site; this with its reports of heavy clays and bad drainage on the southern part of the site tempered Stenton's initial optimism. That apart, it was difficult to know where to begin. There were obvious difficulties: the lack of money and materials, the presence of leasehold interests, the continuing requisition orders on some of the properties. But beyond those there was the simple enormity of the question of where and how to begin in moving the University to a new site. Planning as a subject was in its infancy: circulation patterns, pedestrian precincts and the like were not yet common currency. Those directing affairs at Reading had to learn planning as they planned. There were many false starts. There was no one with the imaginative flair and driving energy of Childs. That was probably as well. There was opportunity for great disasters as well as great achievements.

It may be that Stenton sensed this. At least in presenting his resignation as Vice-Chancellor to Council on 12 March 1948 he commented 'that it was desirable in the interest of the University that the appointment of his successor should take place before the earliest date at which the development of Whiteknights Park was likely to begin'.[2] His own thinking initially was very much conditioned by the earlier history of the estate and the

[1] Council Reports, xxiv, 29 May 1964; Building Development Committee, 4 June 1964.
[2] Council Minutes, ii, 1282, 12 March 1948.

residual problem of the leaseholds. An initial shy, which he drafted on a fragment of paper some time in 1947, arranged the development of White-knights accordingly under the heads of these established properties as follows:[1]

1. *Park House Block*
   Students' Union
   Men's Hall
   Women's Hall

2. *Whiteknights – Blandford Lodge*
   Administrative Block
   Common Rooms etc.
   Hall (to N)
   Science Faculty (to S)

3. *Wilderness*
   Agricultural Faculty and Dairying

4. *Erlegh Park*
   Library
   Letters Faculty
   School of Art
   Hall of Residence

Some, but not much of that came about: the Students' Union is attached to Park House, the administrative block is near Whiteknights, the Plant Sciences building is at least adjacent to the Wilderness and there is a Hall of Residence where Erlegh Park used to stand; but that is little more than coincidence. In any case there was no good ground and little support for such dispersal. However, at this stage the opposite notion of concentration was perhaps just as much a shot in the dark. The report of the first meeting of the Joint Committee of Council and Senate on the development of Whiteknights noted that:

> In view of the extent of the Park (approximately 300 acres) it appeared essential to concentrate the three faculties, the Library and the administrative buildings in one part of the site. The general consensus of opinion favoured the Shinfield Road end of the site for the purpose.
>
> The Committee agreed that the western end of the Park, preferably the part which lies north of the bridle path, appeared the most suitable site for the main faculty buildings, the Library and the administrative headquarters of the University. Members also agreed that, if practicable, Whiteknights House and Whiteknights Park House and the walled gardens surrounding them should be retained and incorporated in the general development of the site.[2]

[1] URC, Registrar, box 70.
[2] Joint Planning Committee, minute 2, 14 June 1948.

That area was where much of the University was eventually to be.

Whiteknights was one end of the planning problem; the other was a matter of priorities. Who was to be the first to move from London Road? Initially it seemed that it would be the Faculty of Agriculture. H. A. D. Neville had already argued strongly in 1943–4 that the proper development of the Faculty after the war could not be encompassed at London Road.[1] For a time he had his way. The priorities listed in 1947 for major building developments in Whiteknights were as follows:

   (i) All buildings for the Faculty of Agriculture and Horticulture, including an Institute of Dairy Technology
  (ii) Two halls of residence to accommodate 120 women and 150 men
 (iii) Department of Fine Art
 (iv) Department of Education[2]

None of that came about as planned. The Departments of Education and Fine Art are still at London Road. Moreover, as claims from other faculties and departments were examined over the next three years the case for Agriculture lost ground. From this welter of discussion one principle emerged which went back to the work of the Development Committee of 1943–4 and to Stenton's negotiations with the University Grants Committee in 1946–7: at Reading residential accommodation was critically important and therefore first priority should be given to a hall of residence. This was agreed in January 1949; it was hoped even to complete the Hall in 1950.[3] Nevertheless, although Stenton continued to press the case with the University Grants Committee, it was still unsettled when he handed over to Wolfenden.[4]

When Wolfenden arrived, therefore, no building had started; indeed, no building had even been given a starting date. Undoubtedly one of the main reasons for this was the inability of the University Grants Committee to provide money for building on the scale required. Also, in the years immediately following the purchase of the estate, the University had to feel its way. Initially, it was far from easy to hit upon an appropriate method of supervising such a large-scale, long-term operation. Immediately on completion of the formalities of the purchase the Finance Committee of Council established a standing sub-committee to deal with the development of Whiteknights.[5] It was too large, it exercised powers of co-option, on occasions it was reinforced by invited members of the planning authorities comprising Berkshire County Council, East Berkshire Regional Planning Committee, Reading Borough Council and Wokingham Rural District

[1] See above, pp. 120–1.
[2] Points for discussion with Major-General Hawkins (of the Ministry of Works), 7 May 1947 (URC, Registrar, box 70).
[3] Report of the Finance Committee, 21 January 1949. The Hall was to be for 150 men.
[4] See above, pp. 151–4.
[5] Finance Committee, minute 3049(c), 28 February 1947.

Council.[1] In June 1948 this sub-committee was superseded by a Joint Planning Committee of the Council and Senate. This again proved large and very soon much of the planning was devolved on a small executive committee consisting of Gerald Palmer, chairman of the Committee from December 1948, the Vice-Chancellor and Betts, Professor of Fine Art.[2] By the time Wolfenden arrived a system was emerging in which it was possible to co-ordinate representative discussion in the main committee with preparatory and executive work by this smaller Steering Committee. Once building projects got under way it was this inner group of Palmer, Betts and Wolfenden, along with the Dean, Professors or others immediately concerned with each building, who exercised immediate control in project steering committees which reported to the main committee. This system was formally confirmed and given constitutional blessing when the Joint Planning Committee was renamed the Building Development Committee in 1957.[3] Betts was the first advocate of this scheme. From the beginning he argued that the planning of Whiteknights had to be done professionally and that architects and other professional advisers would want to work with a small directing group which could advise them on the University's requirements.[4] The chief result was to place an enormous and laborious responsibility on the small inner group which formed the Steering Committee and the core of each project steering committee. The chief burden fell on Gerald Palmer. From 1948 he continued as chairman of the main committee and of all the steering committees until 1964 when he resigned on his appointment as a Forestry Commissioner. He was the central co-ordinating figure who kept a firm and genial control, even on occasion of Wolfenden. His assessment of priorities, based on meticulous investigation and consultation, was usually decisive. His devotion to the University matched that of his grandfather, Alfred. His task was cheerfully borne and is zestfully recalled:

By this time (1963–4) the Building Development Committee had proliferated over twenty steering committees some of which met each fortnight according to need. The Vice-Chancellor, Professor Betts and I were the only members of all the steering committees with the Registrar and Bursar generally in attendance. The Dean and the Head of the Department concerned, or whoever else might be

---

[1] In a meeting of 6 August 1947, these totalled eleven, three from Berkshire, three from East Berkshire, three from Wokingham and two from Reading. This arose from the fact that Whiteknights lay partly within the county authority, partly within Reading, and partly within Wokingham rural district.
[2] At its first meeting the Committee comprised Sir George Mowbray, Stenton, Professors Betts, Guggenheim, Hodges, Miller and Stoughton, Mary Kirkus (the Librarian) and Alderman Mrs A. P. E. Cusden. The sub-committee first appears on 8 December 1948 when it was asked to consider proposals for development from faculties and departments. It reported on these on 11 January 1949.
[3] Building Development Committee, minutes 2–5, 4 May 1957.
[4] Conversation with Professor J. A. Betts, May 1972.

relevant, formed the remainder of each committee. We used to hold
six to eight steering committees in a day and this proved a very good
system for facilitating the execution of business, which was very
necessary at this time of rapid development and increasing numbers.[1]

Few men are able to manage six to eight committees a day. Moreover,
Gerald Palmer's contribution went far beyond the chairing of meetings.
Wolfenden turned to him as a sure guide in all the intricate dealings with
architects and contractors which a series of large schemes necessarily involved.[2] He also brought a formidable experience to bear in many technical
matters. One example must suffice – a memorandum on the Boiler House
installation in Whiteknights Park of February 1957:

> It appears that there is a fundamental discrepancy between, on the
> one hand, the specification laid down by the sub-contractors for the
> heating system in the Faculty of Letters building, and, on the other
> hand, the type of boiler that has been installed on the advice of the
> Heating Consultants. The former specified a continuous supply of
> steam; this presumes a constant pressure related to the calorifiers and
> best provided by an automatically fired boiler. The latter have
> supplied a manually fired boiler which they specified as adequate to
> heat the building with a run of 16 hours out of 24.
>
> Actual running of the boiler has revealed the defects arising from
> this discrepancy. It has in fact been found necessary to flash the
> boiler by hand some twelve times daily, raising steam to 100 lb/sq. in.
> pressure and then closing down to allow the pressure to subside to the
> 40 lb which corresponds to the pressure required for the calorifiers
> installed in the building. When this pressure is reached the boiler is
> again flashed and the cycle repeated as often as may be necessary.
>
> At the Faculty of Letters end, the calorifiers and the time-clock
> controls are designed for a continuous supply of steam at constant
> pressure; under the boiler system installed the steam supply is
> discontinuous and the pressure variable as described above. . . .
>
> A problem has arisen in relation to the disposal of caustic from
> the boilers (this problem is independent of the type of boiler); if this
> caustic is discharged into the lake, as is the present arrangement,
> there will be large-scale damage to fish life and the creation of scum.
> The remedy seems to be a soakaway; but this matter should have
> been brought to the attention of the University at a much earlier
> stage.[3]

[1] Conversation with Gerald Palmer, 5 May 1970.
[2] URC, Vice-Chancellor, Wolfenden papers (unsorted) contain examples. Gerald
Palmer would answer queries, or correct drafts, or suggest courses to be taken in
negotiation.
[3] URC, Vice-Chancellor, Wolfenden papers (unsorted). The draft is roughly typed with
no signature but is corrected in Gerald Palmer's hand. It was based on an earlier report
from the University engineers of 23 January 1957.

Much more followed. Palmer's covering note to Wolfenden ran:

> Dear Jack,
>
> Here is a draft memo. for Preston re boiler house situation. I think
> it should go through you, with any amendments you may care to
> make (and properly typed), with, I suggest, a covering note making
> it clear that we hold the architects responsible for comments and
> proposals for remedy . . .

Wolfenden forwarded the memorandum without amendment.

The establishment of the Joint Planning Committee and the quick emergence of an executive and steering sub-committee had an immediate effect. It funnelled general discussion into administrative action. An earlier proposal that the development of Whiteknights should be thrown open to public competition was soon superseded.[1] At its first meeting in June 1948 the Committee asked Betts to make enquiries and produce photographs of work from which it might decide on a short list of possible architects. By October the Committee had enough evidence to make up its mind and the decision was confirmed in December when the Committee recommended to Council that Messrs. Easton and Robertson should be invited to act as architects for the main university buildings in Whiteknights.[2] This firm became responsible for the initial layout of the new site and designed all except the most recent of the main teaching and administrative buildings.[3] The earlier designs bore the mark of Howard Robertson, but another partner, F. L. Preston came to exercise immediate responsibility both for the general layout of the site and the design of individual buildings. The first of the new Halls was designed by S. Meyrick, architect to the University Grants Committee; this became Whiteknights Hall.[4] The second new Hall, which became Windsor Hall, was designed by Easton and Robertson, but only after the Building Development Steering Committee had considered and rejected a request that the design should be thrown open to competition.[5] All but one of the remaining new Halls were designed by Peter Ednie and Partners.[6]

In addition to appointing architects the Joint Planning Committee, led by its steering committee, set in train two related planning operations. First it sought, received and considered submissions from the various

---

[1] Standing sub-committee on the development of Whiteknights, 23 May 1947.

[2] Joint Planning Committee, minute 16, 8 December 1948.

[3] The Faculty of Urban and Regional Studies was designed by Howard, Killick, Partridge and Amis. The same company designed the most recent of the new Halls, Wells Hall.

[4] Building Development Committee, minute 55, 30 July 1959. This was done at the urging of Sir Keith Murray, Chairman of the University Grants Committee. The Committee had long been concerned at the wide variation in the cost of residential building. See below, p. 193.

[5] Building Development Committee, Report of Central Steering Committee, 2 November 1960.

[6] On the exception, Wells Hall, see n.3 above.

faculties and departments on their requirements in Whiteknights. Secondly it got to work on the overall layout of the new site. The first submissions from departments were ready by January 1949; they were the first task given to the sub-committee of Palmer, Betts and the Vice-Chancellor. The first preliminary report from the architects on the development of Whiteknights was ready for consideration on 16 May 1949. These were matters subject to repeated revision and restatement. Departmental and faculty requirements changed as students numbers increased. These changes and the increasing demand for residential accommodation in turn affected the overall plan. Meeting after meeting considered and reconsidered requests that buildings should be allowed more room for future expansion, or that one building should be brought nearer to another or that something should be done by slight adjustment of the plan to preserve a specimen tree. Over all there were seven major revisions of the site plan before 1968 when new consultants, Bickerdike, Allen, Rich and Partners produced what to date is the final one – 'The University of Reading Development Study: a Short Report'.[1]

Throughout this, especially in the early stages of the planning and building, the work of the committee and the architects shared an approach to the problem which was linked in turn to the assumption that they only had to cater for a relatively small university – 1,500 initially, then 2,000, and then, up to the Robbins Report, no more than 3,000 at most. The approach was summed up by Wolfenden's view that ideally the citizens of Reading should not be aware that they were passing through a University as they walked through Whiteknights. There seemed to be more than enough land; it had the quality of a great park; the establishment of the leaseholds and the walled gardens of Park House and Whiteknights House only gave it additional intimacy. All this was to be preserved as far as possible. As the first report from Easton and Robertson put it:

> The natural charm of the park with its gently rolling contours and wooded glades has been present in our minds throughout the preparation of the designs. The desire to preserve and exploit its possibilities, together with the more practical wish to economize by building along natural contours has resulted in the asymmetrical character which is present in each scheme. These considerations have dictated the scale of the buildings proposed as well as their planning.[2]

This attitude was only undermined gradually. When the student-target was raised to 2,000 in 1957, the Steering Committee of the Joint Committee asked the architects whether 'there was sufficient space in Whiteknights Park to meet the revised need of the University'. The answer was

[1] It is difficult to count the revisions. To distinguish major from minor changes is a wondrous scholastic exercise. I have followed Gerald Palmer's view at this point.
[2] Joint Planning Committee, 11 November 1949.

reassuring.[1] In 1960 the increase from 2,000 to 3,000 led to a special re-examination of the building programme by a committee of Council and Senate. The Committee noted that the Faculty of Letters would have to extend, that the move to Whiteknights would have to be accelerated and that the centre of gravity of the University would have to be shifted there by 1964; but it made no proposal for any major change in the layout of the site.[2] Hence, it was not until the Robbins Report that the assumptions underlying the planning of Whiteknights were called in question, and then by Gerald Palmer.[3]

This approach to the layout of the site was matched by the attitude adopted by Easton and Robertson towards the design of individual buildings. When Howard Robertson submitted the original design for the first of these, the Faculty of Letters, he deliberately set out to provide a modest structure which would sit unobtrusively in the landscape. He was determined not to narrow the context for the work of later architects by a bold individual design. The result was a comfortable, manageable building, pleasant, but of no great architectural originality in itself since this was not the architect's objective.[4] The buildings which followed the Faculty of Letters, the Department of Physics and the Research Laboratory in Sedimentology, were of similar appearance. It was not in fact until the completion of Preston's design of the Library in 1963 that real distinction was attempted or achieved. Until then there was no architectural focus. The effect of both the building pattern and the overall plan was spacious and leisurely, so much so that some professors were somewhat disturbed by a programme which seemed to seek to preserve the appearance of a gentleman's park.[5] The use of ground was lavish. It could afford to be. A basic tenet was that all buildings should be so sited and designed that each would allow for 50% expansion in as many directions as possible. In its final form the plan envisaged buildings generously distributed throughout the south-western sector of the Park, new halls of residence across the valley to the north, a vast running track and sports ground extending into the area where the much needed Temporary Office Buildings still stand, the whole rounded off by a splendid scheme for an Arts and Music Centre with an open air theatre on the south-western brow overlooking the Lake. The scheme is still attractive – in the mind's eye and on the assumption that Reading remained relatively small. In the event it was well that the buildings sited or completed before 1963 were not too far apart. That was

[1] Whiteknights Park Estate Steering Committee, minutes 112, 114, 7 and 13 March 1957.
[2] The Committee was appointed on the recommendation of the Building Development Committee specifically to examine Halls building policy. Its report involved a review of all building development necessitated by the proposed expansion to 3,000 (Senate Reports, xvii, 11 March 1960).
[3] See above, pp. 182–3.
[4] Conversation with Lord Wolfenden, 22 March 1975. The point is expanded in *Turning Points*, pp. 111–12.
[5] Conversation with Professor A. Graham, 28 July 1975.

a simple consequence of academic considerations. The Faculty of Letters included the Department of Mathematics. It followed that the Department of Physics and the other departments in the Faculty of Science had to be within reasonable distance. It was natural to site the Library amidst the departments which were already established in the Park.

By 1968 the old scheme looked out of date. The Report of Bickerdike, Allen, Rich and Partners commented:

> The policy of development in Whiteknights has been to spread buildings thinly, so that parkland rather than buildings dominates. This was apparently determined when people had in mind a small University of some 1,500–2,000 students, when it was practicable for landscape to flow freely among loosely located buildings. Today this has already changed – the buildings are larger and higher; the original Letters building of three storeys is linked to an extension rising to six, while Animal Biology, almost in the centre of the park, will be nine. From the north the academic area already presents the appearance of a virtually continuous wall some 900 feet long, while from the west, a new 'front' to the University has appeared with the Letters extension and the Administration block closing the view from Shinfield Road. The once loosely scattered buildings in a landscape have now become more like a monastery in the park, the area of each now distinct from the other, and therefore capable of development with more independence than formerly.[1]

The new scheme which they now proposed provided for a much greater concentration of academic building, largely free of vehicular traffic, contained within a perimeter road in the south-western sector of the Park.[2] The Report ranged ahead with relentless confidence:

> Our function has been to examine the implications of growth in respect of land, density, movement, landscape, and building forms, and the changes that may be needed not merely to deal with the problems foreseeable up to the 1980s, when the University will likely have some 8,000 students, and the urban area will reach southward around it to the M4, but to peer beyond this period into the more distant future. Ultimate population sizes cannot be predicted, whether for institutions or cities, but it is possible to establish probabilities for a reasonable distance ahead, and in working on such a basis short-term actions can be made viable within the constraints of longer-term plans that keep open vital growth options for the future.[3]

This seemed to mark a radical change and indeed it did so in that it grappled with an entirely new level of expansion. But the principles on which it was

[1] University of Reading Development Study: A Short Report, p. 3.
[2] University of Reading Development Plan (June 1970), paras. 9–11.
[3] University of Reading Development Study: A Short Report, p. 1.

based were derived from the nature of the Park and these had been recognized long ago. Already in 1949, the Joint Planning Committee had reacted to the first Report from Easton and Robertson by requiring a greater concentration of the faculty buildings and the Library on the site which they eventually came to occupy.[1] Again, in 1964, after the consequences of the Robbins Report had been assessed, it was noted that 'the whole complex of buildings [in the Park] should be as compact as possible with a central area free from motor vehicles'.[2] Moreover, in 1968 the Report of Bickerdike, Allen, Rich and Partners was based on a division between the academic buildings concentrated in the south-western sector and the halls of residence sited around the northern perimeter. Just such a division was already envisaged in the first site plan agreed with Easton and Robertson in 1949 – 'six halls of residence, arranged in three groups of pairs for economy of servicing, were placed round the perimeter of the site'.[3] That intention had largely been fulfilled by the time of the Report of 1968.

Hence, the Park imposed its own logic on discussion. It left less room for manoeuvre than the planners imagined. Above all its capacity was finite. Gerald Palmer was right in 1963 in his warning that the land available was limited. Moreover, the local planning authorities were not ready to see an excessive concentration in Whiteknights. For these reasons the last two halls of residence to be built, Sibly and Wells, were sited elsewhere. Later plans envisaged a 'student village' on some site outside the Park. The Report of Bickerdike, Allen, Rich and partners went even further and foresaw the establishment of a precinct between Whiteknights, the old site in London Road and the Royal Berkshire Hospital. Unwittingly, it revived Stenton's vision of 1943.[4]

The start of the development was long delayed. It depended on the provision of funds by the University Grants Committee. In 1949 the University firmly committed itself to giving first priority to a hall of residence for men.[5] The University Grants Committee was far from convinced. Reading already had plenty of residential accommodation; other universities seemed to have a stronger claim. Moreover, in 1949, the Committee's investigation of the comparative costs of expenditure on residential accommodation revealed a disturbing disparity ranging from £1,100 to £2,300 a place; it turned to the architects of the Ministry of Works for advice and enjoined the most stringent economy.[6] Stenton, who was present at the meeting, noted

---

[1] Joint Planning Committee, minute 33, 16 May 1949.
[2] Senate Minutes, iv, 3840, 15 June 1964; Report of the Building Development Committee.
[3] Joint Planning Committee, minute 42, 11 November 1949.
[4] 'University of Reading Development Study: A Short Report', pp. 7–8, 13. For Stenton's comments, see above, p. 138.
[5] See above, p. 186.
[6] Note of a meeting between the Committee of Vice-Chancellors and Principals and officers of the University Grants Committee, 10 November 1949. The main report was presented by Dr A. E. Trueman, then Chairman of the UGC (URC, Registrar, box 70).

that the 'new Hall is in the melting pot'. He was right. The negotiation dragged on with the University Grants Committee revealing diminishing enthusiasm. When the Committee visited the University in November 1950 members suggested that new buildings for a department or departments in the Science Faculty should be the first to be erected, thereby releasing space for the Faculty of Letters at London Road. But if the Committee, holding the purse strings, was powerful enough effectively to turn down the proposal for a Hall, it could not impose its own priorities on the University. To move all the departments of the Faculty of Science was a course scarcely conceivable. No single science department could be asked to risk lengthy isolation at Whiteknights, especially in a Faculty where the teaching time-tables of different subjects were closely interlocked. Hence if it were not to be a hall of residence it had to be the Faculty of Letters. By this time there was little to choose between the worst conditions under which all departments worked at London Road. But the Faculty suffered the worst conditions more than most.[1] The decision made sense and was agreed by both Senate and Council in July 1951. Questions and objections from the University Grants Committee had led to a change of policy but not to the specific change which the Committee had in mind.[2]

For four years after the purchase of Whiteknights, Reading set off on what proved to be a wrong track. Even when it had accepted the view of the University Grants Committee that a teaching building should come first, formal approval and the necessary funds were still delayed.[3] It was not in fact until the summer of 1953 that the proposed building was included in the University Grants Committee's building programme for 1954. There was much rejoicing and trumpeting of the news. Wolfenden himself drafted the press announcement;[4] a reception was held in the autumn to display the

[1] Dr R. Bowen described conditions in the French Department in the London Road houses: 'There was still gas everywhere in the Department, even up the stairs. The only exception was on Desseignet's floor and one room on the floor above where electricity was needed for the recording machines. The room that I had was at the top of the building, right under the eaves, and it had a cupboard door through into the History Department to meet fire regulations. I could either be warm or well-lit, but never the two together, since the gas fire was in one corner and the light in another. I never had electric light until I moved down to the second floor.' (Conversation with R. Bowen, 15 December 1969).
[2] The report of the visitation of the UGC is in Council Reports, xii, 29 November 1950. Following the visitation Sir George Mowbray, Gerald Palmer and Wolfenden were empowered to investigate and negotiate further with the UGC. They obtained very preliminary costs for the construction of new buildings for Botany and Zoology. This came to £300,000 as against £300–500,000 for the Faculty of Letters. There are interim reports in Senate Minutes, iii, 2187, 2194 of 22 January and 26 February 1951. The final report of Senate, in which priority for the Faculty of Letters was agreed *nem. con.* is in Council Reports, xiii, 6 July 1951.
[3] 'I should make it clear that there is, as we see it, no prospect of a starting date for the scheme in the academic year 1951–2, as our new starts have been severely restricted on account of the Defence Programme.' (E. Hale to Wolfenden, 3 September 1951; URC, Vice-Chancellor, Wolfenden papers (unsorted)).
[4] *Ibid.*

plans and drawings; Stenton cut the first sod; the Chancellor, Lord Temple-wood, laid the Foundation Stone; and the Queen, accompanied by the Duke of Edinburgh, finally opened the new building on 22 March 1957, when the students decorated the occasion with the inscribed banner – 'Welcome to the house which Jack built'.[1] But behind the formal celebrations there was a hard, relentless grind in the Building Development Committee and on the site. Betts commented:

> The Building Committee was now to get the first of several shocks when the architects informed them that the first building in the Park would not be a hall of residence nor a Faculty of Letters, but a boiler house, and moreover this must be big enough not only to heat the proposed Faculty of Letters building but also subsequent buildings on the site. It would also be necessary to erect it on the perimeter of the Park. When the Committee realized that the Faculty of Letters was to occupy a central position and when, on completion of the boiler house, the lengthy pipe system, needed to convey water and other services to the building site of the new Faculty arose two feet six inches above the ground, and when they saw the sea of mud inseparable from winter building, their illusions about the joyous adventure of building a new university began to fade.[2]

Innocence soon came to be replaced by experience, imagination by a sense of the practical, guesswork by a shrewd assessment of pros and cons. Not all could learn this; there were those still in the 1970s who confused buildings on the ground with castles in the air; but on the whole those within the University whose interest was aroused took to the problem with zest and remarkable ease. In the autumn of 1953 the Joint Planning Committee tackled the problem of what was to come next after the Faculty of Letters. There were three contenders: the Library, the Department of Physics and the Department of Agricultural Chemistry. It was soon decided that enough could be done for Agricultural Chemistry on the London Road site, but between the other two possibilities a full-dress debate developed in which the Librarian, Mary Kirkus, and R. W. Ditchburn, Head of the Department of Physics, presented elaborate cases to the Committee. The discussion began in November and continued to April 1954 when the Committee decided to recommend that the building for Physics should come next. The report of the final discussion runs as follows:

[1] For some of the above, see plates 32, 33, 36. The cutting of the first turf was the occasion of Stenton's celebrated introduction – 'Unaccustomed as I am to public digging, as indeed to every other form of physical exercise . . .'. For the students' banner, see Wolfenden, *Turning Points*, p. 124.
[2] Conversation with J. A. Betts, May 1972. The boiler house came to the fore in the course of 1954 (Joint Planning Committee, minute 106, 27 April 1954; note of informal meeting 18 June 1954). Its teething troubles seared the memory of the participants in the Committee. For an intervention by Gerald Palmer, see above, pp. 188–9. Putting the heating pipe above ground was a temporary expedient. Money was not immediately available for a long run of underground ducting.

(d) In the ensuing discussion, the following points were made concerning the relative merits of proposals that the Department of Physics or the Library should be the next building to be erected:

(i) That the 'centre of gravity' of the University would not have shifted sufficiently by the time that one Faculty was installed in Whiteknights Park for the Library to be the next building to be needed.

(ii) It was most desirable that the problem should also be considered from the point of view of ensuring continuity of building; again the chances of ensuring such continuity would be greater if the proposal were for a Science Faculty building.

(iii) A proposal for the Library to be the next building, had, in fact, already been made in part to the University Grants Committee; if they were now confronted with a proposal for a Science Faculty building instead they might ask why the plans had been changed.

(iv) That it would obviously be essential to convince the University Grants Committee of any case that might be put to them. In present circumstances a proposal for a Science Faculty Department would probably meet with a more favourable reception.

(v) It might be indicated that if the Department of Physics were the next building to be erected the Library would possibly follow it, but it would be unwise to commit the University to a definite proposal at this stage.

(vi) The buildings and equipment of the Department of Physics were probably more out-of-date than those of any other department in the Faculty of Science; also, Physics might be considered as the science to which most attention was being paid at the present time.

(vii) The Physics Department at present was working under a serious disadvantage in that its buildings were on two sites.[1]

(viii) From the point of view of the balance of the University it would seem that the Department of Physics should occupy the next building.

(ix) If the Department of Physics were the next to move the situation on the present site would be eased more than if the Library were the next to move.

(e) The Committee were agreed that the right policy would be to erect as the next building the Department of Physics. It would appear that the Library should then follow but they felt that at present no formal recommendation on either point should be made to Senate and Council. Instead, the Vice-Chancellor was requested to discuss with the University Grants Committee the prospects of such a proposal meeting with their approval and to report to the Committee at their next meeting.[2]

[1] Viz. London Road and huts at Wantage Hall.
[2] Joint Planning Committee, minute 107, 27 April 1954.

There was caution in that, and experience; it was even hard bitten. There was a growing concern and skill in how best to 'manage' the University Grants Committee. That in turn reflected the increasing influence of the Committee's views, expressed as firm policies or in mere winks and nods, in the discussion of priorities within the University. In September Wolfenden reported:

In May last he had discussed with the Chairman and Secretary of the University Grants Committee the prospect of their giving approval to a proposal that the next building to be erected should be either that for the Department of Physics or that for the Library. He had informed them that, in his own opinion, it would not seem right that the Library should be erected unless and until the centre of gravity of the University was in Whiteknights Park, and he did not think that this situation would arise even when the Faculty of Letters building was occupied. The Secretary of the University Grants Committee had said that it was not for them to decide which building should be the next to be erected, but that he was impressed by the argument concerning the Library.

He had then asked the Chairman and Secretary whether the University might expect that building would proceed continuously once it had commenced. No direct answer was given but he was told that it would certainly be desirable for the University to put forward proposals in good time, as the University Grants Committee obviously did not want to find themselves with money available and no plan ready.

His impression was that sympathetic consideration would be given to a proposal that the next building to be erected should be that for the Department of Physics.[1]

It was only then that the Joint Committee confirmed their decision of April and made a formal recommendation to Council and Senate. They already foresaw that it would have long-term effects:

Since the building for the Department of Physics should be planned as part of the whole Faculty of Science, the Steering Committee should request from the Faculty of Science Planning Committee such information concerning the requirements of the various departments in the Faculty as might be needed for the guidance of the Architects in their planning of the Department of Physics building.[2]

They had in effect given priority to the physical sciences over the life-sciences, and to the Faculty of Science over the Faculty of Agriculture. When priorities were next determined, in the summer and autumn of 1956, the Physics building was followed by the Library and the Department of

[1] Joint Planning Committee, minute 113, 22 September 1954.
[2] *Ibid.*

Geology.[1] In the next round, settled in 1958, the Department of Chemistry took first place.[2]

The Robbins Report brought the building programme to its peak. From the commencement of the Faculty of Letters in 1956 for twenty years thereafter, large buildings were always under construction in some part of Whiteknights. When the programme was at its height between 1960 and 1970 the Park was a major construction site, both at the centre where teaching and administrative buildings followed hot on each other and on the periphery where new halls of residence were springing up.[3] The total achievement was formidable. It is convenient to tabulate it:[4]

	Work begun	Work completed
1954–5	Faculty of Letters	
1955–6	Mansfield Hall, extension	
1956–7		Faculty of Letters Mansfield Hall, extension
1957–8	Department of Physics	
1958–9	St Patrick's Hall, extension	
1959–60	Research Laboratory in Sedimentology	Department of Physics St Patrick's Hall, extension
1960–1	Library Whiteknights Hall	

[1] Joint Planning Committee, minutes 132, 141; 13 August, 9 November 1956. The University Grants Committee gave a broad hint which gave support to the case of Geology by indicating that 'it might possibly include a sum not exceeding £125,000 for the Research Laboratory in Sedimentology in 1959 if the University felt encouraged to go forward with the project after discussion with the oil industry'. It was in this form that the scheme for a new Geology building went forward. At the meeting of the Committee in November it was reported that the Faculty of Agriculture and Horticulture 'did not feel justified in putting forward any proposals for building in 1960 and 1961'. The case for the Library, in contrast, was strongly pressed, partly on the ground that 'when the new Library is in Whiteknights Park the centre of gravity of the University will really be on the way thither and that this might act as an accelerating factor in our total removal to the new site.' (Professor B. C. J. G. Knight to Gerald Palmer, 9 August 1956; see also a joint letter of Professor D. J. Gordon, then Chairman of the Curators of the Library, and Mary Kirkus, 12 July 1956; Joint Planning Committee, 13 August 1956).
[2] Correspondence of Sir Keith Murray and Wolfenden, June to July 1958 (URC, Vice-Chancellor, Wolfenden papers (unsorted) Building Development Committee, 25 February 1958; Council Minutes, iii, no. 1884, 23 May 1958).
[3] See plates 34, 35.
[4] The following table embraces major projects only. Prefabricated buildings or buildings of a temporary nature have been included only where the work was directed by a steering committee of the Buildings Committee or subsequently by a project committee. Work on the London Road site has not been included. Some additions had been made to halls of residence before 1954, chiefly by the purchase and adaptation of houses as annexes for St Andrew's, St George's and Wessex.

1961–2	Chemistry	Research Laboratory in Sedimentology
1962–3	St Andrew's Hall, extension New Sanatorium	
1963–4	Faculty of Letters, first extension Mathematics Windsor Hall Wessex Hall	Library Whiteknights Hall St Andrew's Hall, extension New Sanatorium
1964–5	St George's Hall, extension Geography (prefabricated) Geology (prefabricated) Bridges Hall Childs Hall Buttery	Chemistry Windsor Hall

1965–6	Faculty of Letters,
	   second extension
	Applied Physical Sciences
	Palmer Building
	Sibly Hall
	Senior Common Room
	   (Park House)
		Faculty of Letters, first
		   extension
		Mathematics
		Geography/Geology
		   (prefabricated)
		Wessex Hall
		St George's Hall, extension
		Buttery

1966–7	Whiteknights House Students' Union	Senior Common Room Bridges Hall Childs Hall

1967–8	Physiology, Biochemistry,
	   Zoology
		Faculty of Letters, second
		   extension
		Applied Physical Sciences
		Palmer Building
		Whiteknights House
		Sibly Hall

1968–9		Students' Union
1969–70	Plant Sciences Wantage Hall, extension	

1970–1	Faculty of Urban and
	   Regional Studies
	Bridges Hall, extension
	Childs Hall, extension
	Wells Hall
		Physiology, Biochemistry,
		   Zoology

	Work begun	Work completed
1971–2		Wantage Hall, extension
		Plant Sciences (including the Philip Lyle Memorial Research Laboratory)
		Bridges Hall, extension
		Childs Hall, extension
1972–3	Mansfield Hall, extension	Faculty of Urban and Regional Studies
	Students' Union/Senior Common Room	
1973–4	St Andrew's Hall, extension	Wells Hall
	Students' Union/Senior Common Room	
1974–5		Mansfield Hall, extension
		St Andrew's Hall, extension
		Students' Union/Senior Common Room

In 1956, the year before the completion of the Faculty of Letters, the University's properties were valued in the capital account at £1,280,228. In 1975 the equivalent figure was £16,636,441. The capital account for Whiteknights was over £8,700,000; the capital account for the halls of residence was nearly £5,000,000.[1]

The programme petered out as a result of financial stringency and economic pressures. Reading was cushioned against the first restrictions on the building programme in1965–7 by the fact that it already had a large number of buildings under construction or in an advanced stage of planning.[2] A moratorium on building-starts from March 1969 to March 1970 resulted in the postponement of the Plant Sciences Building. The severe restriction of the capital sums available to the University Grants Committee in 1973–4 led to the suspension, in the planning stage, of three projects: a new building for the Faculty of Letters and Social Sciences, which would have been the third addition to its original accommodation, an extension to the administrative accommodation in Whiteknights House, and a multi-purpose hall with sports facilities.[3] Meanwhile since 1968 all the additions

---

[1] The totals include the University farms and other properties. It should be noted also that they are simply sums of capital expenditure and make no allowance for appreciation or inflation. It would be impossible to adjust them accurately to compensate for these factors.

[2] See the comments of Gerald Palmer as President of Council (*Proceedings 1965–6*, p. 2; *Proceedings 1966–7*, p. 2).

[3] An extension to the Library was also under less immediate consideration.

to Hall accommodation, with the exception of Wells Hall,[1] had been financed by loans amortized on the current accounts of the Halls.[2] The extension to Mansfield Hall was the last to be completed under this scheme. Plans for similar work at St George's Hall had to be dropped because building costs of an extension designed even on the most stringent of traditional lines had risen beyond the University's means. A scheme for the construction of accommodation for graduates on University property outside the Park also had to be abandoned.[3] In this case the University Grants Committee was unable to provide support.

Throughout the last ten years of this development the specifications laid down by the University Grants Committee became more and more stringent. The rooms for academic and administrative staff became smaller, ceilings were lowered, corridors became narrower, the finish was made more spartan, sound-insulation became less effective. Expansion was accompanied by diminishing standards which became less and less easy to accept. The final addition to the accommodation at Mansfield Hall could only be achieved at the barest specification. The Warden and the students at one point doubted whether it should be done at all. When the projected addition to St George's was cancelled the Warden breathed a sigh of relief. When the additional Arts places were under discussion the representatives of the Faculty of Letters and Social Sciences and of the departments which would take over the new accommodation stated that they were not prepared to accept a reduction in the sound insulation below that of the first extension to the Faculty. They meant it. Whether the lines represented on the one hand by the economies required by the University Grants Committee, and on the other by the increasing resistance to less and less adequate building, would have intersected at this point was never put to the test. National economy-cuts intervened. It could be argued that the policy of the University Grants Committee had been finely judged. At times the occasional *grognard* at Reading tended to regard them rather as the front-line troops looked upon the Staff in the First World War. But they were not their own masters.

The expansion of the University can be stated easily enough as figures on a balance sheet.[4] It is less easy to express it in terms of the quality of life. It is some measure of the work of a university that one should seek to do so. Some answers are easy enough: in 1976 the University was equipped with a Library far beyond the dreams of de Burgh or Ure, with laboratories which Crowther or Bassett could scarcely have conceived, with a range of subjects outside the schemes of H. A. D. Neville or the vision of the young Hodges.

[1] Wells Hall, like the Faculty of Urban and Regional Studies, was financed by the sale of the London property of the College of Estate Management. See below, pp. 241–2.
[2] In all cases, including Wells Hall, a proportion of the cost was covered by the UGC. This ranged from the cost of the professional fees and furniture to 50 per cent of the total building cost. On the importance of loan-finance for the students of the University, see below, pp. 311–13, 315.
[3] Allcroft Road.
[4] See above, p. 200.

Halls had sprouted where Pearson, Mary Bolam and others had slowly established a Reading tradition. In some respects there was a clear gain. In 1968 the students obtained a proper Union Building, finally achieving an objective first stated in the 1930s and first embodied in the development plans of the University in 1944. In other respects there was a loss. By 1976 the Acacias, although still a Senior Common Room on the London Road site, had long ceased to fulfil its old function as a focal centre for the staff. The new Senior Common Room in Whiteknights was housed in 1966 in Park House, a building recognized as unsatisfactory for the purpose as long ago as 1954.[1] The addition of dining rooms in 1975 did not fully repair the resulting inadequacies. Perhaps it is in the Halls that Reading has experienced the greatest continuity. Here, the last word, as so often in his heyday, should be left to Childs:

> In designing a hall of residence it is easy to lose sight of the essential thing. The Hall is an instrument of education. If it is mean or pretentious, congested, monotonously schemed, and ungenerously administered, it will not achieve the things we expect of it, any more than poor teaching under poor conditions will achieve what is expected of instruction. Again, the Hall is for youth; and the characteristic of youth is not fixity but growth. The concern of a university with this growth is two-fold: to ensure that each individual has a chance of growing for the best in mind, character, and body; and to ensure that each individual is taken into that fellowship which, beginning in the Hall, merges in the life of the university. A university Hall, therefore, requires of us in respect of its design and character, and in respect of its management, a delicate and thoughtful balance and adjustment between opposed sets of considerations. If we were to build for economy and nothing else, we should build a standardized honeycomb. If we were to build for administrative ease and nothing

[1] In 1954 Park House was in temporary use as a hall of residence. A sub-committee appointed to consider its use, which was attended in its second meeting by G. B. Bisset and Dr R. Bowen as stewards of Senior Common Room, reported as follows:
The Sub-Committee have discussed the questions raised in their terms of reference and others arising out of them, and unanimously recommend:
(a) that the site of Whiteknights Park House should not be used for a permanent hall of residence.
They recognize that eventually it may be necessary temporarily to use Whiteknights Park House for some purpose other than as a hall of residence; it is at present designated on the layout plan as 'Senior Common Room (Temporary)', but in their opinion it could never serve as a permanent Senior Common Room. They are of the opinion that the existing building should eventually be demolished, partly for aesthetic reasons and partly because it cannot be suitably adapted for permanent use.
(b) that no decision should be taken at this stage regarding the ultimate use of the site. While it is unlikely that a Senior Common Room would be required at Whiteknights Park for a considerable number of years, they consider the site to be appropriate for this purpose, but a Senior Common Room would be a building relatively inconsiderable in size in relation to its surroundings. The site might be used for a major block which would include both a Senior Common Room and some other buildings, e.g., a Senate House.

else, we should flatten out or ignore those individualities of habitation and routine which make a sympathetic appeal to most human beings. If we were to build for discipline and nothing else, why not revert to the scheme of Bentham's Panopticon, so that our radial corridors might be raked by the eye of authority with the minimum of exertion? Such vagaries, it may be said, are improbable. But do we sufficiently bear in mind that we build, not to please ourselves, but to provide a fit home for developing youth? In the interests of fellowship, we establish a community. That motive justifies buildings of dignity and character.[1]

The first Hall, Wantage, was a piece of Oxford neo-Gothic; the last were University Grants Committee nondescript.[2] But if Reading has fallen short of Childs's ideal, it is not for the want of trying.

[1] Childs (1933), p. 179.
[2] See plates 21, 22, 45.

Chapter 9

Ways and means 1947–76

The expansion of old and the establishment of new halls of residence was a natural growth at Reading. They followed from the original character of the University which was based in turn on its site and surroundings. It was to be expected also that such development would largely follow the traditional pattern of such Halls, which indeed Reading had done much to mould.[1] Once funds were made available by the University Grants Committee the way ahead could be seen; the development of residence became simply a matter of siting and design, plumbing and furnishing. Occasionally changes of direction might be discussed, especially when it was feared that the provision might not keep pace with the increase in student numbers, and sometimes alternative forms of residence were considered; but in the main the University's course was set. The prime function of the Halls was simply to house the students. Whatever else they contributed, however close they came to fulfilling the ideals which Childs had held, they played little real and no formal part in teaching and research, and here, in the main function and purpose of the University, Reading's course was far from pre-determined. Until the late 1960s, when halls of residence came under attack as symbols of paternalism, there was no great argument about them; the establishment of new ones was largely a matter of numbers and finance. The academic development of the University, in contrast, was the subject of continuous discussion and debate.

Reading's earlier history, of course, had some effect on this. It was and remained outstanding as a centre of agricultural studies. There were departments in the Faculties of Letters and Science with established reputations. Stenton, as Vice-Chancellor, had tried to ensure that none of this would be lost as the University expanded,[2] and on the whole that policy was respected. Furthermore, the custodians of the old established subjects acted as censors of the new. Hence, despite its relatively small size in 1947 and the enormous expansion of the next thirty years, Reading was not like a new university where newly collected staff could commit themselves wholeheartedly to experiment. It was organized in the standard

---

[1] See above, pp. 6–7, 57–74. Sibly Hall and the extensions to Bridges and Childs Hall were designed for self-catering. For student reactions to the design and organization of Halls, see below, pp. 311–13, 315–16.

[2] See above, pp. 162–4.

fashion in departments and faculties. The subjects for which they were responsible were often firmly rooted in traditions derived from Oxford or London. Even so, Reading changed, and at times rapidly.

This change presents at least two important aspects. The first is local, even parochial, and concerns personalities, sometimes the clash of personalities. For example, the contrasting development of the Departments of Agricultural Botany and of Agricultural Chemistry depended to no small degree on the response of T. M. Harris, Professor of Botany, and E. A. Guggenheim, Professor of Chemistry; the one tolerant, co-operative, sympathetic, the other sometimes demonstratively less so. Much depended on personal interest. The development of the study of Italian and ultimately the establishment of a department derived in part from the interest of D. J. Gordon, Professor of English; Italian grew up as a subject within his Department. Again, J. A. Betts was responsible for the establishment and encouragement of the study of Typography which finally emerged as a department, unique in English universities, in 1974;[1] it was Betts also who started the bindery in the Library. Edgar Thomas played a very similar role in the establishment and development of the Department of Agricultural Economics.[2] A. G. Lehmann left his mark on the teaching of foreign language studies; he was also the founder of the Graduate School of Contemporary European Studies. The other graduate institution in the Faculty of Letters and Social Sciences, the Graduate Centre for Medieval Studies, was very much the brain-child of F. P. Pickering. There is no doubt at all that, but for these men, much of this would not have happened. And these are but a few illustrative examples. Many more could be found across the widening spectrum of the University's work. Indeed, the whole academic development of the University could be viewed as a mosaic of individual initiatives disciplined only by accumulated collective experience and the hitherto established pattern.[3]

[1] See above, p. 53.

[2] See above, pp. 113–14, 130–2.

[3] Compare Stenton's last speech to the Court, 1 March 1950. 'Apart from the obvious and fundamental subjects which must be represented in any institution claiming to be a university, our academic growth has always been determined by accidents of personal interest and local situation rather than by deliberate planning. One result of this natural process has been that in all parts of the University there are sections which have come to importance without any impulse and with a very modest amount of financial support from the bodies responsible for academic policy. The Museum of Greek Archaeology, for example, which now has an international reputation, came into being, not through any act of Senate or Council, but simply through the determination of Professor Ure. Even before the War the Senate gave its general approval to a project for the development of Italian Studies within the University, but the present interest in these studies which has carried them into our plans for immediate development, is due to the efforts of a few individuals working in related fields. When all due recognition has been paid to the support which Council and Senate have always given, as their resources allowed, to proposals coming before them, it is impossible to overstress the extent to which the internal development of the University has proceeded from movements arising within its several departments.' (*Reading University Gazette*, xxiii, 2, 30 March 1950, p. 5).

However, there is a second aspect to this. Development took place within an assumption that the University had an educational duty towards the community at large. This was Sibly's starting point in 1943 when he set on foot the examination of post-war development.[1] The duty was defined as time passed by the reports of committees appointed by the government of the day, of which the Barlow Report on Scientific Manpower of 1948 and the Robbins Report of 1963 were the most important, by government projections of the likely numbers in higher education, and by government decisions about the relationship between universities and other sectors of higher education. The University worked within the limits prescribed and aimed at the targets set. To all appearances it ran on a very loose rein. In reality it responded immediately to the guidelines provided by the University Grants Committee, always conforming to the general extent of the advance in student numbers, only differing where circumstances gave room for discussion and argument between the Committee and the University.[2] This close conformity with the general pattern of development was achieved without any strict direction; the University was not like the customer for the Ford Model T, who could have any colour so long as it was black. One reason why the reports of most government committees were accepted so readily is that they coincided with views strongly held and arguments vigorously advanced in Council, Senate and the Boards of Faculties.[3] Hence strict direction was unnecessary.

In practice, therefore, the debate about particular proposals turned on three considerations: cost, academic merit and social needs. The first was over-riding; the other two reacted on each other in varying strengths and with different effects. In the development of the physical sciences, mathematics, computer science and statistics they combined relatively easily in the expansion of urgently needed subjects which were of unquestioned academic standing. But this was not always so. The academic case for the establishment of a Chair of Greek, long advocated first by Ure and then by Cormack, never managed to outweigh the marked decline in the demand for the subject. Reading still has no Chair of Greek; the proposal is long defunct. Similarly the reasons for maintaining the study of Old English in the university of Stenton and Jean Young failed to hold against the changing structure of the English syllabus and the decline of the language component of the course. In these cases, social need, expressed in the form of student demand, carried the day against academic arguments rooted in tradition. That was not inevitable. One of the proposals advanced in the Faculty of Letters and Social Sciences for the Quinquennium 1967–72 was for the establishment of a department of Social Administration. The arguments

[1] See above, pp. 117–18.
[2] For examples see above, pp. 147–8, 172–4, 193–4.
[3] See Sir George Mowbray, above, p. 177. The James Report provides a possible exception, but this was concerned primarily with the non-university institutions of higher education. On this see below, pp. 254–5.

for it were based on the social usefulness of the subject and the high demand
for it. One of the arguments against suggested that the need was already
covered in other universities, but the main case was aimed against the
academic credentials of the subject. Some could see little justification in an
Honours degree in 'form filling' and, rightly or wrongly, that settled the
matter. Reading has no course in social administration. It failed to contribute to the supply of social workers in the late 1960s. It also avoided
contributing to the surplus in the late 1970s. Academic arguments may have
desirable social consequences.

Such assessments embodied an element which was particularly difficult,
indeed confusing. The definition of social need was almost scholastic in its
obscurity. Something depended on elementary common sense; in 1948 the
need for scientists and technologists was obvious to all. But how many more
were required, and how many more the educational system could yield
from how large a pool of talent, were questions which no-one could answer.
This was recognized by the Robbins Committee[1] which complicated the
problem further by recommending that 'all young persons qualified by
ability and attainment to pursue a full-time course in higher education
should have the opportunity to do so'.[2] This placed universities, if not quite
at the whim of the young, at least at the mercy of the social pressures to
which the young in turn were subjected. How many would seek to come to
universities? What would they want to study? At what point might student
demand cease to match any objective assessment of the country's requirements? A further complication was that the increasing flow of young people
into universities led a number of professions to feel that they would lose
access to adequate recruits unless they required a degree as a normal
professional qualification. This contributed to a sudden upsurge in the
demand for university courses in Law and Accounting.

Reading coped with these problems as best it could. In the development
of the social sciences in the 1960s student choice, social need as defined, for
example, by the demand for economists and local government officers, and
academic arguments for the development of these subjects all marched
together. Likewise there was no difficulty in the development of Law from
1972, and even as late as 1975–6, when the establishment of new courses
had largely ceased, the argument of social need based on student demand
was still strong enough to persuade the University to consider courses in
Accounting. However, occasionally the process produced rather odd results.
From 1968 courses in Archaeology were developed within the History
Department, where there were already an archaeological museum and
other resources. The demand for places was high. There was no difficulty

[1] 'While it is possible, for a number of professions and over a short term, to calculate
with a fair degree of precision what the national need for recruits will be, we have
found no reliable basis for reckoning the totality of such needs over a long term.'
(*Higher Education*, p. 48; compare pp. 71–4).
[2] *Ibid.*, p. 49.

in finding posts for graduates. Hence staff appointments were made and by 1976 the University was on the verge of establishing a separate department. This was consistent with the principle enunciated in the Robbins Report that opportunity should be provided for qualified applicants, and the case for Archaeology gained strength from the fact that it brought further diversification to the activities of the Faculty of Letters and Social Sciences. How far it matched any objective social need is more questionable. Can social need be defined except by the demand for places and the opportunity of secure careers? In other areas of work such *laissez-faire* was more difficult to tolerate. By 1972 there was a clear indication that the provision for scientists was not being matched by student demand.[1] Reading responded in a number of ways. Some science departments went out to spread the gospel in schools and thereby attract applicants. Others, especially in the life sciences, which were accustomed to co-operation with departments in the Faculty of Agriculture, developed applied courses. Others co-operated with the School of Education in designing joint graduate courses, thereby seeking to increase the supply of qualified science teachers and so attack what might be one of the root causes of the problem. However, none of these measures introduced more than minor corrections to the gravest imbalance between resources on the one hand and student demand on the other. In 1974–5, faced with the saturation of residential accommodation and the need for increasingly stringent economy, the University took the only sensible course. It put a stop to the further expansion of departments such as English, where student demand was already high and was still increasing. It left elbow-room for an increased intake of students into science departments where student demand was low. Implicitly it rejected the profile imposed on it by the choice of applicants. It took its own view of social needs. That was based not on overweening confidence in its own judgment, but on a long academic tradition which required a reasonable diversity in the work of the University and a reasonable balance between subjects. All the University did was to define what 'reasonable' meant.

That is the context within which men worked towards the future at Reading. It is not one to provide much comfort to those who argue that universities are insufficiently responsive to social needs and that they must be made more accountable for what they do both in teaching and research. Indeed it supports a contrary contention. At Reading all the major difficulties came from without. The University worked to projections which were supplied by or agreed with the University Grants Committee, which were related to national calculations by the Ministry of Education and the

[1] The total number of undergraduates in the Faculty of Science with the First and Preliminary years in parentheses was:

1969–70	1,049 (362)	1972–3	1,059 (345+2)
1970–1	1,057 (385)	1973–4	948 (277+3)
1971–2	1,094 (432+2)	1974–5	865 (321+5)

Department of Education and Science, which in turn were designed to express the policies of successive governments. These projections, repeatedly revised, amounted in the end to a long-term plan. But the plan, when clearly stated in the Robbins Report, was less firm than it seemed, for student choice, and hence the profile of expansion, was not wholly predictable. More important still, the cost of the expansion which it envisaged proved to be beyond the country's immediate means. That mattered more than the vacillations in predicting student numbers.

The development of the academic work of the University fell into two distinct periods separated by the Robbins Report. In the first period the departments of the Faculty of Science, especially the physical science departments, were the main centres of change. Up to the post-war years Chemistry and Physics were not among the stronger departments. They lacked resources; by comparison with departments in the Faculty of Agriculture they lacked prestige; in their reports of 1943–4 the heads of the two departments, H. Bassett and J. A. Crowther, emphasized how much had to be done if their subjects were to be placed properly on the map at Reading. Their concern was shared by E. H. Neville of the Department of Mathematics. In the reports of all three there was perhaps a touch of pessimism born of bitter experience of inadequate resources and insufficient students.[1] By the 1960s an astonishing change had taken place. In 1946–7 there were four members of staff in the Department of Physics, by 1964–5 the number had risen to twenty-seven. In 1946–7 eight students graduated with an Honours degree in the subject. In 1964–5 there were thirty-eight. Measured in these terms the Department had become not simply the largest department in the Faculty of Science, but the largest in the whole of the University.[2] This was true of graduate work as well as undergraduate teaching. Of the 189 Ph.D. degrees awarded in the Faculty of Science between 1947 and 1964, 81 were in Physics. The development of Chemistry was less dramatic numerically. There were four members of staff in 1946–7 and eleven in 1964–5. The growth in the numbers of students graduating with honours in Chemistry was slow; one in 1946–7 and four in 1964–5. However, by then the Department had established a remarkable reputation for its research; out of the 189 Ph.D.s in the Faculty between 1947 and 1964, 42 were chemists. These two departments are remarkable partly because they had much leeway to make up. The Department of Zoology which had secured an established position under Cole also made great advances.[3] And these three departments were simply part of a general growth which completely changed the relationship and balance between the Faculty of

[1] See above, pp. 126–8.
[2] In 1964–5 the equivalent numbers in the larger departments in the Faculty of Letters were: English 11 staff, 21 graduands; French 13 staff, 31 graduands; History 9 staff, 27 graduands.
[3] Of the 189 Ph.D.s in the Faculty 1947–64, 24 were in Zoology.

Science and the Faculty of Agriculture. This can be expressed numerically as follows:[1]

	Science			Agriculture		
	Staff	U/Gs	P/Gs	Staff	U/Gs	P/Gs
1946–7	22	134	13	32	301	6
1949–50	33	238	40	38	308	86
1958–9	50	403	87	45	382	75
1964–5	90	677	160	62	405	83

In 1946–7 the Faculty of Agriculture was predominant in all except postgraduates, who were too small in number to be of great significance. By 1964–5 this situation had been reversed. The Faculty of Science now had 50 per cent more staff than the sister Faculty, 60 per cent more undergraduates and nearly twice as many postgraduates. The whole Faculty had advanced its reputation. The two departments of Chemistry and Physics, which at the end of the war were of no great account, were now of national standing.

Those who took part in or simply watched these developments talk almost inevitably of two men: E. A. Guggenheim, Head of the Department of Chemistry from 1946 to 1966, and R. W. Ditchburn, Head of the Department of Physics from 1946 to 1968. They came to Reading together as professors just at the point where new men with new ideas and energies could have a decisive effect;[2] Ditchburn had taken the advice of C. P. Snow, who predicted that there must necessarily be a great advance in Physics departments and that Reading was 'a good place to be geographically'.[3] Both Guggenheim and Ditchburn were determined to have their subjects properly established. More than that, they both felt that a university where their subjects were not practised at a high level could not fully justify the name. At times they cast themselves in the role of inquisitors in the cause of scientific excellence.

However, their achievements for their departments were very different. Guggenheim had an outstanding national and international reputation for his work in thermodynamics. Young scientists first joining the staff at Reading knew all about him and came expecting to find him at work with

[1] Only full-time permanent or temporary lecturing staff (including assistant lecturers) are counted along with professors and readers. The Department of Mathematics has been included in, and the Departments of Geography and Psychology excluded from, the Faculty of Science. Microbiology has been included under Science; Physiological Chemistry under Agriculture.
[2] Guggenheim had already held an appointment at Reading, as a lecturer in 1934–5.
[3] Conversation with Professor R. W. Ditchburn, 11 August 1975.

a large active team around him. There was none. He did not even have
many research students. He was a brilliant individualist. He saw no great
virtue in expansion. He sought rather the scientific excellence which lay
within the range only of a few. All the rest was ancillary. His approach to
the teaching of his subject was so mathematical that, despite the superb
clarity of his expositions, the students found him very difficult to follow.
When he first arrived at Reading he decided that he would see the students
off on the right lines by taking demonstrations for the Intermediate class,
but he was impractical with his hands and the demonstrations went awry.
When he entered the laboratory for the third Intermediate class he found
all the doors and windows shut, with the blinds down; the students said that
this was to keep the gremlins out.[1] As an examiner he was ferocious. No
shorn lamb could ever expect a tempered wind from Guggenheim. On one
occasion he threatened to fail an otherwise acceptable Ph.D. thesis because,
on the spine of the binding, the title ran from bottom to top rather than from
top to bottom.[2] In his relationships with other departments, even including
the Physics department, he was 'difficult'. In any combined course he
expected simply to lay down what the Chemistry component should be; he
knew, and that was that. Those who shared laboratory facilities with him
had a rough time. Yet he commanded enormous respect, and as a result so
did his Department. 'When you saw the miserable facilities they had',
commented one newcomer, 'the work they did was gorgeous'.[3] So, without
any great scheme devised by Guggenheim, through the simple effect of his
prowess as a scientist and his personality, the Department of Chemistry
advanced. The mechanism of advance was simple. Guggenheim could pick
good men, and good men were prepared to come to and remain in his
Department. P. F. Holt arrived in the same year as Guggenheim. He built
up a research team in organic Chemistry. In the next few years he was
followed by D. Bryce-Smith, M. L. McGlashan, I. M. Mills and J. E. Prue,
all of whom were later elected to professorships at Reading or elsewhere.[4]
It was from this group, especially from Prue, that the drive came for the
numerical expansion of the Department and for the new building in
Whiteknights. Guggenheim saw that they got the necessary resources; in
this he was a ruthless fighter. In such business, as in his own research, he

[1] Conversation with Professor P. F. Holt, 29 July 1975.
[2] The story is not apocryphal. The issue was made the subject of correspondence with the
Registrar who ruled that there was no University regulation on the manner in which the
spine should be labelled. Nevertheless the thesis was rebound and relabelled to
Guggenheim's requirements, and it is pleasant to report that the candidate was successful
and is now a professor in a Canadian university. The importance of the matter is
reflected in the complete inability of the participants to recall whether Guggenheim
wanted the title to run from top to bottom or bottom to top. The version given above has
been verified in the Library.
[3] Conversation with Professor A. H. Bunting, 14 August 1975.
[4] M. L. McGlashan moved to a chair at Exeter and then subsequently to University
College, London. The others all received professorships at Reading.

was far shrewder and better organized, than the volatile first impression might suggest.[1]

The development of Physics took a very different course. Unlike Guggenheim, Ditchburn was very much a departmental man, an empire-builder in the best sense. A barren scene greeted his arrival. The Department was inadequately housed. It was short of equipment; what it had was liable to break down; some of it was in a dangerous condition. Ditchburn's predecessor, Crowther, had appreciated the problem but had not been able to do very much before his retirement.[2] Ditchburn now set about it systematically. He accumulated resources both for teaching and research, from the University, the Science Research Council and from industry. He greatly expanded the intake of students. He seized the opportunity of moving to Whiteknights, skilfully exploiting the fact that the Department was split between the main site at London Road and the huts which the Royal Air Force had left at the end of the war in the grounds of Wantage Hall.[3] He got his building when other scientists were hesitating about committing themselves to a move to Whiteknights. He applied steady and relentless pressure in the interests of his subject. He also showed a shrewd insight into the development of research. Realizing that his own field of vacuum spectroscopy was too specialized to provide the basis for the research work of the Department, he seized the opportunity created by one of his lecturers, Dr H. K. Henisch, who received a contract from the Admiralty for work on semi-conductors. Ditchburn appointed staff to work in this field. By 1951 Reading had become an acknowledged centre. In that year the first big conference on the subject was held there. It attracted two Nobel laureates. Ditchburn felt at that point that he had put the Department on the map. The achievement was possible only because from the

[1] Conversation with Professor R. W. Ditchburn, 11 August 1975. When Guggenheim arrived in 1946 the administrative provision for departments was still negligible. They were simply permitted to call on secretarial assistance from the Registrar's department. Guggenheim acquired a secretary by the simple expedient of monopolizing the service in the Registry. Admitting defeat, the University provided him with both secretary and telephone (Conversation with Professor P. F. Holt, 29 July 1975).
[2] See above, p. 128. In 1944 Crowther was asked by the Bursar, E. H. Carpenter, to estimate the cost of re-equipping the Department. He gave a rough and ready estimate of £10,000. This now seems astonishingly low; nevertheless it was enough to astound the Bursar (Conversation with Dr T. B. Rymer, 10 August 1975). Crowther retired early partly because of ill-health, partly to make way for a successor who could tackle the problem as a long-term task.
[3] This was one of the critical arguments which put the new building for Physics ahead of the Library: 'Professor Ditchburn stated that he did not wish to press the claims of his Department over the general interests of the University, but he felt that he had not in the past stressed sufficiently the problems of the Wantage Hutted Site. It would be expensive to renew the huts on this site; the use of the present Library building for the Department of Physics would be less expensive but probably less practicable; and in any case if the Department of Physics were not the next to move to Whiteknights Park some other measures would need to be taken with regard to the Wantage Hutted Site.' (Joint Planning Committee, 27 April 1954). See also above, pp. 195–7.

start he had made up his mind to stay in Reading; he had been ready to commit himself to a prolonged campaign.

It is important to keep the development of both Chemistry and Physics in perspective. They stand out partly because the two departments had few advantages to start with, partly because their advance called for an outlay of resources which was novel at Reading, partly because their advance was marked by large new buildings in Whiteknights, erected before standards of construction and fitting were eroded by the demand for economy. The other departments in the Faculty were also moving forward. In 1957 the Department of Geology was able to begin work on the Research Laboratory in Sedimentology, financed partly by the University Grants Committee and partly by funds provided by the oil industry both for the building and its equipment.[1] In some departments development came easily; this was true of Geology where Hawkins was succeeded as professor in 1952 by one of his pupils, P. Allen. In others it was more hazardous. Indeed from some points of view it was easier to build on the *tabula rasa* with which Ditchburn was faced on his arrival, than to reconstruct and redirect a department which was already well settled in its ways. A. Graham joined such a department when he succeeded O'Donoghue as Professor of Zoology in 1952. Like Ditchburn he found his department short of the necessary resources. It never bought what it could collect or scrounge. Ian Crichton brought in mussels from local ponds; F. C. Padley, the chief technician, collected crayfish from traps set in the Kennet; one of the functions of the Easter field-course was to collect specimens for use throughout the coming year. It struck Graham that students at Reading were learning the biology of pickled animals. Like many other new arrivals he marvelled at Reading's instinctive penny-pinching; the Department issued outline maps of Great Britain to its students at a penny a time. Again, like many, he noted an enclosed, self-satisfied atmosphere in the place.[2] In the case of Zoology, however, all this was emphasized by the fact that the formidable figure of Cole still overshadowed the Department from retirement, whilst within the Department Dr Nellie B. Eales acted as a kind of guardian angel over all Cole's work. O'Donoghue had scarcely brought in any change; he had developed as an administrator[3] and an entertaining *raconteur* in the Senior Common Room rather than as an active scientist. Graham now wanted change. In 1955 the issue between the old and the new came to a head over his rearrangement of material in the Zoological Museum. Cole intervened

[1] See above, p. 198 n. 1. The grants from oil companies are noted in *Proceedings 1956–7*, p. 8; *Proceedings 1957–8*, p. 9; *Proceedings 1961–2*, p. 10; *Proceedings 1962–3*, p. 10; *Proceedings 1963–4*, p. 12; *Proceedings 1964–5*, p. 13.

[2] See above, pp. 157–8. Graham summarizes this the most succinctly of all the contemporary witnesses: 'the feeling of belonging could have led to the feeling that it was a good place to belong to. People felt that they didn't need to seek information elsewhere on how things might have been done differently.' (Conversation with Professor A. Graham, 28 July 1975).

[3] He was Dean of the Faculty of Science 1944–8 and Deputy Vice-Chancellor 1950–2.

with the Vice-Chancellor and ultimately the matter was referred to Council. Council confirmed Graham's action; it 'declined to limit or further define the departmental autonomy of the Professor of Zoology'; as Wolfenden wittily and perhaps a little unjustly put it 'Cole wanted a museum of a museum'.[1] Even then the determined old man was still dissatisfied and launched a further broadside against the Council's resolutions in May 1956; 'zoological museums', he argued, 'should be allowed to grow and evolve free from periodic cataclysmic disturbance'.[2] Council could find no cataclysm and reaffirmed its decision.[3] From the furore there emerged some good. One of the *pièces justificatives* was an admirable little account, published in *Nature*,[4] of the early development of Cole's zoological collection. Another consequence was that the Council took note of the difficulty of maintaining the collection and gave the Department a supplementary vote of not more than £200.[5] Graham went his way, as steadfast as Ditchburn in Physics. The Department changed, conforming more and more to what he wanted.[6] Increasingly his own work and that of Dr Vera Fretter ensured that it added to its reputation by developing into a centre for the study of molluscs. Research prospered. Research students multiplied.[7] Cole's museum

---

[1] Council Minute, 1728, 9 December 1955. For Wolfenden's comment, conversation with Professor A. Graham 28 July 1975. Cole had founded the collection and this was recognized on his retirement when the Council resolved 'that on the occasion of the retirement of Dr F. J. Cole from the Professorship of Zoology, the Council . . . have much pleasure in the reflection that the Zoological Museum, which is his creation, will remain as a permanent memorial of the professorship which he has held for thirty-three years in the University College and University of Reading. . . . Council further resolved that the Zoological Museum should henceforth be known as "The Cole Zoological Museum".' (Council Minute, 789, 7 July 1939).

[2] Council Reports, xvi, 25 May 1956.

[3] Council Minute, 1752, 25 May 1956.

[4] 'The Cole Museum of Zoology', *Nature*, clxxvii, 555–6, 24 March 1956.

[5] Council Minute, 1752, 25 May 1956; 1764, 26 July 1956.

[6] F. C. Padley, chief technician, commented: 'He had many ideas, but he introduced them very gradually, trying not to hurt anyone's feelings. Over the years Zoology like most of the other science subjects has changed very markedly, chemistry and electronics playing a much bigger part, and I found myself having to learn many new facets of my job. I was having to order many more living animals than we ever did in the old days, trying to keep them alive in more or less artificial conditions. A constant supply of sea water had to be kept in stock. Most marine animals do not like long railway journeys and then being left at the station, hence we would often have them sent on an overnight train and collected first thing in the morning. . . . These new types of classes also meant very much more in the way of basic laboratory equipment, glassware, dishes, test tube racks, thermometers and the like of which we had only a limited quantity. Again it was a case of making new improvisation and I am afraid of borrowing a lot from other departments and I am ever grateful to my colleagues . . . for the generous help they gave me in these transition days. So the weeks and months went by, settling down into a new routine.' (*Recollections*, p. 18).

[7] In 1962–3, for example, a bumper year for the Department, 6 of the 21 Ph.D.s conferred in the Faculty of Science were in Zoology. In numbers of Ph.D. students over the period 1947–64 the Department ran third to Chemistry and Physics, and slightly ahead of Geology. Almost all these students obtained their degrees after Graham's arrival.

remained one of the features of the Department. So also did 'Nellie B.'.[1]

There were trials, therefore, the like of which neither Guggenheim nor Ditchburn had to face, and there were advances and changes in their Faculty for which others were responsible. However, the two of them, supported at times by E. H. Neville, had an importance beyond the purely departmental. Their insistent concern for science in general and their own subjects in particular disturbed the traditionally sympathetic, give-and-take discussions of the Senate. 'With the advent of Guggenheim and Ditchburn', Edgar Thomas recalled, 'Senate became a different place.'[2] Some saw this as a result of Guggenheim's volcanic personality. 'We coined the intransitive verb "to Gugg" ', said Hodges, 'abstract noun "Guggery", which denoted raising Cain and generally laying about oneself'.[3] Others appreciated that while Guggenheim was the more explosive, Ditchburn was the better organized and more persistent.[4] The sun shone after Guggenheim's thunder, but Ditchburn held on, as relentless as a cold north-easter. The effect of their intervention was to change the content and format of discussion. As one dispassionate observer put it, the old hands would ask first what was good for the University, secondly what was good for the Faculty, and thirdly what was good for the Department. Guggenheim and Ditchburn reversed that order, or so it seemed.[5] Some, like Harris, watched with tolerant interest. Among the rest, W. B. Brierley, Professor of Agricultural Botany since 1932, was driven at times to almost apoplectic fury. Yet there was a logic in the line which Guggenheim and Ditchburn were taking and it was one which turned on a distinction between 'real' scientists and others. They were simply insisting that the 'real' scientists should be provided with the resources to do their job properly. How could that be anything but a paramount interest to the University as a whole?

This had a direct effect on the Faculty of Agriculture and its relations with the Faculty of Science. The first year of Guggenheim and Ditchburn was the last year of H. A. D. Neville. He had been Dean of the Faculty of Agriculture, re-elected annually, since 1919. With Percival, Pennington and Brierley he had been one of the chief builders of the Faculty of Agriculture and was certainly its organizing genius, directing even the detail of its affairs in person. He had become a masterly wire-puller in great things and small; he knew as no one else how to get things done.[6] In Edgar

[1] It is pleasant to record that Dr Eales, long after her formal retirement, still manages the Cole Library in the University Library, with the assistance of F. C. Padley. See below, p. 259.
[2] Conversation with Professor Edgar Thomas, 23 July 1975.
[3] Conversation with Professor H. A. Hodges, 24 July 1975.
[4] Conversation with Professor C. Tyler, 8 August 1975.
[5] But compare Ditchburn's remarks on the move to Whiteknights, above, p. 213, n. 3.
[6] Conversation with Sir Harold Sanders, 12 August 1975; conversation with Professor C. Tyler, 8 August 1975.

Thomas's words 'he was a wizard'.[1] Seen from outside the Faculty he created a different impression; P. F. Holt remembered him as a 'small very stubborn man, determined to fight for the interests of his department and his Faculty.'[2] Hence from 1947 the Faculty was without its old watch-dog, and this in circumstances where it was obvious that both the Faculty of Agriculture and the Faculty of Science would have to pay close attention to the areas in which their work overlapped. This was a long-standing problem; it was an inevitable consequence of the syllabuses adopted in the Faculty of Agriculture, and it had been discussed many times before, especially in the reports to the Development Committee of 1943–4.[3] Some argument about the use of accommodation, about who was to teach what, and about the extent to which pure science courses were to be adjusted to the needs of the agriculturalists was probably unavoidable. T. M. Harris later commented as follows:

> In Botany the Professors before me were men of peace, but there were stories of the battles between Keeble (whom I never saw) and Percival of Agricultural Botany. This could explain the fantastic lack of relation between these departments – apart from the fact that I transmitted students to be further and quite independently processed by Agricultural Botany in their final years. I was friendly, but my colleagues, though not unfriendly, had no relations with them. The boundary was so sharp that it totally controlled everyone's thought, and when the question of new departments at Whiteknights arose everyone thought of Botany and Zoology being the natural unit. For some reason, I thought of an alliance with Agricultural Botany and Horticulture, and everyone was at first appalled – but it prevailed. There was the ideal concept of faculties as armies led into battle by their deans (never very real outside dreams) but only very late was there the idea that their lecture timetables were about the most fundamental boundary.[4]

It was easier to resolve matters in this way in the case of Botany than in other subjects. H. A. D. Neville's old Department of Agricultural Chemistry, for example, was responsible for a wide range of subjects the association of which only made sense within an agriculture course: animal nutrition, dairy chemistry, soil science, fertilizers and insecticides. Once Neville had retired the future of the Department became a matter of prolonged controversy, for in 1949 the proposals of the Faculty of Science for the Quinquennium 1952–7 included the establishment of a Department of Physiology & Biochemistry, with a chair in each subject. But these were the essential scientific components in the course in animal nutrition;

[1] Conversation with Professor Edgar Thomas, 23 July 1975.
[2] Conversation with Professor P. F. Holt, 29 July 1975.
[3] See above, pp. 129–30.
[4] Memorandum of Professor T. M. Harris, 5 August 1975. Keeble was Professor of Botany in the University College, 1907–14.

there was a movement, therefore, for the duplication in the Faculty of
Science of work which the Department of Agricultural Chemistry could
claim to be doing already in the Faculty of Agriculture. There Neville's
successor, C. Tyler, came to envisage a curiously similar development,
but one under his own direction. He wanted to see his Department shed
the work on Soil Science and Dairy Chemistry to separate departments,
thereby leaving a central core of Physiology and Biochemistry for which
his Department would be responsible both in the Faculty of Agriculture
and the Faculty of Science. Tyler, in his cause, was as tough and formidable
as Guggenheim and Ditchburn were in theirs; indeed he was prepared to
go on batting in defence of his wicket when all the rest had gone home
to bed. On Guggenheim's side the argument was sharpened by his notion
of 'real' science, by his awareness of the enhanced reputation and superior
resources which the Faculty of Agriculture still enjoyed, and by his desire
to see Biochemistry develop within the orbit of the staff of his own Department.[1] There were moments of embarrassment. In 1958 when it had
been agreed that the old Department of Agricultural Chemistry should be
established in both Faculties with the new title of Physiological Chemistry,
Tyler still had to submit to a debate about the headship of the Department, and, when that had been settled, Guggenheim went on to argue
that only those members of the Department 'who were good enough'
should appear in the *Calendar* under the Faculty of Science. There were
also moments of pure comedy. The design for the new Chemistry building
in Whiteknights made provision for two wings separated by a central
staircase, the one for Chemistry, the other, which was never in fact erected,
for Agricultural or Physiological Chemistry. Guggenheim had the staircase designed as an elegant double helix.[2] It was only partly in jest that
he insisted that this was in order to ensure that the chemists and the 'adjec-
tival' chemists, as he had come to call them, should never meet on the stairs.
But Tyler won the argument.

This prolonged debate had an interesting and important effect on the
planning of the building development in Whiteknights. Guggenheim came
to reject an association with Agricultural or Physiological Chemistry. But
Graham was thinking of developing courses in Agricultural Zoology,[3] while
Harris was ready for an alliance with Agricultural Botany. Initially it was
intended that Chemistry and Agricultural Chemistry should go together
in the new building in Whiteknights. When in 1958 it became clear that

[1] P. F. Holt was an important figure in the field, engaged in 1956 and 1957 in work on
silicosis and pneumoconiosis.
[2] See plate 41.
[3] A Lecturership in Agricultural Zoology to be established in the Department of Zoology
was included in the Quinquennial Proposals for 1957–62. On 9 April 1957, in answering
questions concerning the future size of the Zoology Department, Graham indicated that
'we hope to develop an Agricultural Zoology Department.' (A. Graham to Registrar,
9 April 1957: Building Development Committee, 4 May 1957).

the building would have to be phased, it was agreed that the Chemistry wing would be built first. Guggenheim at this stage was against phasing and the intention to include Physiological Chemistry in the Chemistry building was noted repeatedly over the next few years.[1] Meanwhile plans for a Biology block were emerging from preliminary ideas of housing Zoology and Botany in separate buildings.[2] By 1961 it had been agreed that Botany, Zoology and Psychology should share a building and Microbiology was added to the planned complex in 1962.[3] It was not in fact until the end of 1963, in the discussions following the Robbins Report, that any change was made in the traditional association of Botany and Zoology. Only then was Physiological Chemistry included in the new Biology block with Zoology, Microbiology and Psychology, and it was only in January 1964 that it was finally agreed that Botany and Agricultural Botany should go together.[4] Out of the initial difficulties therefore there came a completely new scheme which in 1963-4 envisaged three closely related biology buildings, one for Animal Biology, the second for Plant Biology and a third for Microbiology and Genetics.[5]

In these areas individual idiosyncracies and academic planning combined to produce solutions different from those first intended. They were probably better solutions. It may be also that the vehemence of Guggenheim, the persistence of Ditchburn and the endurance of Tyler had a more general effect. The pure scientists did not get it all their own way. Edgar Thomas, for example, could argue very cogently that the Faculty of Agriculture would get better scientists, and the science departments themselves would enjoy an enhanced reputation if their work was closely interwoven with that of the Faculty of Agriculture. For him the link with Agriculture brought reinforcement rather than debasement.[6] Others considered that the Faculty of Agriculture got better students and marked to stiffer standards.[7] Hence, although the controversy appeared a little domestic to colleagues in the Faculty of Letters and proved wearisome at times to Wolfenden, it was vigorous and was none the worse for that. In the whole broad area of

[1] Building Development Committee, 25 February 1958; Senate Minute, 2975, 3 June 1958. See also Building Programme 1964-8 for submission to the Central Steering Committee of the Building Development Committee, 19 November 1959.
[2] Revised Building Programme 1957-62 (Building Development Committee, 4 May 1957). At that point it was intended that they should share 5,000 sq. ft. as a teaching provision for the courses which the two departments taught in the Faculty of Agriculture.
[3] Building Development Committee, 6 October 1961, 16 February 1962.
[4] Building Development Committee, 2 December 1963, 10 February 1964.
[5] The intended site for all three was to the north of the Faculty of Letters. Only the Animal Biology building stands there. The Plant Sciences building was ultimately sited close to the Wilderness, where there was sufficient space to establish a botanical garden by the side of the building. The third building has not materialized, nor was there ever room to include Psychology in these developments; nor finally, was it possible to establish a Department of Genetics.
[6] Conversation with Professor Edgar Thomas, 23 July 1975.
[7] Conversation with Professor C. Tyler, 8 August 1975.

the biological sciences it brought departments in the two Faculties closer together. Sometimes an advance delayed in one faculty was achieved in the other. In 1961, for example, after a long wait for the appointment of a statistician in the Department of Mathematics, the Faculty of Agriculture, at the urging of A. H. Bunting, went ahead with the establishment of a Biometry Unit.[1] But there was no hard and fast separation of faculties. In 1951 the Department of Microbiology was established in both the Faculty of Science and the Faculty of Agriculture,[2] and two years later the Department of Psychology was included in the Faculty of Science as well as in the Faculty of Letters.

These developments were part of a broad general advance in the University's size and prosperity. In the Faculty of Letters the Department of German was strengthened by the establishment of a Chair of German in 1952–3. Italian was established, first in 1955 as a separate unit in the Department of English, then in 1960 as a separate department; in 1963–4, that also was strengthened by the establishment of a Chair. Both the Schools of Music and Fine Art were finally included within the Faculty, and a Chair of Music was established in 1950–1. The whole Faculty, apart from these two Schools, gained elbow-room when it moved to Whiteknights in 1957; at last there was room to expand in spacious surroundings. The Department of Physics in 1960, Geology in 1961, and Chemistry in 1965, enjoyed a similar release. The Faculty of Agriculture was confined for the present to the old buildings in London Road, but it was able to expand into the vacated accommodation. Moreover, it could count on an enormous addition to its facilities following the purchase of Shinfield Grange in 1949. This estate of 478 acres, larger even than Whiteknights, provided a base for a new Horticultural Station.[3]

The three Faculties shared a common feature which conditioned the University's response to the Robbins Report. They were all committed in different ways to a preliminary course, involving at least three subjects, which led to the First University Examination. The First University Examination, held after the first two terms, originated in a temporary expedient which was introduced in the Faculty of Letters in 1943 in an attempt to provide a more coherent course for students during the few months available to them before entering the Forces. It took the place of the old Intermediate Examination in the Faculty after the war and was adopted gradually by the other Faculties.[4] In the 1960s it developed into

---

[1] The Unit became the Department of Applied Statistics in 1966 in both Faculties.
[2] From 1969 it ceased to be included in Agriculture.
[3] The Estate was bought for £37,500, £20,000 of which was provided by the UGC. Finance Committee Minutes, 3403, 3427, 6 May and 17 June 1949; *Proceedings 1948–9*, p. 1. See also below, pp. 270–1.
[4] The Faculty of Science abandoned the old Intermediate Examination in 1963 and adopted a First University Examination, held at the beginning of the summer term, in 1965. The Faculty of Agriculture took to the new title in 1953, but did not accept that the examination should be held at the beginning of the third term until 1965–6.

a propædeutic system intended to allow the student to delay final confirmation of his choice of degree course until his first year in the University. This brought advantages and disadvantages. The advantages were all immediate. In dealing with the extraordinarily rapid expansion which the Robbins Report heralded, the University already had a system whereby students could be drawn in from the subjects traditionally taught in school and then enabled, through their experience in the first year and if they so wished, to change to some other course of which they might scarcely have heard before their arrival in the University. This enabled the University to found new departments concerned with 'non-school' subjects with all the greater confidence. It could diversify its activities, knowing that new subjects, properly handled, could generate their own supply of students in the first year. This was related to yet another feature of the University's work which went back to the years before the Second World War. It had long ago provided Honours courses either in Combined Subjects or in Single Subjects which involved some work in other fields.[1] By the 1960s this had become widespread and deep rooted. In 1963–4 there were in the Faculty of Letters twenty-two Honours courses involving two subjects and two involving three subjects. Most of them embodied the traditional association of two different languages, but there were also French and Economics, Philosophy and German, and Social Theory and Institutions. In the Faculty of Science a slightly different effect was produced by a requirement that all Special Honours students should take a subsidiary subject.[2] In the Faculty of Agriculture the syllabus remained as it had been since its foundation, based on a combination of sciences which traversed the traditional boundaries between subjects and from which special studies diverged as the course progressed. Hence all three Faculties, in different ways and to varying degrees, were committed either to mixing or to integrating the accepted disciplines.

Reading had designed a system which, in its wide range of choice, was particularly adaptable to circumstances of expansion. The disadvantages were to become apparent later. These arose from the difficulty of adjusting resources to the consequences of student-choice.[3] There were early indications that these did not necessarily go hand in hand. In considering the advance from the target of 2,000 to 3,000 in 1960 both the Faculty of Science and the Faculty of Agriculture expressed concern that they might not be able to find a sufficient number of adequately qualified students to keep pace with the necessary expansion. At that point Senate accepted that it might be necessary to abandon the principle of rough parity between the

[1] See above, pp. 47–51.
[2] Some of the subsidiary subjects allowed a narrower choice than the principle perhaps implied. For example it was possible to read Physics with the Physical Properties of Materials and vice versa. Cybernetics was also included in the list.
[3] See above, pp. 208–9; below, pp. 237–40.

Faculties on which expansion had hitherto been planned.[1] The consequences were immediate. Already in 1960 the undergraduates in the Faculty of Letters numbered 526, against 313 in the Faculty of Science and 291 in the Faculty of Agriculture. Five years later in 1964–5 there were 900 undergraduates in Letters, against 517 in Science and 307 in Agriculture. In these terms the Faculty of Letters was already slightly larger than the other two together. It was only in fact in graduate work that the numerical imbalance could be redressed and then only to a limited extent.[2] At Reading this imbalance was accepted as a necessary consequence of rapid expansion more than three years before the publication of the Robbins Report. In the expansion which followed the Report little could be done to correct it. The University could increase its numbers, certainly, but only by taking a larger proportion of undergraduate students into the Faculty of Letters. By 1974–5 the undergraduates in the Faculty of Letters numbered 1,875 against 865 in Science and 562 in Agriculture,[3] a ratio of roughly 9 to 7 in the other two Faculties.

No one in the University advocated such a distribution in principle. However, the policies adopted may have contributed to it quite unintentionally. The very same Committee which regretfully accepted the abandonment of parity of numbers between faculties went on immediately to say:

> The Committee is strongly of the opinion that in addition to the extension of existing interests further consideration should be given to the introduction of new fields of study, in order that the range of 'offerings' may be widened and the opportunities increased for the greater number of students envisaged.[4]

---

[1] Development Committee Working Paper on Student Numbers:

(b) The Faculty of Letters would have little difficulty in achieving the annual intake of some 300 that would be required.

(c) The Faculty of Science might find it more difficult to achieve an annual intake of 300. On present reckonings there would be about 100 new students each year in the Pure Maths., Applied Maths., Physics group; about 50 in the Combined Maths., Chemistry and Physics groups; and about 50 in the biological groups including Chemistry. The remainder would have to be in the other groupings, and it is not certain that 100 of these could be found . . .

(d) The Faculty of Agriculture and Horticulture will have difficulty in finding an annual intake of 120 (and 150 would be the absolute maximum) on the evidence of the recent decline in numbers of applications.

(e) It will be necessary for the principle of parity in Faculty numbers to be abandoned. (Senate Reports, xvii, 11 March 1960).

[2] The number of graduate students was as follows:

	Letters	Science	Agriculture
1959–60	47	93	87
1964–5	104	160	98

[3] The number of graduate students in 1974–5 was: Letters 316; Science 520; Agriculture 498. The total of all students in 1974–5 was: Letters 2,204; Science 1,388; Agriculture 1,060. These figures include occasional students and students working overseas.

[4] Senate Reports, xvii, 11 March 1960.

That was the natural and sensible course to follow. It grew out of all the proposals for development which departments had been advancing since 1943–4. It was both academically desirable and socially responsible. Nevertheless it led to a proliferation of new courses in Letters as much as in Science and Agriculture, and the demand for the new courses in Letters expanded very rapidly. Diversification exaggerated rather than diminished the imbalance.

The Government's acceptance of the Robbins Report was made known on 24 October 1963. At Reading academic planning was already under way. In July Sir Keith Murray, Chairman of the University Grants Committee, had written to advise universities to keep going with their building plans and to ask whether they would be able to increase the existing targets for admissions.[1] On 14 October the Senate appointed six working parties to consider possible developments.[2] These took the Robbins Report in their stride and reported to a special meeting of the Senate on 20 November.[3] Their work did much to determine the development of the University in the next decade. They were under some pressure; the Robbins Committee envisaged an emergency programme extending up to 1967–8; hence the working parties were on the look-out for subjects which could be developed rapidly to meet an expanding demand for places. The resulting list compiled for Senate was labelled 'Offerings'. There was room for considerable exercise of the imagination. The 'offerings' included many items which, in 1976, have yet to materialize: American Studies, Asian Studies, African Studies, Anatomy, Veterinary Science, Domestic Science, Medicine and Dentistry. But amidst these, the subjects which Reading could develop quickly and coherently stood out clearly.

In the Faculty of Letters the social sciences provided the most obvious field for development. Hitherto their advance had been slow and hesitant. Up to the war the old Department of Economics in the Faculty was upheld by the single figure of Mabel Buer. When she died in 1943 E. S. Budden was appointed to an independent Lecturership in Political Economy, and a year later the Department was likewise renamed. By this time there was considerable pressure for further development. In the Faculty of Letters Hodges in particular was advocating an extension of social studies in a very broad sense of the term, while in the Faculty of Agriculture, Edgar Thomas was arguing for the proper establishment of a Department of Economics

[1] Chairman of the University Grants Committee to Vice-Chancellor, 24 July 1963 (Senate Reports, xxi).
[2] Senate Minute, 3731. One working party comprising the Deputy Vice-Chancellor and the Deans was responsible for co-ordination and central planning. The others were concerned respectively with Social Sciences, Biological Sciences, Physical Sciences, Earth Sciences, and other Arts subjects.
[3] Senate Minute, 3756. The Reports headed 'Expansion of the University' are in Senate Reports, xxii, 20 November 1963.

specializing in agricultural matters.[1] Budden was slow. Although a learned scholar and a capable teacher, he regarded Political Economy in the old fashioned manner as an all embracing subject within which politics, economics and social studies were all comprised, and which was best studied in the works of the great masters of the past, Adam Smith, Ricardo and Bentham. However, Agricultural Economics developed rapidly in the Faculty of Agriculture.[2] In the Faculty of Letters Budden was given some support; two lecturers in social studies were appointed in 1950;[3] and throughout the 1950s the Department carried a staff of three or four. But he was himself the chief block to further development. He saw no virtue in expansion and he was totally opposed to the subdivision of his subject. Senate showed increasing impatience. The Quinquennial Plan for 1952–7, drawn up in 1951, provided for the establishment of Chairs in both German and Political Economy.[4] A professor of German was appointed in 1953, but nothing was done about the other proposal. The next Quinquennial Plan for 1957–62, drawn up in 1956, was both urgent and blunt; a professorship of Political Economy was listed first among the new commitments with the following comment:

> The Department of Political Economy is the only one in the University which offers an Honours course but which has at its head not a Professor but an Independent Lecturer. It is our opinion that we should delay the institution of a Chair no longer.[5]

In 1960, matters were taken out of Budden's hands with the appointment of P. W. Campbell as Professor of Political Economy. With this the Faculty was at last placed in a position in which it could meet the increased demand for places by extending and deepening its provision for social studies. This was already in hand when the Robbins Report was published and it now went ahead rapidly. In 1963–4 separate Departments of Economics and Sociology were established, with a Chair in each and the old Department of Political Economy became the Department of Politics. The expansion of the three departments was rapid. By the end of 1965 Economics catered for 94 students, Politics for 60 and Sociology for 102, amounting in total to 18 per cent of all the students in the Faculty.[6] In the proposals for the next Quinquennium, 1967–72, further expansion was envisaged; the three departments together were to cater for roughly a quarter of the whole Faculty.[7]

[1] See above, pp. 125–6, 130–1.
[2] Edgar Thomas was elected to a chair in 1945.
[3] Senate Minute, 2181, 29 November 1950.
[4] Council Reports, xiii, 9 November 1951.
[5] Council Reports, xvi, 9 November 1956.
[6] Faculty of Letters, F, Quinquennial Development 1967–72, Breakdown of staff–student ratio December 1965. The figures are of student units and hence include all FUE and combined-subject students. The total of student units was 1,385.
[7] The projected numbers for 1971–2 were Economics 202, Politics 133, Sociology 183, amounting to 518 out of a Faculty total of 2,105 (Faculty of Letters, F, Quinquennial Development 1967–72).

This was not fully achieved.[1] Even so by 1970–1 the three departments were larger than any other departments in the Faculty except for English, Fine Art, French and History. Only in one major respect was the advance checked. Proposals for a Department of Social Administration were put forward in 1963 and renewed in 1967. Some members of the Faculty were far from convinced of the academic merits of the subject. Some of the social studies departments had other interests to advance; none was prepared to give the case first priority. Hence in the Quinquennial proposals for 1972–7 it was overtaken by a proposal for the establishment of Law.[2] The foundation of a Law Department in the Faculty in 1973 was the last major advance.[3]

These developments in the social sciences were numerically the most important in the Faculty in the period following the Robbins Report. There were also other notable advances. A Department of Linguistic Science was established in 1965. That in turn led to the development of Language Pathology and a Centre for Applied Language Studies from 1974. The Department of Geography proceeded to diversify its work so that one section concentrated on Physical Geography in the Faculty of Science while in the Faculty of Letters the study of Human Geography under Professor P. G. Hall moved more and more towards environmental and planning studies. The Department of Psychology followed a similar division between Experimental and Human Psychology, although in this case the main weight lay on the Experimental side in the Faculty of Science. In the Department of History after 1966 increasing emphasis was laid on European History; for a time from 1968 it was the only department in the country where it was possible to take a history course based on European history. All the language departments were moving away from the exclusive

[1] By 1970–1 Economics had reached 185, Politics 147, but Sociology lagged behind at 173 (*ibid.*).
[2] The comment of the Faculty Development Committee was: 'The Development Committee has examined carefully the case for the introduction of Social Administration and has scrutinized the proposals put forward in 1964 and 1967. It has also consulted the Heads of Departments of Economics, Politics, Psychology and Sociology. Some expression of support was obtained, but neither the departments consulted nor the members of the Committee felt that a high priority could be given to this proposal in view of the recommendation that Law should be the major new development, and in view of the desire for growth and expansion by a majority of the existing departments. The fact that this proposal has been in the pipeline since 1964, but has remained unimplemented, was regarded by the Committee as an indication that it had not, in the preceding six years, achieved the status of a compelling development. The Committee therefore recommends that there should be no provision in the Plan for the introduction of Social Administration.'
    The Department of Economics was lukewarm unless the subject was started on a major scale; the Department of Politics gave priority to Law and its own further expansion; the Department of Sociology noted that 'Technical Colleges have been expanding this line on quite a big scale' and avoided including it even after its own list of five priorities (Faculty of Letters, F, Quinquennial Estimates, 1972–7).
[3] For the origins of the Department of Law in the Faculty of Urban and Regional Studies see below, pp. 241, 243.

study of language and literature and towards courses which embraced the study of society, history and institutions. This took root in French first, under the direction of A. G. Lehmann, then in Italian, and finally and more slowly in German, where linguistic study remained strong during the reign of Professor F. P. Pickering.[1]

This development was of general importance for it led to the development of new combined courses, especially of languages and social studies. Indeed the establishment of new departments and of new interests within departments led to the further proliferation of combined subject courses throughout the Faculty. In 1963–4 there were 24 such courses; by 1974–5 there were 79. Time-tabling became difficult: it remained feasible only because not all combinations were taken up at any one time. The Faculty accepted this. Indeed it proved easier to introduce such a course than to remove it from the syllabus, once introduced; there might be a student wishing to follow it next year or the year after. Some departments, especially Philosophy and Classics, came to feel dependent on such courses for an adequate supply of students. But the instinct to experiment with combinations of subjects was something more than an expedient. It went back to the earliest days of the University's independence.[2] It subsumed varied ideas and approaches. The Graduate Centre for Medieval Studies and the Graduate School of Contemporary European Studies were both founded in 1965–6.[3] The first was based on the principle that literary students should acquire some history and vice versa, and that all students should take part in a number of hybrid courses which traversed the traditional divisions between subjects. The second allowed a free, almost random, choice by the individual student of 'offerings' volunteered by historians, linguists and social scientists. The two schools were based on very different principles which in turn affected their internal organization. The Faculty accepted both. There seemed to be no need to decide between the two different rationales which they represented.

[1] For an account of the development of the Department of German up to 1966, which foreshadowed the changes outlined above see W. A. Coupe, 'The Development of German Studies in the University of Reading' (1966), pp. 12–13 (URC, box 256).
[2] See above, p. 49. The readiness to accept combinations which might attract students only at rare intervals had a long history in the Faculty. In 1943 Hodges wrote a paper entitled 'The Idea of a Faculty of Arts' which Sibly circulated to the Principal of University College, Exeter (URC, Vice-Chancellor, box 45). After considering compulsory special subjects Hodges went on – 'The compulsory special subject can obviously be developed so as to take a greater part in the scheme of the degree course, and the end of this line of development is the Honours course in two subjects on an equal or nearly equal footing. In the last thirteen years we have set up several such courses. Philosophy and English Literature, the earliest of them, works very well and is popular with a good type of student. So is Latin and English Literature. So is Economics and Social Psychology. Greek and English has a smaller public, for obvious reasons. *Philosophy and Economics has never had a student at all*' [my italics].
[3] The Graduate Centre had a pre-history, as it were, in the M.A. course in Medieval Symbolism and Iconography provided by Professor F. P. Pickering, who became the first Director of the Centre.

However, the development of the graduate courses and indeed of all the combined subject first-degree courses took place within clearly defined limits set by the administrative structure of the Faculty. It was simply an agglomeration of departments. Responsibility for a subject lay squarely on the shoulders of the head of the appropriate department. Occasionally this was circumvented for immediate practical reasons; in the language departments, for example, posts in history were established without any formal link with the Department of History; but little was done to alter it in principle. Schools of study, associating departments in particular subject-groups, were set up in 1967–8, but they faded away almost at once. There seemed to be nothing for them to do. There was no serious attempt to develop modular courses based on separate units. No one advocated such a policy seriously or with any weight, either on administrative or academic grounds. But if in these matters the administrative structure helped to determine academic development, in another important respect the converse was the case. In 1968 the Faculty was renamed the Faculty of Letters and Social Sciences. A few members of the Board of the Faculty favoured the establishment of a separate Faculty of Social Sciences,[1] but the association of arts and social sciences in combined subject courses was too extended and too complex to allow such an administrative separation. At the simplest level there had to be one single, co-ordinated lecture time-table. Hence the Faculty remained one, a large cumbersome monument to its own history; to the ease with which it had accepted combined subject courses and, beyond that, to the notions which had inspired de Burgh, Hodges, Dyson and others in the earliest days of the University and which had set the Faculty on its course.

In the Faculty of Science development following the Robbins Report was on a smaller scale than in the Faculty of Letters; no numbers-spinner comparable to Social Studies lay ready to hand. Moreover, there was a stricter limit on space; no science department could go in for incremental building as easily or cheaply as the Faculty of Letters. Hence the three working parties concerned emphasized that the easiest way to increase numbers was to expand existing subjects. The working party on Physical Sciences envisaged trebling undergraduate numbers in this field by 1968. The Earth Sciences working party put the maximum increase by 1969 as high as 600, excluding those reading Soil Science. Only in the case of the Biological Sciences was enthusiasm tempered by realistic doubt:

> The Group considers that a 50 per cent increase in the number
> previously envisaged of first-year students following existing courses
> in the Biological Sciences would be both acceptable and feasible –
> if the statements in the Robbins Report that students of the requisite
> quality and quantity will be forthcoming are accepted, as perforce

---

[1] The main pressure came from the Department of Economics. The case was not strongly supported, even in the other Social Science departments.

they must be, even though they are not borne out by the applications for entry in October 1963.[1]

In addition, the working parties proposed several new developments. Much the most imposing scheme was for the establishment of a Department or School of Applied Physical Sciences:

Sir Eric Ashby in his presidential address to the 1963 meeting of the British Association spoke on the theme: the university as a social instrument for investment in man. He thought that, 'it is for their bread and butter service of training men and women for the professions that the public is willing to invest money (in the universities) and it is on their discharge of this service that their efficiency is judged'. It is also apparent that the present political emphasis on training increasing numbers of scientists arises largely from a desire to apply science more widely in the solution of technological, economic and social problems (see Robbins Report, para. 507). This note is concerned with the training of applied physicists, but the general conclusion may well apply to some chemists and mathematicians.

At present some twenty-two per cent of physicists enter industry and this proportion may be expected to increase as physicists become employed in a wider range of industries. The physics degree courses of most universities provide an admirable preparation for academic life, for advancing physics itself, and for the restricted range of industry in which technology is based upon recent scientific discoveries. It is less satisfactory as a preparation for the wider range of industry requiring mainly the application of classical physics. Nevertheless, industrialists value the services of physicists highly and are prepared to go to great lengths to recruit them. The reason for this high valuation is that in a period of rapid technological advance, a training in physics provides a better preparation for innovation and less quickly becomes obsolete than does a training in traditional engineering. The general acceptance of this point is witnessed by the increasing scientific content of engineering degree courses, and by the recent change in the membership regulation of the Institution of Mechanical Engineers to allow admission of suitable physicists to full membership. The disadvantage of the present physics degree courses as a basis for entry into industry, is that a period of further training within industry itself is required before the physicist becomes fully effective. If he enters industry at Ph.D. level, this further period will take him to about the age of thirty. By provision of a training course designed with the requirements of an industry in mind, it should be possible to produce an effective industrial physicist more quickly.

[1] Senate Reports, xxii, 20 November 1963, Expansion of the University, Report of Group C, p. 1.

The proposal is that it is desirable to prepare students for an industrial career by the provision of new degree courses in physical sciences with the requirements of industry in mind.

The objects to be achieved are:

1. To train students to become primarily and pre-eminently good physicists, but
2. To train them in the branches of physics most used in industry. (This would ultimately require several courses each biased towards an important branch of physics, e.g. electricity, mechanics, acoustics, cybernetics, of which only the last is now in existence.)
3. To encourage them to appreciate that the problems of industrial physics can demand the full powers of an able scientist and can stimulate many fields of original activity.
4. To accustom them to the use of the techniques, resources, and working methods available in a first-class industrial laboratory, in particular to accustom them to the support of drawing office and workshop staff and of experimental officers. (Acquiring facility in the handling of such resources normally takes the first two years of a man's working life in industry.)[1]

The chief advocate of this plan was Ditchburn. He later recalled that it was difficult to persuade colleagues in the Faculty of Letters of the virtues of the case.[2] Some found it difficult to appreciate why the strictures which had been directed against Agricultural Chemistry should not be equally pertinent to applied Physics. None the less a Department of Applied Physical Sciences was founded in 1965, marking the beginning of a rapid development in Cybernetics, which had hitherto lain within the province of the Physics Department, and in Instrument Physics and Engineering Science.

At the same time one of the main proposals of the working party on Earth Sciences took effect. A Department of Meteorology, approval for which had already been obtained before the publication of the Robbins Report, was established in 1965. All departments in the Faculty shared an interest in computing. A separate Computer Unit was established in 1969 and an independent Department of Computer Science, which had developed first within the Department of Mathematics, was set up, separately from the Unit, in 1971. The working party on the Physical Sciences in particular placed great weight on the development of Mathematics, especially of Applied Mathematics, in combination with other sciences – 'The recommendations concerning Staff for Mathematics are considered to be crucial to the whole development of this side of the Faculty of Science'.[3]

[1] *Ibid.*, Report of Group D, Appendix v.
[2] Conversation with Professor R. W. Ditchburn, 11 August 1975.
[3] Senate Reports, xxii, 20 November 1963, Expansion of the University, Report of Group D, p. 4.

The pattern of development in the Faculty of Science differed from that in the Faculty of Letters in several respects. Much greater emphasis was placed on the establishment of new chairs in existing departments as a means of giving proper weight to the different branches of established subjects. The working party on the Physical Sciences reported that 'there should be many more professorial appointments within this group of subjects' and it went on to argue that immediate steps should be taken to fill a second Chair of Mathematics which had already been approved in principle.[1] This policy soon bore fruit. In 1963 Guggenheim was the only professor of Chemistry. On his retirement in 1966 there were three.[2] In 1963 there were two chairs in the Department of Physics. In 1974 there were five.[3] In 1963 there was one Chair of Mathematics. In 1974 there were four.[4] The new department of Applied Physical Sciences was established in 1965 with two chairs. Ten years later there were three.[5] Such proliferation was scarcely equalled in any other sector of the University.[6]

The degree structure of the Faculty was recast in 1962–3. The old Intermediate Examination was abandoned in favour of a system similar to that in the Faculty of Letters, and the subsequent course was remodelled on an annual teaching and examining cycle. Initially, combined subjects were provided in a three-subject General Degree course and in the provision of a subsidiary subject within the Special courses. Between 1966 and 1968 this was revised in stages in order to allow students to read either one or two subjects in various combinations within the final course. Here the parallel with the Faculty of Letters ended. In Letters subjects were thrown together in order to broaden the student's experience. In Science the combination of subjects hitherto established in separate departments became an academic necessity affecting both teaching and research.

This was particularly true in the area where Biology mingled with Physics, Chemistry and Applied Mathematics. In 1963 the working party on Biological Sciences reported as follows:

> The Group recommends the creation of a 'Department' of Genetics
> for the study of Genetics, breeding (i.e. applied Genetics) and
> Cytology. Genetics would and should not be a degree subject in
> its own right: the proposed 'Department' would be largely concerned

---

[1] Senate Reports, xxii, 20 November 1963, Expansion of the University, Report of Group D, p. 4.

[2] Organic, Inorganic and Physical Chemistry.

[3] The two chairs at the earlier date were in Physics and the Physical Properties of Materials. The additional chairs were in Physics, Solid State Electronics and Applied Optics.

[4] Two chairs in Applied Mathematics and two in Pure Mathematics.

[5] The original chairs were in Engineering Science and Cybernetics. The additional chair was in Materials Technology.

[6] New chairs were established in Physiology & Biochemistry and in Zoology in the Faculty of Science and in several departments in the Faculty of Letters and the Faculty of Agriculture. It was only in the Department of Economics, which had three chairs by 1974, that the expansion in the Physical Sciences was matched.

with research, but would provide 'service courses' for other departments in the Faculties of Science and of Agriculture. It could be partially staffed at the outset by members of other departments.

The establishment of this 'Department', which could be accomplished rapidly, would lead to only a modest increase in numbers, but to a considerable and very desirable rationalization of teaching and research in this field. . . .

The Group is also aware that there seems to be general agreement that there should be large developments in a spectrum of subjects which are not easily separable into departments. This ranges from Physiology (mainly vertebrate, dealing with whole animals, organs) to Physiological Chemistry and Physiological Physics (the study of the Chemistry and Physics of Physiology, Biochemistry in the wide sense), to 'Molecular Biology' (form and function up to cellular level; cell Physiology, Chemistry and Physics; Chemical anatomy of the cell).[1]

This was not the only group with an iron in the fire. The Report on the Physical Sciences also included proposals for the development of Molecular Biology and Neurophysiology. Tyler was not formally consulted and submitted a written memorandum.[2] The Group reported:

The Committee puts forward proposals . . . for postgraduate studies in the fields of Molecular Biology and Neurophysiology. The Committee received a communication from Professor Tyler saying that whilst he was in favour of the development of Molecular Biology and non-chemical Physiology, he would not like these subjects to be developed at the expense of Physiological Chemistry which covers the integrated Physiology and Biochemistry of a number of topics, e.g. muscles, bones, growth, reproduction and lactation. The Committee considers that equally the presence of Physiological Chemistry should not inhibit the growth of the other two subjects.[3]

This was simply one of several areas of study where the traditional dividing lines were losing much of their significance. Similar changes were taking place on a narrower front on the borderlines between Physics and Engineering or between Physics and Chemistry. Moreover most departments in the Faculty required service courses in applied Mathematics or Statistics or Computer Science.

The results, in comparison with the Faculty of Letters, were paradoxical. On the one hand, the Faculty of Science could not afford to develop a wide

---

[1] Senate Reports, xxii, 20 November 1963, Expansion of the University, Report of Group C, pp. 1–2.

[2] 'Professor Knight has reported to me about meetings which have been held concerning aspects of the teaching of subjects in which we have some interest. It now seems imperative that I should make known my own ideas in these matters as soon as possible . . .' (*Ibid.*, Report of Group D, Appendix iii).

[3] *Ibid.*, Report of Group D, p. 5.

range of combined subject courses. Quite apart from time-tabling difficulties in practical subjects, combining subjects was too important a matter simply to be taken lightly. By 1974–5 there were only sixteen such courses. These were less important in the development of the Faculty than new single subject courses organized in, or in conjunction with, the new departments, especially with the Department of Applied Physical Sciences. There was a notable tendency to develop applied courses in all sections of the Faculty. Botany had already entered upon a closer association with Agricultural Botany. The Mathematics Department took part in founding joint courses in Mathematics and Computer Science and Mathematics and Statistics. The Department of Zoology started a course in Applied Zoology which developed the study of pest and parasite control, the harvesting of economically important species, and conservation. On the other hand, the Faculty was much readier to question the accepted academic and administrative structure. In 1973 there was a prolonged discussion of the possibility of introducing a modular syllabus based on unit courses. The scheme had been applied elsewhere, not least at London, and it attracted considerable support, but in the end it was felt that such a change might make the syllabus less flexible. The main result was to encourage departmental co-operation in shared but integrated courses. This was possible because the Faculty had already gone a long way towards resolving the problem administratively. In 1963 the working party on Biological Sciences reported:

> The Group suggests most strongly that there should be a general
> discussion involving the Faculties of Science and of Agriculture,
> if not all three faculties, on the rationalization of teaching and
> research in subjects which overlap and the possible reorganization of
> the present faculty/department arrangement and degree structure.[1]

The working party on Physical Sciences was of the same mind:

> The Committee believes that there should be a complete review of
> organization within the University so as to consider alternatives to
> the present structure of faculties, courses, teaching arrangements,
> laboratory usage and financial arrangements.[2]

In 1968, after much travail, Schools of Biological, Earth and Physical Sciences were established, and in 1971–2 a School of Mathematical Sciences was added. These Schools came to exercise real and immediate responsibility for their subject groups. In this lay yet another contrast with the Faculty of Letters.

One other difference between the two faculties was more a matter of emphasis. In the Faculty of Science graduate students came to constitute a much greater proportion of the total. Their number rose from 160 in 1964–5 to 520 in 1974–5; they accounted for roughly 24 per cent of the students in the Faculty in 1964–5, and 37 per cent in 1974–5. In the same

[1] *Ibid.*, Report of Group C, p. 3.
[2] *Ibid.*, Report of Group D, p. 7.

period the number of graduate students in the Faculty of Letters and Social Sciences increased by roughly the same factor from 104 to 316, but they constituted a smaller proportion of the total number in the Faculty: roughly 12 per cent in 1964-5 and 14 per cent in 1974-5. These changes in the Faculty of Science were not simply numerical. Up to 1963 it provided no graduate courses at all for the degree of M.Sc. Indeed there was some feeling that such courses diminished the standard of the M.Sc. and hence those which had been introduced in the Faculty of Agriculture were not allowed the accolade; they had to do with the title of Master of Agricultural Science.[1] The working parties on expansion now took a different line. There were suggestions that there might be a Master's Degree by examination in Technical Physics and Chemical Technology and a long list of similar possibilities was advanced in Earth Sciences.[2] The first four courses were introduced in 1965. Ten years later there were twelve. In 1974-5 88 of the Faculty's 250 graduate students were following such courses.

In considering expansion, the Faculty of Science divided into subject groups. The Faculty of Agriculture, in contrast, reported as a whole. Its report was comparatively brief. Although it proposed that numbers should be increased from roughly 370 to 600 in four years and subsequently to 1,000, the Faculty nevertheless shared some of the misgivings to which the working party on Biological Sciences had alluded. It noted that it was engaged on a complete revision of the structure of its courses 'which should make them more attractive and offer a wider range of choices within a general pattern' and it emphasized that expansion would necessitate 'an extensive publicity effort south of Birmingham'.[3] In fact it achieved its targets, but in directions which were not indicated in the Report. It said nothing of graduate courses. These were to become an increasingly important feature of the Faculty's work in the next decade.

In some respects the development of the Faculty was determined by the change in the position of the old Department of Agricultural Chemistry. As it developed into a more specialized department of Physiology & Biochemistry, so it shed some of its earlier responsibilities along the way. In 1964 Soil Chemistry became the responsibility of a new Department of Soil Science. In 1965-6 Food Chemistry and Dairying were brought together, and in 1968 the old Department of Dairying became the Department of Food Science. The Chair of Dairying was likewise renamed and the old Honours Degree in Dairying, for so long a feature of Reading's courses, was finally removed from the syllabus. In other respects the Faculty was breaking new ground important both to itself and to the departments of biological sciences in the Faculty of Science. The Biometry Unit, estab-

---

[1] Conversation with Professor C. Tyler, 8 August 1975.
[2] Senate Reports, xxii, 20 November, 1963, Expansion of the University, Report of Group D, p. 4, Appendix vi; Report of Group E, p. 2.
[3] *Ibid.*, Report of the Faculty of Agriculture, p. 1.

lished first in 1961 under the wing of the Department of Agricultural Botany, emerged as a Department of Applied Statistics in 1966. Just as the Department of Zoology was occupying some of the middle ground between the two faculties by its proposals for Agricultural Zoology and the ultimate establishment of the course in Applied Zoology, so on the side of the Faculty of Agriculture, those leading the way in the study of animal production and crop production were establishing an interest in Genetics. But more than any other faculty, the Faculty of Agriculture stuck together. True, the Department of Agricultural Chemistry developed into something much more specialized, and abandoned some of its earlier wider interests. But all the departments in the Faculty retained an interest in the degree in Agriculture, each contributing essential or optional components. On the side of Plant Sciences the instinct towards co-operation was particularly strong. A joint committee in 1969–70 brought together the Crop Production side of the Department of Agriculture and the Departments of Agricultural Botany, Horticulture, Soil Science and Botany in discussions of developments in this field. In 1971–2 the Departments of Botany and Agricultural Botany came together in a new building which from the beginning they ran very much as a joint enterprise. In 1973 the Departments of Agriculture and Horticulture amalgamated. Such steps would not have been taken at all easily in other Faculties.[1]

To a great extent this was rooted in the academic structure of the Faculty. There was no department which did not rely on the services of some other department in the Faculty or in the Faculty of Science for some contribution to its courses.[2] These courses were still based on the old principle, on which the Faculty's work had always rested, of embodying in a small number of applied courses all the basic scientific training essential to their study. This had been strengthened by the abandonment in 1947–8 of the Diplomas in Agriculture, Horticulture and Dairying. Thereafter, the Pass courses were the Faculty's basic diet. The adherence to this structure also helps to explain the Faculty's increasing interest in graduate courses. Faced with the increasing intensity and diversity of university disciplines, other faculties could afford the luxury of new first-degree courses. The Faculty of Agriculture coped by developing graduate studies. It already provided six courses for the M. Agr. Sc. in 1964–5. Ten years later there were three two-year courses with the title of M. Agr. Sc. or M. Agr. Eng., and no less than fifteen one-year M.Sc. courses.[3] Together these involved every department in the Faculty and covered every major aspect of its work. In 1964–5 the graduate courses attracted only 15 students. In 1974–5 the

[1] The nearest approach, by no means so complete, was made in the association of the Departments of Physiology & Biochemistry and of Zoology in the new building for Animal Sciences.
[2] This remark is not intended to apply to the courses provided by the National College of Food Technology at Weybridge.
[3] Several of these included options which were almost separate courses in themselves. With these options the bill of fare ran to thirty items.

number had risen to 178. By then the Faculty had introduced a preliminary course in which students spent a qualifying year preparing for the M.Sc. work. In 1974–5 39 students followed this course; the total involved in graduate work was 217. In the same year the number working for research degrees in the Faculty was 132. Graduate courses now constituted one of the most important of the Faculty's activities. In some departments graduates outnumbered undergraduates.[1]

There was yet another point in this development. The graduate courses attracted a high proportion of students from overseas, especially from the developing countries. Some, such as the M. Agr. Sc. in Tropical Agricultural Development and the M.Sc. in Agricultural Economic Development, were specifically designed to this end and to prepare British students for work abroad. And this was but one of the many overseas links which the Faculty forged. It provided vacation courses for Voluntary Service Overseas; it assisted in the establishment of faculties and courses in universities in developing countries; professors of the Faculty paid extended visits to universities in Africa, Asia, the West Indies and elsewhere. So widespread became this activity that it is difficult to single out any one achievement. Official recognition of the part which Reading had come to play came with the establishment in 1971 by the Overseas Development Administration of a Chair of Agricultural Development Overseas, which was taken up by A. H. Bunting, hitherto Professor of Agricultural Botany, whose drive and enthusiasm lay behind many of the connections which Reading had built up abroad. But the overseas links were not confined to this one Faculty. In 1961 the University reached an agreement with the University of Khartoum for the joint recruitment of academic staff. The intention was to appoint staff for immediate secondment to Khartoum, but with the guarantee that they might return to Reading for the last year of their appointment and hence be better placed for finding a permanent post at home. A similar arrangement was made with the University of the West Indies in 1964. The agreements also covered the secondment of existing staff at Reading. The resulting intellectual traffic was far from one-way. A member of the Department of Agricultural Economics commented:

> ... the most direct impetus to Development Economics occurred
> when, in 1966, D. S. Thornton (returning from a secondment in
> Khartoum) was appointed to a readership in Comparative
> Agricultural Economics with special reference to developing countries
> and when, a year later, Ronald Tuck undertook a six country tour
> of Africa. Thornton's contribution has subsequently been reflected
> in teaching courses, post-graduate and staff research and in *ad hoc*

[1] In October 1975 there were 44 undergraduates and 55 graduates in the Department of Food Science, and 37 undergraduates and 38 graduates in Soil Science. The figures for graduates include research students. The figures of annual intake present a sharper contrast: in October 1975, 23 undergraduates against 47 graduates in Food Science; 8 undergraduates against 21 graduates in Soil Science.

consultancy work. Much of this work has been concentrated in Botswana, Sudan and Ghana – but a complete alphabetical list of the countries in which substantial contacts of one kind or another have been made is given below.* In 1969, twenty-two different countries were in fact represented at a course held in the Department on behalf of the Ministry of Overseas Development on 'Credit and Marketing for developing countries'.[1]

In the Faculty of Agriculture, indeed in all faculties, development was very much a natural growth. Initially some possible projects were carefully examined and then shelved, some like Architecture, permanently, others like Law, for the time-being. The University could easily develop as fast as was required by extending its existing range of subjects in a logical manner and by taking up schemes which had long been advocated. There was no need to strive for originality and thereby run the risk of artificiality, and there was little readiness to risk scarce resources. In reviewing the possible establishment of Architecture, Lehmann commented as Dean of Letters:

> (a) . . . the money and effort required to create an entirely new department might well produce quicker results if applied to an existing field.
> (b) Architecture involves higher costs (for a given number of students) than many developments in Letters, but probably lower costs than many developments in Science or Agriculture.
> (c) As a contribution to emergency expansion, its effect is likely to be slower than say expansion in certain existing fields (though the evidence of national demand is such as to reassure one that the initial investment could over a ten-year period be justified).[2]

In commenting on the possible introduction of Law, Professor P. W. Campbell was likewise cautious:

> Law is a particularly expensive subject for a university's library. English Law is so very much case law that it is necessary to have long runs of reports as well as statutes, commentaries, and journals. It seems that £6,000 would be necessary as the initial investment and that at least £400 p.a. would be necessary to keep the library up-to-date.[3]

Similar reservations ensured that some proposals were advanced as distant dreams rather than immediate objectives. Medicine, Dentistry and Veterinary Studies, for example, never played a part in the practical planning for the emergency period immediately following the Robbins Report.

---

* Afghanistan, Botswana, Barbados, Ethiopia, Ghana, India, Kenya, Libya, Malawi, Malaya, Mauritius, Montserrat, Nigeria, Sudan, Swaziland, Tanzania, Thailand, Uganda and Pakistan.
[1] A. K. Giles, *Agricultural Economics, 1923–1973* (University of Reading, 1973), pp. 28–9.
[2] Senate Reports, xxii, 20 January 1964.
[3] *Ibid.*

Development was subject to two important conditions. First, as was emphasized repeatedly both within the University and in communications to the University Grants Committee, it was dependent on the provision of the necessary resources, especially accommodation. In the event the University was able to advance as far as it did only through the use of the temporary buildings erected by the Ministry of Works in the south-eastern quarter of the Park. In 1965 the planning authority consented to the use of these buildings by the University for twenty years, and they came into the University's hands between March 1966 and the summer of 1969. They were used to house the Departments of Agriculture, Agricultural Economics, Geophysics, Psychology and Typography & Graphic Communication and part of the Departments of Engineering and Cybernetics, Geography, Physics and Chemistry. Without this additional space the expansion would necessarily have been more expensive or more limited. The buildings were of a type which, in the early days following the purchase of White-knights, had been deprecated by both the University and the planning authorities.[1] Suddenly, in circumstances of rapid expansion in which the specification of new buildings was repeatedly reduced, they seemed more attractive, even relatively spacious. In any case a university which still used temporary huts erected during the First World War could scarcely jib at using temporary buildings erected during and after the Second World War. However, as that precedent suggested, the use of temporary buildings might become a drug-like expedient. Some became overcrowded. Some had to be altered or extended. The habit developed as the University, un-willingly and as a temporary measure while it awaited new buildings, was forced to accept prefabricated huts for the overflow of academic and administrative staff. There, in the centre of Whiteknights, they remain as a memorial to cancelled or suspended building projects, impregnable alike to the attentions of planning authorities and the imprecations of staff and students, the most excrescent of them occupied by none other than the University Accommodation Officer.

The second condition was even more critical. In the discussion of expansion in 1963 and indeed even earlier some doubt was always ex-pressed whether the demand for undergraduate places would in fact keep pace with the planned expansion.[2] Such doubts, born of the instinct and hard-won experience of those who year by year admitted and taught each new generation of students, had to give way to the various national pre-dictions used to bolster and justify the plans for expansion.[3] But the doubters were largely right, and some of the predictions were proved wrong. At all events from 1969 the total number of applications to the University began to fall. In 1968 it amounted to over 16,500. By 1974, in the same Faculties

---

[1] See above, pp. 150–1.
[2] See above, pp. 221–2.
[3] See the revealing remarks of the 1963 working party on biological sciences, above, pp. 227–8.

and Departments, it had dropped to roughly 11,800.[1] This was only partially offset by the addition of a new Faculty of Urban and Regional Studies in 1969 and the establishment of a Department of Law, with its high demand for places, in 1974.[2] In broad terms the causes of the decline were obvious enough. From 1968 to 1974 the numbers taking the Advanced level examinations of the Joint Matriculation Board, for example, never rose by more than 2,000 a year; in 1973 there was a slight fall in total numbers.[3] At the same time the rate of increase of the number of applications through the Universities' Central Council for Admissions also declined; in 1973 there were only 275 more than in the previous year.[4] This occurred at a time when the new universities founded in the 1960s were offering more and more places, especially in the arts and social sciences. Hence a decline in applications to Reading, and indeed to any other similar university, was inevitable. These general conditions were complicated in several ways. First, there was an absolute decline in certain subjects in the numbers entering the Advanced level examination. Latin fell away, understandably, but so also did Mathematics and French. Secondly, the wider choice of university available to applicants and the greatly increased variety in the subjects and courses which the universities now offered meant that the entry into any one course in any one university became much less predictable. As a result expansion became more difficult to control. The actual and the planned profile matched less and less. They never had matched exactly, but that had been hidden by continued rapid expansion; an absolute deficit in numbers in any particular subject or group of subjects could be regarded simply as a lag which could be taken up in future years. Once the demand for places levelled off the mismatch was revealed.

The Faculty of Letters and Social Sciences was the first to be affected, probably because it was in these fields that the new universities expanded most rapidly. The number of applications fell from 11,578 in 1967 to 7,731 in 1974.[5] In the Faculty of Science the decline came later. It remained unaffected up to and including 1971; thereafter the applications declined from 4,896 to 3,148 in 1974. In the Faculty of Agriculture and Food the change was less dramatic, from a peak of 1,332 applications in 1969 to 1,165 in 1974. The reaction to these changes could not be other than

---

[1] The figures are complicated by the reduction, in 1971, of the number of applications allowed on each individual form from six to five. This undoubtedly exaggerates the decline but it does not follow that a simple arithmetical correction should be applied. Even if it were the notional applications which such a correction would provide for 1971 would still fall considerably below the number for 1968.
[2] These raised the total of applications in 1974 to 14,100.
[3] 48,444 against 48,565 in 1972.
[4] 124,634 as against 124,359 in 1972.
[5] The later figure excludes Law, which would raise the total to 8,361. Again, as in the general totals given above and in the figures for other faculties which follow, I have made no correction for the reduction of individual applications from six to five in 1971.

slow. At first it was far from easy to distinguish between a new trend and an intermission. Once the downward trend was seen for what it was, policy could not always be changed immediately, and, once changed, it could rarely take effect other than gradually, from year to year, as the intake was corrected; in some subjects the decline went far beyond anything which the University had power to correct. In the Faculty of Letters and Social Sciences no serious action was taken until 1970–1. Thereafter the proportion of offers made to applicants was increased sharply,[1] and departments with potentially large intakes, such as English and History, were expanded rapidly to the maximum numbers planned for them by the end of the Quinquennium of 1972–7. After fluctuating between 1969 and 1971 the admissions into the Faculty rose steadily from 1972 and by 1973 the recovery was reflected in the overall numbers of undergraduates.[2] In the Faculty of Science there was far less room for manoeuvre. The proportion of offers to applications was already high and further increase probably had a diminishing effect.[3] The decline in applications which began in 1972 was accompanied by a fall in intake from 446 in 1971 to 315 in 1974. From 1971–2 the total number of undergraduates began to fall. In the Faculty of Agriculture and Food there was less of a problem. The number of applicants declined only slightly, and, as it did, the proportion of offers to applications was steadily increased.[4] The intake into the Faculty fluctuated but showed no serious decline until 1974.[5] Except in that year the total of undergraduates was maintained. In both Faculties, as undergraduate numbers wavered or fell, graduate numbers increased.[6]

It was as if the University had been forced on to a treadmill. It had to work harder to stay where it was. In 1967 the three Faculties admitted 1,138 undergraduates. That figure was exceeded by a mere 15 additional students in 1974; in the intervening years it fluctuated between 1,211 in 1971 and 1,049 in 1972. In the same period the percentage of offers of

[1] The percentage of offers to applications rose from 19 per cent in 1970 to 42 per cent in 1974.

[2] The figures for intake into the Faculty rose from 514 in 1972 to 618 (excluding Law) in 1974. In the same period the total undergraduates increased from 2,029 in 1972–3 to 2,204 in 1974–5.

[3] The relationship of offers to applications was 61.6 per cent in 1969 and 73.7 per cent in 1974. However it showed a less consistent trend than in the Faculty of Letters and Social Sciences. It had stood at 70.4 per cent in 1968.

[4] 47.1 per cent in 1967; 63.4 per cent in 1974.

[5] From 1968 to 1973 the intake fluctuated between 185 and 220. In 1974 it dropped to 164.

[6] The figures for the two Faculties are as follows:

	Science		Agriculture & Food	
	u/g	p/g	u/g	p/g
1970–1	1,057	412	614	362
1971–2	1,094	457	601	425
1972–3	1,059	491	608	441
1973–4	948	498	624	481
1974–5	865	520	562	498

These figures include all registered graduate students.

places to applications nearly doubled, from 27 to 52 per cent. Each offer
was less likely to lead to a place filled, either because the applicant failed
to achieve the requirements for the course or because he chose to go elsewhere.[1] Overall however, the proportion of admissions to applications rose
slowly and continuously.[2] This was broadly in conformity with the objectives of the Robbins Committee. More applicants were receiving offers
of places; more of them were being admitted; Reading was keeping pace
with the general increase in the national total of students.[3] But it was
achieved only through great effort. Admissions became a major industry in
the Registrar's Office, the Faculty offices and in each department. And it
was achieved at the cost of accepting students in the subjects which they
wished to read. The University naturally tried to plan the intake; each year
it set targets for entry into each subject, course or groups of courses; but it
was the applicants who finally determined how far those targets were met;
in any one subject the University could prevent an excessive intake, but it
could not make up a deficit. Hence the maintenance overall of the level of
undergraduate admissions was accompanied by increasing disparity
between Faculties and, within Faculties, between departments. By 1975
roughly half of all the undergraduates in the University were in the Faculty
of Letters and Social Sciences, and roughly one quarter were contained in
the five departments of Economics, English, Fine Art, Geography and
History.[4] To each member of the academic staff there were, in the Department of English more than eleven undergraduates, in the Departments of
Fine Art, History (including Archaeology), Politics and Typography
rather more than ten, in the Departments of Psychology and Sociology
rather less than ten. In the Department of Physics, in contrast, to every
member of staff there were rather more than two undergraduates, in the
Departments of Microbiology and Geophysics rather less than three, in the
Department of Chemistry slightly less than four. No one had planned this.
No one wanted this. Yet it followed ineluctably once the principles of
the Robbins Report were adopted for the range of applicants which
British schools produced.

This, however, is not the whole story. The disparity might have been very
much greater. The problem was anticipated and the imbalance to some
extent corrected. Within the Faculty of Letters and Social Sciences it was
appreciated that the Faculty ought not to develop simply by making the
large departments larger. In designing its proposal for the Quinquennium

[1] The proportion of admissions to offers fell from 26.4 per cent in 1967 to 17.4 per cent in
1974.
[2] The proportion of admissions to applications rose from 7.1 per cent in 1967 to 9.1
per cent in 1974.
[3] Between 1967 and 1974 the admissions to Reading varied between 1.9 per cent and
2.4 per cent of the national total. The figure was 2.0 per cent in 1967 and 2.1 per cent in
1974.
[4] Part of the total for Economics was derived from students who were studying the subject
as part of the courses in the Faculty of Urban and Regional Studies.

1972–7 it deliberately sought for diversity; hence the readiness to encourage the growth of Archaeology, Language Pathology and Law. And within the University as a whole it was equally appreciated that one effective way to expand and diversify was to incorporate other institutions. Such notions were not new; they had contributed to the earliest development of the University College.[1] Where such institutions were seeking a home within an established university, and where their work fitted what was done **or** might be done at Reading, the policy made good sense.

Two such moves had considerable results. First, in 1965 agreement was reached on a proposal to embody the National College of Food Technology at Weybridge within the University. The agreement took effect on 1 April 1966.[2] The College added over 100 undergraduates to the Faculty of Agriculture; it was the premier centre in the country for the training of food technologists, and it not only provided a welcome and valuable extension of the Faculty's range in food studies but also brought into the University a healthy experience of 'sandwich' courses in the food production industry. Secondly, in the summer of 1964 discussion began of a possible move of the College of Estate Management from Kensington to Reading.[3] Agreement was reached for the incorporation of the College, to the extent of its degree work, in the University as a Faculty of Urban and Regional Studies from October 1967. This added 380 students to the University in that year. It led to the introduction of new departments and new B.Sc. courses in Estate Management and Construction Management.[4] In building studies it strengthened an interest which had long been maintained in the Faculty of Agriculture. In planning studies it complemented the work done in the Department of Geography. It included a department of Law which was established in the University as a Department of Law relating to the Land; from that the new University Department of Law emerged in 1973. It also brought an enormous material resource in the form of a 'dowry' of £1¼ millions. This was derived from the sale of its properties in Kensington, the realization of other assets and a skilfully managed effort to raise money for the move. It enabled the College to provide funds for the erection of a new faculty building in Whiteknights, which it occupied in 1972. It also paid for the construction of a new hall of

[1] See above, pp. 7, 22.
[2] The College was founded in 1951 and moved to Weybridge in 1959.
[3] Senate Minute, 3883, 12 October 1964. The College was founded in 1919 and was incorporated as a public educational institution by royal charter in 1922.
[4] The titles of the departments underwent some change during the first years of the Faculty's history. The departments which the Faculty inherited from the College were four: Civil Engineering, Estate Management, Law relating to the Land, and Building and Quantity Surveying. The Department of Estate Management took the title of Land Management and Development in 1970; in the same year the Department of Building and Quantity Surveying was renamed Construction Management and was amalgamated with Civil Engineering in a Department of Construction Management in 1972. The Department of Law relating to the Land was absorbed by the new Department of Law in 1973.

residence which came into use as Wells Hall in 1973. By 1974–5 the new Faculty comprised 529 undergraduates and 68 postgraduates.

The staff of both these Colleges became part of the University. The Head of the National College of Food Technology was appointed to a personal professorship. The Head of the College of Estate Management became Dean of the new Faculty; along with some of the heads of departments in the College he also was appointed to a professorship. There the similarity between the two institutions ended. The National College of Food Technology became part of the Faculty of Agriculture and its accession contributed to the adoption of the new title – Faculty of Agriculture and Food – from 1970. The intention was that it should move to Reading as soon as funds were available; they could not be found and it had to remain at Weybridge. Its affairs were managed by a separate Delegacy responsible to the University Council. The College of Estate Management, in contrast, was embodied completely within the University for all its first degree and postgraduate work. The original College remained in being as a separate institution solely to manage correspondence and post-experience courses; although it was housed in the new building at Reading, it was not part of the University. In the new Faculty departments derived both from the College and the University worked side by side.[1] The two departments of Economics merged completely. So also did the Department of Law relating to Land when the new Department of Law was established in the Faculty of Letters and Social Sciences. The Libraries merged; so also did the administrative staff. The whole operation was carried through with remarkable ease and little friction. For this both the University and the College owed much to the wisdom and vision of the Principal of the College, Robert Jardine Brown. He steered the College carefully into its new role. He himself, with genial good humour and ready adaptability, submerged his old office as Principal in his new role as Dean.

The University did not enter upon these arrangements lightly. The proposed merger with the College of Estate Management in particular seemed beset with difficulty simply because of the size of the operation. The establishment of a new Faculty was an adventure, and an adventure into applied studies of a kind which was not likely to arouse the enthusiasm of academic diehards. At the end of 1965 both Senate and Council accepted that no commitment could be given for the Quinquennium ending in 1967. They noted:

> It is by no means certain that it would be advantageous to the
> University to put Estate Management at the top of its list of priorities
> in the Quinquennial submission, since it has no reason to suppose
> that the University Grants Committee would feel inclined to

[1] The University departments originally included in the Faculty were Agricultural Economics, Agriculture, Economics, Geography, Politics and Soil Science. The Department of Engineering and Cybernetics joined the Faculty in 1974.

encourage this field of study in preference to others. Even apart from this assessment of the likely University Grants Committee attitude, the proposal could be included in the University's Quinquennial development, without undue curtailment of developments in other fields, only if the rate of expansion for the Quinquennium were very much greater than now seems likely. The conclusion seems inescapable that the College should be told of these facts and encouraged to try to gain public recognition in the shape of recurrent financial support *before* the completion of its association with the University.[1]

When the matter was brought to a head and finally agreed in the summer of 1966 it was because the College itself overcame difficulties and presented the University with an acceptable scheme.[2] One of the main concerns of the University throughout the negotiation was that the College should not be brought into competition for scarce resources within the University. Even after the merger one or two still voiced their doubts about the College's capacity to underwrite the cost of a hall of residence in addition to the Faculty building. Hence, although the advantages of diversification were emphasized by some and appreciated by many, they did not seem to provide an overriding argument for embodying the College, whatever the terms of the merger. In 1965–7 the growing imbalance within the University seemed remediable; the number of applicants had not yet begun to fall. Hence the case for amalgamation depended essentially on the academic advantage which it brought to each party. The College, as a Faculty at Reading, gained greater control over its degree courses than it had hitherto in working for degrees in the University of London. The University gained in that, in one single stride, it placed itself in the forefront of undergraduate studies in a field bordering on some of its existing work. In the College's Department of Law it was provided with a springboard for a major development which had been carefully examined as recently as 1964.[3] In the College's interests in planning it was provided with a base on which a School of Planning Studies, embodying departments from all four faculties, was established in 1971.

As a result of these activities the University began to acquire a certain reputation. At the time take-overs were in fashion. Mild jokes circulated in Common Rooms at Oxford suggesting that that more ancient institution might have to look to its defences. But Reading's readiness to consider such moves was natural enough. The economic geography of south-east England

[1] Report on the College of Estate Management: Proposed Association with the University (Senate Reports, xxvi, 15 November 1965; Council Reports, xxvii, 3 December 1965).
[2] Senate Reports, xxviii, 13 June 1966.
[3] See above, p. 236. The impression at Reading was that the existence of the Department of Law relating to the Land had a considerable effect in leading the University Grants Committee to support the establishment of a Department of Law in the Quinquennium 1972–7.

continued to play its part. Indeed, the construction of the M4 motorway, the pre-eminence of Heathrow as an airport, the establishment of an Air Terminal at Reading General Station, which in turn accentuated its position as a major stop for express trains, all emphasized the advantages which had led in the previous century to the establishment of the University College. But this was not the only influence at work. The Robbins Report signalled a striking advance in both the resources and prestige of universities. Increasingly, research institutions which lay outside or on the fringe of the university system turned to them for co-operation and support. Increasingly universities had the facility to respond to such approaches. In doing so they frequently received official blessing from the University Grants Committee and interested government ministries. It was not simply that in these circumstances a university could act as a kind of academic almshouse, tendering aid to deserving institutions hit by escalating expenditure. Large industrial concerns also became interested in the opportunities which the greatly increased resources of a university might provide for co-operation in research. In all this Reading had more than a simple geographic advantage. As compared with its more important neighbours, London and Oxford, it was still relatively compact. It could provide a home in which newcomers would be more than small fry in an immense and complicated organization; they would carry weight. Above all in Whiteknights it had a resource which was becoming increasingly scarce and valuable, especially in south-east England: land. In any negotiation Reading could always provide a good site if the other party could find the resources for building. That was a tremendous advantage.

The National Institute of Research in Dairying provided a long standing example of such a relationship. Legally it had always been a part of the University. Yet it preserved its direct responsibilities to the Ministry of Agriculture, latterly through the Agricultural Research Council. It lay within the University, yet was not fully of it, and this dual status was confirmed and given greater precision in 1963 when the terms of a new Trust Deed were agreed and the government of the Institute placed in the hand of a Delegacy which was appointed part by the University and part by the Agricultural Research Council.[1] With this experience behind it, the University could take in its stride all the complex problems which such associations were likely to involve: the allocation of titles and academic staff status, dual interests in the control of research funds and the appointment of staff, co-operation, both formal and informal, in programmes of research. In 1966 the Council and Senate approved general ground rules

---

[1] Council Reports, xxii, 15 March 1963. This was the culmination of lengthy negotiations which extended from 1955 to 1960 when a Joint Committee of the University and the Institute was ready to submit the new scheme of government to the Agricultural Research Council. The final draft scheme was submitted to the University Court on 10 November 1961 (Council Reports, xxi).

for the establishment of a general category of Associated Institutions.[1] The Royal Aircraft Establishment, Farnborough, and the Grassland Research Institute, Hurley, were included at once. They were followed in 1967–8 by the National College of Agricultural Engineering, Silsoe,[2] in 1968–9 by the Agricultural Research Council's Radio-biological Laboratory at Letcombe Regis and the Imperial Chemical Industries' Research Station at Jealott's Hill, Bracknell, in 1969–70 by the Royal Botanic Gardens, Kew, the Agricultural Research Council's Institute for Research on Animal Diseases, Compton, the Tate and Lyle Research Laboratory, Keston, and the River Laboratory of the Freshwater Biological Association, East Stoke, near Wareham, in 1971 by the Summer Institute of Linguistics, in 1973–4 by the Agricultural Research Council's Weed Research Organisation, and in 1976 by the International Seismological Centre. These associations normally involved straightforward arrangements for the interchange of facilities; the Head of the Institution was usually given the title of Visiting Professor in the University. The formalities often did little more than set a seal on practical co-operation which had grown up naturally in the preceding years, especially in research work; in some cases provision was made for running joint courses. One institution expressed its co-operation more permanently: the research and development department of Tate and Lyle Ltd moved to Whiteknights in 1972 and occupied the Philip Lyle Memorial Research Laboratory which the Company built as part of the new Plant Sciences Building.

The main successes came in the Faculties of Science and of Agriculture and Food, where they were a result of natural growth. In other faculties, such arrangements were less securely founded. In 1967, for example, the Institute of Contemporary History which was based on the Wiener Library, London, became an affiliated institution. The University made a financial provision to assist the Institute, and the Director was made a Visiting Professor. In the next few years attempts were made to forge stronger links, especially with the Graduate School of Contemporary European Studies. At one point the University came within a whisker of making a permanent appointment to an established Chair of Contemporary History, to which the Directorship of the Institute would have been attached. But there was little genuine growth. The University was not ready or able to provide funds indefinitely for an out-station in London. It had land available in Reading, but it had no money to provide special accommodation for the Institute's considerable staff or to house its Library's 60,000 volumes. In any case opinion in the Institute was against moving to Reading. In 1972 the arrangement came to an end by the agreement of

[1] These provided for a review of specific arrangements at five-year intervals.
[2] This association lasted until 1975 when the College became a School of the Cranfield Institute of Technology.

both parties.[1] It proved an expensive but salutary lesson.[2] Subsequent proposals coming within the view of the Faculty of Letters and Social Sciences were examined with a more experienced eye.

All these arrangements reflected and advanced the growing influence and reputation of the University. They were particularly important for the Faculty of Agriculture and Food, for in agricultural and related studies the University was building up a unique involvement with the Ministry of Agriculture, the Agricultural Research Council and the Ministry of Overseas Development, on the one hand, and with research and teaching institutes, established with government support, or with research laboratories of great industrial companies, on the other. By the mid 1970s the Faculty no longer threatened to dominate the University numerically as it had in the 1940s, but it still retained, and had indeed augmented, its national reputation. In 1974 the Wolfson Foundation agreed to provide nearly £250,000 over a period of four to five years for research in the Departments of Agriculture and Horticulture, Agricultural Botany and Food Science on leaf protein and oilseeds as protein and edible oil sources. In 1975 the Nuffield Foundation made a grant of £250,000 to meet the costs in the early years of a new Centre for Agricultural Strategy. This established in Reading an independent body which was to analyse and criticize the country's agricultural policies. Professor J. C. Bowman was appointed the first Director.

However, it was not simply a matter of one Faculty of the University benefiting from the principle, as valid in academic as in other walks of life, that to them that hath shall be given. Across the complete range of the University's work men were looking for fresh opportunities, turning outwards to industry, to the great trusts and foundations, to the research councils, to government departments, above all perhaps to the increasing public interest in university education. A whole generation of teachers, scholars and administrators was bred in circumstances of expansion, in which new initiatives, new courses, new departments became commonplace, all the more welcome if the proposals carried with them financial support from external sources. Successful initiative was not confined to the Faculty of Agriculture and Food. The Department of Geology continued to maintain close relations with and receive considerable help from the great oil and petroleum companies. The Imperial Chemical Industries maintained Research Fellowships. The Taylor Hobson division of the Rank Organization made possible the establishment of a Chair of Applied Optics

[1] The sad end to this story in 1976 seems to be that the Institute, for lack of financial support in the United Kingdom, is likely to be moved to Tel Aviv.
[2] The agreement with the Institute involved an annual subvention from the University of £5,000 (Council Reports, xxx, 2 June 1967). The report to Council stated that 'the University would very much hope that the scheme now propounded would be only the first step towards the Institute's becoming a constituent part of the University'. It is fair to say that the affair could well have developed differently if the chief protagonist of the scheme, Professor A. G. Lehmann, had not left the University in 1968.

by the grant of £105,000 in 1966. The Esmée Fairbairn Charitable Trust provided for the establishment of a Chair of International Investment and Business Studies in 1971. The Volkswagen Foundation made grants towards the establishment of posts in the Social Sciences and supported the work of the Graduate School of Contemporary European Studies. The Schools Council made a grant of £75,000 in 1971 for a study of Sixth Form Mathematics in the School of Education. This is to name but a few of the major grants of the period. They manifested a new world which would have astonished Stenton, de Burgh or Cole.

Yet within it there still remained that personal initiative, to which Stenton pointed in his final speech as Vice-Chancellor to the University Court;[1] and such initiative, in which devotion and inspiration mingled, might lead not to some great coup in which an industry, trust or government department agreed to underwrite a project, but to a prolonged hard slog in which resources were pieced together only slowly and with difficulty. The Museum of English Rural Life is a memorial to such an effort. The establishment of a museum of agricultural history was first proposed by Edgar Thomas in 1947. It was brought into being by J. W. Y. Higgs, Lecturer in Farm Mechanization in the Department of Agriculture, who in October 1950 submitted a proposal for the inclusion of such a museum among the new buildings in Whiteknights. At that stage he suggested that the Museum might include a collection of reassembled cottages. That notion was rejected, but the broad principle of the scheme was accepted and the University was duly launched into establishing a museum 'which would serve as a workshop for scholars and historians'. For that ambitious plan it allocated a grant 'not exceeding £200' to enable Higgs to begin a collection. Lady Stenton offered to provide temporary storage in the barn at Whitley Park Farm and that became the Museum's first repository.[2] From that small beginning the Museum advanced rapidly. In 1952 Wolfenden reported that:

> The Museum of English Rural Life had been growing with great rapidity and was already becoming nationally recognized. The development of the Museum had been accomplished under great difficulties. It was hoped that it would become a national institution, but the Curators were of the opinion that if it were to be established on the scale they would like, the University would not be able to meet the expenses that would be involved. The Curators were, nevertheless, firmly convinced that the Museum should remain a part of the University.[3]

The upshot was that the appeal for funds which the University Grants Committee had advocated on its visitation of November 1950 was finally

[1] See above, p. 206, n. 3.
[2] Council Reports, xii, 8 December 1950: Council Minute, 1434, 8 December 1950.
[3] Council Minute, 1511, 23 May 1952.

launched on behalf of the Museum.[1] The moment was well judged. Some-how the project caught the public imagination. Funds came only slowly and were never adequate, but items for exhibition poured in: a gipsy caravan, wooden ploughs, wheelwrights' and blacksmiths' tools, a hand-propelled hearse, cheese-making equipment from Somerset, the contents of a farm brewhouse from Suffolk. Few such extensive museum collections have been built up so quickly. In 1952 the Museum moved into White-knights House. It began to gain official recognition. In 1955 it was opened formally by the chairman of the University Grants Committee,[2] and both the Victoria and Albert and the Science Museums figured among the donors of material for exhibition. By that time it was already receiving nearly 5,000 visitors a year. The public was taking notice. In 1964 it was able to move its collections from various scattered repositories in Whiteknights into a newly constructed but temporary building at the south-west entrance to the park. From this new base it began a fresh venture: the recording and collection of farm records. By 1968 it had surveyed 600 collections. This work was backed by the University Library which stored much of the material. Some county archivists complained that the Museum was making piratical intrusions into their own spheres of interest. But farm accounts had been neglected and the Museum's intervention did much to prevent further loss and destruction. Reading was recognized as an official repository for this class of record. The Museum now had its own specialist library; it had accumulated a vast collection of photographs; with financial support from the Social Science Research Council it had built up an extensive bibliography of works on agricultural history; and it had become the main centre for research in agricultural history in the University. It had in fact become more than a Museum. In 1968 it was re-established as the Institute of Agricultural History and as such it went from strength to strength; in 1975 further accommodation was provided for the display of the large exhibits. In that year the Museum received 9,000 visitors.

This was almost a conjuring act. From nothing the University created an institution which provided a major resource for scholars; an information centre, reference library and repository for farmers, landowners and the agricultural industries; and an absorbing collection for the inspection of the interested public. In 1950 there was enthusiasm, a readiness to get down to work, a grant from the Council of up to £200, and Lady Stenton's barn. In 1975 there was an Institute with a staff of sixteen and a budget of £34,000.[3] It is a fine example of what a University, when left to itself, can do.

However, the University was not left to itself. This achievement represents one extreme of its development, where initiative ran ahead on a loose rein. At the other extreme there were developments in which it simply had to

---

[1] *Ibid.*, and see above, p. 165.
[2] Dr Keith Murray.
[3] This includes clerical and technical staff. Of the five academic staff the two Associate Directors are members of the Department of Agricultural Economics and Management.

conform to a national pattern. In particular it had to toe the line drawn between the universities and other sectors of higher or further education. It also had to accept changes, required by government policy, in its relationships with the local colleges of education. It differed from many other universities in that it was affected by the decisions not only of the Ministry of Education but also of the Ministry of Agriculture, Fisheries and Food. And government policy was not the only determinant: economic change occasionally imposed its own equally categorical requirements.

During its first twenty years the University played a many sided educational role.[1] At the end of the war it was still the local centre for technical and further education. In the British Dairy Institute it still housed a body which was concerned with teaching at less than the standard and depth required for a first degree. In the Agricultural Advisory Service it still had an important administrative, technical and advisory function in which it was responsible to the Ministry of Agriculture. In the Schools of Art and Music it still retained more general commitments alongside its teaching for degrees. Within five years much of this was swept away. The British Dairy Institute was the first to go. As an exercise in private enterprise it was increasingly out of place in a state-run system of education. Dairying had changed from a domestic to a highly capitalized industry. The Institute had to contend with increasing financial difficulties; it could maintain itself only through trading activities which hampered, and were hampered by, its educational function. The new distributing and manufacturing companies would not provide the private support which the farmers had given. Hence the University's agreement with the British Dairy Farmers' Association was terminated in 1944 and the Institute was closed in July 1945; the building and equipment were transferred to the University: the Diploma in Dairying became the responsibility of the Department of Dairying in the Faculty of Agriculture.[2] Other closures followed hard on the Institute: the Department of Domestic Subjects in September 1945, the Department of Commerce in September 1946. By that date all evening classes except for those in Art had been transferred to the Local Education Authority.[3] This marked the foundation of the Reading College of Technology, but for a further decade the classes were still held in the 'Tech. Block' at London Road, which was rented by the Borough Council, until the College had its own new buildings in King's Road.[4] The use of the University as the centre for the Agricultural Advisory Service for the southern provinces also came to an end. From 1 October 1946 the local service was replaced by the

[1] See above, pp. 23–6.
[2] E. L. Crossley, 'The British Dairy Institute and the University of Reading', rept. from *Journal of the British Dairy Farmers' Association*, lxii (1958), pp. 11–13.
[3] These included all classes in foreign languages, commercial subjects, geography and English; in Science, all classes in mathematics, physics, engineering and building; and in Building, all classes in construction, quantities, surveying and geometry (Senate Reports, x, 7 December 1945).
[4] Finance Committee Minutes, 2946, 21 June 1946.

National Agricultural Advisory Service. A formal link with the University was maintained only in the Provincial Agricultural Economic Service which continued in the Department of Agricultural Economics.[1] The School of Art and the three-year Diploma in Fine Art survived until 1965 when they, too, were abolished. By then only the School of Music preserved the old general educational service for the locality. In this case the Department of Music benefited from the broader School, for it enabled it to provide a wider range of instrumental tuition for its students than would otherwise have been possible; it also reinforced the University choirs and orchestra.

In its relationship with the local colleges of education the University again had to conform to national requirements and policies. However, it was left with more and more room for manoeuvre as time passed. Initially the relationship was very close; fifty years later, in formal terms, it had almost come to an end. This was not inevitable, but equally it was not entirely of the University's free choosing. The founding of the University in 1926 coincided with a new policy in the Board of Education which required that training colleges for teachers should be associated with universities or university colleges for the purposes of examination. Reading took this commitment very seriously. It established a Joint Committee of representatives of the University and the colleges, and separate Boards of Studies for each subject under the chairmanship of the appropriate University head of department. When the first examinations for the Teacher's Certificate were taken under this scheme Professor Dewar of the Department of English chaired every Board 'in order to ensure uniformity of standard'; he dealt with a total of 430 candidates. But as Childs indicated in his Report of 1927 the scheme as envisaged at Reading did more than establish an external examining authority:

> If the scheme were merely a device for carrying out a system of external examinations, there would be little to be said about it, for the University of Reading would not have concerned itself with it. The intention of the scheme on both sides goes beyond that. From the first it has been regarded as essential that there should be direct personal relations between the authorities and teaching staff of each training college on the one hand, and the authorities and teaching staff of the University upon the other. Such relations are to be sought through visits, conferences, and consultations: and further it is hoped that in approved cases students from the colleges included in the scheme will be enabled to proceed to the University for a further course of advanced study. All syllabuses of instruction, again, are settled after consultation. The scheme, in short, was intended to be no mere piece of educational mechanism, but to be human, friendly,

---

[1] *Ibid.*, 2915, 10 May 1946. See also A. K. Giles (1973), p. 15. Dr N. S. Barron who was originally appointed as Veterinary Officer on the Advisory Staff continued in a University post as Veterinary Surgeon and Lecturer in Veterinary Science.

and helpful. In that spirit on both sides it has been happily and successfully launched. It means fresh work and responsibility for all concerned: but the training and teaching of more than 600 students in these colleges justify the effort.[1]

The close co-operation which the scheme envisaged was in fact achieved. In 1930 Sibly reported that the Joint Committee had overcome most of the initial difficulties and that a 'spirit of confidence and goodwill had been established and maintained between members of the University and members of the training colleges'.[2] H. C. Barnard, then Professor of Education, later looked back on these arrangements with pride and affection. He used to spend up to three weeks each year visiting each college for three days or so, talking to the staff, chatting with the students, perhaps giving a lecture, perhaps taking a service in a college chapel. Conversely when the college members of the Joint Committee visited Reading they were received as fellow members of staff in the Senior Common Room.[3] Under these arrangements six widely scattered colleges were happily linked with the University throughout the 1930s.[4]

This settled tenor was disturbed at the end of the War. The McNair Report of 1944 noted that training colleges valued their connection with universities and would welcome closer contact 'provided that it takes the form of a partnership between equals and does not lead to the universities having a predominant influence in the training of the students in the training colleges'.[5] That note was to sound louder and louder as the years passed, and its peculiar logic was to undermine the close relationship which had been established. The Report confused matters further through its failure to provide an agreed recommendation on the future pattern of local organization for the training of teachers.[6] In the event the Education Act of 1945 provided for the establishment of local institutes of education under optional administrative arrangements. From this point onwards policies changed more rapidly, both nationally and within the University. In the same period some of the constituent colleges left to establish associations with other, more convenient universities; and other colleges, newly founded, came into an association with Reading for the first time. Initially in 1947 the University decided to reduce its administrative responsibility for the

---

[1] *Proceedings 1926–7*, p. 32.

[2] *Proceedings 1928–9*, pp. 48–9.

[3] Conversation with Professor H. C. Barnard, 25 October 1974.

[4] The Diocesan Training College, Brighton; the Municipal Training College, Brighton; the Bishop Otter College, Chichester; Culham College, Abingdon; the Training College, Portsmouth; and the Diocesan Training College, Salisbury. Of these the Diocesan Training College, Brighton was closed in July 1938.

[5] *Teachers and Youth Leaders* (1944), para. 188, p. 56.

[6] Five members of the Committee recommended that responsibility should be centred on University Schools of Education; five recommended the expansion of the existing Joint Boards (that is at Reading the Joint Committee) to embrace a wider range of interests (*ibid.*, paras. 182, 196 and pp. 48–62).

colleges; it was felt that many of them were too distant and that, with the greatly increased number of teacher-training places, they might swamp a small university: in any case, at Reading, there was a strong tide running against all non-degree work. Hence the University opted for a type of institute which was independently financed by the Ministry of Education, and in which its previous administrative responsibilities were considerably diminished.[1] The University's commitments were also reduced geographically: the colleges at Salisbury, Portsmouth and Brighton now fell to other training areas.

This scheme lasted for a mere seven years. In 1954 the University decided to resort to an alternative option which linked it more closely with the Institute.[2] By now it was responsible for only two colleges, of which only one had been a member of the original six.[3] Wolfenden advocated the change on grounds which were closely similar to those chosen by Childs in setting up the Joint Committee in 1926:

> Fundamentally the change would give the University the chance of
> positive leadership in the education of teachers in this neighbourhood,
> both during their training and afterwards, and of increasing its
> influence and impact on them and, through them, on the schools.
> For a University like ours this might well be regarded as a duty.[4]

As a result a better co-ordinated system was established in which the Professor of Education became the Director of the Institute. That remained intact until 1972 when the whole organization of the Area Training Organizations was called in question in the James Report. The words of the McNair Report were now reasserted far more strongly:

> The association between colleges and universities has continued to
> be one in which universities are the predominant partners in Area
> Training Organizations. Although it would be folly to dissociate the

[1] The Institute was formally established on 26 July 1948. See *Gazette*, 24 March 1948, p. 5 and *Proceedings 1947–8*, p. 3. The constitution provided for the establishment of a Foundation, administered by a Board of Governors, with funds provided by the Ministry of Education. The University had no financial responsibility. The Governing Body consisted of representatives appointed by the governing bodies of the Colleges, the Local Education Authorities and the University; University representation was to be equal to the larger of the other two. However, on the Professional Board, which administered all academic questions, representation was limited to the Colleges and the University which were placed on an equal footing as in the old Joint Committee. See Council Reports, xi, 5 December 1947.
[2] Under this option the University assumed direct responsibility through a Delegacy for administering the Institute through funds provided by the University Grants Committee.
[3] Easthampstead Park, Berkshire, and Bishop Otter College, Chichester.
[4] Council Reports, xv, 5 November 1954. This Memorandum of Wolfenden provides a useful review of the developments between 1947 and 1954. I have relied on it in the above account. A different emphasis, derived largely from the expectations and hopes held within the Department and Institute of Education in 1949 is given by H. C. Barnard and C. R. E. Gillett, the first Director of the Institute in *Through Fifty Years* (Reading, 1949), pp. 43–7.

universities from teacher education and training the time has now come for major modifications of the present relationship.

One strong reason for changing the system is that the colleges have outgrown the pattern designed for them. Since the Robbins Report, and even more plainly since the McNair Report, the colleges have grown in status and confidence . . . A growing proportion of the students possess the formal qualifications for degree work, and such work has been developed in most of the colleges. Many of the colleges are large and aspire to a greater measure of control over their own destinies . . . the colleges have grown up and should be encouraged to move forward to a new degree of independence.[1]

The case was far from convincing. The Government's White Paper of December 1972 noted that:

The radical recommendation of the James Committee that [Area Training Organizations] should be replaced and all their present functions assumed by new bodies virtually divorced from the universities has caused wide misgivings which the Government share.[2]

Nevertheless the White Paper recommended the replacement of the old Area Training Organizations, based on universities, by new regional committees and the old organization ceased to function in 1975.[3] Meanwhile constituent colleges had come and gone. Bishop Otter College, the last of the first six, finally left in 1966. Newland Park College, Buckinghamshire, came in, went out, and came in yet again. In 1964 Easthampstead Park was joined by, and in 1969 was amalgamated with, the new Bulmershe College of Education, which advanced rapidly in size and reputation.[4] Situated in Woodley, within two miles of the University, this was an outstanding example of the large and aspiring colleges to which the James Report referred. It was to become the main problem in the University's discussion of its changing relationship with the colleges.

Within this shifting framework the Institute of Education achieved a great deal. Like others, it was established in 1947 with the intention that it should play a much wider role than the old Joint Committee which was confined to supervizing the work of the constituent colleges. It became responsible for Diploma and M.A. courses. It became a centre of research. It provided courses, long and short, within the field of education: in Speech Therapy, for example, in which it worked with the Department of Linguistic Science, in Educational Guidance, in Adult Literacy and Sixth Form Mathematics, and especially in Agricultural Extension work, in which it

---

[1] *Teacher Education and Training* (London, 1972), p. 49.
[2] *Education: A Framework for Expansion* (London, 1972), p. 26.
[3] *Ibid.*, p. 27; *Proceedings 1974–5*, p. 44.
[4] For a time Bulmershe was renamed the Berkshire College of Education. Since Bulmershe was its initial, and is its present title, I have used it throughout.

established a major centre.[1] All this was accommodated easily enough within the structure of the University; the Institute was treated as a quasi department and then, from 1969, was allied with the Department of Education in a School of Education. However, the constituent colleges, given the direction of their development, were more of a problem. In 1963 the Robbins Report recommended the establishment of the Bachelor of Education degree.[2] That too was accepted. It fitted easily as a combined course in Education and some other subject into Reading's proliferation of combined subject syllabuses. There was a strong feeling that if it was to be done at all it had better be done properly; hence, after some debate, Reading became one of the first universities to admit the B.Ed. as an Honours Degree; it also did its best to make suitable arrangements for subjects not taught in the University.[3] The B.Ed. degree prospered; in 1975 there were 138 successful candidates from the two constituent colleges. However, by that time the James Report had appeared and this was a very different kettle of fish, for it argued that some of the larger colleges 'should be encouraged to offer a comprehensive programme of activities . . . including the development of degree courses for students other than intending teachers'.[4] Bulmershe was such a college. Moreover its Principal, J. F. Porter, was one of the members of the James Committee and a co-signatory of a Note of Extension to the Report which emphasized not only the importance of association between colleges and universities but also 'the implications of the proposals contained in the Report that some Colleges of Education should develop both General and Honours Degree courses,

---

[1] In 1975 the Chairman of the School of Education reported: 'The completion this year of ten years' work in Agricultural Extension and Rural Development was taken to be an opportunity for some reassessment of purpose and programme, and for some modest celebration. Much can be quantified. The Centre started with an Academic Staff of two, and seven full-time students: we now have seven Academic Staff, two invaluable seconded posts from the Ministry of Overseas Development and the Ministry of Agriculture, Fisheries and Food, three staff involved in research and documentation, and 60 students. We have had, each year, about 140 advisory staff on short courses varying from one to three weeks in duration, and in this year the number increased to over 200. We started in a few rooms, and now occupy a few buildings. The work, in 1965, took staff on a few hundred miles of travel in England and Wales: last year, staff travelled a total of some 155,000 miles to 15 countries outside the U.K. We started with a single postgraduate diploma course, and now have two diploma courses, together with two taught Master's degree courses and students reading for both M.Phil. and Ph.D. degrees.

The Centre continues to preserve an even balance between work with the Agricultural Development and Advisory Service and other agricultural advisory services in Britain. This is done for and in "overseas" countries. Probably our biggest need, now that we have established curricula for our courses and relationships with many Extension Services throughout the world, is for a more coherent and ambitious research programme and we shall be tackling this in the immediate future' (*Proceedings 1974–5*, p. 44).

[2] *Higher Education*, paras. 323–41, pp. 112–16.

[3] It was in these circumstances that Religious Studies finally entered the University's curriculum. It also came to accept Physical Education, Drama and Film Studies.

[4] *Teacher Education and Training*, para. 5.36, p. 61.

built on the unit structure' of the newly proposed Diploma of Higher Education.[1] In the event the White Paper envisaged the possibility that some colleges might be completely integrated in the university system on the condition that 'staff, students and courses would need to become equal and integral parts of the institutions concerned'.[2] At Reading that marked the end of the road. The University's link with Newland Park College remained, but the College turned to examine the possibility of an association with the College of Technology at High Wycombe. In the winter of 1971 and the spring of 1972 discussions took place between the University and Bulmershe College. They could be little more than perfunctory within the time-limits allowed by the Department of Education and Science. However, more time would have made no difference, for the James Report had carried the College well outside the range of any possible agreement. It had to ask the University to underwrite Honours Degrees, largely in the Arts and Social Sciences, which were to be based on a unit structure related to a Diploma, of less than degree standard, which had not yet been properly established, still less examined.[3] In effect this envisaged two sets of Honours Degrees in the University of Reading. On the side of the University that was unacceptable. The objection applied equally to the validation of such degrees and to any possible amalgamation of the University and the College. There was little need, therefore, to probe the deep unease, felt in some departments in the University, especially in those heavily involved in the B.Ed., at the prospect of the proposed new degrees. The College turned to the Council of National Academic Awards for validation. By 1976 all that remained was simply to phase out the University's responsibility for the B.Ed.[4]

This was a negative result. It stands in sharp contrast to the successful negotiation with the College of Estate Management. The difference lay to some extent in the fact that the College of Estate Management sought an agreement without the kind of academic stipulations which the James Report imposed. But there was yet another contrast, less obvious but more important. The College of Estate Management brought much needed variety to the University. The association with the Colleges in the B.Ed. on the other hand, had done very little to extend the range of its work. The main effect was to add to the numbers reading subjects within the large

[1] *Ibid.*, p. 78.

[2] *Education: a Framework for Expansion*, para. 154, p. 44.

[3] Senate appointed a committee to consider the James Report. It reported to a special meeting of Senate on 21 March 1972. Its report allowed that there might be a place for the Dip.H.E. as a complement to degree courses and noted that 'the acceptability of the Dip.H.E. would be enhanced by the extent to which universities were involved in approving syllabuses and validating diploma courses'. It recommended limited 'recognition' of diploma courses in the form of a possible exemption from the first part or first year of a degree course, each case being treated on its merits (Senate Reports, 21 March 1972).

[4] Important links remain. For example, the staff and the degree students of the College have limited use of the University Library and the University is represented on the Governing Body of the College.

Arts and Social Science departments; of the 138 successful candidates admitted to the B.Ed. degree in 1975, 100 came within the Departments of English, Fine Art, French, Geography and History. The new modular courses envisaged in the James Report, however novel they might be claimed to be, threatened to add yet more students working in these subjects and in related fields in the Social Sciences.[1] Of that the University was already wary.

These decisions put the final touch to the shaping of the University. The changes which had taken place in the thirty years since the end of the Second World War were of both addition and subtraction. By its own initiative, with the support of the University Grants Committee and through the beneficence of private and public benefactors, it extended the range of its work both in teaching and research. At the same time it abandoned practically all the non-degree courses in which it had earlier been involved. It had emerged fully as a University. Its work was more varied, and there was greater depth in the variety. It had not abandoned its early commitment to applied subjects. If anything this had been increased; but where it had taught for Diplomas and Certificates in Dairying in 1939, it now provided degrees in Food Science; and where it had held classes for the City and Guilds of London Institute in Builders' Quantities it now provided M.Sc. courses in Building Maintenance Management and Construction. It had stuck to the ingrained commitment to scholarship which is the fibre of any University. Indeed it had advanced its reputation into fields which were completely inaccessible to it in the earlier years when its resources were so meagre. For all this it had paid one price: size. It had to accept that it had become a comparatively large university.

Size seems a simple enough problem. In the case of universities it may be measured or calculated in terms of numbers, accommodation, expenditure and the like. It represents the most solid of objective realities by the side of academic standards, for example, or headier ideas of the nature and boundaries of particular disciplines. But objective though it be, there is nothing so vulnerable to subjective assessment as this plain matter of size. That which in one's own department is plainly a function of natural growth, a necessary consequence of the proper development of the subject, may seem in another to amount to nothing more than empire-building; and those new appointments which in academic departments seem to fill the most obvious gaps in teaching and research, may look like unnecessary and sinister extensions of bureaucracy when they are made in the offices of

[1] The Senate Committee noted, with specific reference to the possibility of some form of integration with Berkshire [Bulmershe] College of Education, that 'quite apart from the strength or weakness of the academic case for a close association between the two institutions, the practical obstacles would be severe. The College had some 1,200 students, most of them on the arts side, whose GCE qualifications would be, on average, below those normally required for entrance to this University.' (Notes on meeting of 21 February 1972).

the Registrar or Bursar. Of such impressions the origin partly lies in size itself, for they grow as the small intimate community is swamped by numbers and fragmented by complexities. There is no way entirely to correct them, for they also stem from that ignorance of the general good which often partners deep concern for special interests. Universities sometimes have to put up with the one if they are to have the other. Reading was no exception. However, if increasing size encouraged some misgivings, it also brought obvious benefits, and it was the benefits – the reinforcement of academic and technical staff, the acquisition of new equipment, the access to computers, the availability of secretarial help, even the provision of telephones – which dominated the collective consciousness. There were few ready to deny that growth was good or to question whether it was natural and necessary. Some might wonder whether it was possible, but by the late 1960s only the old hands, with a wry sense of superiority, would say – 'Of course, in the old days, we had to do all this ourselves'. For plainly much of the University's growth was indeed good, and of this, even for those who were habitually afflicted by doubt whenever they looked beyond the range of interest of their own departments, there were two convincing illustrations: the Library and the Research Board.

At the end of the war Reading's Library was still more characteristic of a college than of a university with an increasingly earnest commitment to expansion. The war had caused a cut in the immediate provision for books which was not restored until 1944–5.[1] That apart, the vote of Council, at £1,750, had remained unchanged since 1930. It was plain too that the Library building was inadequate. Already before the war increasing congestion had twice led to a reorganization of the accommodation. In 1936 it was estimated that there was adequate space for the next thirty years, but that was highly optimistic; it assumed an annual growth of no more than 2,500 volumes and no great increase in reader places.[2] Even the small initial expansion of the years immediately following the war precipitated a crisis. From 1945–6 the vote to the Library was increased,[3] and by 1948–9 the rate of acquisition was more than double that on which the predictions of 1936 had been based.[4] The more books and periodicals acquired, the quicker the building approached its capacity. In 1949 the Librarian reported that the available space would be completely filled by 1951. In the event the last shelves were added to the stack in that year, and no more could be done within the building. Thereafter the Library survived only by taking over the accommodation vacated as departments moved to

---

[1] The grant was reduced from £1,750 to £1,400 in 1940–1, partly because of the reduction in academic publications and the cessation of orders from the continent.
[2] D. J. Hewlett, *op. cit.*, pp. 64–6, 75–80.
[3] It was raised from £1,750 to £2,500 in 1945–6 and £4,000 in 1947–8.
[4] The volumes added to the stock in these years were:

1947–8	3,879	1950–1	4,295
1948–9	5,168	1951–2	5,074
1949–50	5,698	1952–3	6,052

new buildings in Whiteknights,[1] and by using some of the war-time hut-
ments in Whiteknights as stores. It was saved from these increasing difficulties by the obvious inadequacy of the old Library and by the decision
that the first new building in Whiteknights should be for the Faculty of
Letters.[2] Once the Arts departments had moved to Whiteknights, the
Library had to follow, and sooner rather than later. The move to a new
Library building in Whiteknights was finally made in December 1963. The
completion of the new building was accompanied by an appeal for books
and funds for books. Within a year over 5,000 volumes and over £1,500
had been received. By the summer of 1964 the Library held over 220,000
volumes and pamphlets compared with just under 100,000 in 1946. Its
accessions for 1963–4 came to over 13,000. The Library grant from Council
was now £20,500. In its new accommodation it could make a brave
showing. An enthusiastic Library staff, aided by equally enthusiastic
students, completed the removal in nineteen working days. The old Library
closed down on Saturday 30 November.[3] The Current Periodicals Room
and Reading Rooms in the new Library opened three days later, on
Tuesday 3 December.

The new Library building was certainly the best in Whiteknights. It was
one of the last university libraries to be built before the establishment of the
doctrine that libraries should consist of vast cubes of conditioned air,
enclosed by concrete, in which books, readers, offices and services may be
moved at will to meet changing fashions and requirements. It was designed
as a readers' library, and the design conveyed the purpose with unusual
directness. It linked a large bookstack which was surrounded by a gallery
for readers, with two handsome reading rooms by means of a formal staircase, the landings of which were intended as exhibition areas. The original
intentions were soon overtaken as overcrowding spread bookcases into the
reading rooms and landings and as places for more readers were required in
the main stack. But at last the University had a building, designed for 600
readers and 500,000 volumes which fully matched its new size and academic
strengths. The new building also reflected some of the special qualities of the
Library. The staff workrooms on the ground floor included a well fitted
Bindery. That went back to the decision taken in 1947 to employ a binder
at London Road. In this Mary Kirkus, the Librarian, had been the driving
force, and Betts, then Chairman of the Curators of the Library, the inspiration. Carpenter, characteristically, had found a room and persuaded the
Finance Committee to provide a small non-recurrent grant for the purchase
of tools and materials. Stenton, in such a matter, needed no persuasion and

[1] The old History Room at London Road, taken over in 1956, and altered to house
18,000 volumes, was the main addition.
[2] For the debate on the respective priority to be given to a new Library and a new
building for the Department of Physics, see above, pp. 195–7.
[3] The old Library subsequently continued in use as an Education Library.

encouraged the project as Vice-Chancellor.[1] By 1953 the Bindery was dealing with 3,000 volumes a year, which as a result never had to leave the University. The top floor of the new building also had a special purpose: it was designed to house special collections. Here the Overstone collection which had been the pride of the old Library[2] was joined by Cole's superb library of 8,000 volumes on the history of medicine and zoology, which was acquired in 1960.[3] Other private collections followed, perhaps the most important being the library of Sir Frank and Lady Stenton which they bequeathed to the University with an endowment for its upkeep. The arrival of this collection after Lady Stenton's death in 1971 and of the Finzi collection of modern poets in 1974 exhausted the special accommodation available for private collections. By 1975 the Library as a whole was approaching saturation. Quite apart from the normal accessions, it had taken in the Library of the College of Estate Management and was establishing a library for the new Department of Law. Ominously its stock had mounted to 452,025 volumes and 56,525 pamphlets; the accessions had risen to more than 20,000 volumes a year. It was once again driven to revive its experience of the 1950s and seek other storage space. It was now a very different library in quality as well as size. Quite apart from the special collections, some sections were outstanding: agricultural studies, especially Agricultural Economics, housed separately in the temporary buildings at Earley Gate, where Edgar Thomas was the inspiration; Medieval English History which was in all essentials the work of the Stentons; Italian History where Dr S. J. Woolf, of the Department of Italian Studies, had brought together a remarkable collection in less than ten years; book design and printing where Betts and later M. L. Twyman were the driving force. It had also achieved some importance as an archive and manuscript repository. In addition to its major holdings for the Institute of Agricultural History, it included, as loans or deposits: the records of Huntley & Palmer, and of Longman and Co.; the estate papers of the Duke of Wellington; and the political papers of Nancy, Viscountess Astor. It also helped to house an important collection of material relating to John

---

[1] 'It is interesting to see how (like so many of the University ventures) it started under the most difficult conditions: one very small room, the minimum of equipment and material, one temperamental binder, a sewing woman, and Mary Kirkus, the Librarian, with a lot of faith in the future of the bindery, and myself, sometimes pushing, sometimes cajoling, but always sure that a good Library needs a bindery.' (J. A. Betts, May 1972).

[2] On the Overstone collection, see Lady Stenton's comments below, p. 344.

[3] Cole, who died in 1959, bequeathed his collection to Dr Eales who subsequently sold it to the Library. Along with twelve collaborators she established an endowment for the upkeep of the Cole Library. She continued Cole's work of indexing and cataloguing, producing two scholarly catalogues *The Cole Library of Early Medicine and Zoology*, parts 1 and 2 (University of Reading, 1969, 1975). See also, 'The Cole Library of Zoology and early medicine, University of Reading', *Nature*, clxxxviii, no. 4757 (1960), pp. 1148–51. It will be observed that Cole took careful steps to ensure the maintenance of his collection. Compare his experience with his museum collection, above, pp. 214–16.

Ruskin which belonged to the Guild of St. George;[1] and, through the generosity of authors and the assiduity of members of staff, it had accumulated numerous literary manuscripts, especially of Samuel Beckett. In 1975 the Library might be near to bursting at the seams, but it had fulfilled the objective defined in the jargon of university policy: it had become a centre of excellence. The collection was highly centralized. Apart from the Education Library at London Road there were few 'out-stations' or independent libraries of any importance. It remained vulnerable, most of all to the inflation of the price of books and periodicals in the 1970s.

The Research Board provided a similar example on a smaller scale. Founded on the inspiration of Childs in 1925, it was carefully tended by Stenton, who acted as its Chairman, re-elected annually, until he became Vice-Chancellor twenty-one years later. During the 1930s it administered the award of up to six senior scholarships, one of which was endowed.[2] It also allocated, for research grants, a small sum which varied between £200 and £300 per annum. This was supplemented on the side of agricultural research by an endowment of £10,000 established by the firm of Huntley & Palmer in 1921, which became available only when the University College became a University in 1926; from this, in addition to grants for research, a fellowship was occasionally awarded. The development after the Second World War was at first very slow. The University's annual provision for research grants still stood at £250 in 1946–7 and had only risen to £400 in 1948–9. In that year there were five senior scholarships, only one more than in 1929–30.[3] Thereafter, however, changes came thick and fast. Two University Research Fellowships were established in 1950; by 1973–4 there were five. In 1957 the Board proposed that fellowships should be established for visiting scholars; in 1962–3 the first Visiting Fellow was elected. By 1953–4 the number of studentships had risen to twelve; twenty years later there were forty-four. The annual grants for research rose to £2,000 by 1960, more than £5,000 by 1965, and in 1973–4 totalled over £13,000. Whereas earlier the Board had largely to confine its awards to existing minor purchases of materials and apparatus, it was now able to support individual research on an international scale in libraries and in the field overseas. It was also able to contribute towards the cost of attendance at

---

[1] On the Guild of St George see W. G. Collingwood, *The Life of John Ruskin* (London, 6th edn., 1905), pp. 312–19 and Edith Hope Scott, *Ruskin's Guild of St. George* (London, 1931). The association with Reading came through the interest of both Betts and Hodges in the Pre-Raphaelite Movement and in Ruskin. Betts got to know of the collection, which was housed in Sheffield, when he was director of the School of Painting at the Sheffield College of Art. He and Hodges became members of the Guild and Hodges became Master from 1950 to 1972, when he was succeeded by Cyril Tyler. The University agreed to house the collection after lengthy negotiations which began in 1952. An exhibition room was provided for it at London Road in 1970.

[2] The Ernest Ridley Research Studentship, founded in 1925 by Mrs Ernest Ridley, in memory of her husband, who was a member of Council of University College.

[3] This figure excludes endowed scholarships.

research conferences.[1] It provided a major facility which, in the size of its operation and in the extent to which it placed funds for the furtherance of research under the direction of members of the academic staff, was one of Reading's best achievements.

In the development of the Research Board and the Library the advantages of size were apparent to all. They were equally real in other, less obvious, aspects of the University's work. For example, the increase in numbers led in 1963 to an entirely new Health Centre in place of the old Sanatorium. The further rapid expansion envisaged after the Robbins Report brought the establishment of a full-time Medical Officer in place of a consultant practitioner.[2] By 1974 there were four medical officers and a dental surgeon. The change in title was deliberate. The old Sanatorium was for the recovery of the sick. The new Health Centre also provided for the education and supervision of the healthy. It was a pioneering venture in which Reading was to the fore, just as it had been, nearly sixty years earlier, in the development of halls of residence. Another equally valued development concerned the students' future careers. This originated in an Appointments Committee set up in 1942, chiefly to organize the placing of women in some recognized form of national service under the Employment of Women (Control of Engagement) Orders, 1942. From a University Committee it grew into a Careers Advisory Service which, by 1974–5, included a Director, four Careers Advisers and secretarial and other staff: it cost nearly £43,000, roughly £26 for every student who obtained a first or an advanced degree in that year.

These were simply two elements in a rapidly expanding section of the annual accounts of the University which were headed 'Student Facilities and Amenities'. However, it was not these which impressed students most immediately and deeply, any more than the Library and the Research Board sprang to the mind of members of staff as two of the most obvious features of the University's new growth. The students, in their course and in their patterns of behaviour, could now exercise choice far beyond the range available to earlier generations. Yet the size of the University made an informal choice more difficult. The staff had far greater resources for teaching and research. Yet the size of the University made the exploitation of these opportunities more complicated. The larger the University the more it had to be administered; the more sophisticated the less room for the amateur, and the more specialized the greater the need for the professional.

[1] In 1973–4 a total of £13,507 was distributed as follows:

(i) £8,022 to 171 applicants towards costs of attendance at research conferences. This included £403 from the Huntley & Palmer Agriculture Research Fund.

(ii) £5,327 to 70 applicants towards travelling and subsistence and other expenses incurred in research in libraries and in the field.

(iii) £58 to four applicants towards the cost of photographic and other copies.

(iv) £100 to one applicant to assist publication.

[2] Report of the Residential Policy Committee: Senate Reports, xxii, 24 February 1964.

In the *Calendar 1946–7* the administrative staff of the University was listed as the Registrar and Tutorial Secretary, the Bursar, an Assistant Registrar and thirty-two assistants. In the *Calendar 1974–5* the Registrar's Office comprised an administrative and secretarial staff of fifty-two, the Bursar's Office an administrative and secretarial staff of nearly ninety. Each was now divided into sub-departments, and in each sub-department there was a senior responsible officer and assistant staff. Who administered what was now, for the academic staff, a matter of arcane knowledge illuminated from time to time by circulars listing the allocation of responsibilities to what for many were simply names and telephone numbers. Yet the administration of the University had done no more than grow in proportion with the rest. It absorbed 7.47 per cent of the University's expenditure in 1949–50 and 7.52 per cent in 1974–5. Administrative costs were 13.9 per cent of academic costs in 1949–50 and 11.74 per cent in 1974–5.[1] A comparative study of relative costs which the University undertook in 1975 revealed that administrative expenditure at Reading was on a par with that of other comparable universities.[2] But this was not what mattered. In 1975 T. M. Harris could still look back with affection to 'Dear old Smithy', Registrar and Tutorial Secretary from 1932 to 1955. In the place of that friendly image, students and staff alike now raised an ogre – 'Admin.'.

[1] The above calculations exclude research grants from external sources. There are naturally slight variations in these figures from year to year, but I have not been able to detect any significant trend. It should be noted that the calculations do not include secretarial posts in departments or those posts which are accounted as Student Facilities and Amenities.

[2] 'University Costs,' a paper prepared for the Committee of Deans by C. Tyler, Deputy Vice-Chancellor, 6 March 1975. The paper was based on the national statistics for 1972–3. Tyler noted some of the difficulties inherent in such calculations – 'comparisons of administrative costs are notoriously difficult between universities. For example, we do not charge part of the personnel and purchasing costs to academic departments, but some universities do. Similarly, there is the administration of the farms and the indirect costs of examinations which in Reading are not charged elsewhere as they could well be'.

Chapter 10

The Governance of the University

The Council was, and is, the immediate governing body of the University.[1]
In the relative tranquillity of his retirement Childs retained a clear
memory of the transaction of its business:

> George William Palmer once remarked to me with satisfaction that
> it was not the Council's way to decide things by counting heads.
> Ayes and noes there must have been sometimes; but rarely, if ever,
> upon questions of moment. Perhaps this absence of division may
> suggest inertness, or the habit of murmuring 'Ditto'. Such an
> inference would be wide of the truth, and, indeed, preposterous,
> when one thinks of the men whose want of capacity it would prove,
> if true. Few institutions can have passed through more trying times
> than the young College at Reading; and few can have owed more
> to the competence of their governing bodies. The true explanation
> of the prevailing accord was very different. The Council was faithful
> to a well-understood and well-tested tradition of procedure. It
> required full information, and this it received. It expected its
> committees and its principal officer to state the facts, and to advise
> upon them, in accordance with their duty. If, commonly, the
> advice was taken, this was not because the Council was a docile
> court of registration, but because the advice commended itself.
> During twenty-six years of office, I recall no occasion when I was
> not aware that the statements which it fell to me to make in Council
> were being heard with close attention. No recommendation involv-
> ing a new principle of action, or a new departure of moment, was
> accepted passively, or as a matter of course. Questions would be
> asked, discussion might follow, and the result might be approval,
> or amendment, or withdrawal. In some ways, perhaps, we were
> fortunate. We had no tradition of disunion or bickering. We could
> not hope to escape difficulties; but the habit of contention or petty
> criticism never took root amongst us. Nearly all our members were

[1] The ultimate authority in the University lies in the University Court which holds one
ordinary meeting a year to receive the Annual Report and Statement of Accounts. It is
the Council, however, which has the sole custody and use of the University Seal. The
various powers of Court, Council and Senate are laid down in Statutes XIII, XV and
XVII, which amplify Articles VIII, IX and X of the Charter.

familiar with the despatch of public business and they were impatient
of talking for talking's sake. Moreover, the Council was not anxious
to interfere in ordinary management, unless such intervention was
shown to be necessary. It was not touchy about its jurisdiction, for
its jurisdiction had never been questioned. At no time did it lay
itself open to any charge of unconstitutional action. In short, we
met and acted in an atmosphere of trust, friendliness, and lively
enterprise. We were business-like, but not formal. Members spoke
sitting: set speeches were not the fashion: our meetings were private.
When Palmer took pleasure in the thought that we put our work
through without formal divisions, he was only noticing something
which is likely enough to happen in English life when sensible and
experienced men get together over business which is outside the
realms of controversy, and yet endowed with an intrinsic interest
so absorbing that it becomes in itself a bond of unity and concord.[1]

Childs failed to provide a similar description of the proceedings of the
Academic Board of the College or the Senate of the new-born University.
He came to the verge of it twice, but on both occasions resorted to a purely
formal account which emphasized his own role as Chairman and Principal
of the academic staff.[2] For him, the Council, not the Academic Board or
the Senate, was the power-house of the institution which he governed and
the centre of all the planning and discussion which underlay the establishment of the University. This reflects his instinctive appreciation of where
authority lay and whence initiative had come.

Fifty years later the authority of the Council remained unimpaired. Its
powers, as defined by the Statutes of the University, had not been reduced
in any respect, nor had they been devolved in any formal sense. Yet the
Council had come to act less immediately. Its capacity to initiate business
had been divided or shared among an increasing number of committees.
Some members of Council felt increasingly out of touch with its business:

Members tended to come out of the meeting and say: 'Well, I did
not quite understand this,' or: 'We did not have enough information
on that, but anyway I went along with it.' When it was suggested to
them that they might have held matters up for discussion they
tended to say that they did not wish to waste time.[3]

---

[1] W. M. Childs (1933), pp. 194–5.
[2] The first and most important example concerned the first bid for University status in
December 1920, when Childs tried to ensure that the issues of the Great Row would not
be revived. 'I spoke to the Academic Board without reserve. . . . Unless we were united,
the university project must come to naught. I, at least, would waste no more time
ploughing sands. If divisions recurred, my intention was to advise the Council to drop
the project. If it seemed that my leadership was an obstacle to unity, my intention was to
withdraw . . . "I ask for unity, not unanimity" ' (*ibid.*, pp. 228–9). He got it. The second
occasion concerned the establishment of the Research Board: 'I invited the Academic
Board to consider "whether any further steps can usefully be taken to encourage and
promote research and original work by members of the academic staff" ' (*ibid.*, p. 256).
[3] Conversation with The Honourable Gordon Palmer, 11 August 1975.

For a time, Wolfenden did something to correct this. After the meetings of the Council had ended he would sometimes talk informally and open a free and easy interchange of information, questions and suggestions. This was much appreciated, but nevertheless it underlined the increasing formality of the Council's business; to Childs it would have seemed strange and unnecessary. The President of the Council had some influence in this. Sir George Mowbray's methods were distinctly brisk; he allowed questions and discussion on occasions, but rarely sought them and cut them very short. That induced lethargy. Gerald Palmer and Sir George Abell, in contrast, set out to revive and sharpen interest by provoking discussion and emphasizing points of importance. But the increasing size and complexity of the University was the main determinant. Size in itself bred committees. Rapidly increasing size bred committee after committee.

Increasing size brought other changes. As the resources of the University increased, it became less easy to separate the administrative and financial business which was properly the concern of the Council from academic matters which lay immediately within the province of the Senate. Inevitably that emphasized the role of those members of Council who were also members of Senate. These steadily increased in number as the political community of the University was enlarged. Originally the Principal was the sole link between the Academic Board of the College and the Council.[1] Then representatives of the Academic Board were added to the Council: two in 1909, three in 1913. The constitution of the new University embodied wider representation of the academic staff: eight at its foundation in 1926, by 1975 twelve, three of whom were elected by a general ballot of the academic staff. If prior to 1909 the academic staff were represented by the Principal, in 1926 they were represented very much by the professors. Fifty years later, in contrast, the non-professorial academic staff had direct representation on both Council and Senate. In 1926 the only formal acknowledgement of the voice of the students was in the consultative committees of the various halls of residence. Fifty years later their representatives attended the meetings of both the Council and the Senate, numerous joint consultative committees of academic staff and students had been established, and students sat on a wide range of deliberative committees which dealt with residence, catering and sports facilities.

Most of these changes came relatively late, many in the last decade. It was not until 1956 that the University began to grow with any rapidity, and not until the Robbins Report that it experienced galloping expansion.[2] It was only then that change began to seem essential. Once begun, it proceeded very rapidly. It was accelerated by forces outside the University system and quite beyond the University's control: by the growing con-

---

[1] 'The academic staff was represented upon the Council by the Principal' (Childs, 1933, p. 33). For an expression of Childs's view of the role of the Principal see *ibid.*, pp. 62–3.
[2] See above, p. 156.

fidence and influence of trades unions, by government pronouncements on
the age of majority, by the financial affluence of young employees in the
1960s and by increasingly influential ideas which were concerned chiefly
with primary and secondary education, but which came to affect attitudes
towards the function and organization of universities. These were matters
which affected every university, and as a result the university world became
less fragmentary. Some changes at Reading arose from events elsewhere or
from general problems which all universities had to solve. Even so, like any
other university, it drew on its own experience and history. In administration more than in anything else, the ghosts of the past linger on, influencing
the present through the remnants of their handiwork. At Reading this
influence drew its strength from the slow development of the College and
University as a small closely knit community. It was reinforced by the
pattern of succession to the office of Registrar. The first Registrar, Francis
Wright, who had been in office since 1895[1] was succeeded in 1927 by
Herbert Knapman, who had been Tutorial Secretary since 1906. Knapman
in his turn was succeeded in 1932 by Ernest Smith who had been Assistant
Registrar since 1928, an office which he held alongside his earlier appointment as lecturer in the Department of Education. Ernest Smith was
succeeded in 1955 by J. F. Johnson, who had been Assistant Registrar since
1950 and had returned as a veteran to graduate in French in 1947. At no
point, throughout the University's history, was there the kind of break
which might have come with the intrusion of a Registrar who came fresh
to Reading's ways.

Childs was not so much the founder as the first interpreter of Reading's
traditions. His enthusiasm for the work of Council and the easy relations
which he was able to establish with the benefactors of the College led him
into proposing a uni-cameral system of government for the University. That
was the origin of the Great Row in which Childs was defeated.[2] Yet,
although the University was ultimately established with the usual bie
cameral arrangement of Council and Senate, Childs's scheme had not
stemmed from mere whim. It was rather his own personal distillation of the
very close working relations which had been established between some
members of the Council and some of the senior academic staff, and these
were real enough to affect the working of the University quite apart from
the central proposal for uni-cameral government which Childs wished to
see established. In 1976 the University continues to rely on a number of
standing committees which include lay members of the Council as well as
members of the Senate or the academic staff. These work very much in the
manner which Childs envisaged for the central direction of the University.
The management of the affairs of the Library perhaps provides the most

---

[1] Wright held the title of Secretary between 1892 and 1895 and had been secretary to the
Schools of Science and Art before the establishment of the College in 1892.
[2] See above, pp. 28–31.

enduring example. This is the responsibility, not of an executive or advisory committee of academic staff, but of a body of Curators, whose functions are defined by the Ordinances of the University. The Curators include lay members of the Council as well as representatives of the Senate. They do not report their meetings regularly to the Council and the Senate as one of their committees; instead they submit an annual Report which the Senate transmits in whole or in part to the Council. The Librarian is responsible directly to the Curators, and the Curators are responsible directly to the Council for the allocation and expenditure of the funds which the Council makes available. This structure was first established in 1921 and has remained unchanged in its essentials thereafter. Even in areas of the University's work where the committees were repeatedly refashioned the instinct to associate lay members of the Council and members of the academic staff remained strong. The College's committees for the management of men's and women's halls of residence were made up in this way; so still are the University's Residential Board and the committees for each individual Hall. Moreover, committees of recent foundation, which had no forerunners in the College, were often cast in the same mould. The Museum of English Rural Life followed the pattern of the Library; from 1952 it was governed by a body of Curators who included at least one member of the Council.[1] Council representatives were also included in the Appointments Committee, which developed into the Careers Advisory Board, the Standing Disciplinary Committee, the Standing Disciplinary Appeals Committee, the Committee for the Sanatorium which became the Health Centre Committee, and others which outlived their purpose and were subsequently terminated. The pattern was not restricted to the outworks of the University's organization, but penetrated to its very heart. The Building Development Committee, which planned the development of Whiteknights, was organized in this way, with four members appointed by the Council and four members appointed by the Senate to serve with the *ex officio* members.[2] The system was perpetuated even where the interests of the academic staff were most closely involved. From the beginning the President of Council was, and still is, an *ex officio* member of the Research Board.[3] Even more strikingly, when, in 1962, the University established a committee to determine and recommend upon the promotion of members of staff to research professorships[4] it was one in which the Council and the Senate enjoyed equal representation. A similar constitution was adopted in 1963 for the Joint Standing Committee on Readers and Senior Lecturers, and

[1] When the Museum became the Institute of Agricultural History in 1969 the Curators were replaced by a Committee which included two appointees of the Council.
[2] The *ex officio* members were in addition to the Vice-Chancellor: from the Council, the President, the Vice-President and the Treasurer, and from the Senate, the Deputy Vice-Chancellor and the Deans of the Faculties.
[3] The President, like the Vice-Chancellor, has ceased to exercise his right of attendance.
[4] Later changed to personal professorships.

it was retained when the two committees were amalgamated in 1970.[1]

Within the Council there was always an informal but coherent working group completely devoted to the interests of the University. At the heart of this, at every period in the history of the University there was a member of the Palmer family. George William and Alfred Palmer were the benefactors who founded the University. But to imagine that their role was limited to that single vital act would be a serious misconception. Alfred Palmer in particular was Childs's guide and counsellor, a continuing source of wise advice. From 1911 he was Chairman of the Council of the College and he continued as President of the University Council until forced to resign through ill-health in 1930. The University marked his unique services in the most solemn way it could: in 1927 it conferred on him the honorary degree of D.Sc., and he remained the sole honorary Doctor until 1935. Alfred Palmer was followed after the War by his grandson Gerald, and by Gerald's cousin, Gordon, both of whom became Presidents of the Council. Gerald especially played a great part in the development of the University in Whiteknights.[2] To some degree he was to Wolfenden what Alfred had been to Childs. Members of other local families were equally committed: Herbert Benyon, the last President of the College and the first Chancellor of the University, Leonard and Noël Sutton, Sir William A. Mount and Sir George Mowbray. Mount was the first Treasurer of the University; his father had been one of the supporters of the College; he was followed on the Council by his son, Sir William M. Mount, who was Treasurer from 1946 to 1950. Sir George Mowbray joined the Council as President in 1933 and remained in that office until 1966. Following in the footsteps of his uncle, Sir Robert Mowbray, who had served on the Council of the College, he proved a formidable and energetic President who bridged the period between Alfred Palmer on the one hand and Gerald Palmer, who succeeded him as President, on the other. This group was intermingled with members of other local families who were drawn from the professions or came in as representatives of local authorities and then continued as co-opted members of the Council. Among these, A. P. Shaw, Treasurer from 1932 to 1946, and Arthur West, Vice-President of Council from 1936 to 1946, were among the most prominent. The Council of both the College and the University had a marked academic flavour. Sir Robert Mowbray was a Fellow of All Souls.[3] Sir George Young, who joined the Council of the College in 1907 to die as a member of the Council of the University at the age of ninety-two in 1930, had been a Fellow of Trinity. The members

---

[1] The Joint Standing Committee on Research Professorships included the President of the Council, the Vice-Chancellor and the Deputy Vice-Chancellor as *ex officio* members. The Deans of the Faculties were added to the *ex officio* membership of this Committee in 1966, but not to the Committee concerned with Readers and Senior Lecturers. They retained *ex officio* membership when the committees were amalgamated.

[2] See above, pp. 182–3, 187–9.

[3] On Sir Robert Mowbray, Sir George's uncle, see Childs (1933), pp. 190–1.

included a representative of the University of Oxford, who was usually able to play an active part in Reading's affairs. Moreover, the University benefited from the proximity of London and the fact that the counties of Berkshire, Oxfordshire and Hampshire were favourite areas of residence and retirement for men of business, for those involved in public affairs and for senior civil servants. Four of Reading's five Chancellors were drawn from such men; others gave readily of their services on the Council and its committees; two, Sir George Abell and Sir Michael Milne-Watson, served as Presidents. These men mixed easily with senior members of the academic staff in committee and on the Council. It was not an exclusively male club. Mrs Eustace Palmer, Alfred's daughter-in-law and Gerald's mother, served as a member of Council from 1932 to 1958 and following in her steps there were Dr Kathleen Field, Lady Helen Smith, Lady Brunner and Mrs Barbara Sheasby. Dr Field helped in the establishment of the Health Centre. Lady Helen Smith served on the Building Development Committee and on the Finance Committee and Standing Committee among others. Lady Brunner became one of the longest serving Curators of the Library.

This inner group within the Council was used to working with an easy informality. Many of its members knew each other professionally or in business or simply as friends. Within the University they all found that they could turn to the Registrar for advice. Most of them soon acquired a deep respect for the business acumen of the Bursar, E. H. Carpenter.[1] They were busy men. Even so their instinct was always to find out more. Their response to the 'troubles' which affected all universities from 1968 was to suggest that there was insufficient opportunity for them to meet the students.[2] Characteristically, Gerald Palmer, then President of the Council, arranged to entertain the officers of the Students' Union along with members of the Council,[3] and his cousin Gordon volunteered to serve for long hours on the University Joint Committee where the views of the students were advanced with exhaustive advocacy.

The Council was at its most effective and its powers were wielded most directly when the University was relatively small. Initially it used few committees. Of these much the most important was the Finance Committee which for many years exercised detailed surveillance of the running expenses of the University and was regularly authorized to act on behalf of the Council during long vacations. Its minutes record what in retrospect seems like a cottage industry. One random example, of a meeting of the Committee held on 11 March 1949, provides ample illustration. Its recommendations include: a non-recurrent grant of £12 to the Department of Agriculture for experiments at Sonning Farm; the sum of £20 to the

---

[1] Gordon Palmer's comment on Carpenter as a negotiator was – 'I don't believe that the University ever paid a shade over the odds.' (Conversation with The Honourable Gordon Palmer, 11 August 1975).

[2] *Ibid.*

[3] See below, p. 317.

Department of Botany for an additional demonstrator; £25 to the Department of English for four lectures by a visiting lecturer and £15 to the same department for the purchase of slides; £25 to the Department of Geography as an increase in its expedition grant; £41.13s.4d. per term to the School of Art for a part-time lecturer; £45 to the Faculty of Agriculture and Horticulture in connexion with the purchase of a projector for film-strips and slides; and an unspecified provision for an assistant part-time shorthand typist in the Faculty of Science. Much of this concerned minutiae which in later years would have been met from departmental funds. Each separate little problem required a recommendation from the Finance Committee to the Council. One of the marks of the old hands among the professors and the deans was the knowledge of pockets of money, funds tucked away here and there, which might be tapped in an emergency without recourse to the Committee.[1]

By the side of such minutiae the Committee also dealt with salaries, the management of the University's endowments and the financial supervision of its farms and other properties. It delegated some of its business to sub-committees which reported on annual estimates, for example, or on the management of the University farms. It could act with remarkable speed and decisiveness. The purchase of Whiteknights provides one remarkable example.[2] In the case of the Shinfield Grange Estate, which was acquired in 1949, its operations were even quicker. Carpenter first got wind that the estate was coming on the market in the spring. Stenton first reported it to the Finance Committee on 6 May. Carpenter and he had already arranged for the University Grants Committee to provide for part of the purchase price; it was now estimated that the University might have to draw up to £15,000 of its reserves in order to complete the purchase. The estate was due to be auctioned on 26 May. The Finance Committee resolved at once that arrangements should be made to complete the purchase.[3] The agreement to purchase was signed on 17 May. The Council gave approval on 20 May. Far from questioning the constitutional propriety of what had happened the members of Council:

> unanimously approved the action which had been taken on their behalf and congratulated the Vice-Chancellor and the Bursar on the expedition with which the deal had been carried out.[4]

[1] The flavour is preserved by Cyril Tyler: 'The Finance Office consisted of Mr Carpenter, then Finance Officer, his Secretary and Miss Reeves. Miss Reeves had a number of old-fashioned account books and if you wanted to check anything she would turn over the pages and come up with: "Here you are – you have so much money for such and such". If I needed anything extra, I would go to H. A. D. Neville who would go along to Miss Reeves and say: "Of those various funds we have got, is there an amount of £5 in any one of them?" Curiously enough, after Neville went, there was no sign of "those various funds" anywhere.' (Conversation with Professor C. Tyler, 11 March 1971).
[2] See above, pp. 141–5.
[3] Reports of the Finance Committee, 6 May 1949.
[4] Council Minutes, ii, 20 May 1949. See also Doris M. Stenton (1968), pp. 409–10.

The support of the University Grants Committee was not always so ready as it had been in the case of Whiteknights and Shinfield Grange. In the winter of 1963–4 the search for suitable land was resumed. It was felt that Whiteknights would be insufficient to accommodate a University which might grow to 8,000 or more.[1] In the course of discussions on the general possibilities of development of the University's properties in Shinfield, Carpenter characteristically discovered that the owners of Elm Farm, which was much closer than the land in Shinfield to Whiteknights, might be prepared to sell part of their estate. Between January and November 1964 the purchase of nearly 90 acres was settled. This time the procedure was less informal; the purchase was managed by a sub-committee of the Finance Committee, and the Finance Committee's report was approved in a special meeting of the Council before the purchase was completed. It was never-theless speedy: on 24 August the University acquired an option which was due to expire on 30 November; the Finance Committee accepted the report of its sub-committee on 16 November, the Council met on 24 November, and Carpenter went ahead with the purchase on 26 November. Moreover, it was carried through despite the evident reluctance of the University Grants Committee, whose officials were not convinced that the University really needed more land, and who argued that the purchase would only make sense if the old site in London Road were sold. There were also difficulties, some of them quite accidental, over the valuation. In the end the University Grants Committee was unwilling to provide a grant-in-aid and unable to recommend an interest-free loan from public funds. How-ever, from the start of the negotiations those involved were determined to conclude the purchase whether financial support was received or not, and the appropriate contingent measures were accepted and approved by the Council when it authorized the purchase. When the obstacles in the way of support were finally recognized as insuperable, there was no lack of confidence. As Gerald Palmer commented, 'the result was very much as we anticipated, and it is a great thing that we can go ahead on our own'.[2] The cost was £420,000: a measure not only of estimated needs but also of Reading's confidence in its own plans.

Such a system of directing the affairs of the University lasted for nearly forty years from its foundation. It worked. It was highly adaptable in practice. It met new needs by establishing new committees, usually endowed with extensive powers or discretion: hence the Whiteknights Development Committee, the Building Development Committee and the committees established from time to time to consider quinquennial plans or other more urgent proposals for the expansion of the University. It brought the active lay members of the Council and senior members of the

[1] See above, pp. 182–3.
[2] Bursar, Elm Farm. Gerald Palmer's comment is in a letter to the Bursar of 20 January 1965 (*ibid.*). The above paragraph is also based on a conversation with E. H. Carpenter, 19 March 1973.

academic staff together in a working partnership. The eight academic members of the Council included the deans of faculties *ex officio*, and the deans were also members of the Finance Committee. They were in a minority on both bodies, but that caused them no concern. Nor were they disturbed that at crucial stages in the development of the University, in planning, in the execution of plans, in recurrent negotiations with the University Grants Committee, the President of the Council or the Chairman of the Finance Committee, Sir George Mowbray, perhaps, or Gerald Palmer, might play a leading role. Nor was the system ultimately changed as the result of some constitutional conflict. It evolved in response to the increasing size of the University. It was the rapidity and enormity of that increase from 1963 onwards that quickened the pace of evolutionary change.

The development of the academic government of the University was not so smooth. It was more formal, its path more bestrewn with the clutter of principle and precedent. The Council inherited an easy-going and effective system of government from the College. The Senate, though descended from the Academic Board of the College, was born of the Great Row, and, although the Great Row led to the establishment of the pattern of government usual in many British universities, the heat which it had produced set that pattern in a hard, crystalline, form which was worn down and re-shaped only slowly and, at times, by friction. For the Great Row was not simply about the constitution of the University; it was also a dispute between the Principal and some of his professors. The professors won, and the establishment of the Senate set the seal on that victory. Most universities between the wars were governed by what later generations might describe as a professorial oligarchy. At Reading that oligarchy could claim some aristocratic authority through its successful insistence, in the face of a powerful Principal strongly supported even among the academic staff, on the joint responsibility of the members of the Senate for the academic welfare of the University. They had fought not only against sharing that responsibility with laymen but also against concentrating it in the hands of a smaller committee:

> In the Senate the powerful initiative of different minds and wills is bent to the highest purpose of a University – the advancement of learning and research.[1]

The professors as a body inherited the fruits of the victory which a minority of them had won. They ruled as the grandees, with an accepted authority all the stronger because it had been tested.

At first this was unobtrusive. Occasionally there was an echo of the old quarrel: Childs sought to add representatives of the wardens to the membership of the Senate, but that, almost brutally, was rejected.[2]

[1] *An appeal against the Form of Constitution proposed for the University of Reading*, p. 7.
[2] See above, pp. 60–1.

> Occasionally, an observer might detect a faint, distant murmur of unease:
>
> Nowadays we talk a lot about 'communication', but Childs put this
> into practice. He was keen to be on good terms with the younger
> teaching staff who were not professors, and he gave dinners in the
> Senior Common Room to which he invited twenty or thirty of us.
> They were formal affairs and we wore dinner jackets, but after dinner
> we sat round the fire and discussed the policy of the University.
> Childs told us what the University was doing and had been doing
> in previous years, and I got the impression that he was a little tired
> of his colleagues on the Senate and wanted to get his ideas across to
> the younger staff.[1]

However, no-one as yet could conceive of bringing in the junior staff to counteract the senior. No one could doubt that the authority exercised by Stenton, or Cole or Hawkins was other than naturally ordained. It was an extension of their academic achievement, a quality of leadership which was accepted because of the respect, even awe, in which their reputation was held. It was felt that the professor knew best, and usually he did. Those on his coat-tails enjoyed the ride.

To say that the professors ran their departments is in one sense tautological, for a department acquired a natural complexion from the interests and character of the professor. He directed it, or left it much to its own devices, according to his lights, with understanding or impatience, in a concerned or casual manner, more or less efficiently. Any gap he might leave was usually filled by a devoted, long serving, perhaps long suffering, lecturer, who acted as a kind of chief-of-staff. Little record survives of this primitive stage of government.[2] Departments were so small that they required little formal administration. Communication was by word of mouth or written by hand; recourse to a secretary was reserved for occasional matters of importance. What remains, therefore, is largely in the memory of the participants, the junior staff and students. Often it is no more than a memory of the professor's personal quirks and oddities, of Bassett's prowess at an advanced age on a bicycle, perhaps, or of Dewar's colourful language. Often, where it touches on academic matters, on Ure's maniacal devotion to Greek for example, or Guggenheim's galvanic insistence on the advancement of research, it is entirely predictable. Sometimes, perhaps rarely, it may reveal how a department worked from day to day: 'You really ought to do an essay', said Stenton to a returned veteran in 1945, 'Go and see my wife and ask her to set you something on the late Anglo-Saxon period'.[3]

[1] Conversation with E. W. Gilbert (Lecturer in Geography 1926–35 and subsequently Professor of Geography in the University of Oxford 1953–67), 6 November 1970.
[2] When the author joined the Department of History in April 1966, there survived from the reigns of Stenton and Aspinall a book used to record all Finals marks in History from 1928 onwards and one booklet of receipts of recent petty cash expenditure.
[3] Conversation with Dr C. F. Slade.

Such informality was not restricted to departments. Some deans directed their faculties in much the same style, as recalled by R. D. Williams:

> I was Secretary of the Faculty of Letters when Cormack was Dean (1948–54), and I was paid £50 a year for doing the very tiny beginnings of what is now done by the Sub-Dean, two Senior Tutors[1] and all their staff. Dewar had been Dean before Cormack; he managed without a Secretary and was inclined to make out lists on the backs of envelopes. At Student Reception (known as the Bazaar), Dewar would hand out little scraps of paper to the different professors – one scrap might have five names on it and another three. The intake of students was such that they could all be personally welcomed and matriculated in Sibly's room.[2]

Dewar was not alone. Percy Allen remembered something very similar of his registration as a student in the Faculty of Science under Hawkins in 1936:

> My first memory of the University was my first Reception. I went to a table somewhere in the Old Red Building and received a slip of paper. I was then told to go and see the Dean of the Faculty of Science, Professor Hawkins. He was in his room in the Department of Geology, scrubbing a fossil clear of its matrix. 'Hello', he said, 'What can I do for you?' (He was still working on the fossil.) I told him that I had come to be assigned to a Tutor. He took a large piece of foolscap, wrote in pencil at the top 'Mr P. Allen – Zoology, Botany and Geology. Professor Cole'. He folded this over very carefully, tore it off, handed it to me and wrote my name on another piece of foolscap. He then returned to scrubbing his fossil.[3]

This relegation of the chores of administration to their proper and secondary place was the preferred fashion. One or two enjoyed administrative power, like H. A. D. Neville who 'suffered from the appalling disability of being repeatedly elected Dean',[4] but that was to court unpopularity. Ruthlessness was not admired. However, Neville's devotion to administration was excusable. His Faculty of Agriculture was more unitary than the others and had more resources. It required more intensive management. Where he led, others in other faculties would soon have to follow.

The constitution of the University provided the appropriate circumstances for this natural, easy, direction by the professors. They were statutory members of the Senate and the boards of faculties. So were the Lecturer in Education, in the case of Senate,[5] and, in the case of boards of faculties, the readers and lecturers in independent charge of subjects. Thereafter there were on the Senate two elected members of the academic staff and one woman member of staff, chosen by the Senate; and, on faculty

---

[1] Now reduced to one.
[2] Conversation with Professor R. D. Williams, 12 July 1971.
[3] Conversation with Professor P. Allen, 12 November 1969.
[4] Conversation with Professor T. M. Harris, 4 August 1975.
[5] This applied up to the establishment of the Chair in Education in 1934.

boards, a number of co-opted members amounting to one-third of the total of each board. Of all these, only the two non-professorial members of the Senate were elected directly by the academic staff; the rest were chosen by the bodies on which they were to serve. The structure was by no means vibrant with democratic impulses; it was not so designed; no one thought it should be. Representation soon took a settled pattern. Wolters acted as one of the representatives on the Senate from 1931 until his election to the Chair of Psychology in 1943; the other, J. Mackintosh, Lecturer in Dairy Husbandry, served from 1932 to 1944; both men were lecturers in charge of subjects. Mary Bolam was the first 'statutory woman' member of the Senate; when she retired in 1928 she was succeeded by Nellie Eales who continued as a member up to 1942. The boards of faculties co-opted those lecturers of experience and long standing who were the chief departmental assistants to the professors, members of staff who could speak for their departments and subjects if the professor happened to be absent. Here, as in the Senate, resignation or retirement from the University were the main causes of change.

This structure remained almost entirely unaltered until 1957.[1] It was scarcely affected by the gradual growth of the University. In 1927 the Senate numbered twenty-one, in 1957, twenty-eight. Both the Senate and the boards of faculties were small enough to work effectively as deliberative bodies.[2] There was little need for committees or working parties. The power of decision was concentrated to a degree which might seem unjustifiable to later generations of the academic staff, but it was real power expressed in open discussion. Still into the 1960s the Senate met to receive reports from the committees of selection to chairs. It debated them fully, in a mood sometimes far removed from silent acquiescence in a committee's recommendation. It was not until 1967 that such committees were empowered to conclude the appointment.[3] By then the Senate numbered sixty.

[1] The only change came in 1956 when the Librarian was given *ex officio* membership of the Senate.

[2] The numbers on the boards of faculties were as follows:

	1927–8	1956–7
Letters	17	20
Science	12	16
Agriculture	18	15

[3] Committees of selection to chairs were, and are, committees of the Council, comprising, up to 1974, the Vice-Chancellor, the Dean of the Faculty, two members of the Council and two professors of the University elected by the Board of the Faculty. Up to 1967 they embodied a recommendation in a report to the Senate. The Senate could ask to see letters of application and testimonials of any candidates if a third of its members so desired; it could not refer the report of the committee but it was empowered to forward it to the Council with its approval or other expression of opinion. These provisions were not a dead letter. The debate of such reports was open and vigorous. On one occasion at least, the Senate's view led the Council to reject the recommendation of a committee of selection.

Under the new procedures introduced in March 1967 committees of selection were empowered to act on behalf of the Council unless the Council in any particular case expressly directed otherwise.

This system of government was never seriously dislocated. It was managed by an inner group in which at first de Burgh, H. A. D. Neville, Stenton and Dewar were the chief figures, followed after the War by the various deputy vice-chancellors and the deans. Occasionally a rogue professor, such as Edith Morley, might disturb the scene, but at the cost of appearing 'difficult'. The level of salaries was always likely to provoke discussion. Nationally agreed scales were not established until 1947. In earlier years vice-chancellors occasionally exchanged information, and this tended to produce a rough parity between one institution and another.[1] Nevertheless, there was some feeling that Reading was particularly parsimonious. Throughout the 1930s the salary of an assistant lecturer remained at £300; as late as 1944 it was only envisaged that it might go up to £350, with a possible increment of £50 if the assistant lecturership was extended for a fourth year. By then it was felt that the University was lagging badly. In October 1946 a report from the non-professorial staff summed this up:

> From the information received from the Secretary of the Association
> of University Teachers it is evident that no other English university
> or university college offers lower salary scales than does Reading
> and many universities offer considerably higher scales of remunera-
> tion. Thus the salary scale for Grade II Lectureships, which can be
> considered as corresponding to the £400–£600 per annum grade in
> this university reaches £800 per annum in many other universities.
> Also the majority of other universities have stated salary scales for
> Grade I Lectureships usually in the range of £700–£1000 per annum
> but sometimes reaching £1,200.[2]

The last remark was pointed at the informality and uncertainty of the arrangements about increments. Here, too, Reading took its own course, described by Sibly:

> As to increments of salary, I think that our position is quite excep-
> tional. In the first place, we have no system of grading; and no
> scheme of automatic increments, though we aim at the greatest
> possible degree of consistency in practice. Secondly, there is no
> prescribed procedure by which salaries are reviewed and incre-
> ments recommended. I inherited an informal system, ten years
> ago, which I have carried on consistently. In this small University
> it seems to work very well; and as far as I know it has never been
> called in question . . . . Every year the Vice-Chancellor reviews
> all salaries, in consultation with the deans of faculties and also

[1] See for example Sibly to the Secretary, London School of Economics, 29 January 1931; Sibly to the Principal, University College, Hull, 22 October 1931; Sibly to Professor G. H. Thomson, Department of Education, University of Edinburgh, 15 December 1931; Sibly to the Vice-Chancellor, University of Wales, 7 May 1945 (URC, Vice-Chancellor, box 45).
[2] URC, Non-professorial staff, Minutes of general meeting, 30 October 1946.

(as far as he considers it necessary) in consultation with the heads
of departments. His recommendations for increments, agreed with
the deans, are put before the Estimates Committee.[1]

That was the situation in 1940. To Sibly all seemed calm. Earlier there
had been some attempt led by J. H. Sacret, Lecturer in Modern History up
to 1931, to organize a local branch of the Association of University
Teachers, but this became moribund and finally dined itself out of
existence.[2] All that remained from this early effort was an ill defined but
increasingly strong sense of grievance which finally took shape after the
War. It was sufficiently justified for those close to authority to feel defensive about it.[3]

In the end Reading found its own characteristic solution. The first
local branch of the Association of University Teachers failed because it
was concerned largely with salaries and smacked of a trade union. An
organization based more widely on the general interests and concerns of
the lecturing staff had a greater chance of success, and the small scale and
coherence of Reading made it all the easier to establish. These characteristics of the place encouraged all members of staff of whatever status to
interest themselves in the growing academic community. At the same time
the direction of the University's affairs was confined to the Council, the
Officers, the professors, whose authority was entrenched in the Senate, and
other senior staff. Between the academic and social reality, on the one
hand, and the formal constitution, on the other, there was a gap. In
January 1944 that gap was filled by the foundation of an association of
non-professorial staff. The moving spirit was E. S. Budden, Lecturer in
Economics,[4] who was one of the non-professorial representatives on the

[1] Sibly to Ernest Priestley, Vice-Chancellor, University of Birmingham, 2 February 1940
(URC, Vice-Chancellor, box 45).

[2] Conversation with Ernest Smith, 22 September 1969. In fact the Branch did not quite
succeed in this act of self-immolation. It left a balance of £13. 2s. 7d. which came to light
when it was refounded in 1947 (URC, Non-professorial staff, Minutes of general
meeting, 19 November 1947).

[3] Lady Stenton commented in one of the few fragments she left on the history of the
University:

In 1912 my husband became Professor of Modern History at Reading at a salary of
£600. He was a Medievalist, but at this date everything that was not Ancient History
was Modern. I remember when Mrs Ure, who as an undergraduate had been a member
of St Andrew's Hall, became, in 1918, engaged to Professor Ure. She was congratulated
by the Warden of St Andrew's, Miss Bolam, on the extremely high salaries professors
received. Actually they received at that time a flat £600, not because the authorities
did not wish to pay more, but because they could not find the money. It was not there.
The impossibility of paying lecturers anything nearly approaching what today would be
thought of as a living wage for lecturers was absolute. Somewhere about this time a
meeting was held to consider the possibility of starting a branch of the Association of
University Teachers in the hope of improving salaries. I did not join it, as I disliked the
idea of a trade union. I had heard enough discussions between my husband and Childs
to realise that salaries were not kept low by malice or even to provide more capital.
(URC, box 256).

[4] Subsequently Lecturer in Political Economy. See above, pp. 223–4.

Senate. He had joined the University only a year earlier, but there was strong support from older hands. D. R. Maxted, of the Department of Chemistry was the first Chairman, Nellie Eales the first Secretary, and both Edgar Thomas and Paul White were members of the first committee. At a preliminary meeting on 12 January, it was decided 'to hold meetings at intervals to discuss matters connected with the University'. At a second meeting held a week later a constitution was established. That foundation meeting was attended by fifty-six members of the non-professorial staff, roughly two-thirds of the total number.[1] Almost at once they slipped into thinking of themselves not simply as a group defined by status, but also as an organization for the drafting of memoranda to the Vice-Chancellor, the Council and the Senate. Within the year they adopted the shorthand 'NPS'; they subsequently confirmed this instinctive claim to corporate capacity by rejecting the titles of 'association' or 'society' as too restrictive.[2]

From the start they displayed remarkable vigour. They held nine meetings within a year of their foundation.[3] The first concern was for information; in the third meeting on 2 February 1944 it was resolved that 'the Non-professorial staff ask that information regarding the decisions of the Council and the Senate, not of a confidential nature, be communicated to them' and that 'the Non-professorial staff think that they are not sufficiently well informed of the proceedings of the faculty boards affecting them and wish for better means of information and more frequent consultation'. They then turned very quickly to matters arising in the general conduct of the University. Proposals for discussion came in thick and fast; so much so that the Committee kept a card index of them. At the fourth meeting on 1 March, they were already launched on a discussion of facilities for research and of a possible improvement in the tutorial system. The discussion of tutorial arrangements led to separate meetings of the Non-professorial staff in the Faculties of Science and of Agriculture and Horticulture; their reports were accepted by a general meeting and it was then agreed that the conveners of the faculty meetings should discuss them with their respective deans; in the Faculty of Agriculture and Horticulture the report recommended changes in the tutorial role of the professors. In a similar fashion a sub-committee established in November 1944 to investigate central services set about its work by interviewing heads of departments. Hence, within a few months an entirely new element was injected into the structure of the University. It had no formal place in the constitution, but it was confident, experienced, persistent and not to be ignored.

Officialdom smiled bravely on this vigorous offspring. Budden reported

[1] URC, Non-professorial staff, Minutes of general meeting, 19 January 1944.
[2] *Ibid.*, 6 June 1951.
[3] *Ibid.*

to the foundation meeting that the Vice-Chancellor 'welcomed the prospect of combined effort and expression of opinion in the Non-professorial staff'.[1] In some respects the Non-professorial staff served a necessary constitutional function. From 1946 onwards they provided an organization for the representation of the non-professorial staff in the quinquennial visitations of the University Grants Committee. Moreover, from the inception they looked to the Vice-Chancellor for a regular address on the development of the University;[2] this provided a formal setting for talks similar to those which Childs had given years before. But, useful though the new organization might be at times, it was to be kept firmly in its place. Non-professorial members of the Senate gained the impression that they were there to be seen and not heard. The Non-professorial staff's discussion of the general policy of the University was likely to provoke questions as to what it had to do with them.[3] Sibly, in particular, felt that there was a settled constitution of the University which was not to be ignored, still less by-passed or subverted. Hence, when the Non-professorial staff's report on central services was finally presented to him in the winter of 1945–6 it received a bleak welcome:

> The Chairman reported that he had had an interview with the Vice-Chancellor concerning central services. The Vice-Chancellor had informed him that the Finance Committee were considering the establishment of a central workshop and that he was therefore unable to discuss this subject. He considered that the establishment of a photographic service was impracticable, and the engagement of a computer out of the question. He would be prepared to discuss the establishment of a secretarial service with the non-professorial staff in the presence of the Deans, the Registrar and the Finance Officer.[4]

That spelt defeat but not surrender. The Non-professorial staff agreed that no further action could be taken with the University authorities. They nevertheless resolved that the committee responsible for the report should consider 'what action, if any, could be taken by the Non-professorial staff without reference to the University authorities in furtherance of the aims set forth in the committee's report'.[5]

In some matters there was a sharper edge to the exchanges. Until the re-establishment of a local branch of the Association of University Teachers at the end of 1947 the Non-professorial staff took responsibility

[1] *Ibid.*, 19 January 1944.
[2] The first of many addresses of this kind was given by Sibly to the ninth meeting on 29 November 1944. In this he reviewed the proposals of the Post-War Development Committee.
[3] Conversation with Professor C. Tyler, 11 March 1971.
[4] Non-professorial staff, Minutes of general meeting, 27 February 1946. There is no indication that the proposed meeting took place.
[5] *Ibid.*

for the discussion of salaries.[1] They received the minor increases of 1944
without enthusiasm.[2] A motion that a meeting should 'convey to the
Council its appreciation of the recent increases in the salaries of members
of the non-professorial staff' was lost by nine votes to eight with eight
abstentions.[3] Feeling strengthened markedly in the next few years. A
meeting of 30 October 1946 voted unanimously that 'the salaries and
academic status of members of the academic staff of this university
having been unsatisfactory for some time, and having now become even
more unsatisfactory, a special meeting of the Non-professorial staff
should be called in order that something may be done'. That was provoked by an increase in professorial salaries. It led to a comprehensive
review of salaries and status by the Non-professorial staff, to discussions
with the Vice-Chancellor, who was already involved in the Council
in a wholesale revision of the salaries and grading of academic staff,[4] and
to arrangements which, except on some questions of grading, did much to
bring Reading into line with other universities.[5] At times in this the
Non-professorial staff came to look much like a trade union. They were
saved from that by the revival of the local branch of the Association of
University Teachers in 1947 and by their readiness to discuss almost
anything which affected the life and development of the University.
Maxted summed this up in reviewing the achievements of the first six
meetings:

[1] The Non-professorial staff kept the possible re-establishment of a branch of the
Association of University Teachers under review from 1944 onwards and were finally
responsible for bringing it about. The matter was the subject of a report by Dr T. B.
Rymer in September 1944, as a result of which it was decided to encourage attached
individual membership for the time being. When the branch was re-established in 1947
there were eighteen attached members, four of whom were professors. By then Reading
was the only University without a branch (*ibid.*, 4 June, 19 November 1947).
[2] For the increases of 1944 see above, p. 276.
[3] Non-professorial staff, Minutes of general meeting, 6 September 1944.
[4] The initial proposals for salaries for 1946–7 put professorial salaries at £1,450, assistant
lecturers on a range of £350–£400 and lecturers on a scale of £400 × £25 to £850.
These were subsequently revised, on the advice of the UGC, to include a cost-of-living
supplement to all salaries below £1,450. The new scales were: assistant lecturers on a
range £400–£450; grade II lecturers £500 × £25 to £750; grade I lecturers £750 ×
£25 to £850. The proposals were agreed by the Finance Committee, the first on
6 September and the revisions on 18 October. The revised scales were put to Council on
1 November (Council Reports x, 1 November 1946).
  The review by the Non-professorial staff, set on foot on 30 October, is attached to
Minutes of the general meeting of 22 January 1947. It is based on the salary scales
pertaining before the above increases took effect. Except in one matter noted below, the
new scales agreed by the Council coincided closely with the proposals of the
Non-professorial staff (Minutes of committee meeting, 24 January 1947). It is apparent
from the timing of these events that the Council decided on the revised scales
independently of the discussions of the Non-professorial staff.
[5] There was as yet no category of Senior Lecturer. The new salary scales still preserved
arrangements whereby an additional salary (in 1945–7 up to £150) might be paid to
Independent Lecturers in charge of subjects or to Lecturers with other special
responsibilities (*ibid.*).

We had enlightening discussions on such matters as finance, the fourth
term and the School of Music. He was of the opinion that such
discussions were in some ways our most valuable function. It was
interesting to learn that we can disagree. There was evidently room
in the University for meetings of the non-professorial staff as well
as for the Association of University Teachers.[1]

Within a few years that argument could be given a much firmer foundation. In bringing its work to the attention of new members of staff it was
claimed that:

The subjects discussed at meetings of members have ranged from
sabbatical leave to the selection of university students, and matters
in which action has followed discussion include: the tutorial system
in the Faculties of Agriculture and Science; the training of laboratory
assistants; the formation of the local branch of the Association of
University Teachers; the proportion of senior appointments; the
circulation of information about Senate committees and meetings
of faculty boards.[2]

These were material successes. The list reveals the dual role from which
the Non-professorial staff derived much of their strength. They were
concerned at one and the same time with the general affairs of the
University and with their own sectional interests. Sectional concerns
helped to keep general interests alive and ensured that they would always
be more than a mere discussion group.

The Non-professorial staff were largely responsible for the first major
amendment in the constitution of the University. This sprang from the
difficulty of ensuring adequate communication between the governing
bodies and the staff. At first, Sibly considered that more frequent issues
of the *Gazette* might meet the bill, but no satisfactory machinery was
devised either by him or subsequently by Stenton. On the other side it
was far from easy for the Non-professorial staff to define what precisely
they wanted to know. The Minutes of a meeting of 15 November 1950
recorded that:

Dr Paul White speaking particularly of faculty boards, appealed
to members to think of the things they would like to have known –
a feat of mental gymnastics to which apparently no one was equal.[3]

The Committee subsequently collected a number of practical suggestions:
the circulation of minutes of the boards of faculties, departmental meetings
of staff, the posting of abstracts of the minutes of the meetings of the
Senate and of the occasional press releases concerning the business of the

---

[1] Non-professorial staff, Minutes of general meeting, 6 September 1944.
[2] 'History and Function of N.P.S.' loosely inserted in the Minute Book 1960–73, but
belonging to 1951 (Minutes of general meeting, 6 June 1951). A later review of the work
of the Non-professorial staff was circulated in October 1965 (Minute Book 1960–73).
[3] *Ibid.*, 15 November 1950.

Council on the notice board in the lobby of the Senior Common Room.[1] But these proposals were combined with an uneasy sense that such methods had not worked well in the past and none were advanced with any conviction. Meanwhile in the meeting of 15 November Magdalen Vernon of the Department of Psychology had argued for another line of policy: she proposed that 'there should be on the Council a representative of the Non-professorial staff who would be empowered to present their wishes to the Council and to report to the Non-professorial staff on matters directly affecting them'. The proposal was received without enthusiasm. It was felt that representation on the Senate had served no useful purpose and that representation on the Council would prove equally valueless. Nevertheless it marked a turning point. In 1952 the Chairman reported on the representation on Council in other universities;[2] and in 1955 the matter was raised in the meeting of the Non-professorial staff with the University Grants Committee.[3] Feelings were apparently less strong at Reading than at other universities.[4] Nevertheless the Council asked the Vice-Chancellor to open discussions with the Non-professorial staff,[5] who in March 1956 submitted formal proposals for the increase of the representation on the Senate from two to six and for the increase of the representation on the boards of faculties from a third to a half, the additional members to be elected by the whole faculty. The case was indefeasible; it was substantiated by simple figures of the increase in the number of lecturers since the original constitution of the University in 1926.[6] The increase

[1] *Ibid.*, 31 January 1951.
[2] *Ibid.*, 4 June 1952. The report stated that Birmingham had one non-professorial member in a Council of 35, Leeds two in a Council of 47, Manchester two members appointed by faculty boards in a Council of 26, and Durham, like Reading, none. Reading was roughly on a par with Birmingham and Leeds in non-professorial membership of Senate.
[3] 'Dr Prue said that in the view of many it was now desirable within the framework of the modern university to permit more academic responsibility at the sub-professorial level, and to provide greater opportunities for participation in discussing, formulating and deciding academic policy. At this University, for instance, there was no non-professorial representation on the Council, two representative members on the Senate, and a 15 per cent representation on faculty boards which tended to be unchanging.' (Report of the Representatives of the non-professorial staff on their meeting with the UGC, 24 October 1955, *ibid.*, 30 November 1955).
[4] 'Notes of meeting between the University Grants Committee and the Council, Tuesday, 25 October 1955' (Council Reports, xvi, 11 November 1955).
[5] Council Minutes, iii, minute 1709, 11 November 1955.
[6] The proposals and accompanying memorandum are attached to Non-professorial staff, Minutes of general meeting, 1 March 1956. The memorandum stated that there were 123 lecturers as against 44 in 1926. It demonstrated that this increase in numbers had not been accompanied by any significant increase in representation. Indeed representation on the Senate had remained unchanged, and representation on the Board of the Faculty of Agriculture had fallen from 7 to 5 while the number of lecturers had increased from 10 to 46. No case was made for increased representation on the Council. In the Council meeting of 11 November 1955, Gerald Palmer had pointed out that each Board of Faculty elected a representative on the Council quite apart from the Dean (Council Reports, xvi).

was accepted by the University and came into force in 1957.[1] Nevertheless, the Non-professorial staff did not have it all their own way. Elected
members could not easily act in the quasi-delegatory role which Magdalen
Vernon envisaged in 1950. The Non-professorial staff had always accepted
without demur that members of the Senate could not report on confidential matters. They had no representation on the Senate through their
officers. The elected members were independent individuals not agents,[2]
and it was only rarely that the Non-professorial staff discussed the
nomination of candidates.[3] Nevertheless, the concerns and proposals
which they advanced up to 1956 all turned on the assumption that elected
members of official bodies were representatives of the non-professorial
staff.[4] That assumption was never explored;[5] since the non-professorial
members of the Senate were elected by the academic staff who were not
members *ex officio* it no doubt seemed natural enough. There can be little
doubt either that the Non-professorial staff envisaged a similar system
when they asked that the additional members of the boards of faculties,
proposed in 1956, should be elected by the whole faculty. But the Senate
took this literally. It recommended that all members of the academic
staff, including professors, should participate in the elections to boards
of faculties. Not only that, it extended the principle to the Senate and
confirmed its committee's proposal that 'all members of the Senate
(instead of as at present, only the two elected members) be entitled to
participate in the election of the six members'.[6] That dryly humorous
provision was of great importance. It provided a solid constitutional
obstacle to any attempt to use the elected members as agents or reporters
of the Non-professorial staff. Henceforth elected members of governing
bodies represented all the staff; on occasions, when the more combative

[1] The proposals were amended by the Senate in one respect: the provision for a
'statutory' woman member of the Senate was abandoned in view of the increase of
elected members to six and 'of the fact that the reasons which appear to have prompted
this arrangement no longer apply' (Senate Reports, xiii, 15 October 1956).
[2] On 31 January 1951, in a discussion of Magdalen Vernon's proposal, several members
'questioned the usefulness of such a seat [on the Council] observing that representatives
on the Senate served no apparent purpose to N.P.S., a point which Dr Paul White, a
present member of the Senate, readily conceded. He considered that being on the
Senate was a useful part of University education for the person concerned.'
(Non-professorial staff, Minutes of general meeting, 31 January 1951).
[3] 'The Secretary reported that he had received a note from Dr Budden informing him
that he was due to retire from the Senate. It was agreed that the Committee should take
any action necessary to ensure that at least one candidate was nominated.' (*ibid.*,
7 November 1945).
[4] For example 'The Chairman replied that the Registrar had confirmed that a change of
the Statutes would be required to permit representation of the non-professorial staff on
the Council' (*ibid.*, 4 June 1952); 'The Chairman explained the reason for calling this
extraordinary meeting. At N.P.S. meetings in recent years there had been frequent
discussion of the question of Non-professorial representation on official bodies ...' (*ibid.*,
1 March 1956).
[5] That is as regards the official records of the general and committee meetings.
[6] Senate Reports, xiii, 15 October 1956.

of them spoke of the University as if it were a family divided, they were pointedly reminded of this principle. In 1957 that was in the future. At the time the change went through unchallenged.[1]

These changes came about without a confrontation. Indeed, even in advancing the constitutional proposals of 1956 great care was taken to avoid treading on tender professorial toes.[2] Moreover they represent but one of the many interests of the Non-professorial staff. In these same years they held a prolonged discussions on the function of the tutorial system, the need for disciplinary regulations, and the role of the halls of residence; the discussions came to include the Vice-Chancellor, the deans and the wardens of Halls.[3] On these and many other matters there was no sense or appearance of two opposed camps. Equally on the side of the professors there were some who were ready listeners if not sympathisers. Cormack, Thomas and Tyler had all been founder-members of the Non-professorial staff. In 1956 Magdalen Vernon, who was still one of the strongest advocates of the dissemination of information about the business of the Senate, joined them as Professor of Psychology. Some of the new professors coming to Reading from elsewhere brought in a wider experience and sought to broaden the enclosed community which they now encountered. Within little more than a year of his arrival in 1963, F. P. Pickering addressed the Non-professorial staff on the position and work of a similar association at Sheffield.[4] He also wanted to see more scope for younger members of staff on the Board of the Faculty of Letters, where long established members were regularly re-elected by open vote; Pickering persuaded the board to ballot and in 1955 the old guard had to make way for younger men.[5] New voices were also heard more frequently

[1] The Committee of the Non-professorial staff took the view that the Senate's scheme was only a 'slight modification' of their original proposal (Minutes, 12 November 1956). In reporting the Senate's recommendations, the Chairman, A. E. Wardman, 'emphasized that people elected would not be non-professorial staff delegates but would be elected by the whole of the teaching staff of the relevant part of the University because the University thought it a good thing that they should be there' (Minutes of general meeting, 5 December 1956). The matter was not apparently debated. In the Senate the whole scheme was carried unanimously except for the provision defining the electorate for the boards of faculties; that was approved *nem. con.* (Senate Minutes, iii, 1 November 1956).
[2] 'During the discussion which followed, the view was expressed that the resolution was too sharp and definite in its proposals. The Chairman pointed out that the Non-professorial staff had been asked to submit definite proposals and that there was little point in forwarding an entirely vague request. As a result of discussion, the wording of the second sentence of the resolution: namely 'It is further suggested that these changes should be along the following lines', was changed to 'These changes might be along the following lines.' (Non-professorial staff, Minutes of general meeting, 1 March 1956).
[3] *Ibid.*, 18 March 1953 to 2 December 1959 *passim*.
[4] *Ibid.*, 1 December 1954.
[5] Conversation with Professor F. P. Pickering, 13 August 1975. An unfortunate consequence of the renovation of the encrusted condition of the Board was that the old guard consisted of members of the distinction of Lady Stenton and Jean Young.

and more tellingly among the Non-professorial staff: J. E. Prue, M. L. McGlashan, E. W. J. Mitchell, A. E. Wardman. Gradually a mutual respect was established so that it became more and more difficult even for the hidebound to regard the Non-professorial staff as 'a slight on the Senate'.[1]

However, there were still some sore points. Despite the re-establishment of the local branch of the Association of University Teachers, the Non-professorial staff continued to maintain an interest in the University's policy on senior appointments. There were complaints at the dilatoriness of the University when it finally came to establish senior lecturerships and readerships,[2] and arguments that the proportion of such appointments at Reading was comparatively very low.[3] On this some of the professors also were pressing for a more liberal policy. Sometimes the Non-professorial staff did no more than urge the University along a path which it had already begun to tread.[4] But it moved very cautiously and the Non-professorial staff returned to the matter repeatedly: in the visitation of the University Grants Committee in 1960,[5] and in discussions with the Vice-Chancellor in 1961 and 1963.[6] By 1963 the ratio of senior to junior appointments was 2:10.7 compared with the ratio of 2:7 suggested by the University Grants Committee.[7] Much of the case was met in 1964 when readerships were conferred on four and senior lecturerships on eighteen

---

[1] The phrase is Paul White's reporting the views of 'some older members of the University.' (Non-professorial staff, Minutes of general meeting, 31 January 1951).
[2] *Ibid.*, 14 February, 6 June 1951.
[3] 'In this University many lecturers have little chance of rising above the top of the lecturer scale, since the percentage of non-professorial staff in the senior lecturer or reader grades is very low (5 per cent) compared with many other universities, where it often reaches the figure of 20 per cent recommended in the 1948 Report of your Committee.' (Meeting with the UGC, 24 October 1955: Memorandum from the Non-professorial staff, *ibid.*, 30 November 1955).
[4] Senior lecturerships were first established in 1951. The Senate accepted the initial proposal for five such promotions with the recommendation that further names be added to the list. Ultimately nine promotions were made (Senate Minutes, iii, minute 2203, 26 February 1951; Senate Reports, x, 26 February 1951; Council Reports, xiii, 6 July 1951; Council Minutes, ii, minute 1465, 6 July 1951). The delay arising from increasing the number provoked the debate in the Non-professorial staff.
It was not until 1955 that the University agreed to confer the personal title of reader (Senate Reports, xii, 2 May 1955; Senate Minutes, iii, minute 2630, 2 May 1955; Council Minutes, ii, minute 1692, 20 May 1955). Four readers were appointed in 1956: Dr Vera Fretter, Lady Stenton, Magdalen Vernon and Jean Young; of these Magdalen Vernon became a professor in the same year. In accepting these recommendations the Senate pressed for greater financial provision for readers and senior lecturers during the next Quinquennium (minute 2696).
Pickering, Guggenheim and others came to argue that the University was excessively stringent in conferring the title of reader. It is noteworthy that in 1956 Lady Stenton was already a Fellow of the British Academy. However, no further readers were appointed until 1960, when two more were added.
[5] Non-professorial staff, Minutes of general meeting, 9 November 1960.
[6] Senate Reports, xxi, 14 October 1963.
[7] *Ibid.*

members of staff.[1] Nevertheless, the proportion of senior appointments
remained a matter for almost perennial discussion. Moreover, the procedures, which placed responsibility for proposing a promotion on the
Head of Department, now came under attack. As early as 1960 there were
suggestions that lecturers might advance their own case for promotion,
or that the case of lecturers of some standing should be automatically
reviewed. In this the Non-professorial staff were moved, as Wolfenden
put it in 1963, 'by the suspicion that some of their colleagues are at a
disadvantage compared with others'.[2] The plain fact was that professors too were human beings and therefore varied in their readiness to
submit proposals for what was becoming an annual round of promotions.
But the procedures were changed only slowly and with reluctance; it was
not until 1974 that a member of staff was permitted to make his own case.
The change was less important in its outcome than it had been in its
origins. Promotions were the issue on which the authority of the Professor
was first and most persistently grudged and questioned.

In different ways all these changes reflected or were a response to the
slowly increasing size of the University. It was this which lay behind the
case for senior appointments, behind the problem of communication and
dissemination of information, behind the desire of junior staff to play a
larger role, and behind the recurrent discussions of tutorial arrangements
or the function of the halls of residence. The constitutional changes of
1957 were a marginal adaptation to this gradual growth, and if the growth
had remained gradual the University could well have continued in this
vein, stretching the framework a little here and there as occasion demanded, without committing itself to any major change in structure. In
fact the Robbins Report imposed conditions which demanded more
urgent and fundamental action. Within the decade following the publication of the Report in 1963 the government of the University underwent a
revolution, on the whole a quiet revolution, so quiet that some of the most
important changes were achieved without any amendment to Statutes or
Ordinances, but one which here and there was not so quiet. A university
which succeeded in avoiding clamour and controversy in this decade
would have been a backwater. Reading was not the centre of the greatest
clamour; it saw no virtue in clamour as such; but it was no backwater.

The change was immediately apparent in the methods used to meet the
accelerated rate of expansion. Hitherto, quinquennial plans had been
prepared by special committees which received recommendations and
memoranda from boards of faculties and heads of departments. Now
working parties were established for subject-groups, and it was on their
reports that the expansion of the next decade was based.[3] The working

[1] Senate Reports, xxiii, 4 May 1964.
[2] Senate Reports, xxi, 14 October 1963.
[3] Senate Minutes, iv, 3731(b), 14 October 1963. See also above p. 223.

parties brought in a broader sweep of opinion.[1] They were empowered to 'take advice inside or outside the University wherever necessary'.[2] Members of the academic staff were encouraged to submit suggestions through deans of faculties. Several such submissions were made and were ultimately included in the list of possible developments;[3] one led to the establishment of an additional working party from whose proposals the Department of Applied Statistics ultimately emerged.[4] There was also much informal discussion. In retrospect it seemed that the University had emerged into a more open world in which general discussion had become not just a permitted luxury, but a practical necessity;[5] the wider the debate, the broader the range of 'offerings' available to meet the projected targets.[6] Moreover, at the time, it was soon appreciated that expansion would entail administrative change. Two of the reports of the working parties called for a review of part or the whole of the University's organization.[7] The natural reaction initially was to provide more of the same, to meet the new urgencies by extending the existing system of committees. The Building Development Committee at once established a Special Steering Committee to deal with the emergency expansion.[8] A Development Policy Committee was set up to co-ordinate all aspects of expansion. A committee of both the Council and the Senate, it provided yet another example of that close integration of academic staff and lay members of the

[1] The working parties were:
    a. *Social Sciences*, Professors Campbell, Vernon, Thomas, Lehmann and Dobinson.
    b. *Biological Sciences*, Professors Graham, Harris and Knight.
    c. *Physical Sciences*, Professors Ditchburn, Mitchell and Rado, and Dr J. E. Prue.
    d. *Earth Sciences*, Professors Allen, Ditchburn and Miller.
    e. *Other arts subjects*, Professors Cormack and Lehmann and Dr C. F. Slade.
Of these neither Prue nor Slade were members of the Senate; Slade was not a member of the Board of the Faculty of Letters. For a further working party see n. 4 below.
[2] Senate Minutes, iv, 3731 (b), 14 October 1963.
[3] C. F. Slade was responsible for a proposal for Archaeology; K. R. Gladdish and E. A. Smith both advocated American Studies (Senate Reports, xxii, 20 November 1963).
[4] A working party on Statistics/Biometry was established on 19 December 1963, comprising R. N. Curnow, who had submitted a proposal, Ditchburn, Tuck, Tyler and Paul White (Senate Minutes, iv, 3759). Of these Curnow, Tuck and White were not members of the Senate; Curnow was an elected member of the Board of the Faculty of Agriculture.
[5] Conversation with Professor E. W. J. Mitchell, 22 July 1975.
[6] The proposals mentioned in notes 3 and 4 above were discussed formally by the working parties or included in their final reports. There was also much informal talk about proposals which, at this stage, got no more than a bare mention, especially Medicine, Veterinary Science and Regional Studies.
[7] The working party on Biological Sciences asked for a review of the organization of departments and faculties where subjects overlapped. The working party on Physical Sciences asked for 'a complete review of organization within the University so as to consider alternatives to the present structure of faculties, courses, teaching arrangements, laboratory usage and financial arrangements.' (Senate Reports, xxii, 20 November 1963).
[8] Senate Reports, xxii, 19 December 1963. The new committee comprised the existing Central Steering Committee of the Building Development Committee with the addition of a representative of the Faculty of Agriculture, a warden and a lay member.

Council on which Reading had relied for so long.[1] It proved to be a piece of makeshift patchwork, soon rendered unnecessary by other changes.

In the summer of 1963 Wolfenden left to become Chairman of the University Grants Committee. His successor, H. R. Pitt, could not take up office until the spring of 1964. Cormack was Acting Vice-Chancellor during an interval which coincided exactly with the planning for the emergency expansion. Endowed with less authority than a permanent Vice-Chancellor, and less certain in his touch than Wolfenden, he resorted at once to more open methods. This contributed to the wide scope given to the working parties and also to another, even more important, change in the pattern of government. When the working parties were established in October 1963 the Deans were required to report on the possible expansion of existing courses and, with the Acting Vice-Chancellor, to co-ordinate the reports of the various working parties. In November they submitted a general survey not only of student numbers and the various 'offerings' of the working parties, but also of building requirements and other capital expenditure. They had in effect acted as a central planning and co-ordinating committee.[2]

Their work was soon extended further into one of the arcana of the University's government – annual estimates. These were always considered first in the Estimates Committee,[3] where, as part of an annual ritual, Sir George Mowbray would prise out of Carpenter the sums of money 'hidden' as his financial 'cushions' in the overall figures, and Wolfenden would press for as large an allocation as possible for academic purposes. The division of this allocation, once the revised figures were agreed, was by tradition the job of the Vice-Chancellor. Here Wolfenden seemed to some to be at his most headmasterly; estimates were a matter of confidence for private discussion between him and each head of department. He might discuss particular items with an individual dean or the Bursar or perhaps one of the lay officers, but the proposals for academic expenditure laid before the final meeting of the Estimates Committee were essentially his responsibility. The procedure had altered little since the days of Sibly and Childs. To a head of department it was something of a mystery, more or less understood, a kind of lucky dip in which fortunes varied, more or less explicably. Some indeed, liked to feel that they were dealing with one man who seemed to have, and to a considerable degree

[1] 'Development Policy: Planning, Procedures, Co-ordination'. The paper was authorized by Sir George Mowbray and Cormack. The new committee comprised, from the lay members, the President and Vice-President of the Council, the Treasurer, the Chairman of the Finance Committee and the Chairman of the Building Development Committee, and from the academic staff, the Vice-Chancellor, Deputy Vice-Chancellor and the deans of faculties (Senate Reports, xxii, 20 January 1964).
[2] Senate Reports, xxii, 20 November 1963.
[3] The Estimates Committee comprised the President, the Treasurer, and the Vice-Chancellor with the Registrar and Bursar in attendance. It reported to the Finance Committee.

did have, the power to decide.[1] Some seemed to gain advantage; developments took place which might not have received priority if they had been openly debated.[2] It was soon apparent that Cormack had neither the will nor the confidence to continue these methods. With Sir George Mowbray's approval he took the Deans into consultation.[3] This was the first step in a process which transferred the consideration of Estimates to the Committee of Deans. It was the preliminary to an administrative reformation. Up to 1963 the Committee of Deans was still concerned with little more than the application of regulations concerning degrees and examinations. By 1966 it had become responsible for the planning, co-ordination and financing of the general development of the University. This was achieved without any major amendment to the constitution; indeed, the new powers of the Committee were never defined in Ordinances. Existing forms were met by requiring the Committee simply to recommend to the appropriate constitutional authority: to the Council or to one of its committees or to the Senate. But the power to initiate was enough.

If this was begun by Cormack it was completed by the new Vice-Chancellor, H. R. Pitt. Pitt came to Reading from the Chair of Pure Mathematics at Nottingham. His arrival was marked by an act, small enough in itself, which at Reading was revolutionary, almost sacrilegious, in its implications. To his great delight, Ronald Tuck, then Senior Steward of the Common Room, was requested by the new Vice-Chancellor to remove the Vice-Chancellor's chair from the dining room.[4] Childs's throne, to which Sibly, Stenton and Wolfenden had in turn succeeded, was jettisoned. That was symbolic. Pitt's authority was to be without artificial aids. He deliberately set out to be a *primus inter pares*. Wolfenden consulted and then decided, or so it seemed to observers. Pitt would encourage and restrain; he could lay down the constraints and limitations, whether moral, academic or financial, with great firmness; but he sought a consensus, a genuine communal decision, in the first instance from senior academic staff. Those who still wished to be led or directed found the new regime mild and apparently formless. In fact it re-fashioned the University as a self-governing community.

The ground was well prepared. By the summer of 1963 the possible administrative consequences of rapid expansion could be foreseen.

[1] Conversation with D. T. Richnell, Librarian, 1966.
[2] The establishment of Italian under the wing of the English Department was achieved in this way. The example illustrates the advantages of the method. However, it may not have been the only way to do it, and the apparent advantage which had been gained for Italian left some discontent in other departments.
[3] The paper on Development Policy (p. 288, n. 1 above) commented: 'It is not the purpose of this paper to discuss the Estimates Committee's procedures: but they are likely to be modified, e.g. the Vice-Chancellor may well consult the Deans before advising the Committee on the importance and degree of priority of proposals for developments'. Cormack took full advantage of this.
[4] Conversation with Professor R. H. Tuck, 20 September 1971.

Quite apart from that, there was considerable concern among heads
of departments that the existing structure allowed the Finance Committee
to make decisions which were essentially academic. In the Long Vacation
of that year the Registrar composed a lengthy review of his own of the
government of the University in which he suggested a possible plan of
reform. The paper was seen by Wolfenden and Sir George Mowbray,
but was shelved on Wolfenden's retirement to await a new vice-chancellor.
Hence when Pitt arrived a scheme of reform lay to hand. Moreover, one of
its essential features, the Committee of Deans, was already coming to play
a new role simply because more and more business was referred to it. In
the course of 1965 it became in effect a general standing committee of the
Senate, responsible not only for miscellaneous matters on which the
Senate required it to report, but also for the continuing review of the plans
for expansion; it was superseding the Development Policy Committee
established in 1963 and was already acquiring functions exercised
hitherto by the Building Development Committee. In 1966 the Committee advanced its own proposals for reform which were based directly
on the Registrar's paper of 1963. After a bland announcement that it had
'taken upon itself to consider the pattern of the University's administration' it pointed out that:

> The University is functioning to a scheme of government that
> basically has not been changed for some forty years. The system
> now in operation, which has developed from the basic scheme by
> the accretion of both procedures and habits, needs to be overhauled
> and simplified if the University is not to be in danger of operating at
> a very low degree of efficiency. . . .
>
> Various intermediate bodies and sub-committees have been welded
> into the original simple 'chain of command' represented by Faculty
> Board – Senate – Council and by Finance Committee – Council,
> with two outstanding consequences. First, the principal bodies rely
> greatly on the advice of the intermediate groups; second, the time-lag
> between the first consideration of any matter and the final decision
> can be irritatingly and sometimes disadvantageously long.[1]

The Committee went on to propose that it should now be established as a
'central co-ordinating committee' with the powers of preparing and
reviewing the development plans for submission to the Senate and the
Council; of preparing, with the Estimates Committee, the quinquennial
estimates; of advising the Estimates Committee on annual estimates; of
preparing and reviewing the building programme for submission to the
Senate and the Council; and of dealing with such matters as the Senate
and the Council might refer to it; although it was to have no executive
power it was nevertheless 'to act at its discretion, whether officially or
unofficially'. Finally, it proceeded to exercise the powers it envisaged by

[1] 'Administration of the University' (Senate Reports, xxvii, 2 May 1966).

proposing administrative reforms, again derived from the Registrar's paper, affecting the Senate, boards of faculties and departments. Without any apparent qualm it noted that the Development Policy Committee should be abolished and that some of the functions of the Building Development Committee would be affected.[1]

The scheme was not accepted without objections and reservations. The Senate approved it on 2 May,[2] and then some members had second thoughts. One group returned to the next meeting of 13 June with the proposal that the 'co-ordinating committee' should be enlarged by the addition of two or three members elected by the Senate.[3] Guggenheim, now in his final term, had one last characteristic fling:

> Any or all of the three deans are of course entitled as members of the
> Senate to put forward any proposals they like, but they have no
> right to describe these proposals as coming from the Committee of
> Deans unless the proposals are within the terms of reference of this
> Committee, which so far as I can find out they are not. The proposal
> purporting to come from the Committee of three Deans should
> therefore have been ruled out of order.[4]

To no avail. After further discussion the Senate confirmed its earlier decision by an overwhelming majority.[5] Doubt had centred on the representative capacity of the Deans,[6] but, as the Vice-Chancellor indicated, that was not the point:

> In his opinion the proposed 'central co-ordinating committee' . . .
> could not be increased in size in the way proposed without detriment
> to its operation. It was a small group which could discuss matters of
> University policy frankly and on an equal basis, and was not intended
> to represent separate interests within the University. Indeed, in his
> opinion this was something to be avoided.[7]

The objective was not representation, but the involvement of the deans, the only members of the academic staff after the Vice-Chancellor and the Deputy Vice-Chancellor who had all the essential information at their fingertips, in the common endeavour of running the University.

The Council also had reservations, but of a very different kind. It was obvious that the scheme would alter, perhaps even undermine, Reading's traditional association of academic staff and lay members of the Council.

---

[1] *Ibid.*

[2] Senate Minutes, iv, 4139, 2 May 1966.

[3] Letter of Professor B. C. J. G. Knight and others (Senate Reports, xxviii, 13 June 1966).

[4] *Ibid.* Guggenheim went on to propose that the co-ordinating committee should be composed of ex-Deans.

[5] The figures were 22 in favour, 2 against.

[6] 'We feel very strongly that a committee of five is too small to represent adequately the interests of an organism so complex and diverse as a growing university containing more than thirty departments and with student numbers likely to increase so greatly.' (Letter of B. C. J. G. Knight and others, n. 3 above).

[7] Senate Minutes, iv, 4173(a), 13 June 1966.

A small committee appointed by the Council to examine the proposals, commented that:

> it would be unfortunate if there were not participation by lay
> members in the preparation and review of the development plan
> before it is submitted to both Senate and Council, especially as
> ultimately it is the Council which must approve the plan and its
> various revisions.[1]

It proposed amendments aimed at maintaining the function of both the Estimates Committee and the Building Development Committee,[2] and it was in that form that the scheme was formally confirmed in the autumn of 1966. Nevertheless it proved impossible and indeed unnecessary to shore up every buttress of the old system. Very quickly the Committee of Deans made some other committees redundant. In 1968, the Estimates Committee and the Building Development Committee were both abolished, and the Finance Committee was superseded by a Standing Committee of the Council. It was to this body of which the deans were *ex officio* members, that the Committee of Deans became responsible in all matters concerning development and estimates.[3] Out of the reservations expressed by the Council in 1966 there emerged a much simpler, more efficient system of central control. The Committee of Deans proposed academic expenditure; the Standing Committee approved it on behalf of the Council.[4]

The Committee of Deans soon proved itself. Its function in preparing estimates was crucial. In this it became to the Council the chief source of information about academic objectives and requirements, and to the academic staff the chief source of supply. Hence it occupied the strategic ground previously dominated by Wolfenden. Even a direct appeal to the Vice-Chancellor was now likely to lead simply to a discussion in the Committee. Some of the consequences of its new functions were not at once apparent. It proved to be representative in a far more subtle manner than was envisaged in 1966. The Deputy Vice-Chancellor was elected by the Senate;[5] each dean by the board of his faculty. Hence there was some political control of the administrative action of the Committee. Within the Committee no dean could use an argument which, *mutatis mutandis*, he was

[1] Council Reports, xxviii, 1 July 1966. The Committee consisted of the President, Sir George Mowbray, the Vice-President, Gerald Palmer, and the Treasurer, C. Fitzherbert, along with the Vice-Chancellor and the Deputy Vice-Chancellor, Professor A. Graham.
[2] Senate Reports, xxvii, 2 May 1966; Council Reports, xxviii, 1 July 1966.
[3] Council Reports, xxiii, 6 December 1968; Council Minutes, iv, 2811, 6 December 1968.
[4] Not all expenditure went through the Committee of Deans. The accounts of the halls of residence and the University farms went direct to the Standing Committee for submission to the Council. The Standing Committee also continued to deal immediately with endowments and property, as the Finance Committee had previously done. It became usual for the Committee of Deans to seek the approval of the Treasurer for urgent items which could not wait on the next meeting of the Standing Committee.
[5] The Senate embodied the result of the election in a recommendation to the Council which made the formal appointment.

not prepared to allow to another dean. Moreover, any dean could speak on estimates or any other matter with the whole weight of his faculty's opinion behind him. There was another unintended but important effect. The Registrar and the Bursar were joint secretaries of the new committee.[1] It took some time before the Bursar brought himself to submit his own departmental estimates to the eagle eye of the Committee, but that was a detailed and temporary difficulty which was far outweighed by the academic backing which the Committee now gave to both the administrative officers. Moreover, the Registrar and Bursar were regularly brought into prolonged business meetings with senior academic staff; they understood each other the better and respected each other the more; in this crucial work of co-ordination academic staff and 'Admin.' were not to be divided.

Inevitably opinion of the Committee of Deans was mixed. One founder-member waxed enthusiastic:

It had the function of an escapement of a watch; a beautiful device
with no constitutional authority or status, but very effective.[2]

However, to an anxious professor seeking to maintain the resources of his department 'no' was still negative, whether it came as before from the Vice-Chancellor, or as now from the Committee of Deans; indeed, a negative coming from the considered judgment of academic peers might be more wounding since it seemed less arbitrary. However, in the late 1960s the Committee had few occasions for saying 'no', and even a negative often meant no more than the postponement of a treasured scheme until the next year or the year after. Hence the Committee enjoyed the advantage of a period of expansion. Within less than a decade it was established in a position of immense strength.

The effects were important. British universities reacted to the financial stringency imposed on them in 1974 in various ways. Some resorted to an overall percentage cut on all spending departments. Others put a moratorium on all new appointments. Others again extended the embargo to replacements, or at least subjected them to a severe review. Many universities constituted new committees to wield the axe. Some simply devolved the detailed control of expenditure on faculties. At Reading the burden was quietly assumed by the Committee of Deans,[3] and that Committee, far from resorting to the easy formulae of percentage cuts or the brutal remedies of surgical embargoes, attempted one of the most difficult of all financial exercises, the readjustment of resources in a period of retrenchment. Guided by a sophisticated calculation of unit-costs,

[1] The Registrar was responsible for agenda, minutes and the general running of the committee. The Bursar was responsible for the financial business transacted. In 1973 the Registrar became sole secretary of both the Deans' and the Standing Committees.
[2] Conversation with Professor A. H. Bunting, 14 August 1975.
[3] The Committee worked under a general instruction from the Standing Committee of the Council, in which the Deans concurred, that it was not to budget for a deficit.

which was the brain-child of the Deputy Vice-Chancellor, Cyril Tyler, it proceeded to review all commitments and expenditure, from books to telephones, paint to grass-seed, and to examine all proposals for appointments and renewals of appointments, whether of academic, administrative, technical, secretarial or maintenance staff. The Committee said 'yes' to some and 'no' to others. It attempted and achieved some readjustment in departmental and equipment votes. In a period of the strictest economy it was even able to provide resources for some new developments.[1] The information on unit costs, on which the policy was based, was distributed to all departments. Much restricted or obscure information on staff-student ratios, departmental and equipment votes, secretarial provision and library grants, was at last revealed. Comparisons necessarily followed, some guarded and public, many more vehement and private. The results were beneficial. All this was a measure of the strength of the new structure, for a selective policy of this kind was harder to explain and harder to bear than simple curtailment in which all suffered at one and the same time. All this was expounded to a general meeting of all the academic staff in 1974. As economies bit deeper in 1975 heads of departments were called together in a special meeting. There were pleas for more regular sessions of this kind, and from a few departments there came a renewed cry for the addition of representatives to the Committee of Deans. One hard-pressed professor was driven to complain that he was responsible, not to the Committee of Deans, but to the University Council, but that stemmed from dire stress induced by that most terrible of all economies, the truncation of the telephone system. None of this had more than a passing effect on the role of the Committee. The Vice-Chancellor and the Deans stuck to the arguments which had buttressed the original constitution of the Committee in 1966,[2] and the Committee survived with its powers unimpaired and its real role enlarged. It was hard work for the Deans.[3] Quite apart from the intensive exercise in economy, the system designed in 1966 required them to see the same business through a series of different meetings.[4] The tedium was relieved by the capacity of even the most simple and apparently harmless item suddenly to behave like a jumping cracker.

The Committee of Deans survived and flourished partly because it proved to be an effective and flexible means of directing the affairs of the University. However, its new role marked an avowed transfer of responsi-

[1] The Departments of Law, Typography & Graphic Communication, Russian and Archaeology were all established in this period. Final approval was also given to the establishment of the Chairs of Accountancy and of Planning. See above, pp. 208–9.
[2] See above, p. 291.
[3] The Deans and the Deputy Vice-Chancellor were provided with some relief. It was agreed in 1966 that they should be supported by a temporary assistant lecturer or the equivalent.
[4] The Committee of Deans itself, the Standing Committee of the Council, the Steering Committee of the Senate, the Senate and finally, the Council.

bility to the academic staff: to the small group of Deans in person and in a very precise fashion, but also to the members of the faculties they represented in a much wider manner. Here, too, there were precise commitments for under the new arrangements faculties were made responsible for devising their own development programmes and for advising their deans on estimates;[1] but there was also a less easily defined relationship. The Dean was the elected officer of his Faculty. He could be questioned, he could be asked for support, he was expected to do his best for his constituents. It may be doubted whether a small co-ordinating committee of the kind devised in 1966 could have withstood all the strains to which it was subjected if its members had not exercised this representative function. Moreover, in 1966 the Deans saw their new role as but one feature in a scheme in which responsibilities came to be devolved and an attempt made to involve more of the academic staff more immediately in the development of the University. They noted the 'ever-present difficulty of satisfying the need or desire for all interested parties to be consulted'. They proposed that business which had hitherto belonged to the Senate should be transferred to boards of faculties.[2] They recommended that each faculty board should undertake a complete review of the structure, organization and government of its faculty. In arguing that departmental plans for development should be submitted for evaluation to faculty committees, they commented that they 'did not see any other reasonably democratic way of ensuring that particular and general proposals are weighed together and given and seen to be given fair and proper priorities'.[3] Finally, in returning to the old problem of the involvement of the academic staff at large, the Committee asserted:

> that many problems would disappear if all, as distinct from most, heads of department took their staffs into their confidence and discussed with them matters both of particular and of general concern to them. It feels very strongly that this practice is the only real solution to present difficulties of communication.[4]

That feeling was shared by an increasing number. It had been expressed repeatedly by the Non-professorial staff. However, this was the first occasion on which it had received an official ungrudging blessing.

These proposals gave preliminary shape to ideas of reform which went back to 1963 and beyond. They reached down from the central planning committees of the University to the organization of faculties and departments. These lower regions of government were bestrewn with obstacles. The ghost of Childs still stalked abroad. The new professor would find to his

---

[1] Senate Reports, xxvii, 2 May 1966.
[2] The admission of higher degree students, permission for higher degree students to work elsewhere, decisions on requests to change courses or to defer examinations.
[3] It was noted that this did not remove the right of a head of department to discuss his estimates directly with the Vice-Chancellor.
[4] Senate Reports, xxvii, 2 May 1966.

surprise that he was 'doctored' democratically in the Common Room,[1] but 'professored' most earnestly in the corridor; and behind such oddities of titular convention there were real difficulties and raw grievances. The old authority of the professors was becoming less firmly defined and understood. From 1965 all new professorial contracts included provisions for rotating headships of department.[2] This was adopted as a means of relieving professors periodically of the increasing burden of administration, but it also undermined the old dominance, for no professor could easily rule autocratically if he was looking over his shoulder at his successor. There were other, less formal, gradual shifts in attitude. Within the environment of rapidly growing departments some professors readily abandoned any pretensions to autocracy. Naturally, some did so more readily and more radically than others. Such variations in their response, inevitable in the circumstances, were a source of constant irritation. One professor might consult the staff of his department genuinely on all important matters of policy; another, often revealing himself by his references to '*my* staff', might simply expect them to do his bidding. One professor might come to hold formal departmental meetings; another might not.[3] In some departments the hard-won secretary was very much the professor's personal assistant; in others all members of staff might have access to secretarial services. Some professors delegated a great deal; others kept the reins in their own hands. Some were assiduous in advancing the claims of the staff of their departments; others seemed to pass their lives blithely unaware that desire for promotion or advancement was a natural human feeling. Some were efficient administrators and respected as such in their departments; others had to be sustained with affection, exasperation or despair. The professors themselves were not immune from irritations. Some accepted change only grudgingly. Some felt that consultation and discussion only led in the end

---

[1] The democracy of the Common Room extended beyond mere titles. When in one of its meetings it was proposed that the Registrar should count the votes, J. E. Prue at once asked – 'Sir, do we know the Registrar?'.

[2] Senate Reports, xxvi, 11 October 1965; Council Reports, xxvii, 29 October 1965.

[3] The Deans' statement that 'most' professors discussed matters with their staff was somewhat hopeful. It should not be taken to imply a formal organization. In most departments at this stage departmental meetings were held to determine examination results; but even these had only been established with difficulty in some departments and some professors still tended to settle results in a private talk with the external examiner. On other matters departmental meetings were a rarity. None were held in the Department of History prior to Aspinall's retirement in 1965. Guggenheim apparently held *one* meeting during his tenure of the Chair of Chemistry but 'nothing ever came of it.' (Conversation with Professor P. F. Holt, 29 July 1975). It should be remembered, however, that a formal organization of departmental meetings is very much a function of size. Before the rapid growth of departments in the late 1960s much business was settled efficiently and informally over coffee. New departments took to the new style of organization more rapidly. In the Department of Politics, founded in 1964, 'effective responsibility for the Department' was 'exercised by its members acting collectively at staff meetings.' (P. W. Campbell, 'The Department of Politics: notes on the Department's first decade: 1964–1974').

to conclusions which they could easily reach on their own. Many, however ready to consult their colleagues, were likely to regard democratic complexities as unwelcome intrusions into the limited time which they had available for their own research. For most of them, committees were to be endured rather than enjoyed.

Such feelings and reactions discharged themselves at intervals into the discussions. The debate was further complicated by the fact that much of it took place within the old machinery which was itself the object of reform. To those outside it often seemed slow and inadequate. Where official channels proved dilatory or ineffective the Non-professorial staff stepped in, and this in turn heightened contrasting views. Sometimes the debate turned to inessential symbols. For example, professors were still held directly responsible for the research done in their departments. That was never challenged. However, the professors were recorded as supervisors of research students, even where the real work of supervision was done by other members of staff, whose names might or might not be mentioned. Moreover, the professors alone were required to act as examiners, whilst the real supervisors might or might not be consulted or included. That, understandably, was a grievance. It was raised in the Non-professorial staff in 1960 and discussion continued at intervals both there and in boards of faculties on to 1969. It was not until 1970 that the Senate agreed that the professor should appear as a supervisor only if he was really doing the work.[1] The original position was both attacked and defended vigorously. Within it there were real issues, involving the role of the supervisor as an examiner and the extent to which a professor might delegate his responsibilities. The rest concerned appearances.

Many of the proposals advanced by the Deans in 1966 had already been discussed at intervals in the Non-professorial staff. The effect of the Deans' paper was to re-open the debate and, in a longer term, to contribute to a shift in emphasis. Up to 1966 the Non-professorial staff's interest in the government of the University had centred on representation and communication. After 1966 they turned increasingly to the management of departments. They had raised this, among other matters, during the visitation of the University Grants Committee in 1960.[2] However, senior appointments apart, they had not proved very ready to question the professor's responsibility for the management of his subject and hence for the running of his department. This now changed. In a discussion of the composition of the Senate, occasioned by the Deans' proposals, the Non-

---

[1] Non-professorial staff, Minutes of general meeting, 20 January 1960, 24 May 1961, 25 June 1969, 20 May 1970; Senate Minutes, 4759 (a), 21 January 1970.

[2] 'We feel that with the impending foundation of several new universities there is much to be said for a re-examination of the structure of university organization. We believe that the non-professorial members of an academic staff should have the opportunity to contribute in the same way as the professors to the framing of academic policy, both in the departments and in the University.' (Memorandum from the Non-professorial staff, 17 October 1960, Non-professorial staff, Minutes of general meeting).

professorial staff agreed unanimously that nothing could be done until the proper organization of departments and faculties had first been settled.[1] There for the time the matter lay. It was reopened in 1969 as a result of a discussion in the Committee of Deans and the Senate of the headship of departments with only one professor. The Non-professorial staff commented acidly on a scheme for the professor temporarily to transfer the headship to some other senior member by noting that it seemed 'to make it possible for him to shed his duties while retaining his rights'.[2] The scheme was dropped for the time being in the Senate, but it had done enough to start a train of action in the Non-professorial staff. The matter was put to the Committee and then to a sub-committee.[3] A referendum held in 1970 revealed for the first time the depth and extent of feeling. Thirty-six per cent of the respondents wanted to see readers and senior lecturers made eligible for headships of department; 56 per cent wanted to have the head elected by the department, subject to confirmation by the Council, and 64 per cent wanted such a system to be mandatory on all departments. Seventy-five per cent were in favour of transferring certain 'powers' to departmental boards, with varying majorities in this group favouring the inclusion of academic policy, development, estimates, the allocation of resources and recommendations concerning syllabuses; large minorities also wanted to give the boards control of the general arrangements and organization of the department, the nomination of examiners and supervisors, tutorial matters and academic appointments.[4] These ideas were embodied in a paper submitted to the Senate in 1971. This was more circumspect: it referred not to 'powers' but to 'ultimate responsibility'.[5] One of the concerns was that an unsatisfactory head of department should be brought under control, even removed from office. No one explained what might be done with an unsatisfactory departmental board. Such was the tide of opinion.

The Non-professorial staff was not the sole forum for discussion. The Senate had followed up the recommendations of the Deans by establishing a Steering Committee.[6] Both the Senate and the Council had been busy reviewing their membership. Each faculty board had re-examined the structure of its faculty, and the constitutions of the boards were being revised. Hence the Non-professorial staff's proposals came at a time when minds were adjusted to wide ranging discussion; the first question was usually not 'why?', but 'why not?', and that was an open door to new ideas. To no avail. The working party which reported to the Senate on the

[1] *Ibid.*, 7 December 1966.
[2] *Ibid.*, 30 April 1969.
[3] For the report of the sub-committee see *ibid.*, 4 December 1969.
[4] *Ibid.*, 3 December 1970. The percentages given above are of all returns to the questionnaire. These totalled 243.
[5] Senate Reports, 5 May 1971.
[6] Consisting of the deans and three elected members of the Senate, this was designed to 'pre-digest' the Senate's business.

Non-professorial proposals in May 1972 accepted the establishment of departmental boards with restricted but binding powers,[1] but the Senate jibbed. It returned to the matter repeatedly in the summer and autumn of 1972 and its final recommendation agreed in February 1973 was simply that:

> the head of each department be required to hold meetings of the academic staff of the department on at least three occasions during each academic year, for full consultation on such departmental affairs as seems appropriate to the head and/or other members of the department.[2]

The scheme for departmental boards, with its strong constitutional implications was lost and the very term abandoned in what was no more than an advice to heads on how a department might be run. Few recommendations were ever more delicately framed to meet professorial sensitivity:

> The Senate wishes each department to be organized as it suits its members, within the basic rule. It may be that some heads and their departments would like to have guidance on the allocation of functions within a department, and the following scheme is therefore provided to show how this might be done. It is intended solely as an illustration of one method; it is not mandatory; and the list is not comprehensive.[3]

That in effect was a re-assertion of professorial responsibility. It was further emphasized by the Senate's insistence that the appointment of a non-professorial head should be subject to 'the agreement of a clear majority of the professors in a multi-professorial department, or the agreement of the professor in a uni-professorial department'.[4] To the Non-professorial staff, which had scented victory in the Report of the Senate Working Party,[5] this

[1] The working party was set up in the meeting which received the Non-professorial staff's paper, 5 May 1971 (Senate Minutes, 4970).
[2] Senate Reports, 28 February 1973; Senate Minutes, 5318, 28 February 1973. The discussion began in the Senate on 11 October and was continued in subsequent meetings during the winter and spring. The crucial change converting departmental boards into regular departmental meetings was made in the first discussion in October – 'The concept of the departmental board was too formal and should not be adopted.' (Senate Minute 5229, 11 October 1972). Subsequent discussion is recorded in Senate Minutes 5259 of 22 November 1972, and 5283 of 24 January 1973, by when all but the final drafting was completed.
[3] The 'basic rule' mentioned was the recommendation that there should be at least three departmental meetings per year. The 'guidance' suggested that a head might consult colleagues, at his discretion, on promotions, staff and student problems and fund raising, and that he might consult a group of colleagues, chosen by himself as the occasion required, on the organization of duties, estimates, the nomination of examiners and the preliminary stages of staff appointments. Matters on which all the staff might be consulted included syllabus framing, marking duties and policy in undergraduate admissions. The code, spelt out in considerable detail, never acquired any mandatory status.
[4] Registrar's circular, 'Conduct of Departments', September 1973, para. 10.
[5] 'The Chairman outlined the revised document and it appeared to members of the Committee that, if the document were approved, it would be to the advantage of N.P.S. members.' (Non-professorial staff, Minutes of Committee, 17 November 1972).

was a sad end to a long campaign. One of the more tempestuous members of the sub-committee which had produced their original scheme proposed that they should resort to organized non-co-operation with their professors, but that never got beyond the Committee.[1] In the end a general meeting confined itself to a resolution deploring the long delay in completing discussions on the working party's proposals in the Senate, regretting the Senate's rejection of the scheme for departmental boards, and stressing its disapproval of the principle that the consent of the professors should be necessary for the appointment of non-professorial heads.[2]

There the matter rested. If it was not victory for the Non-professorial staff, it was equally not defeat. After 1973 no Head could work without formal consultation with the staff of his department in departmental meetings. Arrangements varied from one department to another. In some something approaching the scheme of departmental boards emerged in practice; in others meetings perhaps achieved little more than an improvement in communications. But, in whatever form, they became commonplace. They were not the only important change. Non-professorial headships were now accepted both in multi- and uni-professorial departments; so was the principle that non-professorial heads should have the same powers and duties as professors. *Ad hoc* committees considering the continuation of a professorship about to become vacant were now obliged to consult the non-professorial staff of the department, and committees of selection to chairs now included a member representing the department.[3] On the whole the Senate had settled on an acceptable compromise, at least for the time being. The Non-professorial staff's motion of disapproval was a final grand gesture. They continued to meet for discussions as before, but this was their last major attempt to alter the structure of the University. The steam went out of their debates. The record in the old minute books of both the Committee and the general meetings ended abruptly in 1973. By this time departments had settled to their own systems of government. Those whose prime concern was to challenge or defend professorial authority were a small minority. Time told in favour of shared responsibility. One department set a standard for another and, where the headship of a department rotated, one professor established practice for another. The trend was towards more rather than less consultation.

The discussion of these affairs was at times vigorous, perhaps even heated. But the constitution and traditions of the University did not readily allow a confrontation. The Non-professorial staff continued to accept that the elected members of the Senate could not be treated as non-professorial

[1] Non-professorial staff, Minutes of Committee, 30 January 1973.
[2] *Ibid.*, and Minutes of general meeting, 20 February 1973.
[3] These matters, embodied in the Report of the Senate Working Party on Conduct of Departments, were discussed and resolved in the spring and summer of 1973. The results were embodied in the Registrar's circular, 'Conduct of Departments', September 1973.

representatives required to report to their own general meetings.[1] The referendum of 1970 revealed some curious currents of opinion. Forty-six per cent
of the respondents wanted the Deans to participate in some way in the
choice of heads of department.[2] Only 23 per cent wanted departmental
boards to intervene in matters of salaries, increments and promotions. Only
32 per cent wanted the boards to deal with routine administration. So some
still saw a continuing role for heads of departments whether as confidential
advocates or as 'dogsbodies' attending to the routine chores. In the end the
sub-committee of the Non-professorial staff recommended that although
heads should be elected by all full-time members of staff of a department,
they should be left with some initiative and should not simply be reduced to
the role of chairmen.[3] This was not democracy rampant. Nor was autocracy
entrenched on the other side of the debate. Twice, in 1966 and in 1969,
discussion was triggered by proposals from the Committee of Deans. Some
of the professors took a keen interest in the Non-professorial staff's schemes;
P. W. Campbell was a co-opted member of the sub-committee which
drafted their first paper, and there were many formal and informal interchanges in which interested professors took part. The argument lacked the
marked political complexion which it acquired in some other universities.
Over the years Reading had become more fertile ground for political
debate. The even tenor of the Common Room had not been disturbed by
the Munich crisis; vociferous argument in 1938 would have been bad
manners. The Suez crisis, in contrast, split the staff in 1956; special meetings
were held to discuss possible representations. Even so, the political element
in the arguments about internal reorganization was very slight. Reading
tended to treasure its political extremists and savour them as part of the
rich variety of human behaviour. Hence the debate was never overheated,
as it was occasionally elsewhere, by a serious political challenge to professorial authority or by the dismissal of staff on grounds which could be
alleged to be political. Political beliefs clearly inspired one or two of the
participants, but detracted from, rather than added to, their weight.

Political views in this narrow sense merged in an inconsistent and un-
predictable fashion into wider concepts of how a university should be

---

[1] Non-professorial staff, Minutes of general meeting, 7 December 1966. On this
occasion reference to 'non-professorial representatives' in formal motions on the agenda
was amended to 'non-professorial members'. The general feeling at this meeting was that
the non-professorial members of the Senate were full members and were not there to
represent sectional interests. The link between this and professorial participation in their
election was fully appreciated and a motion that professors should not have a vote in
order to emphasize the representative function of non-professorial members was not put
to the meeting. Compare, however, a less formal occasion recorded in the Minutes of the
Committee, 6 May 1968 – 'Nominations for Senate: Dr Tiffin was asked to approach
Dr Vince to see if she would stand as N.P.S. representative'.
[2] Against 40 per cent who did not.
[3] Non-professorial staff Report of Sub-Committee on Headships of Departments,
18 May 1970.

governed. It was felt that principle was involved. This feeling was concentrated, or at least expressed most vociferously, in the Faculty of Letters
and Social Sciences, where it touched professional concerns and academic
interests.[1] This was reflected in the revision of the structure of the faculties
which followed the Deans' proposals of 1966. The Board of the Faculty of
Agriculture needed little formal alteration; the Faculty was already highly
integrated; all that was done was to establish for each section of the courses
boards of studies which included all the staff involved, and which, with the
heads of departments, took responsibility for the operation of the syllabus.
That, along with new committees to deal with development and estimates,
was all that was needed. The Faculty of Science went in for a more radical
change. In 1968 the old Board was dissolved. It was replaced by committees
of schools, each responsible for academic policy within one of the broad
divisions of the Faculty,[2] and by a small Board of the Faculty comprising
the Dean, ex-Dean, chairmen of the committees of the schools and an
equivalent number of elected members. This met some resistance from a
few professors who continued to insist on their former right to *ex officio*
memberships of the Board. However, it was a businesslike attempt to isolate
the academic discussions peculiar to each school, to involve more staff in
the work of the Faculty as elected members of the committees of the
schools, and to combine the work of the schools in a small, directing Board
of the Faculty. The scheme worked and was renewed with little amendment
after an experimental period of three years. In the Faculty of Letters and
Social Sciences the approach was very different. Here 'participation'
became the guiding principle. In 1971 a working party reported that:

> there is strong evidence in the Faculty of a desire for change in the
> composition of its Board. It would identify as major reasons for this
> situation the apparently widespread beliefs within the Faculty that
> the Board tends to consist largely of senior members of the Faculty,
> that other members cannot make their views effectively heard and
> that the Board's deliberations may not in consequence pay due
> attention to what are regarded as serious issues by non-Board
> members.[3]

After an arduous debate the Board of the Faculty finally accepted the
working party's proposal which greatly increased the number of elected
members and arranged for election on a departmental basis. Henceforth
each department, according to its size, had a ration of elected members;
a similar method was used for elections to some of the Faculty committees.

[1] The Sub-Committee which drafted the Non-professorial staff proposals was made up
of E. A. Smith (President), Department of History, N. L. J. Montagu (Secretary),
Department of Philosophy, Professor P. W. Campbell, Department of Politics, J. E. Prue,
Department of Chemistry, R. S. Tayler, Department of Agriculture and S. J. Woolf,
Department of Italian Studies.
[2] The Schools were Earth Sciences, Biological Sciences and Physical Sciences.
Mathematical Sciences was separated from Physical Sciences as a fourth School in 1972.
[3] Board of the Faculty of Letters, 3 February 1971.

No one was to be an elected member of more than one body; no one was to stand for immediate re-election. The co-opted element of the Board was reduced to six. The working party, the membership of which overlapped the Non-professorial staff's sub-committee on the conduct of departments,[1] also proposed initially that professors who were not heads of department should no longer enjoy *ex officio* membership of the Board. That was defeated by one vote.[2] With that the argument ended. 'Participation' wasted away into infeasibilities. The papers of the meetings of the Board were made available to all staff in departmental offices. Not many looked at them. It was proposed that all departments should hold meetings after the circulation of the Board's agenda but before the meetings of the Board. That proved difficult to organize; in any case there was no great demand for such meetings. The Board solemnly decided by a vote of fourteen to eleven that, for an experimental period of one Session, any member of the Faculty could attend the meetings of the Board as an observer. No one ever came. The Faculty had met, indeed exhausted, the demand for 'participation'. It was left with a large Board, much given to prolonged debate.

By 1971 each faculty in its own way had adjusted itself to the new, larger scale of its operations. Meanwhile the debate about the conduct of departments was progressing, to be resolved in 1973. The old problem of communication was being solved. The University, at the urging of the Registrar, finally introduced a regular *Bulletin* to replace the *Gazette* in 1969, and this, along with faculty news letters, provided an efficient supply of information on the affairs of the University.[3] Committees had multiplied at all levels. Probably most of those who wished to play a part in the affairs of the University could look forward to doing so. Energy and interest were no longer channelled towards the Non-professorial staff as the only ready outlet. But probably it was just as difficult as ever for a young member of staff to get something done. Earlier it had depended upon the nod of a professor. Now it turned on a safe passage through the narrows of procedure which canalized the work of boards and committees. One thing was certain: it would take longer. In discussing the supervision and examination of higher degree students in 1960, T. B. Rymer remarked that the increase in student numbers would necessarily bring about greater devolution without any changes in regulations. J. E. Prue, on the other hand, pointed out that many of the regulations were a relic of Reading's old status as a college and should accordingly be abandoned.[4] The one a physicist and the other a chemist took diametrically opposed views, yet each accepted that change was inevitable. The arguments were often about detail, about superficial

[1] E. A. Smith and S. J. Woolf. The latter was a member only for its earlier proceedings.
[2] Board of the Faculty of Letters, minute 1968, 2 June 1971.
[3] A *Staff Journal* was also produced between 1967 and 1970. This was initiated by the Non-professorial staff; the first editor was E. A. Smith. It provided a forum for discussion rather than an information service.
[4] Non-professorial staff, Minutes of general meeting, 20 January 1960.

appearances, about the precise formulation of principles which encapsulated what was already happening in practice. But the core of the problem, the adjustment of the government of the University to a larger scale, was real enough. Many, of course, took no part. In 1970, when interest was aroused, roughly half the academic staff answered the Non-professorial staff's referendum on the conduct of departments. But the active participants in the debate were far fewer, and those with a taste for the regular slog of work in committees were fewer still. Hence the peculiar fact that the opening up of the government of the University was reflected in many minds by the fiction of 'Admin.', which was imagined inaccurately to be a vast, wilful and complex machine clanking along predetermined lines which allowed for no pause or diversion. This too was an inevitable consequence of increasing size, and of the fact that most members of staff were absorbed by the immediate work in hand. The change in the pattern of government was something happening outside their immediate experience, in distant areas which they scarcely ever needed to penetrate. If they had been asked a different set of questions in 1970 they might well have answered that their real desire was to work with a professor of academic distinction who would encourage their interests, listen to their views, and protect their studies both in the syllabus and in providing resources for teaching and research. That would have been a plea for an ideal. So also was the response to the questions actually put. Reality was different from both. It was made up of the daily round of teaching and research, and many, indeed most, devoted themselves to that with little reference to the governmental context.

This changing context had still wider boundaries. Following the Deans' recommendations of 1966 the constitution of the Senate was re-examined. It was soon agreed that there should be no substantial alteration,[1] but the discussion re-opened the question of the elected membership. The Non-professorial staff continued to press for an increase,[2] and in 1968 it was agreed that the directly elected members should be increased from six to one-fifth of the *ex officio* membership; that roughly doubled the number.[3] By this time, however, the whole problem of representative government had been changed by the intervention of the students. This affected the attitude of the academic staff in two obvious ways. First, their own proposals were determined to some degree by the demands of the students.

[1] Senate Reports, 10 May 1967.
[2] Non-professorial staff, Minutes of general meeting, 7 December 1966; Minutes of Committee, 2 November 1966; 21 April 1967. It was broadly agreed in the meetings that the Non-professorial staff should seek for an elected membership amounting to one-sixth of the total.
[3] Senate Reports, 4 July 1968; Senate Minutes, 4545, 9 October 1968, 4564, 20 November 1968. *Ex officio* membership was also given at this time to the Chairman of the Wardens' Committee; that did something to meet the case which the wardens and Childs had pressed in 1926 (see above, pp. 60–1). The Non-professorial staff supported the Wardens' case but did not want it to be 'linked in any way with Non-professorial staff representation.' (Non-professorial staff, Minutes of Committee, 21 April 1967).

For example, the Non-professorial staff had little interest in direct representation on the Council until the Council decided to invite student
representatives.[1] Again, they did not question the rule that members of
staff should be of at least some standing before they could play any part in
elections, until students joined the governing bodies.[2] Secondly, and much
more important, the students' campaign forced the academic staff to recast
some of their assumptions. To seek a wider role for themselves in the government of the University was one thing; for the students to do the same was
quite another, especially since the students' interest, like their own, reached
from the Council and the Senate to the organization and conduct of
departments. It was not easy to change deep rooted attitudes. There was
no more than a mere handful of members of staff who held so radical a
political philosophy that they were ready to accept what they would
perhaps have described as 'student power' as an integral part of the government of the University. The rest, relying not unreasonably on the difference
and disparity between teachers and pupils, gradually and in an empirical
fashion adjusted their inherently liberal views to make room for an increasing but limited degree of participation by the student body. But the change
in attitude was slow and halting. When student representation on the
Senate was first discussed in the Non-professorial staff committee in 1967 it
was felt that the best solution was for them to elect three members of staff
as their representatives.[3] When the question was raised again in a general
meeting in April 1969, not even this minimal concession was allowed; a
motion that the Non-professorial staff did not support student representation on the Senate was passed by a comfortable majority.[4]

The involvement of students in the government of British universities had
a long history.[5] At Reading, on the eve of the Second World War, *Tamesis*
already revealed a hubbub of opinion on teaching and tutorial procedures,

[1] 'The Chairman reported that in view of the request by students for membership of
Council, he had been asked whether the N.P.S. also wished to be represented.'
(Non-professorial staff, Minutes of general meeting, 30 April 1969). In the subsequent
discussion it was noted that the members of the Council elected by the Senate and the
faculty boards might be non-professorial. J. E. Prue asked whether the N.P.S. wished to
underline different categories of staff but the meeting ultimately accepted his view that,
if students were to be represented, then there should be an additional category of
members elected from and by the whole academic staff, the number to be 'not less than
that of the student representatives.' (*ibid.*).
[2] *Ibid.* In 1969 electors had to be of not less than five terms' and candidates of not less
than three years' standing. Such limitations were plainly impossible in the case of
students; they were abandoned in the case of the staff in 1970 (Senate Minutes, 4870,
7 October 1970).
[3] Non-professorial staff, Minutes of Committee, 21 April 1967.
[4] *Ibid.* Minutes of general meeting, 30 April 1969. The motion was carried by 23 with 9
against and 8 abstentions. An important argument in the debate was that the presence
of students in the Senate would lead to decisions being taken 'underground'. Members
were also concerned that student representatives would be mandated.
[5] Among the extensive literature on this E. Ashby and Mary Anderson, *The Rise of the
Student Estate in Britain* (1970) provides a most valuable summary.

the content of courses, the purposes of university education and the like.[1] However, the War intervened, and although discussion of both academic arrangements and disciplinary regulations continued after the War, nothing much came of it for some time. Even in the early 1960s there was little indication of what was about to happen. In 1964, for example, it was decided to appoint a full-time medical officer. The President of the Students' Union asked that the students might be represented on the committee of appointment. The Residential Policy Committee rejected the request but indicated that:

> It was prepared to invite a representative of the student body to discuss particular matters with it as and when the occasion seem to make this necessary.[2]

That minimal concession was a fair reflection of the state of opinion on student representation in the governing bodies of the University. The students were equally enmeshed in the assumptions of the time. In 1963 a young man was sent down because a female student had been discovered in his rooms after permitted hours. The Union held an emergency meeting and the President subsequently wrote a strong letter of protest to Cormack, then Acting Vice-Chancellor, who referred the matter to the Senate. The letter revealed the upheaval to come only as distant undertones:

> If one brings in the moral aspects of this case, as one rightly should, it is clear that the University has in no way made itself clear on its responsibilities in this field. No calendar rule prohibits students fornicating (indeed, I presume no student could be punished if caught in the afternoon), but the confident assertion by many students that their morality is always their private concern is untenable. It is clear that before the University punishes so severely students in Mr . . .'s position it should make clear when the demands of public decency require such punishment to be meted out. Yet even if public decency does require heavy punishment for such an offence, what parent these days would agree that a person's career should be ruined because of it? I was asked to bring these views to your notice, Sir, and in addition I should remark that the Union decidedly did not agree with the movers of this motion that a form of public demonstration was the best way of advertising our views.[3]

Much of that would soon seem antiquated. Moreover, it was not simply that opinion both in the governing bodies and among the students was still carried along by regulations and conventions which kept students in their place and infused them with a traditional code of private and public

[1] See above, pp. 95–6.
[2] Senate Reports, 24 February 1964.
[3] P. J. A. Cook to the Acting Vice-Chancellor, 18 December 1963 (Senate Reports, xxii, 20 January 1964). The Minutes of the Senate and the Council contain no record of any discussion of the case.

behaviour. There were also curious cross-currents which were soon to alter direction. On 22 October 1963 the Union passed the following motion:

> This House instructs Reading University Students Union Debates Committee to hold a debate between Sir Oswald or Max Mosley and a Socialist speaker of equal calibre, provided that permission be obtained from the Senate to hold such a debate on University premises. This House therefore instructs the President of the Union to ask the Senate for such permission.

The President accordingly wrote, emphasizing the importance of freedom of speech. The Senate rejected the request; it was concerned to avoid the public disturbances which such a meeting might cause.[1] None of this could have happened a decade or so later. The Senate might still have been concerned about the possibility of disturbance, but the President of the Union could no longer have sought to justify such a proposal, if he could now have dreamed of making it, by a simple appeal to the principle of freedom of speech.[2]

Change came suddenly in 1967. At Reading, as probably at many other universities, much of it seemed to come from outside and hence seemed all the more precipitate. The most important single external influence was the Latey Report of July 1967, which led to the reduction of the age of majority from 21 to 18.[3] It was recognized at once that, with the University no longer *in loco parentis*, the whole system of disciplinary regulation would have to be revised. The Latey Report was followed in July 1969 by the Report on Student Relations from the Select Committee on Education and Science.[4] That was used to provide powerful support, buttressed by collected evidence from all universities, not only for the revision of disciplinary regulations, but also for student participation in many of the University's procedures. Meanwhile a number of legal actions involving other universities had an effect. Much the most important was the Aston judgment of February 1969 which accelerated the establishment of a procedure for

---

[1] The matter was first reported to the Senate by the Standing Committee on Clubs and Societies on 25 February 1963 when a scheme to found a European Society was associated with a proposal to invite Max Mosley (Senate Reports, xx, 25 February 1963). The Committee recommended that University premises should not be made available 'having regard to happenings elsewhere', and that was adopted (Senate Minutes, iv, 3641, 25 February 1963). The second submission in October arose from further discussion in the Students' Union. The Senate reaffirmed its position (Senate Minutes, iv, 3750, 18 November 1963).

[2] In 1974 the National Union of Students formally decided to deny any platform to 'fascists' and 'racists'. It should be noted that in 1963 the constitution of student clubs and societies still required approval by the Senate.

[3] *Report of the Committee on the Age of Majority* (Cmnd. 3342, July 1967).

[4] *Report from the Select Committee on Education and Science; Session 1968–9 Student Relations* (449, July 1969). The committee was established in November 1968. Its general conclusions are contained in vol. i of the *Report*. Vol. vii contains an important collection of evidence on welfare, discipline and participation in the universities.

appeal against examination results.[1] Not all such influences were so precise. The National Union of Students made great advances in the 1960s. The increase in the number of students which followed on the Robbins Report added to its strength. It came to be accepted as the authoritative voice of the student community both by select committees and the national press.[2] Behind this, as behind the Latey Report, lay the fact that the age-group from which the students were drawn was coming to enjoy increasing economic importance. It constituted a commercial market; it acquired, or was provided with, its own tastes; it started 'trends'.

The route to a new constitution in which the students would play a part in the government of the University was bestrewn with hazards and difficulties. First, the Latey Report made assumptions which proved to be quite unrealistic. The Committee argued that:

> Colleges will go on demanding that students read books, go to lectures, write essays and stay in a fit state to do so; they will continue to require that the young people do not enjoy themselves with trumpets and strumpets to the point where it keeps other people awake. But the confusion that springs from *in loco parentis* situation will be removed.[3]

Confusion there may have been but it was Platonic order itself when compared with what was to follow, for the issue was rarely trumpets and never strumpets, but rather the invention of new arrangements, necessitated by the Report, for the orderly government of the university; and the challenge came not from trivial disorderliness, but from organized disruption. The real shape of the problem was soon revealed. On 21 November 1969 Gerald Palmer, then President of the Council, reported as follows:

> Certain events relating to university discipline and its disturbance have taken place recently, and it seems proper to report them to Council before the meeting on the 5th December.
>
> The initial event took place on the 30th October in connection with a conference on the applications of satellite technology held, under the auspices of N.A.T.O., in the Department of Physics. Anti-N.A.T.O. slogans were painted on the Department during the night of 29/30th October. A student demonstration was organized in the

---

[1] Summaries of the various judgments on test cases are conveniently collected in *Academic Freedom and the Law* (National Union of Students and National Council of Civil Liberties, London, 1970). For the Aston judgment see p. 61.

[2] See Ashby and Anderson, pp. 91 ff. The *Report from the Select Committee on Education and Science* (1969), pp. 12–38 also provides a brief review which includes parallel developments in western Europe.

[3] *Report of the Committee on the Age of Majority* (July 1967), para. 463. Although the Committee mentioned university authorities in para. 451 its discussion and recommendations referred in detail only to colleges. It summarized the views of the Association of Teachers in Colleges and Departments of Education and of the National Union of Students. The list of those providing evidence did not include either the Committee of Vice-Chancellors and Principals or the Association of University Teachers.

form of a sit-in in the building in the morning of 30th October, which continued into the afternoon and resulted in attempts to prevent the delegates returning to the conference room after lunch. This, in turn, led to a certain amount of physical disturbance involving, amongst others, the Head of the Department, the Registrar and the Head Porter.

On the following day, the 31st October, a peaceful sit-in took place, but no attempt was made to obstruct the delegates entering the lecture rooms. As is within the knowledge of those who attended, that same afternoon (31st October) Council met as usual with student members present for the first time. At the end of the agenda I started to give an account of the foregoing events when a body of some 25 to 30 students entered the Council chamber and one of them began to read some kind of petition. I told the intruders to leave at once, which request they ignored – so, since the whole of the agenda was complete apart from discussion of the sit-in, I declared the meeting closed and all members of Council left the room, paying no attention to the intruders. The latter, finding themselves without an audience, left about ten minutes later.

The Vice-Chancellor returned from the United States a few days later and decided there was a *prima facie* case for referring to the Standing Disciplinary Committee five students who had been identified for their activities in connection with the disturbance on the 30th October. The hearing was fixed for Thursday, the 13th November.

Meanwhile, on the evening of the 10th November, an emergency meeting of the Students' Union was held and attended by some 400 students. This meeting passed several resolutions by large majorities in effect condemning the fact that the five students were being referred to the Standing Disciplinary Committee.

The following afternoon, 11th November, the University Joint Committee held its first meeting. The Committee made an encouraging start. When, however, the formal agenda was completed there was a demand from student members for discussion of the question of discipline with particular reference to the resolutions passed by the Students' Union meeting the previous night. After a long discussion it was finally fairly generally accepted that the Standing Disciplinary Committee procedure must continue; but that the University Joint Committee should, in the near future, undertake a review of the existing Regulations for Discipline (which had, in fact, been agreed with student representatives only two years ago).

On Thursday, the 13th November, the Standing Disciplinary Committee met in the morning and were informed that there were two barristers present to represent the five students. There is nothing in the regulations or procedures to permit legal representation; and the Disciplinary Committee itself had, of course, no legal adviser present; its members, however, agreed to see the two barristers to hear what they had to say, but not in the presence of the students.

The outcome of this discussion was that the Committee felt bound to take legal advice as to the position and the case was adjourned *sine die*. Legal advice is now being sought.

This account of the events leading to the present situation has been reduced to the barest possible outline, but I thought it might serve a useful purpose in enabling members of Council to grasp the skeleton of a rather complex situation which may take some time finally to resolve. I have deliberately avoided discussing the details of the events and, still more, the legal questions involved.[1]

Discipline in the old sense was now impossible. The University had drawn up new disciplinary procedures and regulations in 1968.[2] These now proved ineffective. They were revised after much discussion during 1970 and 1971.[3] The revision was unacceptable to the Students' Union which voted to reject 'the conception of discipline as something imposed by the Administration upon the students'.[4] Nevertheless, the regulations were approved by the Senate in their revised form. An attempt was made to apply them in May 1973 following an occupation of the central administrative building, Whiteknights House. The process had to be abandoned on a technicality. Once again the regulations were revised to repair the deficiency.[5] In fact the Disciplinary Committee never worked effectively. For individual peccadilloes it was unnecessary. For disruption it was no cure. Indeed it exaggerated the ill, for disciplinary proceedings tended to convert narrow political demonstrations into broad campaigns in defence of individual students. The main result was to produce potential martyrs.

---

[1] Council Reports, 6 February 1970. The Standing Committee on Discipline subsequently decided not to proceed 'solely in view of the delay which had occurred.' (Senate Minutes, 4767, 25 February 1970).

[2] They provided for a Standing Disciplinary Committee consisting of the Vice-Chancellor, one lay member of the Council and two members of the Senate. The President of the Union was entitled to attend, but only as an observer since it was not considered 'right for a student to be in the position of being involved in the imposition of sanctions, especially those of rustication or expulsion, on another student'. The regulations allowed an accused student to bring a 'friend' drawn from the current students or the academic staff (Senate Reports, 19 June 1968).

[3] Senate Minutes, 4904, 18 November 1970, 4947, 24 February 1971. The discussion is summarized in Senate Reports, 24 February 1971. The main revision was to establish an Appeals Committee in addition to the original Disciplinary Committee. A representative of the students was also added to the Disciplinary Committee; since the Students' Union refused to recognize the new regulations, he never attended.

[4] The vote was taken in an emergency meeting of the Union on 2 February 1971. It was 58 for and 48 against (Senate Reports, 24 February 1971).

[5] The Vice-Chancellor was a party to the action and therefore could not act on the Committee. Since the student representative never attended there was doubt whether the Committee, so reduced from five to three, could be considered quorate. Ordinances were subsequently amended to provide alternates for the Vice-Chancellor.

Recognition of this came gradually in fits and starts with each succeeding incident over the next four years. In 1969 the Vice-Chancellor reported to the Senate that the assumptions on which he had acted were:

1. The point at which an orderly peaceful demonstration turns into a breach of order is that at which physical obstruction to the lawful processes of the University takes place, even though no overt force is used; and

2. A student is individually responsible for his or her actions and there could be no question of 'collective responsibility'. Any student breaking a University regulation is at risk of disciplinary action, regardless of what happens to any other students involved in an incident.

That was endorsed by the Senate,[1] and formally neither the Vice-Chancellor nor the Senate ever abandoned these principles. But a number of occupations of women's Halls organized in June 1970 as a protest against Hall rules led to a more elastic response. The Vice-Chancellor then explained that:

Although he had volunteered to intervene if the Wardens had thought it necessary, they had decided that it would be more expedient to handle matters themselves. This proved to be right and the overall response of those affected had been unsuccessful to some extent, since it had led to a feeling of anti-climax; but it was hardly likely to serve as a long-term solution. The main obstacle to disciplinary action in situations of this kind was the difficulty of identifying the students concerned.[2]

That hinted at a change in attitude which became more pronounced in the next three years. On 28 February 1973 a group of students, pursuing the current campaign against the increase in Hall fees, invaded a meeting of the Senate. The Vice-Chancellor terminated the session; members forced their way out; no action was taken against the invading students. It took a tragic occurrence and a remarkable set of coincidences to provoke a disciplinary reaction. The Bursar, E. H. Carpenter, died at his desk in Whiteknights House on the morning of 16 May 1973. Despite repeated pleas, and despite full knowledge of what had happened, the students' action committee decided at lunch-time to occupy Whiteknights House in pursuance of the fees campaign. Senate held one of its regular meetings in the afternoon. One member suggested that members of Senate, instead of recording their disapproval as in the past, might go to Whiteknights House to identify the intruders. At the end of the meeting the Vice-Chancellor asked whether there were any ready to take up the suggestion. He found that he had a posse. The posse found that it had a leader. There was no going back. There was no need, as in a better publicized incident up the

[1] Senate Minutes, 4733, 19 November 1969.
[2] Senate Minutes, 4818, 17 June 1970.

Thames, for the Registrar to effect an entry through a rear window. At Reading the Vice-Chancellor went in through the main door. In a few minutes offices were cleared of astonished students, as many as possible were identified, and they were left in the lobby to recover from the shock. Within the hour, shepherded by the Security Officer, they retreated to the Union building carrying their banners furled. Direct action had been met by direct action. But it was no victory. The imposition of fines led to the organization of a massive demonstration against the Vice-Chancellor on the afternoon of 13 June. The Disciplinary Committee was unable to proceed with the charges and they were dropped.[1] Nor was that a victory for the action committee of students. The demonstration of 13 June proved little more than that the militant left could muster between 200 and 400 students by calling on those of like mind in other universities and colleges: London, Oxford, Bristol, Southampton, and elsewhere.[2] It did the students' cause no good.

   This was an aberrant incident. It occurred at a time when the campaigns of the political activists were underpinned by more general discontent produced by the widening gap between the students' grants on the one hand and the residential charges on the other. Whenever grievances concerned Halls, their rules, their management, their charges, then Reading was vulnerable. Even so the political spark in the place was not explosive. Many students were ready to support the rent strikes of 1973, at least for a time; but only a small minority was ready to take part in disruption. Dramatic though they seemed at the time, the occupations, the marches and the protests were of little consequence. Most of the students, like most of the staff, were getting on with their work. A Union meeting of over 400, in a University numbering over 5,000, was counted well attended. Many of the more sweeping Union resolutions were the work of badly attended meetings.[3] At the heart of the disruption there was a hard political core, made up in part of International Socialists, well organized, voluble, if somewhat tedious. Between 1969 and 1973 they gained great influence in the Students' Union and at times controlled it. They greatly complicated the task of the

[1] See above, p. 310.
[2] See plate 43.
[3] See above, p. 310, n. 4 for a resolution on discipline of 1970. Among the more bizarre occurrences was a Union meeting of 15 May 1969 which passed a motion instructing its delegates on the Joint Working Party on Student Affairs (on which see pp. 313–14, 317 below) 'to petition for 50 per cent student representation on the University Council', with 58 in favour, 4 against and 19 abstentions, and also adopted a recommendation that 'this Union deplores the continuation of First University Examinations and instructs the Executive to petition for their abolition, and in pursuit of the policy, to take action to bring about the abandonment of F.U.E. re-sits this June' with 86 in favour and 45 against (Miss Jennifer Pope, President of the Union to Registrar, 15 May 1969). These numbers should be compared with the vote of 10 November 1969 protesting against the disciplinary proceedings upon participants in the demonstrations of 30 and 31 October 1969 (on which see above p. 309). This was carried 370 in favour, 20 against, with 30 abstentions.

University, for they dominated the students' side of any joint discussion in
the governing bodies or in University committees. However, in all but a few
departments it was apparent that although they were the students' representatives, they were scarcely representative of student opinion. Their
influence declined rapidly after 1973, and in 1974–5 a new President of the
Union was able to tidy up the debris of ill-will which they left. Their
activity had three main effects. First, it led the University to tolerate a
more disruptive pattern of behaviour in practice than it was ready to allow
in principle. Secondly, that was achieved at the cost of intermittent but
serious interruption of the work of the administrative staff in Whiteknights
House; they became a buffer absorbing the first shock and thereby ensuring
that it would be the only one. Thirdly, it had an incongruous influence
on the discussion of the students' case. They would argue that without their
'direct action' the students would have 'gained' less, less quickly. There is
something to be said for that. An apt illustration is provided by the events
which followed the publication on 7 October 1968 of the joint statement
on the role of students within the universities, made by the Committee of
Vice-Chancellors and Principals and the National Union of Students.[1]
At Reading the Vice-Chancellor commented on the statement in his
Report to the Council on 1 November and added that 'he was generally
confident that serious disruption was unlikely to occur at this University';
the Council endorsed that view and, apart from certain precautionary
steps, took no immediate action.[2] By 6 December, the date of its next
regular meeting, disruption had become a real and immediate threat.
Occupations had occurred at Bridges and St George's Halls and the militants had established an organization entitled 'Action for a Free University'
which had the avowed aim of 'democratizing the University in all its
aspects'[3] and was seizing the initiative from the elected Officers of the
Students' Union. The Council met in an atmosphere of crisis, after hurried
and urgent consultations between the President of the Council, the Vice-
Chancellor, the President of the Union and others. Following their lead,
the Council now agreed that the Committee on Residence would review
residential policy and that a Joint Working Party of members of the Council,

[1] This 'concordat', which triggered a wide discussion of student participation in most
British Universities, is in Council Reports, 1 November 1968. It is discussed in Ashby
and Anderson (1970), pp. 91, 116–20.
[2] Council Minute, 2786, 1 November 1968.
[3] These events were summarized in a letter from the Vice-Chancellor to members of
Senate and wardens of halls, 3 December 1968. For the objectives of 'Action for a Free
University' see the information circulated with the above and a leaflet circulated by the
A.F.U. 13 January 1969 – 'Action for a Free University has from the start of its short
existence affirmed its goal to democratize the university in all its aspects. This involves
both student autonomy in the regulation of their own domestic concerns, and a much
greater say in their academic life. However, more to the point, A.F.U. is strongly
opposed to the structure in this university in which decision-making rests with a small
elite. For too long the decisions affecting students' lives have been made by either a small,
unqualified, administrative elite, or by exclusive, small and select committees'.

academic staff and students should be established to examine all aspects of
the joint statement of 7 October. The Council also received a student
delegation at this meeting.[1] No one could doubt that there had been a
marked acceleration; the headline in the local paper – 'Students win
urgent probe into grievances' – was not far from the mark.[2] But if the
militants had achieved that they had lost much else. Both by word and
action they soured the relationships of student representatives with
academic and administrative staff on the Council, on the Senate and in
University committees. They were best met with patience, fortitude and a
powerful sense of humour.

There was yet another complication, already apparent in Gerald
Palmer's remark in 1969 that the students were rejecting disciplinary
arrangements to which they had agreed only two years earlier. The time-
scales of the students and the staff were quite different. To the undergraduate student involved in the affairs of the University two years was a
long time; anything more was pre-history.[3] The staff, on the other hand,
were accustomed to think and work within a framework of agreed procedures, rulings and precedents accumulated over a lengthy period. There
was no way to resolve this difficulty. Experience soon showed that it would
be necessary to repeat explanations for each succeeding generation of
students. It was less easy to grasp that students' views changed quickly. For
example, in 1966 the Students' Union asked the Senate to agree that the
President of the Union should be allowed to take a 'sabbatical' year if he so
wished. The case was based on the argument that the President's duties
were unique within the Union; in countering a possible argument that
similar requests would be made for other officers the submission stated that
members of the Executive other than the President could 'simultaneously
carry out both academic and Union commitments.'[4] The Senate agreed to
the request on the understanding that 'no similar concession be made to any
other Officer of the Students' Union.'[5] By 1975 such a concession had been

[1] Council Minutes, 2817, 2818, 6 December 1968.
[2] *Evening Post*, 7 December 1968. It was not, however, obvious to those not in touch with
events on the Council that the main concern was not one of protecting the Council from
the students but of supporting the elected officers of the Students' Union against the
militant group which founded the A.F.U. This was made perfectly clear in the
Vice-Chancellor's letter of 3 December (see p. 313, n. 3 above). The President of the
Union had already been provided with the proposals which were to be put to the
Council on 6 December when he met the Union Executive on 3 December and the
General Meeting of 5 December. This enabled him to survive the immediate crisis, but
he was replaced in office in January 1969.
[3] It is worth noting that at Reading most of the militant leaders were undergraduates.
The very first three were postgraduates doing one-year courses; all of these came from
other Universities. Subsequently, postgraduates were involved in the affairs of the Union,
but their main contribution came in improving the students' facilities, especially the
provision for sports.
[4] Senate Reports, xxviii, 13 June 1966.
[5] Senate Minute, 4172, 13 June 1966. An earlier request had been rejected in 1964
(Senate Minute, 3875(b), 12 October 1964).

sought and agreed for three other officers and a request for a further two was under consideration. The difference in time-scale also underlay widely diverging attitudes towards the future. The staff had to live with the changes they brought about and would be answerable for future generations of students. The students were gone before many of the changes they advocated could take effect. Nothing emphasized this contrast so much as the unwillingness of the students to accept a comparatively small charge on Hall fees to cover the loan financing of new residential accommodation from which they and their successors would benefit.[1] That they themselves benefited from earlier benefactions was the only comment left to their seniors.[2]

All these difficulties were made manifest by the agitation which began late in 1968. However, by that date, the University had already come to involve the students in discussions. On the recommendation of the Committee of Deans the Senate agreed to establish a university staff/student committee as early as January 1965.[3] It was through this body that the cases for a sabbatical year for the President, for consultation about Hall rules, for the revision of disciplinary regulations and for greater student participation in the government of the University, were first advanced. Although its discussions were somewhat desultory[4] something had been achieved by the autumn of 1968: student representatives joined the Committee on Residence in that term; the regulations on discipline had just undergone their first revision;[5] the Senate was considering a recommendation for the establishment of staff/student committees in departments, based on a proposal submitted by the President of the Union in May 1967.[6] Moreover, beside the work of this Committee there were other less formal developments. On its own initiative the Geography Department

[1] For this development see above, p. 201.
[2] See the remarks of Sir George Abell, President of Council in *Proceedings 1970–1*, p. 8.
[3] The Deans reported as follows: 'At present the only link which the Students' Union has with the University 'authorities' is with the Vice-Chancellor. The Committee is of opinion that it would be wise to establish some form of procedure which would bring the Students' Union into closer contact with other members of the University in order that there might be discussion of problems and proposals. It accordingly recommends that an informal Staff/Student Committee be appointed consisting of members of the Senate, members of the Academic Staff and members of the Students' Union. It considers that no formal terms of reference should be set for this Committee except that it should discuss, informally, matters of common concern.' (Senate Reports, xxiv, 18 January 1965). The original staff members of the Committee were Professor A. H. Bunting, Professor P. W. Campbell, Professor A. Graham, Professor A. G. Lehmann and Dr K. Robinson (Senate Minute 3922, 18 January 1965). The students were represented by the President and four others.
[4] It held six meetings in all, the first in May 1965. It was intended to meet every term, but it never met in the summer term after 1965. The meeting of the autumn term 1966 was cancelled as there was 'no item of importance to discuss'. In the autumn of 1967 the staff members met alone to discuss a paper on departmental staff/student committees presented by the President of the Union in May.
[5] Senate Reports, 19 June 1968.
[6] *Ibid.*, 21 June 1967.

established a staff/student committee which was quoted as a model
example by the President of the Union in his own submission. The discussion of his proposals led to the establishment of a similar committee in the
Department of Politics,[1] and other departments soon followed suit.[2] Yet
again, new residential schemes were under discussion. As early as January
1964 the Building Development Committee indicated to the Council and
the Senate that it was considering a 'student village'.[3] A year later this was
presented as a detailed scheme for the establishment at Elm Farm of a
'village' for 3,000 students along with 150 academic staff, including
married quarters for 100 domestic staff and a full provision of the necessary
social facilities.[4] Study-bedroom blocks were envisaged with central
catering facilities; some tentative provision was made for supervision by
responsible staff;[5] but it was clear that the scheme was far removed from the
traditional hall of residence and that in such accommodation many Hall
regulations would be quite inapplicable. It went forward; Sibly Hall,
completed in 1968, was the first and so far the only building to be constructed.[6] Meanwhile the Committee on Residence was examining the
possibility of converting existing Halls to mixed residence. A working party
made up of two wardens and two students reported favourably in June
1968.[7] St Andrew's Hall became mixed in October 1969. By 1975 it had
been followed by all but three of the rest.[8] This was part of more general
changes in attitude which were becoming apparent by 1968. Hall rules were
slowly relaxed; visiting hours were extended; staff/student committees
were involved experimentally in the government of some Halls.

From 1968 it was not so much the direction as the pace of change which
altered. Consultative committees proliferated: a new University Joint

[1] P. W. Campbell, 'The Department of Politics: notes on the Department's first decade:
1964–74'.
[2] Some, following suggestions made in the Staff/Student Committee, used the student
academic societies as a basis for departmental committees. This was later viewed with
suspicion by the militants.
[3] Building Development Committee, 13 January 1964.
[4] The report was presented by the Residential Policy Committee, 4 February 1965
for the Building Development Committee on 11 February, the Senate on 22 February
and the Council on 12 March. The Senate and the Council approved it (Senate
Minute, 3945, 22 February 1965; Council Minute 2406, 12 March 1965).
[5] 'It is not possible at this stage to say what accommodation would be needed for
wardens nor whether it should be integrated with or separate from student residences.
A decision cannot be made until the system of management of the village has been
further discussed. It seems fairly certain, however, that in each student unit there will
need to be a resident officer-in-charge.' (Report of Residential Policy Committee,
loc. cit).
[6] The scheme envisaged that numbers would rise to about 7,000–8,000. In fact they
settled well below that. See above pp. 156, 237–40. The scheme also encountered
difficulties with the Planning Authorities which were never fully resolved.
[7] Report of the Committee on Residence, 10 June 1968 (Senate Reports, 19 June 1968).
[8] St Patrick's, Wessex and Whiteknights. It was subsequently decided that Wessex would
become mixed in October 1977.

Committee replaced the old Staff/Student Committee in 1969;[1] consultative committees were established in the faculties; in 1970 the Senate finally gave formal approval to the establishment of staff/student committees in departments;[2] a similar committee was established for the Library. Representation on governing bodies and committees advanced almost as rapidly. It was accepted most readily in residential affairs where the interests of the students were immediately involved and where there was a long tradition of consultation between wardens and students. The student representatives added to the Committee on Residence in 1968 were increased in number a year later; students were included in the initial establishment of the Halls Corporation Board of Management in 1973; and in these years they came to be included on project committees concerned with residential building.[3] The Council was responsive. Some members were keenly interested in, if not a little puzzled by, the new urgency of the students. Gerald Palmer, who in his years as President went out of his way to meet and entertain the Officers of the Union and others, was closely involved in the establishment of the Joint Working Party in 1968.[4] The Working Party foundered,[5] but discussion which began there led not only to the establishment of the Joint Committee but also to a decision to invite three officers of the Students' Union to attend the meetings of the Council for a preliminary period of two years.[6] The arrangement was subsequently renewed. The Senate was much more reluctant. Many of its members viewed academic matters as the exclusive preserve of the staff and in May 1969 they decided by a narrow majority not to add students as full members.[7] It took two more years and much negotiation before the Senate finally agreed that students should be invited to attend on the understanding that there would be areas of reserved business from which they

[1] Council Minute 2862, 30 May 1969. The committee first met in October 1969.
The original composition was the President of the Council, the Vice-Chancellor, the President of the Union and the Senior Vice-President, two members of the Council, two members of the Senate, four members of the Non-professorial staff, two members of the Presidents' Committee and six members of the Students' Union. The number of Union members was subsequently increased; the balance in the committee was maintained by increasing the number of elected staff *pari passu*. These were now elected from, and by ballot of, all members of staff.
[2] Senate Minute 4842, 17 June 1970. See above, p. 315.
[3] The President and Senior Vice-President joined the Board of Residence in 1968. Two representatives of the Union and two representatives of the Presidents' Committee were added in 1969. The Halls Corporation Board of Management included the President and two other students.
[4] The Council members of the working party were Sir George Abell, Gerald Palmer, the Honourable Gordon Palmer and Lady Helen Smith.
[5] The militants demanded public meetings with the right of interruption by observers, a rotating chairmanship and a joint secretaryship. A Union meeting of 15 May finally withdrew the students' representatives.
[6] Council Minute 2863, 30 May 1969. The students were the President of the Union, the Senior Vice-President and the Past President or President Elect.
[7] The voting was 24 to 21 (Senate Minute 4653, 7 May 1969).

would be excluded.[1] However, by 1971 many members of the Senate were deeply disenchanted with the Students' Union. They rejected Union or directly elected representatives other than the President. Instead they designed a more academic pattern comprising, in addition to the President, the Chairman of the Postgraduate Society and one undergraduate from each faculty staff/student consultative committee, which in turn was made up of one student from each departmental staff/student committee.[2] That ingenious system of indirect election was a hedge against political intrusion. The case for representation on boards of faculties was but feebly pressed by the students and was not seriously entertained.

At the time these changes were seen by some to portend a new era. They were asserted as principles:

A University is an academic community, a partnership of interests, in which each part should contribute to the whole. This University is made up of both staff and students; both are essential parts of the whole. Yet at the highest level, where the ultimate decisions are made, there are no students. If the views and interests of all members of the community are to be taken into account when decisions are made it is *essential* that student representatives be present to make student feeling known.

A large proportion of the running of a university is by definition of importance to students; they are numerically the largest group within the university. Many of the decisions taken in both Senate and Council, then affect students directly; but members of Senate and Council have no formal way of assessing student opinion on the policies which they consider. This means that they are taking decisions with less information than is necessary.

The Students' Union feels that student representation on Council and Senate would be as valuable to these two bodies as it would be to students. We are quite sure that students can play a valid part in the running of the university in spite of the rapid turnover in personnel.[3]

That was the essence of the students' case. It seemed challenging. The Vice-Chancellor commented mildly that it 'embodied a very positive element of change, which would have to command very strong support if it were to be accepted'.[4] However, it seemed more positive than it was to prove in practice. That may be illustrated by one detailed element in the case: the question of mandation. The students argued that their members of the Senate would be considered to be delegates in that they would, before the

[1] The Joint Committee pressed the students' case again in July 1970 (Senate Reports, 2 July 1970) and it was finally decided to ballot all members of the Senate. This time the vote was marginally in favour of admitting students in some form (37 to 30; Senate Minute 4882, October 1970).
[2] Senate Minutes 4932, 4950, 5 May 1971.
[3] 'Student Membership of Senate and Council', a paper submitted by the President of the Union and a delegation of students to the Senate, 26 February 1969 (Senate Reports, 26 February 1969).
[4] Senate Minute 4632, 26 February 1969.

Senate meeting, discuss in the Union or some other composite body matters which were of concern to students; put the Union view on these to the Senate, and vote accordingly; and report back the Senate's decisions thereon.[1]

Much of the discussion both in the Senate and in the Council, where the same demand was made *mutatis mutandis*, was concerned with this proposal[2] and the arrangements finally agreed were designed to exclude it as far as possible.[3] In fact the danger was chimerical. The schedule which determined the circulation of papers for the meetings of the Senate and the Council scarcely allowed sufficient time for the preliminary meetings which the students envisaged, especially since they were not notably adept in their own administrative arrangements. In the event 'mandation' was never a serious problem; as the Registrar pointed out it was 'an emotive and ill-defined term';[4] its appearance in the discussion only led the authorities to emphasize that students who joined the Council or the Senate would be required to assume all the responsibilities which full members of those bodies carried. Most of them did so willingly and readily. As time passed, and the inherited experience of the student members deepened, so they fitted increasingly easily into the routine of the governing bodies. That was not what the student leaders had intended in the heady days of 'Action for a Free University', but to members of the Council and the Senate it marked the return of common sense. The students had been absorbed into the government of the University.

The effects are not easy to estimate. Within a single department staff and students might co-operate easily and effectively. In the Department of Politics, for example, the staff/student committee, comprising all the staff and an equal number of students, played an important part in decision-making, discussing 'the degree structure, syllabuses, the contents of courses, teaching arrangements, participation in classes, examination arrangements and the establishment of a departmental students' library financed by subscriptions'.[5] It was described as 'a committee which works'; that comment coming from one of the most militant of student leaders, was indeed an accolade. In University committees also there was a ready give and take wherever staff and students settled to work on practical problems. But on a larger scale the results were most obvious where they were most negative. One effect of the Latey Report and the agitation which began in 1968 was to change the structure of Hall regulations which the Committee on Residence had begun slowly to amend in that year. Following a report

---

[1] *Ibid.*
[2] The Vice-Chancellor informed the students' delegation in the Senate on 26 February that 'he was more worried about the question of mandation than confidentiality. He felt that a mandated member might not be able to make a useful contribution' (*ibid.*).
[3] 'Student representation on Senate and Council', a paper prepared by the Registrar (Council Reports, 30 May 1969; Senate Reports, 7 May 1969).
[4] *Ibid.*
[5] P. W. Campbell, *op. cit.*

of a working party of October 1970 it was agreed that rules governing visiting hours should be the concern in each Hall of a committee consisting of the Warden and of representatives of the Senior and Junior Common Rooms. The old assumption which linked such rules to questions of sexual morality was formally abandoned. Hall rules became a practical question concerned with security, the exclusion of unwanted guests, excessive noise and anti-social behaviour. The working party even recognized that 'students generally do not wish to be protected' and asserted that it was 'not the wish of the University to force its protection on individual students in matters relating to residence'.[1] It was less easy to pinpoint positive achievements. For example, in its first year, the Joint Committee spent much time discussing assessment and examinations. The first report which it presented in July 1970 led to the establishment of a Senate Committee on examinations which reported early in 1973.[2] That report in turn led to a revision by some boards of faculties of marking procedures for the First University Examination. That was a definite result, but it was achieved long after the students who first launched their criticism of the First University Examination in 1969 had left the University. And if that seemed dilatory the introduction of assessment methods and the revision of procedures in the Final Examination seemed both dilatory and diffuse. Necessarily important changes could only take place after a two-year interval,[3] and they came bit by bit, department by department, faculty by faculty.

It was not easy for those who launched large-scale proposals for 'reform' in the Joint Committee to appreciate that there was a hierarchy of responsibility which was not susceptible to political pressure. The Joint Committee might propose, but departments would dispose. The organization of the University was more federal, even perhaps more democratic, than student reformers allowed. Hence there was some sense of frustration, a feeling that reforms were delayed, blocked or lost in a maze of committees. In some frustration gave birth to realism. One of the arguments advanced by members of the Senate who supported student membership was that:

> Although the students misinterpreted the role of the Senate, seeing
> it as a forum for debate rather than a managerial organ, nevertheless,
> membership would have a therapeutic effect, binding them into,
> and making them more responsible members of, the academic
> community to which they could make a distinctive contribution.[4]

It would be difficult to prove that the therapy changed fanatics into committee-men, but it certainly deterred the one and encouraged the other.

[1] Report of the Committee on Residence (Senate Reports, 18 November 1970; Senate Minute 4904, 18 November 1970).
[2] Senate Reports, 2 July 1970, 24 January 1973.
[3] The University accepted that syllabuses should not be revised during a student's course except in exceptional circumstances, e.g. the death or resignation of an essential member of staff. Additions to syllabuses, however, could be and were frequently made at less than the two-year interval.
[4] Senate Minute 4632, 26 February 1969.

Chapter 11

Reckoning

One last word. I do not want to see this University too big. We have,
in our modest way, certain particular virtues which distinguish
this University from others. I do not propose to try to rehearse them
all now, for this is not an occasion for immodesty. But they all depend,
in the last resort, on a sort of intimacy, a domesticity, if you like,
which means that we do really know each other, that we are, consciously or unconsciously, members one of another, a real community,
sharing each other's aspirations, disappointments, failures and
successes. If we ever lose that we shall lose the deep sense of personality
which this University abundantly possesses. We shall do everything
we can to meet national needs and to do our national duty. But we
should betray not only our own heritage but the whole ideal of all
university life if in doing that we were to lose our own soul.

That was how Wolfenden concluded his annual address to the Court
almost exactly thirty years after the foundation of the University.[1] The
gods jested, for even he could not have foreseen that, within a decade, he
would be responsible, as Chairman of the University Grants Committee,
for leading Reading and other universities through the travail of the
Robbins Report. Ten years later that speech would have rung hollow or
seemed to express mere fantasy, for the old Reading was then having to
come to terms with the rapid growth in Whiteknights. Whether, in that, the
University lost its soul, whether there was some quintessential characteristic, some ethos, which was threatened or destroyed, is a matter not of
evidence and fact, but of language and logic. It is a question whether the
changing relationships and new tasks which increasing size involved merit
such heightened language. For no one budgets for a University's soul; the
genius loci submits no estimates.

Many of those who took part in the expansion considered that change was
not only acceptable but necessary. To Bryce-Smith, who joined the
Department of Chemistry in 1956, 'the place was like a cottage university . . .
many departments were far too small to be able to teach their subjects with

[1] *Reading University Gazette*, xxix, 2, p. 5, 28 March 1956, reporting the meeting of the
Court of 29 February.

the breadth appropriate to modern times'.[1] A. H. Bunting, who came to the Chair of Agricultural Botany in the same year, was conscious enough of Reading's outstanding reputation in agricultural studies, but he came to feel nevertheless that it smacked of an agricultural college, very much devoted to farming, here and there almost anti-scientific in some of its attitudes; hence he could claim that 'one of our big jobs in the 1960s was to transform it'.[2] To those who were part of the change, therefore, especially to those newly come to Reading, the expansion of the University was an absorbing achievement, just as its foundation had been to their predecessors a generation earlier. Even so, the newcomer, like the older hand, expressed some regrets. In 1970 Bryce-Smith could look back on his fourteen years at Reading and feel that something had been lost in the transition from a 'cottage university':

> Relationships between members of staff were much closer than at present – both liking and disliking. In particular, one knew far more members of other departments than is the case now, and conversation in the Senior Common Room was far more general. For instance, there would be impassioned debates on morality and during the Suez Crisis the Common Room was split down the middle. This was possible in the intimate atmosphere of those days, but would not occur today when large numbers of staff use the Common Room simply for lunch and coffee. But in 1956 you went to the Common Room for entertainment, and it was full of highly colourful personalities, with strong feelings, who helped to create the atmosphere. Now if you raise your voice in discussion, people look at you over the tops of their newspapers. Something has been lost, for the Common Room was then a gracious place, with catering to match. One example of the gracious life was our game of bowls which was surrounded with an elaborate and humorous ritual, but the fact that the woods are now gathering mould is a further example of our diminishing corporate activities.[3]

Though concerned with apparent trivia, that perhaps touches on some part of Wolfenden's 'soul'. It may also reflect the common human experience that the last stage but one (or even two) always seems to have been the best. At Reading that feeling was particularly strong. Ask the older hands about the last twenty years and they will talk of buildings and resources. Ask them about the earlier years and their eyes will light up. In that sense of a golden past there are elements which have little or nothing to do with Reading as such; the year 1939 was a climacteric not just for the University; but there is also a bed-rock of fact which is not to be ignored. The early years of the University not only seem the best to those who can recall them. In some ways they were the best.

[1] Conversation with Professor D. Bryce-Smith, 7 October 1970.
[2] Conversation with Professor A. H. Bunting, 14 August 1975.
[3] Conversation with Professor D. Bryce-Smith, 7 October 1970.

That may be illustrated in mundane fashion by the table overleaf of numbers and resources 1928–74. Admittedly numerical information of this kind is frequently a snare. There are also particular dangers in making comparisons which require extensive adjustment to the changing value of money. Nevertheless, some parts of the story are made plain beyond any serious doubt. First, it is clear that from the 1950s the ratio of students to staff increased. Before the war it never rose above five. By the late 1960s it always exceeded seven, and even that began to seem very low as the economies of the middle 1970s began to take effect. Secondly, the revenues and expenditure increased considerably. To sum it up there were more staff, teaching many more students, but they were provided with more resources with which to do it. But, thirdly, that was not a continuous progression. In the 1930s the staff not only enjoyed a more advantageous staff/student ratio than in the late 1950s; they also seem to have had equivalent or even greater resources measured in real terms and *per capita* against the total of staff and students. It was not in fact until the 1960s that these rose consistently above the level of 1948. Fourthly, that increase was relatively small. Between 1938–9 and 1973–4 the number of students and teaching staff increased nearly eight-fold. In the same period the ratio of students to staff increased by 54 per cent and the *per capita* expenditure in real terms by 25 per cent. There would appear to have been some economies of scale.

These trends underlay and gave solidity to the nostalgia of the older staff. It must be said at once that a comparatively small increase in *per capita* resources was of enormous importance to the teaching and research of the University. It brought in its train technical and secretarial assistance, administrative support, costly equipment, essential laboratory materials and a library worthy of a large university. It is against that, which some perhaps accepted too readily as a matter of course, that the sense of a better past, lost beyond recall, must be set. But that feeling did not find its only source in relatively simple matters like the increasing physical size of the University or the increasing ratio of students to staff. As generation succeeded generation and year succeeded year, each member of staff had to contend with the developments in his own subject, slow in some, rapid in others, increasingly complex in all, and all tending to force him into a narrower vision and a more specialized experience. The band of scholars whom Wolfenden could still imagine in 1956 sharing each others' interests tended always to become a company of specialists increasingly fragmented into smaller and smaller academic groupings. At the extreme, the sense of common endeavour amounted to little more than the recognition of common employment by a large organization. Hence the cry of the local branch of the Association of Scientific, Technical and Managerial Staffs:

> Effectively the universities are now part of the *education industry* and – like other workers – academics need a *trade union* which acts together with workers and professionals in other industries . . . .

Numbers and resources 1928–74[1]

Session	Registered students under tutorial supervision	Teaching staff	Staff/ student ratio	Total expenditure in £	Expenditure per unit (staff and students) in £	Corrected expenditure per unit in £	Percentage (recurrent grant of total income)
1928–9	713	150	4.75	94,589	109.60	598.90	35.60
1934–5	708	143	4.95	107,312	127.30	805.70	42.85
1938–9	698	146	4.80	129,747	153.70	883.50	47.50
1948–9	1,019	182	5.60	281,877	234.70	686.30	52.60
1953–4	1,161	241	4.80	396,605	282.90	668.90	81.70
1958–9	1,476	260	5.70	696,910	401.45	819.30	80.90
1963–4	2,003	305	6.60	1,393,683	603.85	1,099.90	78.75
1968–9	4,996	656	7.60	3,712,657	656.90	981.90	77.90
1973–4	5,816	783	7.40	7,316,226	1,108.70	1,108.70	81.00

[1] Any table of this kind must be to some degree arbitrary. Opinions will differ about what should and should not be included. However it is doubtful whether any of the possible variants would affect the general picture presented by the figures to any great degree. The following notes will help to explain the procedure followed:

(a) The initial and terminal years have been selected in order to exclude the initial expansion which followed the granting of the Charter on the one hand and the onset of the economies which began to take effect in 1974–5, on the other.

(b) The figure for students is the gross figure of registered students under tutorial supervision. It excludes the large number of students who before the war followed evening courses and similar training; the staff engaged solely in teaching these courses have also been excluded. The presentation of statistics was altered in 1969–70. The effect is to exaggerate very slightly the figure for student numbers for 1973–4.

(c) The National Institute for Research in Dairying has been included both in staff numbers and figures for expenditure.

(d) The figures for total expenditure are the gross figures from the Income and Expenditure Account for Teaching and Research for the years in question. A deduction of approximately 5 per cent has been made from the totals of 1928–9, 1934–5 and 1938–9 for the costs incurred in teaching students not under tutorial supervision. This is somewhat arbitrary since the departments involved, such as Commerce and Domestic Subjects, also had pupils under tutorial supervision. No deduction has been made for the School of Music which was a continuing commitment throughout the whole period.

(e) The corrected expenditure per unit is to a base of 1 January 1974 = 100. The index used is that provided by 'The Internal Purchasing Power of the Pound' (Central Statistical Office, May 1975), table 2, p. 4. Since this table already compounds three indexes, I have hesitated to add a fourth by introducing the Tress-Brown index into the calculations.

For those teaching and research staff who have strong ideas and convictions about their work, ASTMS will work to gain increased influence both on the administration here at Reading and the decision-makers at the national level. *Only a union which unites academics with other university workers, such as technicians, research and administrative staff can expect to deal effectively with our present problems.*[1]

In so far as that struck any spark, it was in the breasts of the younger members of staff. Yet it was but one of many responses to the size and diversity of the University. Another was provided by two young research students in the Department of History who in 1965 founded a Society for the History of Ideas. That took root. It remained relatively small, its meetings rarely numbering more than forty. But it still survived in 1976 as a forum in which physicists, philosophers, psychologists, historians, biologists and classicists could talk to each other on academic matters.

In the end therefore there remains a series of kaleidoscopic impressions. Yet there is perhaps one clear distinction which separates the pre-war from the post-war Reading. Up to the Second World War Reading strove, quite self-consciously, to be different. It took pride in its small scale, its residential system and its readiness to attempt much with minimal resources. The self-satisfaction which newcomers tended to notice was a kind of protective barrier around characteristics which were emphasized partly by design, partly through necessity, partly through the zest engendered among the participants in the enterprise. After the war, in contrast, Reading sought, in a less clear-minded fashion, to be more like other universities. It wanted equivalent resources and it had in the end to accept a roughly equivalent size.[2] That too engendered a zest in the participants but not one which emphasized any unique quality in the place to the extent experienced by the pre-war generation. The change in direction took time. It began with the Development Committee of 1943-4.[3] It was complete when the Registrar, himself a Reading man, pointed out in the summer of 1963 that the University was no longer a small and intimate institution.[4] A few resisted and obstructed the change.[5] Many more accepted it while still asserting that the University must not lose its intimate family characteristics which the change inevitably undermined.[6] And the change was not centred in Reading alone. As Reading sought to match the resources of other universities so they sought to match Reading's residential system. In this, by 1957 when the University Grants Committee published its *Report on Halls of Residence*,[7] Reading had long ceased to provide an

1 'ASTMS for Reading University', a leaflet issued by the local branch, 1975.
2 See above, pp. 156-7.
3 See above, pp. 120-132.
4 See above, pp. 174-5.
5 See above, pp. 157, 174.
6 In this Wolfenden's view expressed above, p. 321, was broadly representative.
7 HMSO.

example to the rest. Indeed, there was now some concern lest it should fall behind where it had once led.[1]

There was a further and wider contrast. Before the war the staff at Reading felt that they had to struggle to survive as a University: they were masters of their own fate. After the war they could scarcely avoid the conclusion that although they now enjoyed increasing resources their fate was determined elsewhere. That change can be expressed in a simple arithmetical fashion; up to 1939 the recurrent grant never reached 50 per cent of the University's total income. After 1953–4 it never fell much below 80 per cent. Those who paid the piper called the tune. Reading was never ordered to expand. It simply received a number of requests, or suggestions which it was not in a position to refuse.[2] Likewise, it was never ordered to contract; it was simply placed in a position in which it had to economize. These policies did not originate in Reading. They came from the University Grants Committee, the Department of Education and Science and the various governments of the day. They embodied inaccurate predictions of the number of university places required and the number the country could afford. This work is not the proper place to discuss whether error could have been avoided. Only one comment is perhaps permissible; there would appear to be no good reason for making Reading or any other university more directly dependent on the source of error, especially since error works through the system like an undamped oscillation. When the Treasury or Queen Elizabeth House sneezes, university departments catch cold; and colleges of education die.

These changes were inevitable. They were inevitable psychologically. Professors and heads of departments wanted the resources to do a proper job; with scarcely an exception each individually undermined the small-scale characteristics of Reading which collectively they sought to maintain.[3] They were inevitable politically and financially. The University never considered a future divorced from government aid. In any case such a future would have been quite impracticable. In June 1911, the University Endowment of £200,000 was founded by three people: George William Palmer, Alfred Palmer and Lady Wantage.[4] The Building Appeal launched in 1929 brought in approximately £70,000 after a campaign lasting eight years. That was roughly one-fifth, in real terms, of what had been possible in 1911 alone.[5] In 1974 the £200,000 of 1911 would have been equivalent

---

[1] See the comment of Miss Ursula Martindale, Warden of St Andrew's, in a discussion of the *Report on Halls of Residence* in the Non-professorial staff – 'As pioneers we suffered from a serious lack of amenities by comparison with newer halls of residence.' (Non-professorial staff, Minutes of General Meetings, 11 December 1957). See also above, pp. 173–4.
[2] See above, pp. 147–8, 171–4.
[3] See above, pp. 124–5, 160–2.
[4] See above, p. 12.
[5] See above, p. 34.

to £2,000,000. Even if some benefactor had provided that, welcome though it would have been, the resulting endowed income would have done no more than top up a recurrent government grant which amounted in that year to £6,000,000. Given the level of students' fees, there was no way in which any conceivable benefaction could give the University independence or even restore it to the more limited dependence of 1926.

Reading therefore responded to changing attitudes and policies in the country at large. The University took more students; its staff did more research. The expansion of research was absorbed comparatively easily; it had been an objective of the University since its birth. The increase of students was a different matter. There was much discussion of standards. Wolfenden himself commented in his address to the Court in 1956:

> And what about standards? My own opinion about this question is perhaps rather crude. I cannot get away from the elementary view that in fact at the present moment university standards, not just here but throughout the universities as a whole, are dictated by the simple numerical fact of the number of university places there are. I suspect that there are very few university places deliberately left vacant on the ground that candidates of sufficient merit have not presented themselves. Indeed, the schools are apt to complain that the standards required are too high. In short, I believe that standards are determined by the candidates themselves in their mutual competition for the places available. So this standard may be different in different departments of one university at the same time, or in similarly named departments of the same university, from one year to another. So, you see, I personally believe that to talk of 'university standards' as if they represented something absolute, or even relatively permanent, is a misconception. Granted always the minimum qualifications – which in these days guarantee nothing, either for the student or for any university – the standards are empirically fixed by the candidates themselves, from one year to another. The present total number of university places in the country at large has been arrived at by a series of accidents; it has no absolute validity in relation to the size of the population of this country. Many people think it is too small; a few think it is too big. However that may be, and nobody seems to know how it ought to be determined, it is that fact, the simple arithmetical number of places available, which seems to me to determine the standards of admission. And that will continue to be true whatever that arithmetical number may in the future be.[1]

That was a faultless analysis. But if it hints at the lower standards sometimes accepted for courses which were not in great demand, it has to be set against an earlier change: the termination of the certificate and diploma

[1] *Reading University Gazette*, xxix, 2, pp. 4–5.

courses.[1] Taking that into account there was probably little overall difference in the intellectual quality of the students.

However, there were obvious changes in other respects. Following the Latey Report of 1967 the students could no longer be placed firmly *in statu pupilari*. They came to play an increasing role in the general affairs of the University. Within their own age-group they were less isolated than their predecessors had been. Taking weekends during term to go home or visit friends, once granted only in special circumstances, was now a frequent and accepted practice. This, and the paid work which many undertook during the vacations, kept them in touch with the increasing affluence of young people outside the universities. Yet mix though they might with their peers, and adult though they might be in the eyes of the law, there were few who enjoyed any real financial independence. Hence there was an area of adult responsibility in which most of them were innocent. The low level of student-grants, the lack of any scheme for student-loans and the dependence of many on parental contributions never allowed them to achieve the full maturity which their claim to a say in the government of the University subsumed. Some played at politics just as their predecessors had played rugby or decorated the social scene. Others, for many different reasons, became casualties. There were not many of these, perhaps no higher a proportion than in earlier generations, but now, in a larger university, with the firm control of warden and tutor no longer reinforced by disciplinary regulations, other steps were necessary. In 1973 the University appointed a Counsellor, supported in 1975 by part-time assistants and then in 1976 by a second Counsellor. To a degree the work became self-generating. One of the deans took to concluding his annual address to new students by saying: 'Finally, ladies and gentlemen, if you find you do not need to call on the excellent services provided by the University Counsellor, don't worry: you're normal'. What de Burgh might have said may safely be left to the imagination, where it properly belongs.

What then is the soul of the University to which Wolfenden referred? Its quality stems from relationships: of staff to students, of both to the subjects they follow, of the University to its immediate physical environment and beyond that to the outside world. Those relationships have changed and are still changing; often the University has had no choice but to face up to them, and in that context the plea to sustain the soul of the University

---

[1] On this see above, pp. 50–2, 121–2, 249–50. Sir Harold Sanders's subsequent impression was – 'These diploma students did not do the Intermediate Examination; they did not know much science and indeed they had not got the same qualifications as the degree students on entry; they did the practical side. They were rather hearty, some of them were farmers' sons, and on the whole they were not up to degree work. The general feeling in the Faculty of Agriculture was that it was "a pity to abolish the Diploma since the students were nice chaps, but it had to go". There was some concern in the Faculty whether the required number of degree-students would be forthcoming, but in fact it scarcely ever fell short.' (Conversation, 12 August 1975).

against necessary and inevitable change has been little more than squashy sentimentality. But suppose that the essential characteristics which go to make up that soul include adaptability, then that is a test-bed on which all its other characteristics are to be tried. And if some of the relationships established in the past can be sustained in the present then that is as near a soul as a university is likely to achieve. In 1976 in reviewing the first fifty years of the University, Sue Reid commented:

> Reading today is a university which neither trumpets its own virtues nor yields its secrets casually. It is a quiet, undramatic place and the assortment of architectural styles which distinguish the buildings scattered throughout Whiteknights Park gives little hint of the considerable intellectual power within. . . . Reading, in a sense, is not an innovatory university, but one which has always known what universities are about, and got on with the job. . . . Flexibility is one of Reading's great strengths. There is a seeming ease with which academics get together there to plan joint courses, or simply to work together. It also makes the very best use of its existing facilities.[1]

There are echoes in that of Stenton's letter to Pollard with which this work began;[2] there are echoes of the early enthusiasms of de Burgh and many others for combined courses and special subjects; and in the last sentence there is a reflection of the long years of parsimony and perhaps of a distant glint in the eagle eye of E. H. Carpenter. There has been pathos in the change which Reading has undergone, for it has lost some of its early character. In the 1930s it was an outstanding example of a small residential university. Now, in a national conspectus, it is just another campus university. The cry against expansion that – 'We shan't know each other any more' – has been proved to be largely true; and those who knew Reading earlier may well feel – 'We are hence, we are gone, as though we had not been there'. But it is not all loss. It is rather the price paid for the study of a far wider range of subjects, to a far greater depth, by a far larger body of students, researchers and scholars. Moreover they are not all gone. Barnard still visits the Common Room at the Acacias. Harris and Ditchburn still come to the campus to work in their laboratories. Until her death in 1976 Nan Ure still tended the collection of classical antiquities which she and Percy Neville Ure accumulated long ago. And Nellie Eales still visits the Library, where, supported by the faithful F. C. Padley, she directs the affairs of the Cole Library. The soul of a University is not defined by the relationships of the moment. Its essential quality was summed up long ago by the eighteenth-century antiquary Thomas Hearne, Non-juror, cantankerous waspish controversialist, but an assiduous scholar whom Stenton revered:

> The dignity and splendour of a university lie not in the size of its

---

[1] *Times Higher Education Supplement*, 19 March 1976.
[2] See above, pp. 3–5.

buildings nor in the number of people living in comfort and indolence, but in a multitude of learned and studious men.[1]

Those who have belonged to the community of Reading would be content with that.

[1] For the quotation and the circumstances see Harry Carter, *A History of the Oxford University Press* (Oxford, 1975), i, 267–8. The best short account of Hearne is in D. C. Douglas, *English Scholars 1660–1730* (London, 1951), pp. 178–194. The Non-jurors originated in the clergy who refused to take the oath of allegiance to William and Mary after the Revolution of 1688.

Officers of the University

Chancellor

1926–35	J. H. Benyon
1935–7	Sir Austen Chamberlain
1937–59	Viscount Templewood (formerly Sir Samuel Hoare)
1959–69	Lord Bridges
1970–	Lord Sherfield

Vice-Chancellor

1926–9	W. M. Childs
1929–46	Sir Franklin Sibly
1946–50	Sir Frank Stenton
1950–63	Sir John Wolfenden
1963–4	Professor J. M. R. Cormack (Acting Vice-Chancellor)
1964–	H. R. Pitt

President of the Council

1926–30	Alfred Palmer
1930–2	Leonard G. Sutton
1933–66	Sir George Mowbray
1966–70	Gerald E. H. Palmer
1970–4	Sir George Abell
1974–5	The Hon. Gordon W. N. Palmer
1975–	Sir Michael Milne-Watson

Vice-President of the Council

1926–30	Leonard G. Sutton
1930–2	Sir Leslie Wilson
1932–6	H. G. Willink
1936–46	A. G. West
1946–66	Gerald E. H. Palmer
1966–74	The Hon. Gordon W. N. Palmer
1974–5	Sir Michael Milne-Watson
1975–	R. A. O'Conor

Treasurer

1926–30	Sir William A. Mount, Bart.
1930–1	Leonard G. Sutton
1931–2	Sir George Mowbray
1932–46	A. P. Shaw
1946–50	Sir William M. Mount, Bart.
1950–3	Gerald E. H. Palmer
1953–5	M. Lubbock
1955–9	The Hon. Gordon W. N. Palmer
1959–63	Major L. M. E. Dent
1963–8	C. Fitzherbert
1968–70	Sir George Abell
1970–4	R. O. Steel
1974–	S. R. F. Drake

Deputy Vice-Chancellor

1926–34	Professor W. G. de Burgh
1934–46	Professor F. M. Stenton
1946–50	Professor A. W. P. Wolters
1950–2	Professor C. H. O'Donoghue
1952–4	Professor H. G. Sanders
1954–64	Professor J. M. R. Cormack
1964–8	Professor A. Graham
1968–76	Professor C. Tyler
1976–	Professor E. W. J. Mitchell

Registrar

1926–7	Revd. F. H. Wright
1927–32	H. Knapman
1932–55	E. Smith
1955–	J. F. Johnson

Bursar

1926–36	J. S. Simpson
1936–41	E. B. Morgan

A reorganization of the financial administration of the University resulted in the disappearance of the post of Bursar until its reinstatement in 1946

1946–73	E. H. Carpenter
1974–	R. H. Giddings

Deans of the Faculties[1]

Dean of Faculty of Letters (Letters & Social Sciences from 1968)

1926–34	W. G. de Burgh
1934–48	R. Dewar
1948–54	J. M. R. Cormack
1954–7	D. J. Gordon
1957–60	F. P. Pickering
1960–6	A. G. Lehmann
1966–9	P. W. Campbell
1969–72	F. R. Palmer
1972–6	J. C. Holt
1976–	R. Davis

Dean of Faculty of Science

1926–30	H. Bassett
1930–6	J. A. Crowther
1936–40	H. L. Hawkins
1940–4	A. A. Miller
1944–8	C. H. O'Donoghue
1948–52	T. M. Harris
1952–4	A. A. Miller
1954–6	E. A. Guggenheim
1956–60	B. C. J. G. Knight
1960–3	A. Graham
1963–6	P. Allen
1966–9	E. W. J. Mitchell
1969–72	G. W. A. Fowles
1972–5	C. Kaplan
1975–	H. M. Frey

Dean of Faculty of Agriculture & Horticulture (Agriculture from 1961, Agriculture & Food from 1971)

1926–47	H. A. D. Neville
1947–51	H. G. Sanders
1951–5	R. H. Stoughton
1955–9	E. Thomas
1959–62	C. Tyler
1962–5	E. L. Crossley
1965–71	A. H. Bunting
1971–4	R. H. Tuck
1974–	R. N. Curnow

Dean of Faculty of Urban & Regional Studies

1967–72	R. Jardine Brown
1972–5	C. W. N. Miles
1975–	P. G. Hall

[1] All deans have been professors except A. A. Miller, who did not become Professor of Geography until 1943.

Professors of the University and Librarians

Many of the professors in the following lists were first appointed to chairs in the University College. In such cases the date of appointment is noted in parentheses. The titles of some professors have been changed from time to time. The following list is arranged alphabetically by the latest title of the professorship. Earlier titles are given in parentheses. Subsequent titles are noted with the date of the change. Terminal dates which simply represent a change in title are enclosed in square brackets. Personal professors are included under a separate heading. Visiting and part-time professors have not been included.

Established professors

Agricultural Botany
  J. Percival 1926–32 (1909)
  W. B. Brierley 1932–54
  D. W. Goodall 1954–6
  A. H. Bunting 1956–73 (*see Agricultural Development Overseas*)
  W. Williams 1974–

Agricultural Chemistry
  H. A. D. Neville 1926–47 (1919)
  C. Tyler 1947–[1958]
Changed to *Physiological Chemistry* 1958

Agricultural Development Overseas
  A. H. Bunting 1974–

Agricultural Economics
  Edgar Thomas 1945–65
  R. H. Tuck 1965–[1970]
Changed to *Agricultural Economics & Management* 1970

Agricultural Economics & Management
(*Agricultural Economics*)
  R. H. Tuck [1970]–
  T. E. Josling 1974–

Agricultural Systems
  C. R. W. Spedding 1975–

Agriculture
  S. Pennington 1926–33 (1920)
  R. Rae 1933–44
  H. G. Sanders 1944–54
  A. N. Duckham 1954–68
Divided into *Animal Production* and *Crop Production* 1966–8

Animal Production (*Agriculture*)
  J. C. Bowman 1966–

Applied Mathematics
  J. N. Hunt 1964–
  K. W. Morton 1972–

Applied Optics
  H. H. Hopkins 1967–

Applied Physical Sciences
  P. D. Dunn 1965–[1966]
Changed to *Engineering Science* 1966
  P. B. Fellgett 1965–[1966]
Changed to *Cybernetics & Instrument Physics* 1966

Applied Statistics
  R. N. Curnow 1968–

Botany
  W. Stiles 1926–9
  J. R. Matthews 1929–34
  T. M. Harris 1934–68
  V. H. Heywood 1968–

Building Technology
  W. D. Biggs 1973–

Chemistry
  H. Bassett 1926–46 (1912)
  E. A. Guggenheim 1946–[1965]
Changed to *Physical & Inorganic Chemistry* 1965

Civil Engineering
  L. A. Beaufoy 1967–72

Classics
  P. N. Ure 1926–46 (1911)
  J. M. R. Cormack 1946–65
  A. W. H. Adkins 1966–74
  R. D. Williams 1974–

Computer Science
  R. W. Hockney 1970–

Crop Production (Agriculture)
  E. H. Roberts 1968–

Curriculum Research & Development
  J. Wrigley 1967–75 (*see Education*)

Cybernetics & Instrument Physics (Applied Physical Sciences)
  P. B. Fellgett [1966]–

Dairy Bacteriology
  R. Stenhouse Williams 1926–32

Dairying
  E. Capstick 1938–45
  E. L. Crossley 1947–68
Changed to *Food Science* 1968

Economics
  J. H. Dunning 1964–74 (*see International Investment & Business Studies*)
  P. E. Hart 1967–
  E. V. Morgan 1975–

Education
  F. A. Cavenagh 1934–7
  H. C. Barnard 1937–51
  C. H. Dobinson 1951–68
  R. Wilson 1968–
  J. Wrigley 1975–

Engineering Science (Applied Physical Sciences)
  P. D. Dunn [1966]–

English (English Literature)
  R. Dewar 1940–9
  D. J. Gordon 1949–
  W. F. Bolton 1968–70
  C. G. Salvesen 1971–

English Language
  Edith J. Morley 1926–40 (1908)

English Literature
  R. Dewar 1926–40 (1912)
Changed to *English* 1940

Estate Management
  C. W. N. Miles 1968–

Fine Art
  A. W. Seaby 1926–33 (1920)
  J. A. Betts 1943–63
  C. M. Rogers 1963–72
  M. Froy 1972–

Food Science (Dairying)
  F. Aylward 1968–

Food Technology
  E. J. Rolfe 1967–

French
  J. Desseignet 1926–51 (1920)
  A. G. Lehmann 1951–68
  C. Smith 1967–
  F. W. Leakey 1970–3
  W. G. van Emden 1974–

Geography
  A. A. Miller 1943–65
  T. G. Miller 1965–7
  P. G. Hall 1968–
  R. A. G. Savigear 1969–

Geology
  H. L. Hawkins 1926–52 (1920)
  P. Allen 1952–

German

    F. P. Pickering 1953–74
    W. A. Coupe 1974–

History (Modern History)

    A. Aspinall [1963]–1965
    J. C. Holt 1966–
    H. S. Thomas 1966–

Horticulture

    R. H. Stoughton 1933–57
    O. V. S. Heath 1958–69
    P. A. Huxley 1969–74

Inorganic Chemistry

    G. W. A. Fowles 1966–

International Investment & Business Studies

    J. H. Dunning 1975–

Italian

    L. Meneghello 1964–

Law

    R. Jardine Brown 1967–72
    P. Jackson 1973–

Law Relating to the Land

    W. A. West 1967–

Linguistic Science

    F. R. Palmer 1965–

Materials Technology

    J. E. Gordon 1967–

Mathematics

    E. H. Neville 1926–54 (1919)
    R. Rado 1954–[1965]
Changed to *Pure Mathematics* 1965

Meteorology

    R. C. Sutcliffe 1965–70
    R. P. Pearce 1970–

Microbiology

    B. C. J. G. Knight 1951–69
    C. Kaplan 1968–

Modern History

    F. M. Stenton 1926–47 (1912)
    A. Aspinall 1947–[1963]
Changed to *History* 1963

Music

    R. E. Woodham 1951–

Organic Chemistry

    D. Bryce-Smith 1965–

Philosophy

    W. G. de Burgh 1926–34 (1907)
    H. A. Hodges 1934–69
    D. D. Raphael 1970–2
    A. G. N. Flew 1973–

Physical & Inorganic Chemistry (Chemistry)

    E. A. Guggenheim [1965]–1966

Physical Chemistry

    H. M. Frey 1966–

Physical Properties of Materials

    E. W. J. Mitchell 1961–

Physics

    J. A. Crowther 1926–46 (1924)
    R. W. Ditchburn 1946–68
    C. W. McCombie 1964–
    G. W. Series 1969–

Physiological Chemistry (Agricultural Chemistry)

    C. Tyler [1958]–[1966]
Changed to *Physiology & Biochemistry* 1966

Physiology & Biochemistry (Agricultural Chemistry, Physiological Chemistry)

    C. Tyler [1966]–
    G. M. H. Waites 1969–

Political Economy

    P. W. Campbell 1960–[1964]
Changed to *Politics* 1964

Politics (Political Economy)

    P. W. Campbell [1964]–

Psychology

A. W. P. Wolters 1943–50
R. C. Oldfield 1950–6
Magdalen D. Vernon 1956–67
M. Treisman 1967–72
R. Davis 1973–

Pure Mathematics (Mathematics)

R. Rado [1965]–1971
F. M. Arscott 1972–4
J. D. M. Wright 1971–
C. St. J. A. Nash-Williams 1975–

Quantity Surveying

J. Bennett 1975–

Sociology

S. L. Andreski 1964–

Soil Science

E. W. Russell 1964–70
D. J. Greenland 1970–

Solid State Electronics

E. A. Faulkner 1970–

Zoology

F. J. Cole 1926–39 (1907)
C. H. O'Donoghue 1939–52
A. Graham 1952–72
G. Williams 1967–
K. Simkiss 1972–

I. M. Mills, Chemical Spectroscopy 1966–
J. D. Mounfield, Food Technology 1966–7
R. C. Newman, Physics 1975–
G. H. R. Parkinson, Philosophy 1974–
J. E. Prue, Chemistry 1972
H. G. R. Sellon, French Civilization 1940–1
B. Szigeti, Physics 1969–
K. D. White, Classics 1971–4
R. D. Williams, Classics 1971–4

National Institute for Research in Dairying

H. D. Kay 1932–58
Sir Ronald Baskett 1959–67
S. J. Folley 1964–70 (Research professor)
S. K. Kon 1964–5 (Research professor)
B. G. F. Weitz 1967–

Librarians

S. A. Peyton 1926–41
A. Mary Kirkus 1941–59 (Acting Librarian
    1941–3)
D. T. Richnell 1960–7
J. Thompson 1967–

Personal professors

J. R. L. Allen, Geology 1972–
D. K. Bailey, Geology 1974–
W. F. Bolton, English 1965–8
D. Crystal, Linguistic Science 1975–
Margaret C. Davies, French 1975–
T. Evans, Physics 1968–
W. Hirst, Tribology 1970–
P. F. Holt, Chemistry 1973–5
Olwen H. Hufton, History 1975–
G. C. Lepschy, Italian 1975–
W. B. Lockwood, Germanic and Indo-European
    Philology 1968–
V. Mallinson, Comparative Education 1967–75
P. H. Matthews, Linguistic Science 1975–
G. W. Maynard, Economics 1967–

Appendix 3

'Remarks on policy' from the final statement of W. M. Childs as Vice-Chancellor, 7 January 1929

from *Proceedings, 1927–8*, pp. 47–56

For a discussion of this statement see above, pp. 38–9. Compare also earlier statements of 1926 and 1928 (above, pp. 18–20, 33–4).

As I look back over my long association with the College and University, and in particular over my twenty-six years of office as Principal and Vice-Chancellor, it is perhaps natural that the course of action which has carried us from rudimentary beginnings to our present strength should seem to me to have been guided throughout by definite and consistent principles. In reality, however, when taking a retrospective view of this kind, one is liable, perhaps unconsciously, to error. Those who have to lead a difficult enterprise may be more opportunist than they like to suppose. Without doubt they often have to do things, because they can no other: and expedients of the moment, if they turn out well, have a way of presenting themselves afterwards as moves in a far-sighted campaign. If the University of Reading did not exactly grow up in absence of mind, it has owed much to the English characteristic of doing the obvious thing as soon as possible without worrying too much what would happen next.

Without losing sight, however, of this steadying reflection, it is still possible to find in our common effort, prolonged over so many years, some governing ideas. Some of these I now place on record.

1 Our idea of a university

We have always held that a university is an independent society in one place. Institutions in different places may associate together and call themselves a university. Such arrangements may be defensible and may answer their purpose. Nevertheless, they are a departure from the historic ideal, and at Reading we have held to our belief. Various suggestions involving partnership or dependence have in the past been mooted and then put on one side. We have deemed it wiser to take the risks of passing through a period of relative smallness and of effort to justify our existence, rather than to embarrass ourselves with alliances, or to lose anything of the solidarity and the quickening spirit which go with local independence.

In conformity with this idea that a university is a society in one place, we have always required that full-time members of the academic and administrative staffs shall reside in Reading.

2 Government

We have held that the whole University should be responsible to a single authority, functioning through the Senate and Council. It may perhaps be said that the British Dairy Institute and the National Institute for Research in Dairying are exceptions to this principle, for both have governing bodies of their own. The exception, however, is more apparent than real, a matter rather of form than of substance. Both institutions are in truth and in spirit conscious of inclusion within the University. Their affairs are so intermixed with those of the University, the share of the University in their respective undertakings, and the share of their members in the work of the University, are so much matters of course and daily practice, that the formal points which distinguish their administration from that of other parts of the University constitute no difficulty and attract little notice. The existing arrangements, it is true, might lead to difficulty, if persons on either side set to work to make it; but difficulties of this origin can be exorcized by no system of government whatever. Apart from the case of the two Institutes, which by their reputation and loyalty contribute much to the strength of the University, the University executive is paramount without exception or question. All the University Halls, for example, are controlled by the Council. It is, of course, possible that a Hall might be proposed as a private or public venture, under external authority. But it could not become a Hall of the University except by consent of the Council, which would have the right and duty of laying down conditions to be satisfied. At Reading we once had experience of such institutions, and, without seeking to prejudice proposals which may be made hereafter, it is enough to say that early in our history we found it advisable to go boldly and without qualification for the policy of complete control. The success of our residential system is proof of the soundness of this policy.

3   The three faculties the basis of the University

The fundamental basis of the University is to be found in the three faculties of Letters, Science, and Agriculture and Horticulture. The decisive assertion of this fact belongs to the year 1911 when the University Endowment Fund of £200,000 was given to enable the College to qualify for university status by developing its work in these faculties. A further view was then taken and has been repeatedly expressed, namely, that for a considerable period, the end of which is not in sight, it would be wise to concentrate energy upon the development of these three faculties, and to refrain from contemplating proposals for the addition of new ones. This view was endorsed by the Privy Council and by the University Grants Committee at the time of the granting of the Charter.

The three faculties, as stated, constitute the fundamental basis of the University. A distinction, however, of some interest may be drawn between the Faculties of Letters and Science and the Faculty of Agriculture and Horticulture. Letters and Science together represent the historic 'Faculty of Arts', the foundation of all universities in all ages. Agriculture and Horticulture represent, in harmony with the geographical situation of Reading, those technical and applied sciences which every university in the modern world is bound to develop. If the historic significance of the third faculty is thus less than that of its older sisters, its power of appeal to the practical man is greater, and its opportunity for achieving national distinction is probably broader and freer. The practical bearing of these considerations on policy is this. These three faculties are indispensable. There can be no

university without Letters and Science: the Charter itself provides that 'degrees representing proficiency in technical subjects shall not be conferred without proper security for testing the scientific or general knowledge underlying technical attainments'. On the other hand, unless Letters and Science were reinforced by Agriculture, the University could not fill the part in public and practical life which is incumbent upon it. It was for these reasons that the University Endowment deeds of 1911 named these three faculties as the basis of the University of the future. The policy was not new in 1911; after that date it became fundamental. The Council are, therefore, bound to care impartially for the welfare of each of these faculties. The faculties need not be, and are not, equal in size or in cost: but none of them can be given the cold shoulder, or suffered to lapse into inefficiency or insignificance. Upon them and each of them the University depends.

4   Art and Music

This care for the three faculties is, and has always been, consistent with care for studies of a different order. Chief among such studies are Fine Art and Music. The School of Art existed before the College was founded in 1892: it was the largest single element in the first combination of activities which made a College possible. The inclusion of the Art School in 1892 was accompanied by legal undertakings which presumably still hold good. But apart from this, and far more important than this, the University, like the College before it, owes to the School of Art a distinction and an influence of the highest value. A strand of colour and charm, a point of view neither literary nor scientific, thus enter into our common life. Utilitarian studies are very well; scholarship and research are very well; but the intellectual realm also includes other provinces, among which are beauty and colour, and the principles which the creative artist is called upon to study and to master. The School of Art at Reading has earned honourable distinctions; but, as I think, its greatest service to our society has been the upholding of standards, principles, points of view, and methods of study – the presentation, in short, of a view of life, distinctively its own – which help to broaden and diversify the outlook of our community.

A like argument applies to Music. Whether a School of Music with a staff of teachers providing lessons in different branches of music to pupils, many of whom come to the University for no other purpose, should be permanently maintained upon its present scale and basis is, in my judgement, a question for future policy. But it is surely inconceivable that the University should not strenuously and generously do its utmost to make music a living and constant influence in its life. A movement of this kind, pregnant with hope and promise, is now vigorously on foot. It has already in a short space and with slender means achieved much. I appeal to all who care for the well-being of our University, to all who realize our responsibility not merely for the instruction but for the education of our students, to all who wish to see the University the centre and home of noble influences, to support and cherish it.

The association, then, of aesthetic studies, Music and Art, with academic and technical studies is one of the most arresting of the lines of policy which the history of the College and University presents. It is, perhaps, our oldest tradition as a seat of studies. It is one of those distinguishing characteristics which make Reading interesting to the public, and for that reason as well as for others it should be jealously preserved.

5 Halls: a vital factor

Residential Halls were resolved upon for two reasons, both of which are of standing validity. The first was that the population of Reading and the neighbourhood was insufficient to supply enough students either for a College or a University. Students must also be attracted from distant places, and as soon as this began to happen the conditions of their residence forced themselves upon attention. The second reason was our conviction that the old collegiate system of residence formed a vital part of true university education. There is no need to dwell upon this familiar theme, but I record here three facts. The first is that the very first memorandum which I as Principal (or Principal-elect) addressed to the Council in 1903 was a plea for the immediate development of hostels. The second fact is that Reading was the first of the new universities and colleges to adopt wholeheartedly the residential principle. In doing so we broke new ground. We set an example. We have lived to see the identical principles, which guided us in the founding of Halls, authorita-

tively expounded for the benefit of universities in general in a government report; and what we have done has been closely studied by every modern university in England, and by some outside England. The third fact is that the letter of the Privy Council (1926) named our system of residential Halls as the foremost ground for recommending the grant of a university charter.

'Residential Halls' stand, indeed, for a policy at Reading too simple and too fundamental to require comment. They have proved themselves to possess a power of appeal to the public which has been not merely useful but indispensable to our advance. No question about the future of the University can be framed which is more pregnant with significance than this: will Reading, which was the first to institute Halls on right lines and to incorporate them into its being, also have the imagination and the courage to pursue a progressive policy and to keep the lead thus won? A difficult task: not so difficult as the task of twenty-five years ago. In the coming years there will be a call not for new Halls or larger Halls alone. There will be a call for a generous and constructive statesmanship, able to handle and co-ordinate the resources already at command, and to expand and enrich them, in such a way as to present to the world a university acknowledging and carrying out the full ideal that university education means a comprehensive and equal care for the training both of mind and of character.

A further point is to be noted. From the first, we have held the view that no teaching shall be given in university Halls. Teaching is exclusively a university function and prerogative; and history shews that there are dangers, probable or improbable under modern conditions, in permitting the rise of tutors in Halls, as distinguished from teachers of full university status and responsibility.

6 Friendship the basis of strength

I have spoken of the University as a society, and I have referred more than once to its life. I find myself perpetually coming back to this view of our enterprise as something social, something which means or should mean fellowship, comradeship, friendship. I think that amongst us we have succeeded in giving to our College and University something of this attractive character. I should say, judging by impressions gathered during many years, that with few exceptions people who come to us whether as teachers or students enjoy their life here, and that when they leave they look back upon it with pleasure and satisfaction. If so, has there been anything in our policy which has helped to bring this about? I will mention two things which seem to me relevant. (1) We have a Senior Common Room, which is well-housed and a real centre of life. Common Room is one of our oldest institutions. It is the domain of the whole academic staff. The only official dignities in Common Room are those of the elected Stewards. Seniors and juniors meet there on terms of equality. Members of Council also come and are welcome. Somewhere, in all institutions and forms of government, there is a place where power is generated. Ideas may come in solitude, or among two or three thinking together; but if ideas are to be put into practice in a community, they should be able to count upon a friendly audience. This is what Common Room does for us; this is perhaps the main reason why all of us should support it. There in the dining room and the smoke room, in the garden and on the bowling green, we come to know one another not as professors and lecturers but as comrades and friends. If the secrets of progress and success could be certainly traced, I am sure we should have to go to Common Room to find not a few of them. The University is happy to possess it and the generosity with which it has been treated by the Council is a valuable tradition of wise policy. (2) From the beginning, members of the academic staff have cultivated friendly relations with students. In the early years, some of us did much to initiate and help corporate activities of many kinds. That tradition is still upheld, and the help that is given is both appreciated and important; but initiative and responsibility have naturally and rightly passed into the hands of the students themselves. There remains, however, a wide sphere for personal influence. That the teacher should also be a friend is a great ideal, difficult of practice when numbers become unwieldly. Nevertheless, it has high claims upon all of us. The common life of the University cannot achieve the best that is possible unless there is a good understanding behind formal teaching and disciplinary regulations. Here as elsewhere in life, personal relations are the testing criterion. We have reason to be proud of the loyalty and good sense of our student body; they have done their share to make the University;

never once in a quarter of a century have I appealed to them in vain. But there would be no such record, if authority in the University had held aloof from student interests, and unless on both sides there were the confidence and goodwill born of personal association.

7 *Local relations and local service*

The University is in Reading and bears its name. If the idea of founding a College at Reading came in 1892 from Christ Church and Oxford, the translation of the idea into fact was the work of a group of Reading and Berkshire people, acting under the leadership of the first Principal. The great benefactions which saved the College and made a university possible came from Reading and Berkshire. A host of Reading people raised later on the Reading Citizens' Endowment Fund. From the beginning, leading persons in the town and county have patiently and ably co-operated in administration and management. From very early days also the Town Council of Reading and the Berkshire County Council have given support in the form of annual grants. Many local persons, not directly connected with the executive, have supported the College as annual governors, and the University as 'Friends of the University'. One special function of high importance has always linked the College and University closely with the town: namely, the maintenance of Evening Classes, mainly for the benefit of wage-earners. The policy which recognizes Evening Classes as beneficial in a high degree both to public education in Reading, and to the hold of the University upon local opinion, is one which requires no defence. Universities in great cities, where the municipal authorities are able not only to support the University but also to finance their own technical colleges and institutions, may not feel called upon to undertake evening instruction. Circumstances in Reading are widely different and make necessary another policy.

All these considerations enforce the doctrine that the University of Reading should ever seek to serve the town and neighbourhood, and to be friends with them. Like every modern university, our University is at once national and local. It draws students from all parts: but its home is in Reading and Berkshire. Some may say that this fact, and the obligations which flow from it, can never be overlooked. I reply that they will not be overlooked so long as some person or persons make sure that they are borne in mind. An academic community is a little world in itself; much of its work may well seem to have little concern with locality. The citizen, on his side, is often shy of the academic attitude. Close and friendly contact and reciprocal support are not inevitable; nor will they happen or continue except by an effort of will on both sides. Local public opinion is behind the University to-day: but it was not always so. It supports us partly because every citizen of insight and common sense has long ago come to recognize the value in many ways of the University to the town, and partly because the University by a great variety of services and efforts, some large and many small, has shewn that it realizes its local obligations. It may sound pretentious to say that a university, in addition to performing wider functions, ought to be a centre of local enlightenment; but it is true, nevertheless. Here too in the tradition of local service and local friendliness is a line of wise and right policy.

8 *Library and research*

The University Library and the Research Board stand for two fundamentals in any policy of continuous development. Their importance needs no emphasis here. Each of them, however, possesses characteristics which are not accidental. (1) We deliberately built up one great central Library rather than adopt suggestions at one time current that departmental libraries would be a simpler and more convenient solution. The question has long been settled, but it is interesting to remember not only that our policy has accelerated the growth of the Library, but also that already our Library building and its contents are the most impressive thing that the University possesses. The Library reminds us all, and particularly the student, that a university is something far greater than a collection of departments. (2) The Research Board means the concentration of individual enthusiasm and ability in scholarship and research into a joint effort to make the spirit of research permeate the whole University. I have always regarded this Board, to which the Council readily and most wisely have given generous support, as expressing the very essence of the true university idea. University departments must be run by specialists; but if specialist workers do not pool their ideas, their experience, and their enthusiasm for the benefit of the University to

which they belong, the University gains much less from their presence than it ought to gain. Perhaps I may be allowed to say that, at meetings of the Research Board, I have been greatly impressed by the complete impartiality and generous interest with which my colleagues there from all sides of the University view any proposal, no matter its quarter of origin, that is laid before them. I am sure that any piece of organization, such as the Research Board, which gives play and power to a catholic enthusiasm of this kind is serving the interests of the University in the best and most vital way.

9 *Simple buildings*

Many years ago we fought out the issue of the plain workshop *versus* the 'architectural' building. We decided for the workshop type partly because we had not enough money for expensive buildings, and partly because we realized that for many purposes, e.g., laboratories, studios, and classrooms, the simple building is more satisfactory for a variety of reasons. Experience has borne out this opinion. Experience has also taught a further thing: that if buildings of plain and modest elevation are set amid lawns and gardens the effect, given time, will be good. Except for the University Hall, the Library, and Wantage Hall, the University possesses no buildings that markedly arrest attention. Nevertheless, no one finds serious fault with the appearance of our buildings (except that we need enlargements and more of them) and visitors seldom fail to approve the general effect. The future will settle these problems in its own way: but the policy which has justified itself so far will always deserve consideration.

10 *Benefactors and their motives*

It has fallen to my lot to have had some share in raising very large sums for the benefit of the College and University. I hear it said sometimes that people will not give large sums unless you can promise them some material return: something that will directly promote industry and commerce and make the community richer than it was before. It may be so; I can see that it may well be true in certain circumstances: but it has not been true of the cases with which I have been called upon to deal. I recall no instance of a benefaction, large or small, which has not been prompted, quite simply and candidly, by the large hope of doing good, particularly by broadening the avenues to the best kind of education so that better men and better women may be the outcome, and also by enabling knowledge to advance. I also recall, and in several instances, that one of the hindrances to action which had to be overcome was the distaste for advertisement and notoriety. Reading no doubt has been fortunate in its benefactors: but even if this be so, experience here warrants the belief that great gifts are inspired, as nearly all great action is inspired, not by considerations of material profit and loss, but by a broad and high ideal. The University must present that ideal, and those who are commissioned to speak for it must be able to interpret and express it. They stand for a high cause, and they must believe in it.

Appendix 4

The Library: by Doris Mary Stenton

The following note on the Library is the only part of the history of the University for which Lady Stenton left a continuous account. She completed a revised draft of this section shortly before her death in 1971. Her account is presented with the minimum of editing; one or two sections are included from preliminary drafts, especially where they call on her own reminiscences. Lady Stenton herself incorporated comments and corrections supplied by Sydney Peyton in a remarkably informative letter of 24 July 1971. This is preserved, along with Lady Stenton's drafts, in the University Archives, Stenton Papers.

When my husband first came as a student to join Frank Walker at Reading he cannot have realized how poor the Library was, a few books in a single bookcase, for the main part the gift of Christ Church, as a purple stamp in each volume recorded. No purple stamp marks the most valuable book then in the Library, a copy of *Bracton's Notebook* edited by F. W. Maitland, the first Frank ever saw. Happily it is still there. In those days the room where the books were kept was modestly called the Reading Room, not the Library, and one of the 'privileges of students' was 'free use of the Reading Room when it was not being used for a class'. Childs hardly says anything about the slow building up of a Library in his early chapters. He knew well enough that books were the first necessity of any teaching institution, but students to be taught were even more important and people to teach them. Childs could only advance step by step, and perhaps it was as well that he could not make large purchases of books in the nineties. He would probably not have bought the right books and certainly not the right bookcases. We inherited one of Childs's bookcases and found it quite unusable. Far too narrow shelves, unsteadily supported on pegs, made it a shelf only for very little books.

The first real library we had was the upper floors of the Acacias, the house in London Road where the founder of the firm of Huntley and Palmer, George Palmer, had brought up his family. It must have been a very pleasant family home when his sons, George William and Alfred Palmer, were boys. Set in what was then the outskirts of Reading, itself a country town, in a lovely countryside, hardly as yet touched by the materialism which has ruined it. That the early members of what has become the University of Reading came to love it and settled in it for life is not surprising.

By modern standards this first library can hardly be described as a Library, though I remember it as a very pleasant place looking out over the garden and Senior Common Room lawn, but we had no full-time proper Librarian until after the First World War when Childs invited S. A. Peyton to accept the post at a very modest salary. We had few large books, but we were fortunate in beginning when we did as we were able to get a full set of the *English Historical Review*, begun in the late eighties. We were given all the volumes of the *Victoria County History* as they came out by Lord and Lady Wantage, and their heirs have kept up the practice. Slowly the number of our books increased. When an inspection took place in January 1907 we had in the Library 4,330 books, but despite this pitiful number Childs was already thinking that we might some day become a university. In 1913 the Library was still fewer than 8,000 books. When George William Palmer died in October 1913 it was found that he had left £10,000 to the College without stipulating how it should be spent. His brother Alfred and his sisters suggested that it should be spent on a Library in his memory. They promised to provide an endowment fund for its maintenance. This generosity meant that we had the assurance of a genuine

Library with an income which did not depend on any government grant. By the express wish of George William Palmer's brother, Alfred, and of his sisters the family name was not connected with the Library. The major portion of the income of the endowment was devoted to the maintenance of the Library, but a fixed proportion was to be used for the purchase of books too expensive to be obtained by departmental funds. This amounted to £250, but shrank to £225 when war-loan interest was reduced.

Here I must regretfully record what I feel was Childs's great mistake, perhaps his only mistake, in his hitherto wise management of the affairs of the infant College. At the same time I must admit that in all probability no one would have managed better. Unlike America we had no established tradition in this country of giving generously to found libraries in our new universities. Our own founders, the Palmers, were establishing a new tradition. When the news of the library to be built for us was told by Childs to Lady Wantage, daughter and heir of Lord Overstone, she told him that she had determined to bequeath to the University the library which her father had built up at Overstone Park in Northamptonshire. This library had been made by the Victorian economist J. R. McCulloch (1789–1864) and purchased by Lord Overstone. McCulloch had catalogued it and added 'critical and biographical notices'. In his preface he said that he had not sought for rarities but well printed and handsome volumes and fine bindings. The library contained not only English, but also French, Italian and Spanish books. In his own purchases Lord Overstone had followed much the same line as had McCulloch. When the library passed into our hands it contained about 7,500 books and many economic tracts and pamphlets.

The Overstone books remained in store until Lady Wantage died in August 1920 and they could be brought to Reading to await completion of the Library. They had been in store earlier before they came into Lord Overstone's hands. Peyton tells me that there was a rumour, which he failed to pin down, that when they were awaiting removal to Overstone Park a fire in the repository caused some loss. There was, however, no sign of fire or water having caused damage, but a comparison of the catalogues of McCulloch and that of Lord Overstone showed some

discrepancies. Peyton found that when the books came to Reading the bindings of some of them were in a deplorable state, particularly those bound in calf. The Council made a grant of money for their repair and a man was appointed to do the work. It was a lengthy business getting the work done and the whole collection treated with leather dressing. The collection is particularly rich in fine examples of eighteenth-century French binders' work, which deserved spending on preservation.

To come back to Childs's 'mistake': it was rather a whole galaxy of errors, beginning with and stemming from his admiration for Bodley and his desire to make a library which could stand comparison with Bodley. It meant that he was more concerned with the impression which the first appearance of the Library would make than on its competence as a working institution. Our Library consisted of two wings connected by a cross building which was the entrance hall, with a ceremonial entrance facing the lawn and never opened, and two swing doors opposite, looking towards the main block of teaching and administrative offices known as the Old Red Building. This description highlights at once some of the defects of the Library. The entrance constantly swept by draughts from the two swing doors was cold and draughty and difficult to keep clean. Not only had the librarians no hot water, but for several years they lacked any electric points. The lift was a small hand-hauled affair holding barely fifty octavo volumes. The possibility of bringing books direct to the Library for unpacking rather than unloading them and carrying them there was another point he overlooked. There was no adequate stack provision, so that Peyton had to look around and make use of every vacant space, into which he could introduce readers or books.

We began with only the upper floor shelved and furnished for readers. This had twenty-two alcoves and seats for 150 readers. In September 1928 the lower east reading room was opened. This accommodated sixty-two readers and 12,000 books. It was not long before Peyton had arranged to shelve the landing and to put the catalogue outside the door of the main reading room. The parliamentary debates and the catalogues of our main national collection were put there. Eventually six small basement chambers were shelved, as funds permitted, to accommodate 30,000 volumes.

The Library staff first consisted of the Librarian, S. A. Peyton himself, two part-time assistants and a porter, Pocock; then from 1928 until the early 1940s, two full-time graduates, a part-time typist and two porters, Pocock and Siney. That with so small a staff the Library was well run and fully catalogued and no opportunity missed of acquiring books needed to fill gaps is testimony to the ability of the Librarian and the hard work which the staff was ready to put in.

All through the thirties our annual income was £2,025: £1,800 voted by the Council and £225 from the endowment. Every five years there was a quinquennial grant from the University Grants Committee. These were indeed as Peyton describes them 'the days of our poverty' when we had to be content with about sixty pounds a subject apart from journals which were all bought together. It may well be asked 'How did we manage to get the books we did?' The answer is the gifts of our kind friends, and penny scraping, and watching the second-hand catalogues, and trying to get in first with orders. A most generous friend was Mr R. H. Mardon of Shiplake, a member of our Council, who at various times gave us five £100 cheques. When a Paris bookseller was offering for £108 all the volumes up to date of the catalogue of the Bibliothèque Nationale, and the Council could not find the money, Peyton wrote to Mr Mardon who sent a cheque by return. Lord Winchelsea, through the kind offices of our friend Canon Foster of Lincoln, provided us with Hansard and parliamentary publications. The editor of the *Berkshire Chronicle*, Mr Rivers, gave us £1,040 to help research in medieval history. This was, to the best of my memory, the gift which allowed us to buy the better part of the Rolls Series. Sir Charles Firth, Regius Professor of Modern History at Oxford, and a notable collector of books, was one of our most generous friends. He was a great buyer of books to work at them. Like my husband he always wanted to have the books he was working on in his own possession. Since his interests covered a wide field, this meant a large library from which he was quite ready to give to others when he had finished his immediate work. When Peyton went over to see him he always said 'Bring a case with you' and it always came back full. Nor did ill health or even death end his beneficence. In 1936 Lady Firth gave from her late husband's library the whole of the Navy Record Society. It was a fortunate thing that on the science side at this time the Library was served by two scholars as keen as my husband was, Dr Cole and Dr Hawkins, both of whom were collecting books and both of whose collections have come to the Library. Miss Kirkus's will assured her money to the Library and made it possible for Dr Cole's books to be bought at once.

The appointment of Peyton as our Librarian was a piece of sheer unadulterated good luck. Until his appointment we had struggled on from hand to mouth, making do, certainly without any real Librarian. One must always remember that at this date real Librarians were very thin on the ground. De Burgh looked after the Library with the help of students for a time. Professor Ure and his wife acted for a bit. When I became a student in 1912 Miss Cobb of Banbury was helping in the Library. She belonged to a family which had been much concerned with the local government of Banbury and my husband's diary for 1919 notes on 10 February, 'Saw about Miss Cobb's books'. I remember accompanying Frank and Peyton with Pocock and his truck to see if Miss Cobb would, as she suggested, have any books for us. We came away with a truck load and a great sense of satisfaction. It is an example of the way in which Peyton and my husband never let any opportunity of adding to the Library pass. We were very sorry when Peyton left us. In 1941 he was invited to go to Sheffield where elaborate plans of rebuilding and expansion were going ahead. While we mourned the departure of Peyton we could not expect to keep him. Things might have been much worse for us. Peyton had been training his successor, Miss Mary Kirkus, who had acquired her qualification in librarianship at London University. As soon as she came here Peyton had urged her to take a degree in History. From that she went on to an M.A. and a Ph.D., both good degrees, by research. Peyton helped her in her work and she stayed at the Library to work in the evening. She was made Acting Librarian in 1941 and Librarian in 1943. Her main difficulties in carrying on the work of the Library in the years that followed were to find space for the books which of necessity increased yearly, and to keep the catalogue and binding up to date. It is only of recent years that university libraries have been given the staff that they need and indeed must have if their work is to be adequately done. Miss Kirkus organized her staff very wisely; each one had his or her section of work for which he took responsibility. She herself had taken over charge of Spanish books. It was Mary Kirkus who started the Bindery. She consulted Peyton, who doubted whether she would find it possible. But she began with one man in September 1947. Our man had bound 694 volumes by 1948 and another 204 had been bound by commercial firms. In 1948 another man was needed.

The death of Mary Kirkus [1959] ended a most fertile and valuable period in the history of the University Library, a period when its development was watched over not only by an able and devoted company of librarians under a competent and well trained head but also by an eminent scholar with a wide knowledge of books and their authors.

Just before he retired my husband in speaking of the Library to the Council of the University said that the advance might easily be underestimated: 'With resources never comparable with its significance in the life of the University, and by the gauntest economy in essentials, the Library before the war had been brought to a state in which it might be considered adequate to the needs of our undergraduate population. In many sections the interests of the heads of departments had led to the formation of special collections which would support a graduate student in the beginnings of research. Other sections were brought into being by the insistence of individuals, moved by the importance of the subjects they were encouraging. The anthropological section is the creation of the Professor of Psychology. The result of this unregimented development is that some acquaintance with the Library is necessary before its real strength can be justly measured. . . . We may fairly claim that in quality though not as yet in size we possess a Library appropriate to a university. I have dwelt upon the method of its growth because I believe it illustrates what I believe to be the principal factor determining the growth of the University as a whole. The University is a living organism which in the past has shown that it can adapt itself, if not easily, at least effectively, to varying conditions. Great changes lie ahead of it; grave dangers, but also brilliant opportunities. I will merely record my own confidence and amid the excitements of an uncharted future it will retain the vitality in all its parts which had carried it through the more obvious though less exciting dangers attendant on its past'.

Note: There is a slight discrepancy between the Library's annual income given above, p. 345, and that noted on p. 40, n. 3. Lady Stenton relied at this point on a figure supplied by Peyton.

Report of the Committee appointed by Senate to consider the needs of the University after the war, 10 April 1944

This document is the starting point of the expansion of the University. Its genesis is discussed above, pp. 117–36.

In interpreting its wide terms of reference, the Committee has consistently borne in mind what it conceives to be the realities of the situation. It has not attempted to plan an ideal university. The primary task before it was to consider the developments which it would be necessary for the University to undertake at the end of the war. Its duties were made at once more definite and more urgent by a letter of 8 November 1943 from the Chairman of the University Grants Committee asking for a statement of the development policy of the University, with an approximate estimate of the annual costs which it would involve. In all its meetings subsequent to this date the Committee has borne in mind the fact that its report, if accepted by Senate, and ultimately by Council, would form the basis of a set of practical proposals to be presented to the University Grants Committee. No indication was or could be given by the Grants Committee of the capital sum or the increase of recurrent grant which the University might hope to receive. Under these conditions, the Committee was compelled to use its own judgement as to the scale of the developments which it would put forward. In doing so, it preferred to err on the side of moderation. The proposals which it now advances are not, it is believed, disproportionate in cost to the scale of the grants which, on general grounds, the University might reasonably hope to receive.

In framing these proposals, the Committee has been assisted by a set of memoranda from the various heads of departments in the University, and by the reports of meetings of heads of departments convened by the deans of each of the three faculties. It has not been possible to adopt the entire series of proposals contained in these several communications. This is essentially because of the Committee's desire to keep its programme within its judgement of what is reasonably possible. It would, however, be difficult to over-estimate the value of the guidance which the Committee received from these careful, and in many cases highly detailed, memoranda.

The Committee has not attempted to deal with the main University activities of teaching and research in general terms. The proposals which it now submits have all been framed with these activities in view, and if carried into effect will all, in different ways, make for their advancement. The bearing of the proposals on the development of university teaching at Reading will be evident from their very nature. Their significance for the expansion of research within the University lies beneath the surface. But it is clear that the proposals for new departmental buildings, for an increase in the numbers of the permanent academic staff, for an enlarged provision of research scholarships, and for the institution of new schools of study, when combined with the financial statement annexed to this report, will facilitate a very notable increase in the volume of research conducted within the University. In the opinion of the Committee the extension of opportunities for research was one of its fundamental duties, and throughout its sessions it consistently endeavoured to make provision for this end.

It was obvious from the first that the proposals which the Committee would send forward could not be regarded as all of equal urgency. The range of possible and desirable expansion in one direction or another is so wide that its various aspects cannot easily be brought into a common focus. For practical reasons, the proposals with which the Committee has been required to deal have been divided into two groups. The first comprises the developments which, in the opinion of the Committee, it is desirable to undertake within a term of approximately five years after the end of the war. These developments form the substance of the present report. The second group includes matters of long-term policy. Among them may be mentioned the acquisition of fresh land for university buildings and the use that should be made of such an enlarged site, the establishment of new halls of residence for men and women students, and the creation of new large-scale departments of university activity. In what follows, the Committee has attempted to distinguish between proposals which are of imminent urgency and those which, though desirable, and in many cases necessary, should, in its opinion, be postponed until the main lines of post-war settlement have been firmly laid down.

In the early part of its proceedings, the Committee arrived at certain general principles which influenced the whole course of its subsequent discussions. The chief of them were the undesirability of planning (a) for a great increase in the numbers of the University, or (b) for a large-scale expansion of its extra-mural activities; (c) the necessity of reducing, and so far as possible, of eliminating courses of sub-university standard; and (d) the imperative need of increasing salaries paid to members of the teaching staff.

(a) In regard to the first of these points, the Committee was conscious of a dilemma which under the conditions of the moment is insoluble. It would be unwise to assume that the population of Reading will in any approximate future grow to a point at which it will support a great regional university. Any considerable expansion of the University body would, therefore, seem to depend on the foundation of more halls of residence. The University, which has been based on a residential system, is anxious to maintain and so far as possible to extend its provision of residential facilities. On the other hand, the difficulties presented by the absence of any available site and by the gravity of the financial implications inherent in the establishment of a new Hall are more serious than those which arise from the undertakings necessitated by the immediate requirements of the University. The Committee therefore felt that the University would be well advised to postpone the provision of a new hall or halls of residence until it could assess the urgency of the accommodation problem more precisely than was at present possible, and to

reconcile itself reluctantly and for the time being to the attempt to find such increased accommodation as may be necessary either by enlargement of existing Halls or by extension of the existing system of licensed lodgings.

(b) In regard to the second point, the Committee was of the opinion that university activities, in the strict sense of the phrase, should be the first charge upon any new resources that might become available, and that although the existing services rendered by the University in the field of adult education should be continued and enlarged, they should not be so extended as to cover any area much wider than the Borough of Reading and its immediate neighbourhood.

(c) The policy of reducing 'sub-university' activities falls into line with the general policy of concentrating the University income on the maintenance of courses leading to graduation, and on post-graduate study and research. An important step in this direction has already been taken by the decision of the Council to close the Department of Domestic Subjects in 1945.

(d) The inadequacy of the salaries at present paid to members of staff was felt by all members of the Committee, and it was agreed to recommend that the improvements of salaries should take precedence over all other forms of recurrent expenditure which an increased grant from the Treasury might make possible. The Committee, however, considered that the detailed increments by which this improvement should be brought about fell outside the scope of the Report to the Senate, and it was agreed that the Vice-Chancellor should annex the requisite proposals to this Report for consideration by the Council.

The concrete proposals put forward by the Committee may be conveniently set out under the three heads of (A) Grading and salaries of staff, (B) Buildings, (C) Developments within the individual teaching departments.

(A) Grading and salaries of staff

It was unanimously agreed to recommend that the following grading scheme shall apply to full-time appointments on the non-professorial teaching staff subject to such exceptions as the Council may make from time to time in individual cases.

(i) *Assistant Lecturers*

Appointments shall be made for a period of three years at a fixed salary, with a prospect of promotion to the grade of Lecturer subject to satisfactory service. The maximum period of tenure of an Assistant Lectureship shall be four years. An increment of salary may be given for the fourth year. Promotion to the grade of Lecturer shall be accompanied by a substantial increase of salary.

(ii) Lecturers

Appointments shall be made in general for a period extending to the normal age of retirement. Annual increments of salary shall be given up to a prescribed level. Further increments shall be subject to a resolution of the Council. The University shall retain the right to make appointments at a salary above the minimum approved for the grade.

(iii) Independent Lecturers

The salary range to be the same as for Lecturers, with such additional emoluments as the Council deems appropriate in each case.

(iv) Readers

The title of Reader shall be given only in special cases, and shall carry no additional emolument.

The Committee were unanimously of the opinion that the salary of professors should normally be uniform, but that the Council should reserve the right to appoint at a higher salary in special cases.

(B) Buildings

I. MAIN UNIVERSITY SITE

The Committee was unanimously agreed that three main principles should be observed in the disposition of the new buildings on the main University site, (i) that if possible no encroachment should be made upon the area at present under grass on this site, (ii) that so far as might be practicable, the three faculties of the University should all be accommodated on this site, (iii) that an attempt should be made to house the various departments within each faculty in proximity to one another.

In addition to the buildings needed for the accommodation of the teaching departments, the Committee took into consideration the problem of providing (1) a Senate and Council Chamber, (2) a small hall, (3) a Students' Union building, (4) improved accommodation for St David's Hall, (5) reconstructed main entrance to the University, (6) extended book-stack accommodation for the Library. In order to bring the entire building programme into an intelligible relation to the site, and to obtain an approximate

estimate of the expenditure which would be involved, Mr Verner O. Rees was invited to meet the Committee. After hearing Mr Rees's views on the general problem, the Committee requested him to prepare a block plan showing the developments which, in his opinion, were practicable on the main site. A copy of this plan is annexed to this Report. It is clear to the Committee that many detailed modifications of this plan will be necessary. The plan is only submitted as a general indication of the character of the proposals.

After prolonged discussion, the Committee came to the opinion that partly in view of anticipated building restrictions, and partly on grounds of expense, it would not be practicable in the near future to carry through the whole of the programme indicated on the plan. It finally decided to recommend (i) that the Students' Union building should for the present be postponed and that accommodation for the Union should be provided in one of the houses in Portland Place, (ii) that St David's Hall should remain in the house in Portland Place which it at present occupies, (iii) that the basement book-stack for the Library, shown on the plan, should be postponed to a period subsequent to the developments under review.

The Committee recommends that the following buildings should, if possible, be erected in the first five years after the war:

1. A Council and Senate Chamber and a Committee Room

This is an immediate and urgent necessity for its own sake and in order to release the ground floor of the west wing of the Library for the erecting of a book-stack.

2. An Education and Languages Block

This would release accommodation in Portland Place for the Students' Union and St David's Hall.

It would necessitate the moving of the Buttery northwards from its present position.

3. Accommodation for the Faculty of Agriculture and Horticulture

(a) The completion of the second storey of the Central Chemistry Block to house Agricultural Bacteriology during the building of (b).

(b) The erection of a two-storey building for departments of the Faculty of Agriculture and Horticulture in the south-west corner of the site.

4. Biological Block

The erection of a two-storey building for the

departments of Botany and Zoology, together
with suitable accommodation for the Cole
Museum of Zoology.

This building would release the existing
Zoology Museum for the School of Art and the
existing Botany Block for the Department of
Physics.

5. A reconstructed main entrance

The reconstruction of the main entrance to the
University providing an adequate lobby, porters'
lodge and telephone exchange. This should include the construction of certain covered ways
and the provision of suitable cloakroom accommodation for the University Hall.

Emergency Accommodation

To provide emergency accommodation likely to
be needed in the immediate post-war period the
Committee recommends:

(i) The acquisition of a house or houses in the
immediate vicinity of the University for the use
of the Faculty of Letters.

(ii) The erection at the south-east corner of the
main site of a prefabricated building for the use
of the Department of Physics.

II. HALLS OF RESIDENCE

In regard to the existing halls of residence, the
Committee is aware that considerable alterations
are needed both at Wessex Hall (for women) and
at St Andrew's Hall (for women). In each Hall
more adequate dining-room accommodation and
kitchen facilities are necessary, and there is
urgent need for a Junior Common Room proportionate to the number of students resident in the
Hall. In the case of Wessex Hall an immediate
improvement of amenities could be secured by the
erection of temporary buildings, which would
not prejudice the future development of the site.
At St Andrew's Hall more student-rooms, which
are urgently needed, could most economically
be provided in a second storey to a new dining-
room. Further residential accommodation for
men students could be most readily found by
extending the buildings of Wantage Hall on land
already owned by the University. The Committee
recommends that action should be taken on these
lines so far as may be possible during a period of
five years after the end of the war. They are,
however, of the opinion that the finding of
adequate accommodation for students can only
be solved by building a third hall of residence
for men students and by rebuilding Wessex Hall
on a larger scale.

(C) Departmental proposals

I. EXPANSION OF EXISTING DEPARTMENTS

In discussing the development of the departments
and schools of the University, the Committee
considered it wise to concentrate attention in the
first place on the strengthening and expansion of
activities already in being. The establishment of
entirely new forms of study and research raises
problems of more general policy, and is best
considered separately (below C II). In framing its
proposals, the Committee was guided throughout
by the memoranda submitted by heads of departments and deans of faculties. It did not attempt
to balance the claims of different faculties and
departments against one another, nor did it
consider itself bound by any arbitrary limitation
of expenditure. But in this connection the Committee fully realizes that the general increase of
salaries which is now inevitable will greatly
increase the charges involved in its recommendations under this head. It is well aware that, for
this reason it may prove impossible to carry out
more than a limited portion of the programme
which it is now suggesting.

The detailed proposals which the Committee
recommends for consideration are as follows:

Faculty of Letters
Department/New requirements
Classics/A new Professorship, in place of an
existing Lectureship.
French/One Lecturer or Assistant Lecturer.
Education/One Lecturer.
Political Economy/One Assistant Lecturer will
be needed if, as the Committee hopes, the
University institutes an Honours Degree in
this subject.
German/One Lecturer in place of a part-time
assistant.
History/One Assistant Lecturer.
Psychology/One part-time Assistant in
Psychiatry.
No new appointments are suggested in either
Philosophy or English.
Faculty of Science
Department/New requirements
Geography/One Assistant Lecturer.
Zoology/One Lecturer in Entomology.
Botany/One Assistant Lecturer qualified in
Ecology.
Chemistry/One Assistant Lecturer.
Physics/One Assistant Lecturer.
Four Laboratory Assistants for Geography (1),

Zoology (1), and Physics (2).

No new appointments are suggested in Geology.

Faculty of Agriculture and Horticulture

Department/New requirements

Horticulture/One Assistant Lecturer.

Dairying/One Assistant Lecturer.

Agricultural Botany/One Lecturer in place of an Assistant Lecturer, and one Assistant Lecturer.

Agricultural Bacteriology/One Assistant Lecturer.

Agricultural Economics/A full-time Independent Lecturer.

Veterinary Science and Physiology/Additional provision for part-time assistance.

Senior scholarships

The Committee considered the question of new student demonstratorships for which there were urgent requirements from the Faculties of Science and Agriculture. It was of the opinion that this question was interlocked with the more general problem of increasing the number of senior scholarships, which is common to all three faculties of the University. Without attempting to distribute these appointments among the faculties, the Committee came to the opinion that it was desirable to provide a total establishment of twelve new senior scholarships or research studentships of this type for the whole University. In the Faculty of Science and the Faculty of Agriculture and Horticulture the holders of these studentships or scholarships might undertake part-time duties as student demonstrators.

School of Art

The Committee does not recommend any new appointment of the grade of Lecturer or Assistant Lecturer, but considers that the equivalent of a Laboratory Assistant should be provided for the School. A reorganisation of the existing staff of the Department will be sufficient to provide for any probable expansion of its activities in the immediate future.

School of Music

No proposals are offered.

II. NEW DEVELOPMENTS

Faculty of Letters

The Committee received evidence of a widespread feeling that the University would be well advised to attempt a considerable expansion of its work in the fields of modern languages and literatures at the earliest possible moment. The feeling took the practical shape of a proposal for new Lectureships in Italian and Spanish which

would make possible the ultimate development of a School of Romance Languages within the Faculty.

In adopting this proposal the Committee wishes to record that in its opinion the institution of Slavonic and Scandinavian studies and a considerable expansion in the Department of German are both desirable. They do not, however, suggest that these last developments should form part of the immediate post-war programme of the University.

Faculty of Science

The Faculty of Science does not propose any new developments exclusive to itself. But on the border line between the Faculties of Letters and Science the Committee recommends the appointment of an Independent Lecturer in Applied Mathematics. It is of the opinion that this appointment should replace an existing Lectureship in the Department of Mathematics, but that it would involve the engagement of a new Assistant Lecturer.

Faculty of Agriculture

Both the general work of the Faculty and the notable recent increase in legislation affecting the agricultural industry make the provision of instruction in at least elementary Law extremely desirable. The Committee recommends that the appointment of a Lecturer in Law should form a part of the immediate post-war programme of the University. It is of the opinion that the services of such a Lecturer might prove of value to the Faculty of Letters, particularly in relation to possible developments within the Department of Political Economy.

Library

The problem of the University Library stands apart. It affects each of the university faculties and cannot be dealt with except as a matter of general university policy. The Committee had before it a report from the Librarian which indicated the present position of the Library and its needs in regard to expenditure and staffing.

The recommendations already included in this Report – especially those relating to possible developments in the Romance Languages – will, if carried out, necessitate the purchase of books on a considerable scale. The Committee is also of the opinion that a large expenditure will be needed in order to acquire the books which it has not been possible to purchase during the war, and that for practical reasons it will be necessary to spread this expenditure over a number of years. It therefore considers that in addition to the capital sum needed for the Library equipment of new university departments, it will be necessary for the University to provide a much larger annual grant for the purchase of books than has at any time been made in the past.

In regard to the staffing of the Library, the Committee recommends the appointment of two Junior Assistant Librarians in addition to the pre-war staff.

(signed) Franklin Sibly

Appendix 6

Notes on the purchase of Whiteknights Park submitted to the University Grants Committee, 7 October 1946

There are two drafts of this document: one in University Records Centre box 70 and one in Bursar's Office, 28/10, 1. Both were corrected by Stenton. The following is taken from the first; the second carries a note by Carpenter referring to the submission to the University Grants Committee.

The sections added or corrected in Stenton's hand are printed in italic. For comment on the purchase price given below see above, pp. 142–4. Those familiar with the condition of certain sections of the park in wet weather will detect a note of optimism in the statement that 'the soil is mainly gravel'. This first impression was corrected by an accurate survey directed by Hawkins. On this see above, p. 184.

The University of Reading has received from the Trustees of Whiteknights Settled Estates an offer to sell to the University the property known as the Whiteknights Park Estate, Reading. The University has already acquired 7½ acres of this site, and the remainder of the estate is 281 acres of which the Ministry of Works is acquiring 14½ acres for temporary office accommodation. The area now offered to the University amounts to 266½ acres. The price is £150,000.

The offer has come to the University at an opportune moment. The reports submitted by heads of departments in answer to the letter of July 8 addressed to the University by the University Grants Committee show that within five years, even at a moderate rate of expansion, it will be impossible for the three faculties of the University to be accommodated on the main university site. Small properties, which can be used towards the relief of this congestion are being acquired by the University. But there remains the fundamental difficulty of developing a university on a scale appropriate to modern needs within the limits of a built-up area, and no adequate solution of this difficulty for a university based on our present site has hitherto appeared. The acquisition of the Whiteknights Park Estate would at once permit the formation of a long-term plan for the development of the University, and would *invite ultimate* expansion to an extent much exceeding the number of 1,300 students – *a number which itself, could only be reached if the University were successful in acquiring a series of substantial properties in its immediate neighbourhood.*

The purchase of this estate would at once set in motion the beginnings of a process which, in course of time, would transfer the University from its present site in London Road Reading to Whiteknights Park. Neither the duration nor the cost of this process can at present be estimated except in the most general terms. It can only be said at this stage, that the Whiteknights Park Estate is well fitted to be the site of a university. It is a piece of genuine parkland occupying a plateau to the south of the town of Reading. It adjoins properties already in the possession of the University – notably its playing-fields, which already are much too small for the use that is made of them. It is easily accessible from the town and within a short distance of the older University halls of residence. *The soil is mainly gravel, and the site presents no irregularities of contour likely to interfere with its development for university purposes.*

F. M. Stenton

Regulations for discipline and Hall rules: selected documents

The report of the committee of 1921 is derived from the Registrar's office. The Hall rules of 1922, 1930 and 1932 are held in the University Record Centre.

It would be unnecessarily complicated to present a detailed account of changes in the University and Hall regulations and rules for students. Some of the later changes are discussed above (pp. 307–16). The following documents mainly illustrate the situation at an earlier period. The first is the report of a special committee of 1921. It indicates how Reading defined *mens sana in corpore sano* at that time. It is possible that Mrs Childs chaired this committee. The remaining selections are of the Regulations for Discipline of 1926–7 and of Hall Rules of dates varying between 1922 and 1932. Since the Rules were drafted by the Halls' management committees they were closely similar, if not identical, from one Hall to another. The main differences lay between the Rules for Men's and those for Women's Halls.

An example of Hall Regulations of 1975 and extracts from Regulations for Discipline of 1973 are added for comparison.

Report of Special Committee, University College, Reading, 16 March 1921

RELATIONS OF MEN AND WOMEN STUDENTS

We have considered several points arising under this heading:

(*a*) *The question of men and women students going for walks together*

While we think it undesirable to issue a College rule on this subject, we consider that practice should be governed by common sense and discretion. This is the more necessary because the wardens of women's Halls are frequently asked by parents what precautions are taken in such matters. We think it should be understood that if a man student wishes to take a woman student out for a walk, he should make his request to the Warden of the woman student's Hall, and that the Warden should act according to her discretion and according to her knowledge of the individuals concerned, and should satisfy herself that the privilege if granted will be respected.

(*b*) *The question of motor-cycling excursions*

We are strongly of opinion that there should be a College regulation prohibiting both men and women from carrying passengers on the rear carrier of their motor-cycles. The regulation is required in the interests of safety.

As regards excursions in which a man student proposes to take out a woman student in his side-car, we are not in favour of making a College rule on the subject. Nevertheless, in view particularly of the risk of accidents or breakdowns, we consider that the wardens of women's Halls, if asked to give leave for such excursions, should inform the students concerned that it is necessary for the consent of the woman student's parent or guardian to be obtained. Subject to such consent being obtained, we do not think that the College is called upon at present to take further action.

(*c*) *River excursions*

We consider that the custom whereby women students in Halls do not go upon the river on Sundays should be maintained.

(*d*) *Women students' head-gear*

Our attention has been called to the fact that women students are not infrequently seen in the town without hats. We do not think that this practice brings credit upon the College. We think that there should be an understanding that women students going into the town should either wear cap and gown or ordinary costume.

OPEN-AIR EXERCISE FOR STUDENTS

1. It is doubtful whether all students obtain sufficient exercise in the open air. Some apparently need a stimulus to take such exercise. We think that wardens and tutors should do their best to persuade students who neglect outdoor exercise to be more sensible in this respect.

2. It would be very advantageous if the number of hard tennis-courts (at present only two) could be increased.

3. We think that if a small and simple guide-book could be produced and sold at a cheap rate, giving particulars of the best walks within a radius of ten miles from Reading, it would serve a useful purpose. Such a guide-book should give particulars of routes, footpaths, places where tea, etc. can be obtained, and a few details about churches, buildings and earthworks of interest. There might also be included a few notes about geology, field botany, etc. etc.

TUTORIAL SYSTEM

We are not satisfied that the tutorial system is doing all that it ought and might.

Difficulties arise from e.g. (1) the fact that the number of students to be dealt with is often too large for the staff available, (2) the fact that there is a great difference in the efficiency of individual tutors.

We believe that it is desirable for the Academic Board to give this matter very careful attention, and among other measures to issue to all tutors a short statement of the duties which a tutor is expected to perform.

FUTURE OF THIS COMMITTEE

We believe that our meetings and deliberations have fulfilled a most useful purpose. Our discussions have brought out different points of view and at the same time a predominant measure of agreement on principles of importance. We, therefore, suggest to the Academic Board that the question of giving the Committee a permanent existence deserves consideration. Some of the matters upon which we have reported call for continuous attention; and we therefore think that it would be advantageous if the Committee were made permanent and if it were required to meet at least once a term.

If it is decided to make the Committee permanent, we recommend that Mrs Childs, as Chairman of the Women's Halls Committee, be added to it.

OUR REPORT

Having regard to the fact that our Report deals with several questions of a confidential character, we recommend that the risk of accidental publicity, involved in the making and circulation of many copies, should be avoided, and that the Report should be read to the Academic Board by the Principal.

University Regulations for the Discipline of Students 1926–7

FOR ALL STUDENTS

1. All students are required to conduct themselves in a quiet and orderly manner.

2. Students are required to pay for damage done by them to University property, and fines may be levied for breaches of discipline.

3. Smoking is permitted in the University Gardens, in the Students' Common Rooms, in the Buttery, and in the open cloisters and corridors. Smoking (or carrying lighted pipes, etc.) is prohibited within the buildings and in all enclosed corridors and lobbies (including the main entrance lobby).

4. Rules framed by the Curators of the Library (in respect of the Library), by the Dean of the Faculty of Agriculture and Horticulture (in respect of the Farms and Horticultural Station), by the Dean of the Faculty of Agriculture and Horticulture and the Manager of the British Dairy Institute (in respect of the Dairy Institute), or by members of the Academic Staff for the conduct of their lectures or classes, have the force of Regulations for Discipline.

5. All students are required to attend their prescribed lectures and classes with regularity and punctuality. *Note:* If a case of infectious illness occurs in the place of residence of a student living at home or in lodgings, the student should at once discontinue attendance at University classes, and should inform the Tutorial Secretary of the reason for absence.

6. The University is closed to all students at 10.15 pm. Officers of Students' Common Rooms and university societies must arrange to terminate their meetings and entertainments in time for this Regulation to take effect, unless they have the written permission of the Vice-Chancellor for an extension of time.

7. All students following full courses of day study must reside in a University hall of residence,

unless they reside with their parents or guardians, or unless they hold the permission of the Vice-Chancellor to reside elsewhere. Such permission will not be granted except for special reasons. Students (not residing with their parents or guardians) referred to in this Regulation are in ordinary circumstances required to reside in a hall of residence if there is room for them and any permission to reside elsewhere is given upon the understanding that, if required, the student will migrate to a hall of residence upon the occurrence of a vacancy.

8. Students who do not reside in a University hall of residence are required to inform the Tutorial Secretary at once of any change in their address.

9. All students are answerable to the Vice-Chancellor for their general conduct. No Degree of Bachelor or Diploma or Certificate of the University will be granted to any candidate whose record as a student of the University is not deemed satisfactory by the Senate.

FOR STUDENTS UNDER TUTORIAL SUPERVISION

1. Students under tutorial supervision are required to be present at the Reception of Students in the University Hall on the days before the beginning of the Autumn and Lent Terms, at the Examinations (Collections) at Easter, and at the Interviews at the beginning of the Summer Term.

2. Each student's time-table of lectures and classes must be approved by his or her tutor, and no student may cease to attend a course of lectures or classes included in the approved time-table without obtaining the tutor's consent. A copy of the time-table must be given at the beginning of each term to the Tutorial Secretary.

3. No student may be absent (except through illness or other unavoidable circumstances) from a lecture or class included in his or her time-table unless the consent of the lecturer has been first obtained.

4. When a match in connexion with the Athletic Club, involving absence from lectures or classes, is to be played, the club secretary concerned must submit to the students' tutors the names of any students for whom leave of absence is desired, and must also submit the list of students, as approved by the tutors, to the Vice-Chancellor for his sanction, at least two clear days before the match takes place.

5. In the event of absence without permission from a lecture or class a student must send, on the day when the absence occurs, a note (giving the reason of absence) to the Tutorial Secretary. On resuming attendance after absence for more than one day a student must notify to the Tutorial Secretary the fact of his or her return to classes.

6. No student may enter for an examination, whether held by the University or by any other examining body, without previously obtaining the permission of the University.

FOR STUDENTS IN RESIDENCE

1. Students who do not reside with their parents or guardians may not remove from the hall of residence or rooms appointed for them by the University without the consent of the Vice-Chancellor.

2. Students who reside in a hall of residence must comply with the rules which are in force there.

3. Students in residence may not be absent from their rooms for a night without the permission of the Vice-Chancellor.

4. Students in residence may not leave Reading before the end of term, or remain in Reading after the end of term, without the permission of the Vice-Chancellor.

5. No student in residence is permitted to keep or to have at his or her disposal a motor vehicle, whether car or cycle, unless he or she has applied for permission to the Censor of Discipline and signed a form of undertaking approved by the Senate.

FOR STUDENTS WHO ARE UNDERGRADUATES

1. Undergraduates must wear Academic Dress (a) at all lectures and classes, other than practical classes, (b) at all official interviews with the Vice-Chancellor or with any member of the Academic Staff, (c) at all University Examinations, (d) on other occasions, as may from time to time be officially notified. (This Regulation does not apply to practical work in laboratories, studios, and workrooms.)

2. Students who are graduates of other universities should wear the Academic Dress of their university in place of the Academic Dress of the University of Reading.

The Vice-Chancellor has power to exempt senior students from any of the Regulations, but it is understood that such students assist in maintaining the discipline of the University, and that they continue to be answerable to the Vice-Chancellor for their general conduct.

Wessex Hall Rules *c.*1922

1. Prayers are said daily at 8.0 am, except on Sunday.

2. It is understood that members of the Hall will attend a place of worship on Sunday.

3. Hours for meals are:
Breakfast, 8.5 am (on Sunday, 9.0 am)
Lunch, 1.10 pm
Tea from 4.30 to 5.30 pm
Dinner, 7.30 pm
Students are expected to be punctual at meals, and to change their dress for dinner.

Students who wish on a particular day to be absent from any meal or to take lunch or dinner at a special time are requested to inform the Warden at breakfast-time.

4. Except by special permission from the Warden, students must be in the Hall by dinner-time, and must not leave the Hall after dinner without the Warden's permission.

5. Students are expected to conduct themselves quietly when in the Hall. The morning and evening are considered as times for study, and quiet is maintained between the hours of 9.0 am and 1.0 pm, 5.30 pm and 7.30 pm, and after 8.45 pm. Students are expected to be in their rooms at 10.30 pm on week-days, and by 10.0 pm on Sundays.

6. The Warden should be consulted regarding invitations, and before river or other excursions are arranged. River excursions on Sunday are not permitted.

7. Any member of the Hall wishing to leave Reading during term must apply to the Warden for the form provided for the purpose, at least five days before the period of leave desired begins. The form must be signed by the student's tutor, then by any members of the Staff from whose lectures and classes the student will be absent, then by the Warden, and finally submitted to the Principal of the College for his approval.

8. The Committee for the Management of Women's Halls of Residence reserves the right to the use of students' rooms during vacations, or in the absence of students from illness or other causes. No reduction in maintenance charges will be made for absences during a portion of the term.

9. Students must not go on the river unless they produce a swimming certificate or the written permission of their parents.

10. Care must be taken of the furniture, and additions to the furniture provided may not be made without the approval of the Warden. Pins or nails must not be driven into the walls. A charge will be made for damage done to rooms or furniture.

11. Students are requested to be careful in the use of light. All lights are extinguished at 11.0 pm on week-days, and at 10.30 pm on Sundays. No methylated spirit nor anything inflammable may be kept by a student in her room.

12. Students may have tea in their rooms by arrangement with the Warden, and may entertain visitors, but such visitors must leave the Hall not later than 6.0 pm. Visitors staying in the Hall are charged the Hall fees.

13. Students may not receive gentlemen visitors in their rooms.

14. No student may go to the kitchen or ask the servants for anything without first consulting the Warden.

15. No responsibility can be accepted for articles sent to the laundry, unless such articles are plainly marked with the student's name and initials.

16. If a student is unwell, the Warden must be informed at once, and no other student may enter her room without permission.

Rules for Women's Halls of Residence, 1932

1. Students must observe the silence hours in Hall. The Hall is closed normally at 10.30 pm. All lights must be extinguished by 11.0 pm, unless extension of time has been specially granted.

2. No student may be absent from Hall after dinner without the Warden's permission. Senior students are allowed certain privileges with regard to leave until 10.30 pm on a limited number of nights each term.

3. Visitors must leave the Hall by 6.0 pm. Men visitors may not be received in students' rooms without the permission of the Warden.

4. Students may not go on the river unless the Warden has the written permission of their parents or guardians.

5. Any case of illness must be reported to the Warden immediately. Unless a student's parent or guardian has nominated a doctor, the Warden

will select one to attend the student when necessary. No student may consult a doctor without the Warden's knowledge.

6. Any student wishing to leave Reading during term must apply to the Warden for the application form at least five days before the period of leave desired. Attention is drawn to the University Regulations upon this subject.

7. Musical instruments, gramophones, etc., may not be played on Hall premises except at times and in places authorised by the Warden.

The Committee for the Management of Women's Halls of Residence reserves the right to the use of students' rooms during vacations or in the absence of students through illness or other cause.

Students will be held responsible for any damage done to rooms or furniture.

Students are warned against leaving money or valuables in their rooms or in cloakrooms. The University cannot accept responsibility for any losses that may be incurred.

Wantage Hall: Rules and Customs 1930

General

It is necessary that quiet be maintained throughout the Hall in the evening, in order to facilitate study.

It is particularly requested that on Sundays, quiet be strictly maintained throughout the precincts of the Hall.

Noisy behaviour at any time is an offence against the rules of the Hall and the interests of its members: it will be seriously regarded.

Pianos in private rooms may not be played before 1.0 pm or after 8.30 pm. No other musical or sound-producing instruments may be introduced into the Hall without the Warden's consent.

Gramophones, loud speakers, fireworks, firearms or airguns are prohibited.

The keeping of dogs or other animals within the precincts of the Hall is prohibited.

Tampering in any way with the fire-extinguishing apparatus is forbidden; and attempts to enter or leave the Hall through windows or by other irregular ways will render a student liable to suspension.

Students are required to pay for damage done to Hall property. In case of damage by students who refuse to give their names in response to the Warden's notice, the cost of repairs will be charged to all students on the staircase concerned, or in the Hall.

Students leave the Hall after lunch on the last day of each term, but a student whose work renders it necessary for him to stay in Reading during any part of a vacation must reside in the Hall. The permission of the Warden must be applied for in good time, and it is to be noted that for certain periods in each vacation the Hall is closed.

Rooms

Every student is responsible for the condition of his room. Rooms are officially inspected every term, and all damage to rooms, furniture, or electric light fittings, not attributable to reasonable wear and tear, will be charged to the account of the occupant of the room. A charge of two shillings will be made for each nail driven into the walls or woodwork. Picture hooks can be bought from the Porter.

Students may introduce additional furniture into their rooms, but none of the furniture or electric light fittings provided by the Hall may be removed from the room to which they have been assigned.

Students must provide their own towels.

Rooms may be changed with the Warden's consent.

The Hall does not accept responsibility for articles of value left by students in their rooms.

Quadrangle

Students are requested not to walk on the grass, or to enter a room by the window. Games must not be played, or stones, balls or other missiles be thrown in the quadrangle or buildings.

Junior Common Room

The Junior Common Room is open from 7.45 am to 10.0 pm. Ladies are not admitted. The Common Room Committee, which is elected annually by the students of the Hall is recognized as an essential part of the organization of the Hall. It possesses the right of approaching the Warden, either through its Chairman, or as a Committee, upon any matter affecting the welfare of the Hall, or the interests of its members. The Warden will expect that all such representations will be made to him through the agency of the Committee. He will himself consult the Committee upon matters affecting the Hall, whenever he deems it necessary. The recognized status accorded to the Committee as an essential part of the organization of the Hall carries with it the obligation and understanding that the Committee will on all occasions exert itself to maintain the welfare and best standards of the Hall.[1]

Lights

Lights in the Common Room and Corridors are switched out at 10.0 pm.

Students are requested to exercise strict economy in the use of electric light, and to switch off the light on leaving their rooms, lavatories, etc.

Smoking

Smoking is prohibited in the Dining Hall.

Bicycles

A portion of the basement is reserved for the storage of bicycles. It is closed at 9.0 pm. Bicycles, with the exception of those referred to below, must not be brought into the quadrangle, or past the Tower Gates. Bicycles brought to the Hall after 9.0 pm may be left within the gates for the night, but they must be removed by 9.0 am.

Cars

A limited number of cars and motor bicycles can be stored in the Hall garages. A small charge is made. Motor bicycles may not be stored at the Hall, except in the Hall garages.[2]

Pianos

There are two Hall pianos. The piano in the Library is intended for the use and enjoyment of those who have a serious interest in music. That the spirit of this intention may be fully carried out, students wishing to use the piano in the Library are requested to apply to the Warden for permission. This permission will be given for the Session, subject to the student's adherence to the conditions laid down.

The hours for use of the piano in the Library are: week-days, 4.0 to 10.0 pm; Sundays, before 10.0 pm and at other times during the day if the Library is otherwise vacant.

The hours for use of the piano in the Common Room are: week-days, 1.0 to 9.0 pm; Sundays, before 10.0 pm.

Health

Every student is required on admission, and subsequently at the beginning of each term, to furnish a Certificate of health, on the form provided for the purpose. The Certificate must be given to the Warden on the student's arrival at the Hall.

Illness

All cases of illness must be reported at once to the Warden, or, in his absence, to his representative.

Laundry

The collection and delivery of students' personal laundry is undertaken weekly, but no liability can be accepted by the Hall for any loss or damage incurred. Payment for laundry is charged against the student in his battels account, and rendered at the end of term. No laundry is collected in the last week of term.

Leave of Absence

Any student wishing to be absent from Reading for a night must apply to the Warden at least five days beforehand, on the form provided for the purpose, which is obtainable from the Porter. No deductions will be made from the stated charges for maintenance on the ground of absence from the Hall.

Visitors

It is requested that any member of the Hall desirous of entertaining a guest for the night in the Hall will apply beforehand to the Warden for permission.

A guest-room is kept for the use of occasional visitors at a stated charge for each night.

The possibility of admitting guests for the night in addition to the guest accommodated in the guest-room must depend upon whether or not any of the rooms ordinarily occupied by members of the Hall are vacant on the occasion.

Guests (men) may be entertained at meals in the Hall, or at tea in rooms, if due notice has been given. Charges are made in battels as follows: Breakfast, 1/6; Lunch, 1/6; Tea, 6d.; Dinner, 2s.

Ladies are not admitted to the precincts of the Hall unless the permission of the Warden has been obtained. When such permission has been granted, the visit must terminate before 7.0 pm.

Battels

Battels are rendered terminally.

Tea

Tea will be served in students' rooms. Each student must provide his own crockery and equipment for this meal.

---

[1] This paragraph was included in the information on all halls of residence, both men's and women's, although it was not always included in Regulations. It survives, in a slightly amended form in the information or regulations on Halls of 1976. See the Regulations of St George's Hall below, p. 361.

[2] In the surviving printed leaflet the whole of this section is neatly deleted except for 'Motor bicycles may not be stored at the Hall'. This was possibly an aftermath of Sheep Night. See above, p. 68.

Dinner in the Hall

Academic dress will be worn.

Senior students and scholars sit at the tables nearest to the High Table.

Grace will be said before dinner.

Hours during Term

Week-days:

Prayers in Hall at 8.0 am. Attendance is voluntary.

Breakfast at 8.5 am

Lunch from 1.15 to 1.35 pm

Tea from 4.30 to 5.30 pm

Dinner at 7.0 pm. In the Summer Term, Dinner at 7.30 pm

Sundays

Prayers in Hall at 9.0 am. Attendance is voluntary.

Breakfast at 9.5 am

Dinner at 1.15 pm

Tea at 4.30 pm

Supper from 8.0 to 8.30 pm.

Breakfast will not be served after 8.20 am (Sundays, 9.20 am); Dinner after 7.20 pm, or in the Summer Term after 7.50 pm (Sundays 1.35 pm).

The Tower Bell

The bell is rung on week-days at 7.15 and 7.45 am; and at 5 minutes before 7.0 pm (in the Summer Term at 7.25 pm), on Sundays at 8.15 and 8.45 am and 1.10 pm.

The Gate

The gate is opened at 7.0 am and closed at 9.0 pm. After 9.0 pm no student is allowed to leave the Hall.

Students are admitted between 9.0 and 11.0 pm by the Porter, who will record their names and report to the Warden.

All students must be in the Hall before 11.0 pm. All non-resident persons must leave the Hall before 11.0 pm.

St George's Hall: Regulations, 1975

The Junior Common Room Committee, which is annually elected by the students of the Hall, is an essential part of its organization and possesses the right of approaching the Warden, either through its President or as a committee, upon matters affecting the welfare of the Hall or the common interests of its members. The recognized status accorded to the Committee carries with it the obligation and understanding that it will, on all occasions, exert itself to maintain the best standards of the Hall.

The Hall reserves the right to the use of students' rooms during vacations or in the absence of students through illness or other cause.

Students will be held responsible for any damage done to the fabric of the building or to furniture.

The University does not accept any responsibility whatsoever for loss of, or damage to, property or articles of any kind which are brought or kept anywhere on Hall premises i.e. buildings, car parks etc.

REGULATIONS

1. The Hall is locked at midnight but residents have their own keys to enable them to return later.

2. In accordance with University Regulations, students who wish to be absent for the night must inform the Warden on the appropriate form obtainable in Hall and, where necessary, also obtain their Tutor's permission.

3. Students may entertain visitors in their rooms between 10.0 am and 3.0 am each day. No visitors, however, may come into Hall after midnight, except on Fridays and Saturdays when a visitor, who must always be accompanied by a resident, may be brought in until 1.30 am.

4. Students are expected to observe the silence hours in Hall (i.e. after 11.0 pm no one should be disturbed by other people's activities), and to act at all times with consideration for other members of Hall.

5. Musical instruments may not be played on Hall premises except at the times and in the places authorized by the Warden. Radios and record players should at all times be played so that they do not disturb other residents, and amplifiers and stereo equipment may be operated only through headphones.

6. Car parking is limited and members of Hall may not park cars on Hall premises without special authorization and will be fined if they do so. It is a University regulation that first-year students may not keep a car in Reading.

7. All students are required, during their period at the University, to register with a local medical practitioner, who may be one of the University medical officers or a general practitioner of their own choice. The Halls do not have their own sick bays, but students who are ill go to the University Health Centre.

University Regulations for Discipline 1973 (Selected passages)

GENERAL

The purpose of these Regulations is to state clearly what is expected of students in their lives as members of the University.

All students are, of course, bound by the laws of the land and there are offences against the laws which, even if they are committed on University property, the University has no option but to refer to the Police.

In addition the University, like any other society or collective body, must have rules to be observed by its individual members and these must include sanctions against their infringement. The maintenance of the standards of scholarship, personal integrity and communal life essential to the existence and good name of the University must, however, depend mainly on the responsibility accepted by its members for organizing their academic work, their personal lives and their participation in the University community. It depends in particular on their accepting and where necessary helping to enforce the decisions taken by the University as a whole.

Freedom of discussion is basic to a university and all its members must tolerate and protect the expression of unpopular opinions. The right to freedom of speech must not, however, be exercised in ways which adversely affect the rights and freedom of others.

ACADEMIC OBLIGATION

During Term students are expected to remain within the University's jurisdiction.

In Vacations students are required to complete such work as may be directed.

Students are expected to keep all academic engagements (including examinations, departmental tests, lectures, classes, tutorials, interviews) and to present written work as and when required by the Academic Staff unless excused in advance. In the case of examinations, leave of absence must be sought from the Registrar.

Any student who is unable owing to external circumstances to fulfil an academic engagement of an individual nature (e.g. a tutorial or interview) is expected to inform the member of the Academic Staff concerned. If it is necessary because of illness, injury or other circumstances to be absent from several engagements, the student must inform his or her Warden or Tutor.

Students who fail to meet academic engagements without showing cause may become subject to disciplinary procedures.

No student may enter for an examination, whether held by the University or any other body, without the prior permission of the Registrar.

RESIDENCE

All undergraduate students under 21 years of age on entry must during their first year in the University live in the hall of residence or approved lodgings to which they are assigned by the Registrar. Other students may make their own arrangements for accommodation, provided that (except for first-year students over 21 years of age) they have the permission both of their Warden and of the Registrar to do so and provided the accommodation is in or near Reading.

Sources

Oral evidence

A record of conversations and other oral evidence collected in the course of this work is held in the University of Reading Record Centre (URC). Transcripts are filed in box 256.

University records

Reference is made to records under the number allocated in the University Record Centre. Records which have not yet been transferred to the Record Centre are identified by the appropriate Office reference.

Reports and minutes are identified by the appropriate University body and the date of the meeting to which the minutes refer or to which the reports were submitted.

Manuscript, unprinted and privately printed sources

Except where noted all the following items are held in the University Record Centre.

Allen, P., 'Professor L. R. Wager, F.R.S.' 'Geology Newsletter' no. 4, Reading, 1966.

Appeal against the form of constitution proposed for the University of Reading, Reading, 1914.

Barnard, H. C., ed., *The Education Department through fifty years*, Reading, 1949.

Campbell, P. W., 'The Department of Politics: notes on the Department's first decade, 1964–1974', Department of Politics, 1974.

Childs, W. M., *University College, Reading: its Aims and Character*, 1916.

Childs, W. M., *University College, Reading: the University Question*, 1916.

Coupe, W. A., 'The development of German Studies in the University of Reading', 1966.

Dodgson, J. W., Diary 1939–49.

Hewlett, D. J., 'Reading University Library 1892–1967', Thesis submitted for the Fellowship of the Library Association, 1970.

Hodson, F., 'Professor Hawkins: an appreciation', University of Reading Geology Newsletter, no. 7, 1969, pp. 1–7.

Morley, Edith, 'Reminiscences', 1948.

Padley, F. C., 'Recollections', 1963.

University of Reading, History of the University: letters and miscellanea.

Willis, Vera, [Mrs Hodges], Diary 1931–4 (in the possession of Mrs Hodges).

Reports of government and other official bodies

Curriculum and Examinations in Secondary Schools, HMSO, London, 1943 (the Norwood Report).

Education: a framework for Expansion, Government White Paper, HMSO, London, 1972.

Higher Agricultural Education in England and Wales, HMSO, London, 1946 (the Loveday Report).

Higher Education, Cmnd. 2154, HMSO, London, 1963 (the Robbins Report).

Post-War Agricultural Education in England and Wales, Cmnd. 6433, HMSO, London, 1943 (the Luxmoore Report).

Report from the Select Committee on Education and Science, Session 1968–69, Student Relations, Cmnd. 449, HMSO, London, 1969.

Report of the Committee on the Age of Majority, Cmnd. 3342, HMSO, London, 1967 (the Latey Report).

Scientific Manpower, Cmnd. 6824, HMSO, London, 1946 (the Barlow Report).

Teacher Education and Training, HMSO, London, 1972 (the James Report).

Teachers and Youth Leaders, HMSO, London, 1944 (the McNair Report).

Other publications

Allen, P., 'Herbert Leader Hawkins', *Biographical Memoirs of Fellows of the Royal Society,* xvi, 1970, pp. 315–29.

Anon., *Academic Freedom and the Law,* National Union of Students and National Council of Civil Liberties, London, 1970.

Anon., 'The Cole Library of Zoology and early Medicine, University of Reading', *Nature,* clxxxviii, 4757, 1960, pp. 1148–51.

Anon., 'The Cole Museum of Zoology', *Nature,* clxxvii, 1956, pp. 555–6.

Ashby, E. and Anderson, Mary, *The rise of the Student Estate in Britain,* London, 1970.

Burgess, H. F., *The National Institute for Research in Dairying,* Reading, 1962.

Childs, W. M., *The new University of Reading: some ideas for which it stands,* Reading, 1926.

Childs, W. M., *Making a University,* London, 1933.

Crossley, E. L., 'The British Dairy Institute and the University of Reading', *Journal of the British Dairy Farmers' Association,* lxii, 1958, pp. 5–8.

Gibbings, R., *Four aspects of the work of Robert Gibbings,* University of Reading, 1975.

Giles, A. K., *Agricultural Economics 1923–73,* University of Reading, 1973.

Holt, J. C., 'Doris Mary Stenton', *American Historical Review,* lxxix, 1974, pp. 265–7.

Huxley, Elspeth, *Love among the daughters,* London, 1968.

Kirkus, Mary A., *Robert Gibbings: a bibliography,* ed. Patience Empson and J. Harris, London, 1962.

Major, Kathleen, 'Doris Mary Stenton', *Proceedings of the British Academy,* lviii, 1972, pp. 525–35.

Padley, F. C., 'The technical staff before 1930', *Staff Journal,* University of Reading, no. 7, 1969, pp. 13–16.

Pevsner, N., *The Buildings of England: Berkshire,* London, 1966.

Shell, University of Reading, Students' Union, 1934–76.

Slade, C. F., 'Doris Mary Stenton 1894–1971', *Liber Memorialis Doris Mary Stenton,* Pipe Roll Society, new series, xli, 1976, pp. 1–32.

Smith, E., *A History of Whiteknights,* Reading, 1957.

Staff Journal, University of Reading, 1967–70.

Stenton, Doris M., 'Frank Merry Stenton', *Proceedings of the British Academy,* liv, 1968, pp. 315–423.

Tamesis (formerly *Students' Magazine* of University College, Reading), Reading, 1926–73.

University of Reading, Bulletin, Reading, 1969–76.

University of Reading, Calendar, Reading, 1926–76.

University of Reading, Gazette, Reading, 1926–64.

University of Reading, Old Students' Magazine (formerly *Old Students' News*), Reading, 1926–75.

University of Reading, Proceedings, Reading, 1926–76.

Wake, Joan, 'Frank Merry Stenton', *Northamptonshire Past and Present,* iv, 1968–9, pp. 181–4.

Wolfenden, J. F., *Turning Points,* London, 1976.

Index